MODERN PRINT ACTIVISM
IN THE UNITED STATES

The explosion of print culture that occurred in the United States at the turn of the twentieth century activated the widespread use of print media to promote social and political activism. Exploring this phenomenon, the essays in *Modern Print Activism in the United States* focus on specific groups, individuals, and causes that relied on print as a vehicle for activism. They also take up the variety of print forms in which calls for activism have appeared, including fiction, editorials, letters to the editor, graphic satire, and non-periodical media such as pamphlets and calendars. As the contributors show, activists have used print media in a range of ways, not only in expected applications such as calls for boycotts and protests, but also for less expected aims such as the creation of networks among readers and to the legitimization of their causes. At a time when the golden age of print appears to be ending, *Modern Print Activism in the United States* argues that print activism should be studied as a specifically modernist phenomenon and poses questions related to the efficacy of print as a vehicle for social and political change.

T0304158

Modern Print Activism in the United States

RACHEL SCHREIBER
California College of the Arts,
Oakland and San Francisco, California, USA

Routledge
Taylor & Francis Group

LONDON AND NEW YORK

First published 2013 by Ashgate Publishing

Published 2016 by Routledge
2 Park Square, Milton Park, Abingdon, Oxfordshire OX14 4RN
711 Third Avenue, New York, NY 10017, USA

First issued in paperback 2016

Routledge is an imprint of the Taylor & Francis Group, an informa business

British Library Cataloguing in Publication Data
Modern print activism in the United States.
   1. Periodicals – Publishing – United States – History – 20th century. 2. Periodicals – Publishing – United States – History – 19th century. 3. Publishers and publishing – Social aspects – United States – History. 4. Journalism – Social aspects – United States – History. 5. Social problems – Press coverage – United States. 6. Women – Press coverage – United States. 7. Right and left (Political science) – Press coverage – United States. 8. Social change – United States – History – 20th century.
   I. Schreiber, Rachel.
   070.5'72–dc23

Library of Congress Cataloging-in-Publication Data
Modern print activism in the United States / edited by Rachel Schreiber.
   pages cm
   Includes bibliographical references and index.
   ISBN 978-1-4094-5477-9 (hardcover)
   1. Periodicals—Publishing—United States—History—20th century. 2. Periodicals—Publishing—United States—History—19th century. 3. Publishers and publishing—Social aspects—United States—History. 4. Journalism—Social aspects—United States—History. 5. Social problems—Press coverage—United States. 6. Women—Press coverage—United States. 7. Right and left (Political science)—Press coverage—United States. 8. Social change—United States—History—20th century. I. Schreiber, Rachel, editor of compilation.

   Z480.P4M63 2013
   070.5'72—dc23

2012041825

ISBN 13: 978-1-138-24828-1 (pbk)
ISBN 13: 978-1-4094-5477-9 (hbk)

Contents

List of Figures *vii*

Featured Journals *xi*

List of Contributors *xiii*

Preface and Acknowledgements *xvii*

Introduction 1

1 Print Culture and the Construction of Radical Identity:
Juliet H. Severance and the Reform Press in Late
Nineteenth-Century America 15
Joanne E. Passet

2 Changing Feelings: Fallen Women, Sentimentality, and
the Activist Press 29
María Carla Sánchez

3 "She Will Spike War's Gun": The Anti-War Graphic Satire
of the American Suffrage Press 43
Rachel Schreiber

4 Publishing a "Fighting Spirit": Marianne Moore in the
Little Magazines During WWI 65
Nikolaus Wasmoen

5 Holiday Activism: *Good Housekeeping* and the Meaning
of Mother's Day 87
Katharine Antolini

6 "Give this copy of the *Kourier* magazine to your friend.
You will help him. You will also help society": 1920s KKK
Print, Propaganda, and Publicity 105
Craig Fox

7 Productive Fiction and Propaganda: The Development and
Uses of Communist Party Pamphlet Literature 123
Trevor Joy Sangrey

8   Containment Culture: The Cold War in the *Ladies' Home Journal*,
       1946–1959   145
       Diana Cucuz

9   Challenging the Anti-Pleasure League: *Physique Pictorial*
       and the Cultivation of Gay Politics   161
       Whitney Strub

10   Calendar Art: How the 1968 SNCC Wall Calendar Brought
       Activism Indoors   179
       Lián Amaris

11   *Amazon Quarterly*: Pre-Zine Print Culture and the Politics
       of Separatism   193
       Tirza True Latimer

12   Crafting Public Cultures in Feminist Periodicals   205
       Elizabeth Groeneveld

Works Cited   *221*
Index

List of Figures

3.1   Lou Rogers, "Arms vs. Army," *The Woman's Journal*,
      March 20, 1915.   44

3.2   Lou Rogers, "She Will Spike War's Gun," *Judge*,
      September 14, 1912.   46

3.3   Laura Foster, "Hand in Hand," *Judge*, June 30, 1917.   46

3.4   James Montgomery Flagg, cover for *The Woman Citizen*,
      October 27, 1917.   48

3.5   Charles Dana Gibson, "Gibson Girl."   48

3.6   Alonzo Earl Foringer, "The Greatest Mother in the World,"
      ca. 1918.   50

3.7   Guenther, "Get Behind ... ," ca. 1918. Image courtesy of
      the Library of Congress.   51

3.8   H.J. Glintenkamp, "The Girl He Left Behind Him,"
      the *Masses*, October 1914.   53

3.9   C.D. Batchelor, "The Girl She Left Behind Her,"
      The Woman Citizen, May 25, 1918.   54

3.10 Lou Rogers, "The Girl He Left Behind Him," *The Woman
      Citizen*, August 25, 1917.   55

3.11 C.D. Batchelor, "Behind the Man Behind the Gun,"
      The Woman Citizen, October 6, 1917.   57

3.12 C.D. Batchelor, "Win-the-War Women: The Munition
      Worker," *The Woman Citizen*, April 13, 1918.   58

3.13 C.D. Batchelor, "Win-the-War Women: The Farmer,"
      The Woman Citizen, October 6, 1917.   59

3.14 C.D. Batchelor, "Win-the-War Women Selling for Uncle Sam:
      The Speaker," *The Woman Citizen*, June 29, 1918.   60

3.15   C.D. Batchelor, "Win-the-War Women: The Knitter,"
        The Woman Citizen, June 1, 1918.   61

4.1   *Poetry: A Magazine of Verse*, vol. 5, no. 2, November 1914.
        Image courtesy of the Modernist Journals Project.   80

4.2   *Others*, vol. 1, no. 6, December 1915. Image courtesy
        of the Modernist Journals Project.   83

4.3   Marianne Moore, "To Statecraft Embalmed," *Others*,
        vol. 1, no. 6, December 1915. Image courtesy of the
        Modernist Journals Project.   85

5.1   Maternity Center Association, "he's 9 months ... ," 1931.
        © Childbirth Connection. Used with permission.   89

5.2   Maternity Center Association, "If the Public only Knew!"
        1931. © Childbirth Connection. Used with permission.   93

5.3   Maternity Center Association, "16,000 White Carnations,"
        1931. © Childbirth Connection. Used with permission.   101

7.1   A. Refregier. Cover art, *They Shall Not Die! Story of Scottsboro
        in Pictures*, 1932. Used with the generous permission of
        Walter Goldwater Radical Pamphlet Collection, African
        American History Collection, D-207, Special Collections,
        University of California Library, Davis.   131

7.2   A. Refregier. "Inside the Court," *They Shall Not Die! Story
        of Scottsboro in Pictures*, 1932. Used with the generous
        permission of Walter Goldwater Radical Pamphlet Collection,
        African American History Collection, D-207, Special
        Collections, University of California Library, Davis.   132

7.3   A. Refregier. "The Two White Prostitutes," *They Shall Not Die!
        Story of Scottsboro in Pictures*, 1932. Used with the generous
        permission of Walter Goldwater Radical Pamphlet Collection,
        African American History Collection, D-207, Special
        Collections, University of California Library, Davis.   133

7.4   Cover art, *The Negroes in a Soviet America*, 1935. Used with
        generous permission from the collection of Saul Zalesch,
        <http://www.ephemerastudies.org>.   140

9.1   *Physique Pictorial*, vol. 5, no. 1 (Spring 1955). Used with permission of the Bob Mizer Foundation.   162

9.2   *Physique Pictorial*, vol., 5, no. 1 (Spring 1955). Used with permission of the Bob Mizer Foundation.   165

9.3   *Physique Pictorial*, vol. 6, no. 1 (Spring 1956). Used with permission of the Bob Mizer Foundation.   169

9.4   *Physique Pictorial*, vol. 6, no. 1 (Spring 1956). Used with permission of the Bob Mizer Foundation.   174

10.1   Julius Lester, "1968 Calendar: Student Nonviolent Coordinating Committee." © Julius Lester.   181

10.2   Julius Lester, "1968 Calendar: Student Nonviolent Coordinating Committee." © Julius Lester.   185

10.3   Julius Lester, "1968 Calendar: Student Nonviolent Coordinating Committee." © Julius Lester.   187

11.1   Unidentified artist, cover, *Amazon Quarterly: A Lesbian Feminist Arts Journal*, Fall 1972.   195

11.2   Gina Covina, illustration, *Amazon Quarterly: A Lesbian Feminist Arts Journal*, February 1973.   197

11.3   Carol Newhouse, photograph, frontispiece for *Amazon Quarterly: A Lesbian Feminist Arts Journal*, March 1975.   200

11.4   Gina Covina, drawing, back and front cover of *Amazon Quarterly: A Lesbian Feminist Arts Journal*, December 1973.   203

12.1   Norman Yeung, *Shameless* (cover), Summer 2004.   209

12.2   Page from *Venus*, issue 25 (Fall 2005), p. 6.   214

Featured Journals

Adonis (1954–1957)
The Advocate and Family Guardian (1835–1941)
Amazon Quarterly: A lesbian feminist arts journal (1972–1975)
American Journal of Eugenics (1907–1910)
American Spiritualist (1868–1872)
Banner of Light (1857–1907)
Bitch: Feminist response to popular culture (1996–)
BUST (1993–)
Dawn (1922–1924)
Drum (1964–1967)
Eastern Mattachine Magazine (1956–1966)
The Egoist (1914–1919)
Four Lights: An Adventure in Internationalism (1917–1919)
The Freewoman (1911–1912)
The Friend of Virtue (1838–1867)
Good Housekeeping (1916–)
HUES (1992–1999)
The Illustrated Hydropathic Review (1853–1855)
Imperial Night-Hawk (1923–1924)
Kourier (1924–1936)
Ladies' Home Journal (1889–)
The Masses (1911–1917)
The New Freewoman (1913)
ONE (1953–1967)
Others (1915–1919)
Physique Pictorial (1955–1968)
Physique World (1954)
Poetry (1912–)
Religio-Philosophical Journal (1865–1895)
ROCKRGRL (1995–2006)
The Searchlight (1912–1923)
Shameless: talking back since 2004 (2004–)
The Suffragist (1913–1924)
Tomorrow's Man (1956–1959)
Truth Seeker (1845–1846)
Universe (1973–1974; 1976–1987)
Venus Zine (1994–2010)
Water-Cure Journal (1845–1862)
The Woman Citizen (1917–1927)

Featured Journals

List of Contributors

Lián Amaris holds Master's degrees in Interactive Telecommunications and in Performance Studies, both from New York University, where she focused on transmedia storytelling and audience experience. Her work spans the fields of new media, visual arts, performance, storytelling, and interactivity. She has numerous publications in books and journals, and has presented her original research at international conferences. Her artwork has been shown in such venues as The Guggenheim Museum and The San Jose Museum of Art. She has three years' experience as a full-time digital media professor, was a researcher and editor for media theorist Douglas Rushkoff for over two years, and was a 2011 writing resident with Volunteer Lawyers for the Arts.

Katharine L. Antolini received her Ph.D. in History from West Virginia University. Her dissertation, "Memorializing Motherhood: Anna Jarvis and Her Struggle for Control of Mother's Day," chronicles the life of holiday founder Anna Jarvis and explores the cultural representation of motherhood as expressed through Mother's Day celebrations in the early twentieth century. She is currently a professor of History and Gender Studies at West Virginia Wesleyan College and a member of the Board of Trustees at the International Mother's Day Shrine and Museum in Grafton, West Virginia, which commemorates the "birth place" of Mother's Day in the United States.

Diana Cucuz is a doctoral candidate at York University in Toronto, Canada, specializing in US, women's, and cultural history. Her dissertation focuses on representations of women in propaganda disseminated in the Soviet Union during the early Cold War. Her research interests include the intersection of foreign and domestic policy, and how politics impacts society and culture, particularly women. She received her M.A. from McMaster University in Hamilton, Canada. She has taught courses on social and cultural history, US history, the history of childhood, and women's and gender history, and currently teaches at Ryerson University in Toronto.

Craig Fox earned his Ph.D. in history at the University of York. His first book, *Everyday Klansfolk* (Michigan State University Press, 2011), examines the widespread popular appeal of the interwar Ku Klux Klan in middle America, and was selected by the Michigan Department of Education as part of its *Notable Books* program for 2012. He has also contributed to the PBS show *The History Detectives*, and his principal research interest is the social and cultural history of Jazz Age America. His next project will focus on the life and stage career of one of the forgotten entertainers of the Vaudeville age.

Elizabeth Groeneveld is Faculty Lecturer in Women's Studies at McGill University. Her book on late twentieth- and early twenty-first-century feminist periodicals that made the transition from zine to magazine, *Making Public Cultures:*

Feminist Periodicals on the Cusp of the Digital Age, is under contract with Laurier University Press, and her current research focuses upon the relationship between texts and textiles within feminist periodical publications, particularly zines. Her work appears in the *Canadian Review of American Studies*, the *Journal of Gender Studies*, and the edited collection *Not Drowning, But Waving: Women, Feminism, and the Liberal Arts*.

Tirza True Latimer is a licensed contractor and was a founding partner of Seven Sisters Construction, a feminist building collective operating in Berkeley, CA, in the 1970s–1980s. She is now Associate Professor and Chair of the Graduate Program in Visual and Critical Studies at California College of the Arts, San Francisco. She has published work from a lesbian feminist perspective on a range of topics in the fields of visual culture, sexual culture, and criticism. She is coeditor, with Whitney Chadwick, of the anthology *The Modern Woman Revisited: Paris between the Wars* (Rutgers University Press, 2003) and the author of *Women Together / Women Apart: Portraits of Lesbian Paris* (Rutgers University Press, 2005). She is co-curator, with the art historian Wanda Corn, of *Seeing Gertrude Stein: Five Stories*, organized by the Contemporary Jewish Museum, San Francisco, and the National Portrait Gallery, Washington, DC. She is co-author of a companion book bearing the same title (University of California Press, 2011).

Joanne E. Passet is a Professor of History at Indiana University East. As someone who holds a Ph.D. in library and information science from Indiana University and a Ph.D. in US history from the University of Wisconsin, Madison, her research interests have centered on women and print culture history. Her books include *Cultural Crusaders: Women Librarians and the American West, Sex Radicals and the Quest for Women's Equality*, and *Sex Variant Woman: The Life of Jeannette Howard Foster*. Her current project is a biography of lesbian feminist editor and publisher Barbara Grier.

María Carla Sánchez is Associate Professor of English at the University of North Carolina, Greensboro. Her publications include *Reforming the World: Social Activism and the Problem of Fiction in Nineteenth-Century America* (Iowa University Press, 2008) and *Passing: Identity and Interpretation in Sexuality, Race, and Religion* (New York University Press, 2001), as well as articles on nineteenth-century US literatures. She is currently at work on a study of sentimentality and war in US and Mexican literatures.

Trevor Joy Sangrey received a Ph.D. from the History of Consciousness Department at the University of California, Santa Cruz. The dissertation "'Put One More "S" in the USA': Communist Party Pamphlet Literature and the Productive Fiction of the Black Nation Thesis" explores how social movements use print culture to effect change with a particular focus on African American radicalism. Trevor's teaching and research engages questions of difference in print ephemera and digital spaces, with a particular focus on race, transgender, and sexuality studies. Trevor currently teaches at Washington University in St. Louis in the Women, Gender, and Sexuality Studies program.

Rachel Schreiber is Associate Professor and Director of Humanities & Sciences at the California College of the Arts in Oakland and San Francisco, California. Schreiber is an artist and cultural historian whose work focused on gender and labor rights, and histories of activism. Her first book, *Gender, Activism, and a Little Magazine: the Modern Figures of the* Masses was published by Ashgate in 2011. She has published articles in journals including *Feminist Studies* and the *Journal of Modern Periodical Studies*, and exhibited her visual work internationally.

Whitney Strub is Assistant Professor of history at Rutgers University, Newark, NJ, where he also teaches American Studies and Women's & Gender Studies. His book *Perversion for Profit: The Politics of Pornography and the Rise of the New Right* was published in 2010 by Columbia University Press, and his work on obscenity and sexual politics has also appeared in *American Quarterly*, *Journal of the History of Sexuality*, *Journal of Women's History*, and *Journal of Social History*.

Nikolaus Wasmoen is a Ph.D. candidate in English at the University of Rochester. His research explores modern and postmodern poetry, focusing on the role of literary editors and editing in the shaping of individual oeuvres and the formation of transatlantic modernism. He serves as a project assistant to the Blake Archive preparing manuscript and typographic works for electronic scholarly editions. He has also taught writing courses on the intersections of rhetoric, genre, and media at the University of Rochester.

Preface and Acknowledgements

In November 2010 at the Modernist Studies Association (MSA) conference in Montréal, I had the pleasure of being part of a panel led by Chris Reed on the topic of sexuality and modernist magazines. The discussion following the presentations generated a question in my mind, which was how effective has print culture been in contributing to on-the-ground social and political activism? To explore this question, I convened a panel at the MSA conference the following year in Victoria, British Columbia titled "The Efficacy of Activism in Modernist Magazines." The panel generated an engaging discussion and it was immediately clear to me that a book-length project was in order.

During the time between then and now as these contributors and I have prepared this volume, questions about the intersections of activism and mass media have become increasingly salient. Activism has been very prevalent in global news of the last few years. As an activist and a historian of activism, it has been gratifying to see, once again, news on front pages of people around the world working to address economic, political, and social inequities. As an educator, it has been extremely satisfying to teach and write during a time when my students have participated in activism and interrogate the injustices they see around them. The media that has spread news of these engagements has equally been a topic of discussion, in popular and academic circles. Activists in the United States, Egypt, Libya, and elsewhere eagerly exploited the most readily available and least expensive methods of mass communication to communicate with their constituencies and to create visibility for their causes. In so doing, they generated vibrant cultures of activism that have been rich topics for scholarly exploration. For these activists, and for my students, the media of choice are the web, texting, Twitter, and Facebook. For the activist moderns in this book, print was the privileged form of communication.

Various scholars among the Modernist Studies Association, the *Journal of Modern Periodical Studies*, and the Modernist Journals Project (among other groups) have devoted themselves to understanding the role of magazines and print culture in the formation of modernisms. I begin by acknowledging this engaging and productive milieu, which has contributed greatly to the ideas presented in this volume. The presentations given by the participants of the panel in Victoria were instrumental to the formation of this project: Phyllis Alsdurf, Julian Hanna, María Carla Sánchez, and Margo Thompson. Tirza True Latimer and Nikolaus Wasmoen were also involved in the project at this early date.

My Ashgate editor Ann Donahue has been a great aid in seeing this project through. I also thank Eric Olson, copy editor extraordinaire, and Ashgate editor Kathy Bond Borie. I am deeply appreciative of the women of my writers' group, from whom I have learned so much and whose critical capacities have shaped this work: Kim Anno, Paula Birnbaum, Alla Efimova, Martha Klironomos, Tirza True Latimer, Jordana Moore Saggese, and Jennifer Shaw. I also wish to acknowledge the California College of the Arts for generous funding. Finally, thanks to all my friends and family whose support feeds my work in myriad ways. In particular, I wish to express my gratitude to my partner in life and love, David Gissen, for all the ways that sharing our lives makes projects such as these possible.

Introduction

Since the earliest days of their widespread distribution, periodicals and other serial print forms have been sites where editors and authors expressed impassioned viewpoints intended to move readers to action. In the United States print technologies and the means for distribution expanded exponentially beginning in the late nineteenth century and continuing into the twentieth. Concurrently, a large influx of immigrants joined the ranks of industrial labor and, together with their native-born coworkers, activated one of the most (if not *the* most) radical periods in American history as they addressed increasing economic inequity and unjust labor practices. Meanwhile, middle-class Progressives worked to improve society according to their own ideals. As the nation headed towards intervention in the Great War, heated debates arose about what the role of the US should be in policing the globe. Within this climate, activism took many forms, from wave upon wave of labor strikes, to Progressives' pleas for legislators to protect women and children, to anarchist violence in opposition to capitalism. One of those forms was print activism.

"Print activism" is a term I use here to refer to print media's role in social and political activism throughout the long twentieth century. Beginning in the late 1800s with the industrialization of print technologies and the prolific expansion of networks for distribution of printed materials to readers, activists relied on newspapers, magazines, pamphlets, calendars, and other print forms to amplify their voices. Print activism continued throughout the century as the central vehicle by which activists on all points of the political spectrum—left, right, and center—spread their opinions, elicited support, created networks among like-minded individuals, and attempted to establish cohesive group identities for the larger world.

In the early twenty-first century, the "Arab spring," notable for its use of social media, and a national Occupy movement, which similarly depended upon networked media to communicate central information, have made it clear that print is no longer the central medium for eliciting, enjoining, and imploring engagement with various activist causes. For these reasons, print activism can now be periodized as a twentieth-century phenomenon, one that is inherently modern not only in its contributions to modern culture but also for the ways that it enabled American moderns to connect with one another.

Each of the essays in this book investigates this phenomenon; together they explicate the varied ways that those working for social and political causes participated in the spread of information that a rapidly expanding and increasingly ubiquitous serial and ephemeral print culture enabled.

Gutenberg printed the first Bible using movable type in 1455, and from that moment on print and literacy became the most significant vehicles for the spread of information. "For the past five hundred years, most of humankind has been informed by print," writes print culture historian Wayne Wiegand.[1] Until the nineteenth century, books—mostly read by elites—were the central format for the distribution of this knowledge in the West. The eighteenth and nineteenth centuries saw the rise of the newspaper, the periodical, published pamphlets, and other ephemeral non-codex forms. However, the function of the newspaper shifted dramatically in the 1830s; where previously newspapers had simply listed commercial news, they now began to operate as vehicles for editors' opinions. The new form primarily responsible for this shift was the penny press, which differed from previous subscription-based newspapers in a number of ways. The penny press was cheap, hawked on street corners for a penny in single issues, in contrast to the six-penny subscription services mailed solely to people's homes. And unlike earlier publications that were tied to specific parties, the penny press was politically independent.

Technical developments in printing and distribution also aided in the expansion of journalism and the penny press. In printing, the invention of the steam-powered press greatly increased the speed of the printing process. Where a printer circa 1600 using a hand-operated Gutenberg press could produce a maximum of 240 pages in one hour, by the early 1800s a steam-powered press could turn out 2,400 in that same hour.[2] In 1847 an American inventor named Richard March Hoe patented the rotary, or web press, which fed a continuous sheet of paper around a cylinder, far more efficient than its more time-consuming predecessors that took paper one sheet at a time. This method of printing, still in use today, increased the number of pages printed to as many as 1,000,000 per day.[3] In the United States, the mass industrialization of printing coincided with the dramatic expansion of the railroads, both their saturation into spaces that had already experienced European contact as well as their transcontinental reach. The expansion of the railroads enabled broader distribution of consumer goods, including not only newspapers but also the goods advertised in them.

These technical developments of production and distribution do not, however, themselves explain the ways in which the content of the press evolved. Rather, they were preconditions that enabled burgeoning industrial production to identify and attain new markets. Specifically, it was in this period of print media that the sponsorship of advertisers began to not only address individuals' wants and needs but to actually construct those desires. As Michael Schudson writes,

---

[1]   W.A. Wiegand, "Introduction: Theoretical Foundations for Analyzing Print Culture as Agency and Practice in a Diverse Modern America," in *Print Culture in a Diverse America*, ed. J.P. Danky and W.A. Wiegand (Urbana and Chicago: University of Illinois Press, 1998), 1.

[2]   Philip B. Meggs, *A History of Graphic Design* (New York: Van Nostrand Reinhold Press, 1983), 163.

[3]   Ibid., 183.

> Until the 1830s, a newspaper provided a service to political parties and men
> of commerce; with the penny press a newspaper sold a product to a general
> readership and sold the readership to advertisers. The product sold to readers
> was "news ..."[4]

This change altered forever the relationship between publishers of magazines and
newspapers and their readers, in that publishers were now delivering an audience
to advertisers. As a result, these media became expressions of capitalist culture
via the creation of consumers. By the turn of the twentieth century print culture
had become a mass culture, in consonance with the consumer revolution that
expanded its markets, the technical developments that enabled its production, and
the increased ease of transportation via rail that allowed for its mass distribution.

Alongside this growing mass print media and its uses to promote and spread
capitalist culture, a tangent print culture emerged as well. As the costs associated with
publication declined, print became a viable form of communication for a broad range
of groups, and the radical press expanded as well. Motivated less by profit and more
by the desire to spread a message, the radical press took advantage of the emerging
possibilities for print and flourished in varied types of publications. Throughout the
nineteenth century pamphlets had been used, often by religious groups, to distribute
sermons and other ideological professions, but their print runs were small and
their distribution limited. With the availability of industrialized printing methods,
newspapers, magazines, broadsides, and other forms appeared, using text and image
to give voice to a wide range of people and, equally important, connecting readers to
these authors and to each other. Geographic diversity was no longer a limitation, and
diverse ideological positions gained voice. As laborite culture and activity increased
alongside industrial production, union publications—both official organs as well
as others more generally aimed at socialist, communist, and other labor-related
groups—served to increase membership and raise awareness among non-members.
The large influx of immigrant populations created markets for both newspapers and
literature, often in the native languages of these new Americans.[5] Literary culture
itself was no longer limited to official culture; the so-called "little magazines" spread
avant-garde literary culture far beyond what would have been possible through book
publication alone, engendering its own cultural milieu.

In connecting these audiences, such publications contributed to the formation
of alternate and counter public spheres whose members imagined themselves as
part of larger collectives. Jürgen Habermas famously defined the public sphere
as "a realm of our social life in which something approaching public opinion can
be formed."[6] Although such opinions form any time private individuals assemble

---

[4]   M. Schudson, *Discovering the News: A Social History of American Newspapers*
(New York: Basic Books, 1978), 25.

[5]   Susan L. Mizruchi, *The Rise of Multicultural America: Economy and Print Culture,
1865–1915* (Chapel Hill: University of North Carolina Press, 2008), 3.

[6]   Jürgen Habermas, "The Public Sphere: An Encyclopedia Article," *New German
Critique*, no. 3 (Autumn 1974): 49.

and converse, for Habermas the rise of the public sphere as the site and bearer of public opinion is only possible through the medium of print. Habermas specifically identifies the shift in newspaper usage outlined above as a critical element in the rise of the public sphere.[7] Similarly, Benedict Anderson identifies the central role of print in assembling groups of discreet individuals into what he terms "imagined communities," or groups of people who believe that they share common ideas. For Anderson, the move to mass print enabled the spread of these ideas; where "manuscript knowledge was scarce and arcane lore, print knowledge lived by reproducibility and dissemination."[8]

The coming together of capitalism and print led to a massive increase of public participation in the formation of public opinion and the identifications of individuals as members of collectivities, but in the long run the potent combination also turned into a limitation to a truly democratic milieu. Habermas writes idealistically of the bourgeois public sphere as a moment during which public opinion was cohesive and true freedom of expression was evident, but the commodification of news media ultimately led journalism to "abandon its polemical position and take advantage of the earning possibilities of a commercial undertaking."[9] Ultimately, the public sphere experienced a structural transformation, and, within late capitalism, we can no longer speak of a truly democratic public sphere. Whereas for Habermas the corporatization of the media has led to the inability of mass media to truly communicate public opinion, for Anderson the rise of print contributed to the death of linguistic diversity, and this fatality, alongside the interactions between print and capitalism, led to the rise of nationalisms. Both of these theoretical frameworks provide a temporal structure in which print activism can be clearly codified: it prospered within the proliferation of mass media and subsequently declined as mass media became, in the latter portion of the twentieth century, increasingly univocal due to the monopolization of public media by a limited number of multinational corporations. Once this shift had occurred, the Internet and other forms of social media overtook print as the most efficient and democratically promising form of communication for countercultural and antiestablishment individuals and collectives.

Habermas's theorization of the public sphere has been roundly criticized for its idealization of an arena dominated by the bourgeoisie—that is white, wealthy men—and its lack of attention to public expressions of other groups. It is perhaps heretical then, to invoke his ideas in relation to the efforts of activists who most often operated from the social margins in their efforts to communicate their ideas. While acknowledging this contradiction, the emphasis here and the important point to be drawn from both Habermas and Anderson is the centrality of *print* to their arguments. Moreover, it is Habermas's identification of print as a form of *activity* that has obvious

---

[7] Ibid., 53.

[8] Benedict Anderson, *Imagined Communities: reflections on the origin and spread of nationalism* (London: Verso, 1983), 37.

[9] Jürgen Habermas, "The Public Sphere: An Encyclopedia Article," 53.

cogence for defining print activism. Habermas relies on American pragmatists including Charles Sanders Peirce and John Dewey, identifying in pragmatism the potential within liberal democracy for emancipation through communicative action.[10] Pragmatism is a branch of philosophy that asserts a tight link between theory and practice. Within pragmatism, "practice" can be thought of as "action," and an "activist" may be described as someone who favors action over theory.

In addition to the American pragmatists, the contemporaneous German philosopher Rudolf Eucken developed a theory of "activism"—in fact, the *Oxford English Dictionary* cites Eucken as the first person to coin the term, defining his philosophy as "the theory or belief that truth is arrived at through action or active striving after the spiritual life."[11] If there is a similarity between Eucken's use of the term and the definition within pragmatism, it is that both use the word "activity" to designate the need to apply ideas to the practical, social problems faced in real life. Both of these philosophical strains began to use the word "activism" in the first decades of the twentieth century, and this may be the basis of the word's introduction into popular usage as well.

The word "activist" first appears in American print in The *New York Times* in 1915.[12] Writing of pro-war agitators in Sweden who were attempting to push that nation to enter war on the side of Germany, the *Times* describes activists as those who spread propaganda in their efforts to agitate for war. Several articles appear in American papers in the next few years associating these Swedish activists with pro-German propagandizing, counterposing activists to a range of groups from the "indifferent masses" to conservatives.[13] Throughout World War I, the term increased in usage, most often describing individuals accused of subversive support of Germany and anti-American activities. A book review published in 1922 on Eucken's work, in fact, identifies his ideas of activism as "merely a cloak for the spirit of aggression and pushfulness which prevailed in Germany before the war."[14] The review's author identifies in Eucken's philosophy of activism roots of what turned out to be the philosopher's pro-German militancy during the war.

The first major Red Scare swept the United States in the years 1919–1920, spreading paranoia about anyone critical of US policies. The seeds were sown by the American government's anti-German publicity during the war, and following it, explains historian Todd Pfannestiel, many Americans mistakenly believed that Germans controlled the Russian revolution. Therefore, they "had little difficulty in transforming their government-inspired hatred of Huns into hatred

---

[10] See M. Aboulafia, M. Bookman, and C. Kemp, *Habermas and Pragmatism* (New York: Routledge, 2002).

[11] *The Oxford English Dictionary* (New York: Oxford University Press, 1989), 130.

[12] "Sweden's Leaders Fight War Agitation," *New York Times* (9 October 1915), 3.

[13] "German Peace Propaganda is on in Sweden," *San Francisco Chronicle* (21 April 1917), 1; "Oppose Socialist Aim," *The Washington Post* (5 March 1918), 4; "Huns False to Peace," *The Washington Post* (27 April 1919), 2; "Sweden's Leaders Fight War Agitation," 3.

[14] Austin Hay, "Idealist of Imperial Germany," *New York Times* (30 July 1922).

of Bolsheviks."[15] Further, this same thinking led many to look at the labor union activism that had surrounded them since the turn of the century and connect it to Bolshevism. Ironically, American Socialists vehemently opposed US intervention in World War I, but the term "activist" initially implied someone agitating *for* war. The link owes to the mistaken assumption that Socialist opposition to war was grounded in the desire to aid a German victory.

By the 1920s the term "activism" had come into regular usage in the press, and was most often associated with far left groups including socialists, communists, and anarchists. This association was also possible because these groups had often debated the appropriate form of "activity" to attain their ends. Such debates often centered on the idea of "direct action." While it is unclear when the term "direct action" first came into usage, one of the earliest appearances of the phrase in print is in American anarchist Voltairine de Cleyre's paper on the topic. De Cleyre cites the popular understanding of the term as designating "forcible attacks on life and property" fueled by the media in its reporting on anarchists. In distinction from this use, de Cleyre defines direct action as instances where any individual "who ever thought he had a right to assert, ... went boldly and asserted it, himself or jointly with others that shared his convictions."[16] De Cleyre includes strikes and boycotts, and further identifies examples from American history, including the actions of John Brown, the secessionists, Quakers, and others. Direct action is typically counterposed to political action, whereby electoral means achieve representation that will lead to desired results. By contrast, direct action is based in people's agency to act on their own behalf. Definitions that emanate from the Left do not limit direct action to radical activity but rather identify direct action as any instance where people act directly towards a stated goal. "It is merely another name," wrote William Mellor in 1920, "when employed by the workers, for the strike; when used by the employers, for the lockout."[17]

In American print, the term "activism" has thus been used consistently to designate the actions of radicals, subversives, and other fringe groups. Its usage in the *New York Times*, for example, begins as we have seen in 1915 but peaks in the 1960s in reporting on the civil rights, anti-war, and other countercultural movements of that era.[18]

---

[15] T.J. Pfannestiel, *Rethinking the Red Scare: The Lusk Committee and New York's crusade against Radicalism, 1919–1923* (New York: Routledge, 2003), 7.

[16] <http://dwardmac.pitzer.edu/Anarchist_Archives/bright/cleyre/direct.html> (accessed 28 December 2011).

[17] William Mellor, *Direct Action* (London: Leonard Parsons, 1920), 5.

[18] The word "activism" appeared in *The New York Times* 37 times between 1915 and 1960. Between 1961 and 1969 this number rose to 260, and in the following decade went to 1,050. It is important to note, however, that around this time the phrase "judicial activism" comes into regular usage as well. "Judicial activism" refers to a judge's reliance not on the law, but on personal or political conviction.

"Activism" was thus a term that originated, and appeared most frequently in print, to designate radical, anti-establishment actions. In popular usage, however, the term has come to designate a far broader field of activity. Within this volume print activism is not limited to left wing causes, though clearly they predominate. Essays by Joanne Passet and Trevor Joy Sangrey demonstrate the ways that print culture announced and distributed political positions from individuals and groups considered radical in their time. These authors explore the exponents of free love and Communist responses to the Scottsboro trials—positions that would not have been represented in the mainstream press. Similarly, Craig Fox examines a cause that was outside the confines of mass culture and certainly clandestine, but Fox's essay, on the print culture of the Ku Klux Klan, steers us to a topic that was marginal because of its illegal status. In between, several authors, including Katharine Antolini and Diana Cucuz, advance the idea that magazines in the very center of the mainstream consumer society—*Good Housekeeping* and the *Ladies' Home Journal*—could advance a particular cause within the space of their pages. Print activism is found, it seems, on all points along the political spectrum.

In defining "print activism" this broadly, we might then ask, what counts as activism? Activism typically describes activities such as marching, demonstrating, protesting, and other events that involve a physical, bodily activity. Can "printing" or "publishing" truly be added to this list of activist practices? Returning to Habermas, indeed print played a determining role in the public sphere—its formation couldn't have happened without the dissemination of ideas that print enabled. The term "print culture" illuminates print as an arena of culture that might be understood in the sense of the medium found in a Petri dish: an environment in which something can grow and spread. When culture is understood as productive, rather than merely representational, it then becomes quite possible to think of print culture not merely as a site of record for movements that propose social or political change, but as a means that historical agents use, as they might other means, to bring about such change.

Print activism therefore indeed must be understood as one among other strategies employed by modern social and political movements as they strived to achieve their goals. The propagation of mass print as a feature of American society occurred concurrently with the proliferation of activism of all kinds. The above historicization of both of these features of American society squarely frames print activism as a Modernist phenomenon, a frame that also coalesces various aspects of modernity. Activism of all kinds appeared largely in response to features of modern life. Mass industrialization, accompanied by the tremendous growth of American cities, created working conditions that were met by mass movements of protest and organization. The growth of these cities owed in part to shifts from agrarian population centers to urbanities, but also to an influx of immigrants who brought with them radical modern ideas from Europe. Print culture was the central technology by which these ideas and movements spread among metropolitan populations, and from urban centers to the rest of the country. As such, print culture in particular became a means by which Americans understood themselves as moderns, via their connections to others within the larger modern society.[19]

The reach of print culture, which as we have seen relied on modern technological preconditions, set the stage for print activism. As we have also seen, as the production of goods increased, producers sought new markets that were created largely through the advertisements that print brought directly into consumers' homes. Print culture is itself a commodity, one that is imbricated in the increasing commodification of life and culture at the turn of the twentieth century. Print activists therefore always negotiated their communicative strategies within this commodified medium. As the essays in this volume demonstrate, this happened in a variety of ways. In one case, a mainstream ladies' magazine, perhaps the quintessential site for commodification through print, was the site for an activist campaign. Other print activists discussed in this volume claimed a space distinctly outside of commodity culture. In the later part of the century, for example, several magazines performed feminist critiques of the intensive marketing aimed at women by creating alternate spaces within their serials.

Earlier in the century, literary figures wrote for the "little magazines," which manifestly claimed the journals to be distinct from commodity culture. But as literary theorist Lawrence Rainey and others have shown regarding these claims made by the little magazines, the Modernist mythologies posed by these writers that set literary culture apart from consumer culture must be questioned because the Modernist work of art, by its very claims of autonomy, "invite[d] and solicite[d] its commodification [whereby it was] integrated into a different economic circuit of patronage, collecting, speculation, and investment."[20] The commodification of culture was inescapable; regardless of one's positioning vis-à-vis such culture, one was still engaging with it and therefore connected with the production of modernity. Mark Morrisson, too, in his analysis of little magazines argues that "Modernists' engagements with the commercial mass market were rich and diverse."[21] Influenced by the suffragists, socialists, anarchists, and others who adapted themselves to the demands of the mainstream press, Modernist authors also responded to the commercial milieu, thereby "complicating the polarization of modernism and mass culture."[22]

---

[19]   See, for example, Christine Stansell's book *American Moderns*. Stansell paints a picture of New York City in the early part of the century as a place where bohemian artists and writers were infatuated with immigrant political culture. Christine Stansell, *American Moderns: Bohemian New York and the Creation of a New Century* (New York: Henry Holt and Company, 2000).

[20]   Rainey, *Institutions of Modernism: Literary Elites and Public Culture* (1998), quoted in Peter D. McDonald, "Modernist Publishing," in *A Concise Companion to Modernism*, edited by D. Bradshaw (Malden, MA: Blackwell Publishing, n.d.), 224.

[21]   Mark S. Morrisson, "Pluralism and Counterpublic Spheres: Race, Radicalism, and the *Masses*," in *The Public Face of Modernism: Little Magazines, Audiences, and Reception, 1905–1920* (Madison: University of Wisconsin Press, 2001), 5.

[22]   Ibid., 6.

For all of these reasons, *Modern Print Activism in the United States* adds to a growing body of scholarship that re-examines previously held ideas about Modernism, particularly the fallacious distinctions between high and low culture, intellectuals and masses, and culture and politics. This last binary in particular merits special attention here, for the essays in this volume demonstrate the ways in which print culture was a vital political force. Not only did print culture document the struggles of modern life, but through it a wide range of individuals activated each other within contested domains. Far from being tangential to on-the-ground activism, or merely providing documentation of "real world" events, print culture was integral to activist efforts of all kinds.

The 12 essays in this book illuminate the range of these efforts. The authors examine the writing, visual culture, and particular forms of print used in print activism. Organized chronologically, the essays begin at the turn of the twentieth century by examining two very different women's movements that arose concurrently with the rise of mass print culture. In "Print Culture and the Construction of Radical Identity: Juliet H. Severance and the Reform Press in Late Nineteenth-Century America" Joanne E. Passet examines the print-based trajectory of radical reformer and free love advocate Juliet H. Severance and her campaign to promote women's mental independence, sexual health, and the abolition of marriage. Passet demonstrates not only the ways that Severance made use of the burgeoning alternate press to disseminate her ideas, but the ways that print culture helped Severance shape her ideas about reform and women's social roles. María Carla Sánchez, in "Changing Feelings: Fallen Women, Sentimentality, and the Activist Press" addresses how social reform media regularly employed sentimental narrative strategies at the turn of the century as a means to recast the place of the "fallen woman" within larger bodies politic.

Nikolaus Wasmoen's essay and my own entry bring us into the era of World War I. In "'She Will Spike War's Gun': The Anti-War Graphic Satire of the American Suffrage Press" I study the visual culture of the suffragist press to uncover the ways that suffragists fought against US intervention in World War I. Wasmoen, in "Publishing a 'Fighting Spirit': Marianne Moore in the Little Magazines During WWI," investigates Marianne Moore's early publications during the war as examples of a politically engaged Modernist art whose full political dimensions are disclosed only in light of the networks of artists, writers, editors, and readers constellated by little magazines in America and Britain.

Following World War I, the Depression and ensuing fears of Communism elicit activism from mainstream to right wing and anti-Communist causes. In "Holiday Activism: *Good Housekeeping* and the Meaning of Mother's Day," Katharine Antolini tracks the Maternity Center Association's efforts, through *Good Housekeeping*, to recast the meaning of Mother's Day to promote the health of pregnant women and infants. Craig Fox's essay "'Give this copy of the *Kourier* magazine to your friend. You will help him. You will also help society': 1920s KKK Print, Propaganda and Publicity" addresses the mainstream success enjoyed by the Ku Klux Klan in the 1920s, tracing the abundant print culture that promoted the KKK in this era and the ways that KKK periodicals served as a cohesive source of solidarity for a group that operated undercover. Moving into the post-World War II era, Diana Cucuz demonstrates in her essay "Containment Culture: The Cold War in the *Ladies' Home Journal*, 1946–1959" how a mainstream magazine simultaneously promoted a discourse of domesticity that relegated women to the home while also locating women on the forefront of upholding American values and containing domestic communism and Soviet expansion. This efflorescence of activism in mainstream and right wing arenas did not come, however, at the expense of left wing activism, as Trevor Joy Sangrey shows in "Productive Fiction and Propaganda: The Development and Uses of Communist Party Pamphlet Literature." Sangrey focuses on pamphlets published by the Communist Party of the USA in the 1930s and 1940s in support of the Black Nation Thesis. In particular Sangrey looks at the CPUSA's response to the Scottsboro Nine trials and their support for the defendants.

As we head towards the 1960s and another wave of widespread, radical left activism, three essays explore aspects of rights movements based in minoritarian communities and their desire to establish their identities. Whitney Strub's essay "Challenging the Anti-Pleasure League: *Physique Pictorial* and the Cultivation of Gay Politics" explores the male physique magazines of the 1950s and '60s that scholars of queer studies have regularly dismissed as superficial and apolitical—in the author's words, they have been seen as "mere pictorial flesh-fest." Contrary to this supposition, Strub closely reads letters to the editor published in *Physique Pictorial* to show how these magazines were, in fact, often textual sites for an extremely rare, open expression of gay desire taking place at the very height of the homophobic "lavender scare." Lián Amaris focuses on the civil rights movement in "Calendar Art: How the 1968 SNCC Wall Calendar Brought Activism Indoors." The Student Non-Violent Coordinating Committee published a wall calendar in 1968 featuring photographs by Julius Lester with the intention of bringing positive images of African American life into the homes of Southern blacks. Amaris examines the calendar, finding in it the performance of a quotidian activism operating within domestic space. And Tirza True Latimer addresses lesbian separatism in "*Amazon Quarterly*: Pre-Zine Print Culture and the Politics of Separatism," studying the journal as a site of cultural connection among lesbians across the US and as a publication that strove to foster economic, social, and cultural self-sufficiency among women.

Finally, Elizabeth Groeneveld's essay "Crafting Public Cultures in Feminist Periodicals" concludes the volume by transitioning us into the twenty-first century and the full flowering of the Internet age. Her essay examines a cadre of independent feminist periodicals that began, in the mid-1990s and early 2000s, to discuss and promote the reclamation and repoliticization of crafting activities. Groeneveld historicizes these journals by situating them within the long history of feminist periodicals, as well as within their more immediate contexts of DIY punk and zine culture. In the 1980s and '90s, zines adopted inexpensive, low-tech, readily available means of reproduction—centrally, photocopying—to enable a grassroots countercultural print culture. Where Latimer's essay examines the precursors to zines, the magazines at the center of Groeneveld's essay exemplify the publications that emerged from that same culture and their status as transitional objects that lead towards web-based publications.

There are, as is immediately evident, a number of themes that run as threads along this temporal trajectory, and the essays could have been grouped in sections to allow these themes closer proximity. The chronological organization is therefore not the definitive through-line, but its advantage is twofold. One, it allows us to consider print activism's appearance alongside the unfolding of other major events of the century, such as World War I or the Civil Rights movement. Two, although there are several distinct themes that pull forward in certain essays while receding in others, many of the essays highlight more than one, and therefore a thematic organization would have required choosing one over another. For example, clearly women's rights and feminism appear consistently throughout the volume, in the essays by Passet, Sánchez, Schreiber, Antolini, Latimer, and Groeneveld. However, my essay equally attends to activism around World War I, and Antolini's might have been grouped with other essays that look at activism in the mainstream press.

Another lens through which to focus on common themes among these essays would be the methods and strategies of the activism being performed. For example, both Sánchez and Wasmoen consider activism in literature, and Sangrey may be added to this category for this author's claim that the CPUSA pamphlets in support of the Black Nation Thesis featured "productive fictions." Several authors, including Sangrey and Amaris, look at forms other than the serial. Periodicals occupy a special place in print activism because of their subscription basis, their delivery directly into the homes of readers, and their dialogic nature wherein readers respond via letters to the editor to previous issues as in Strub's essay.[23] Non-periodical forms therefore function quite differently. As has been discussed, pamphlets, such as the CPUSA publications discussed by Sangrey, have a long history as vehicles for proliferating a cause. Amaris's focus is on another non-periodical printed form—the calendar—which posits an interesting hybrid between serial and non-serial. SNCC chose the calendar specifically because of its entry into domestic space, and its diachronic status might be understood to mimic that of a monthly subscription.

---

[23] Though not part of her contribution to this book, Joanne Passet has earlier published a fascinating study of sex radical culture between 1853 and 1910 that similarly explores the dialogic nature of readers' letters to editors. For this book, she mined 3,439 letters to the editors of sex radical journals in order to assess responses to the issues raised in these publications. See Joanne E. Passet, *Sex Radicals and the Quest for Women's Equality* (Urbana and Chicago: University of Illinois Press, 2003). The other groundbreaking study to evaluate reader response in this way is Janice Radway's book *Reading the Romance*. The focus is not on an activist cause yet the book warrants mention for the ways that it illuminates print culture to be a two-way, rather than one-way, form of communication. See Janice Radway, *Reading the Romance: Women, Patriarchy, and Popular Literature* (Chapel Hill: University of North Carolina Press, 1984).

If attentiveness to the form of the print culture is one important thematic, another might be the various ways that activists use print to mobilize readers. For example, while some of the essays, such as those by Fox and Sangrey, explore print activism that appeals to readers to join a cause outright and to participate in activities beyond the space of the publication, others, such as those by Passet, Sánchez, and Cucuz, use moral suasion to move readers to a particular stance. Still others, such as those by Strub, Latimer, and Groeneveld, serve to create networks of readers who identify as part of a collectivity, and this readerly identification is central to the very form of activism under consideration. Of course, there is overlap here again. The publications discussed by Passet and Groeneveld, for instance, offer instructions and advice regarding the movement in question. And certainly Fox's essay on the KKK served the function of networking, particularly important to a movement that perforce operated under cloak of anonymity. Clearly, print activism took many forms and employed myriad strategies in its effort to achieve its aims.

The diversity of strategies leads to a concluding question: is it possible to assess the efficacy of print activism? Even in cases where we can see the overall success of a movement, it would be difficult to evaluate the role that any one strategy versus another contributed to such success. The appearance of a topic in print form may signify its mainstream acceptance, such as in the case of the Mother's Day campaign or the Cold War, or it may indicate the need for a group to use print to locate its members under the radar, as with Klan members and gay men during the "Lavender Scare."

Though the question of efficacy is difficult, if not impossible, to answer with true certainty, the essays in this volume nevertheless expose the important contributions made by print activism to the broad array of social and political causes pursued by Americans throughout the twentieth century. Perhaps more importantly, close examinations of print activism illuminate details about these movements that would be obscured were this significant aspect of activism not considered. The picture that emerges is of a mutually reinforcing schema: activists relied on print to amplify their voices, but moreover, the technological apparatuses of twentieth-century print culture not only fostered, but set the stage for the modern culture of activism that we see spreading to all points on the political spectrum throughout the century in the United States. Of course, it is advisable at the same time to be wary of being overly optimistic about the possibilities that print activism made available. It is easy, for example, to utter pronouncements that are excessively utopian regarding access to print culture (both for producers as well as for readers), without due attention to class distinctions that keep some Americans from full participation in public print culture. Further, the complex relationship between print culture and commodity culture certainly must have limited the possibilities for print activism in certain ways.[24] Finally, as is clear

---

[24] An interesting example is found in *Ms.* magazine, which operated for 19 years before announcing that it would be run ad-free. The move was announced as an ideological positioning intended to free the magazine from constraints imposed by advertisers.

from the essays in this volume, democratized forms of communication and media are not solely employed by noble movements but by nefarious causes as well. All of these lessons also offer the opportunity to bring a more critical awareness to the Internet Age as the utopian promise once thought to inhere to widespread literacy and the availability of printed information shifts to claims of World Wide Web accessibility, and social media aid the efforts of those working for social justice as well as those working against it.[25] Nevertheless, though these lessons carry forward, clearly print activism was a vital force throughout the twentieth century for a wide range of Americans who sought to understand their roles within the modern society and find ways to perform as agents in advancing a variety of causes.

A rare publication in its ability to continue to operate as non-profit, *Ms.* is run by the Feminist Majority Foundation and where it was once a bi-monthly publication, it now appears quarterly.

[25] See, for example, Roberto Gomez's fine (yet disturbing) study of interrogation and execution videos on YouTube produced by Narco gangs in Mexico, intended to intimidate their opponents and the general Mexican population. Roberto Gomez, "A New Digital Media Regime: Narco Warfare Through Social Media," in *Sightlines* (San Francisco: Visual & Critical Studies, California College of the Arts, 2012).

Chapter 1
Print Culture and the Construction of Radical Identity: Juliet H. Severance and the Reform Press in Late Nineteenth-Century America

Joanne E. Passet

> For the cause that lacks assistance,
> For the wrong that needs resistance,
> For the future in the distance
> And the good that I can do.
>
> —Juliet H. Severance[1]

"I am ashamed of professed Liberals," declared Juliet H. Severance in 1893, who are "so ignorant as not to perceive that this [the Comstock Act] is the club with which the church intends to beat out the brains of the Liberal movement." Enacted in 1873 to prohibit the sending of obscene material through the mail, the Act was used to prosecute a number of Severance's friends, among them the sex radical publishers Victoria Woodhull, Moses Harman, and Ezra Heywood, as well as authors Ida Craddock and Lois Waisbrooker. Calling for action, she demanded that readers of a weekly freethought paper, the *Truth Seeker*, take up their pens to "[a]gitate the subject. ... Awaken a public sentiment against it. Write what we please and print it, and send it through the mails to whom we will at any and all costs."[2] They should persist, Severance demanded, even if it meant prosecution and imprisonment. Few followed her advice to the point of risking arrest, but thousands devoured her words in the sex radical and freethought press where such controversial ideas as free love, marital rape, and the sexual double standard could be discussed. With their dissenting ideas validated by print, readers of these publications began envisioning themselves as part of an alternate public sphere, one that fostered a sense of collective power while creating print-based tools they could use to challenge the mainstream and proselytize their cause.

According to historians Carl F. Kaestle and Janice A. Radway, radical voices reached wider audiences than their advocacy of marginalized causes might suggest. Improved access to education and decreased publishing costs made

---

[1]   Juliet H. Severance, "To my Fellow Workers," *Religio-Philosophical Journal* (19 November 1870), p. 2.

[2]   Ibid.

printed works increasingly affordable, and even radical leaflets and newspapers permeated late nineteenth-century American culture. As an increasingly diverse range of groups—for instance, those identified by race, ethnicity, radical rhetoric, or political positions—advanced their views in print, their messages acquired a degree of legitimacy and, in turn, access to mainstream readers. Anthony Comstock and his agents waged a valiant war against vice, but over time their efforts to maintain cultural hegemony could not withstand the onslaught of divergent viewpoints. Indeed, as cultural historian Paul Boyer notes, "print material once deemed inappropriate was increasingly published by established houses or eager newcomers."[3] As Severance's reform career illustrates, the persistent championing of socially marginalized ideas—in print and from the podium—contributed to the larger cacophony that shaped the worldview of Progressive-era Americans.

An amalgam of nineteenth-century religious, reform, and third-party political movements, Juliet Severance's life offers an excellent opportunity to explore how social radicals used print culture to construct identity, build community, and challenge socially and legally sanctioned ideas. As the historian Genevieve McBride argues, many nineteenth-century women "empowered themselves by becoming wise in the ways of power, especially the power of the press."[4] Like most social reformers of the era, Severance never achieved significant wealth, but print culture provided her with an opportunity to establish herself as a physician and as someone who offered a valid social critique and plans for a better world. An outsider by virtue of her marital status and uncompromising advocacy of the rights of chattel, wage, and marital slaves, she became a well-known name nationally among health reformers, Spiritualists, freethinkers, sex radicals, and anarchists.[5] The epistolary nature of the many nineteenth-century reform periodicals to which she contributed, among them the *Water-Cure Journal*, the sex radical *Lucifer, the Light-Bearer*, the freethought *Boston Investigator* and *Truth Seeker*, and the Spiritualist *Banner of Light, Religio-Philosophical Journal*, and *Woodhull & Claflin's Weekly*, enabled tens of thousands of readers to read and respond to her ideas, thus serving as incubators for social change.

---

[3]   Paul Boyer, "Gilded-Age Consensus, Repressive Campaigns, and Gradual Liberalization: The Shifting Rhythms of Book Censorship," in *Print in Motion: The expansion of publishing and reading in the United States, 1880–1940, a history of the book in America, Volume IV*, edited by Carl F. Kaestle and Janice A. Radway (Chapel Hill: University of North Carolina Press, 2005), p. 286.

[4]   Genevieve G. MacBride, *On Wisconsin Women: Working for their rights from settlement to suffrage* (Madison: University of Wisconsin Press, 1993), p. xvi.

[5]   Her name changed three times during her life: Juliet H. Worth from 1833–1852, Juliet H. Stillman from 1852–1862, and thereafter Juliet H. Severance.

* * *

Print culture played a primary role in transforming Severance from a farmer's daughter into a physician. Born on a Madison County, New York dairy farm in 1833, Juliet H. Worth was the 13th of 17 children, and her formative years provided a solid foundation for subsequent engagement in social and political reform. As a young girl she learned important lessons about the impact of patriarchal marriage on women by observing her mother and sisters. The farmer's wife, she explained in a speech that was subsequently published in the agricultural press, was on an "everlasting treadmill of domestic drudgery" and for her efforts owned "nothing, not even herself, her husband or the children."[6] The Worth family's religious heritage fueled the young girl's tendency toward nonconformity and her commitment to activism. From her father she absorbed such Hicksite Quaker views as obedience to the inner light and a tendency to question authority. In *The Quakers in America*, historian Thomas D. Hamm explains that followers of Elias Hicks often adopted ultraist, or extreme, positions and could be found within the antislavery, women's rights, and nonresistance movements. From her mother's Seventh Day Baptist faith, young Juliet learned that women and men are inherently equal and that people had a duty to improve themselves and the world around them. Noted for worshiping on Saturday, the Seventh Day Baptists championed beliefs that provided her with a solid foundation for future participation in the American freethought movement, especially freedom of conscience and the separation of church and state.[7]

The reading of numerous religious, medical, and social reform periodicals, consumed in conjunction with rural newspapers, promoted a reading culture and, according to historian Nicholas Marshall, helped transform rural families like the Worths into "a broad-based potential constituency for the great social movements."[8] In the wake of the countless abolitionists, health and dress reformers, revivalists, temperance advocates, mesmerists, and phrenologists who traveled the "Burned Over District" of upstate New York in the 1830s and 1840s, enthusiastic converts turned to books, newspapers, and periodicals to feed their newfound interests and to find others who shared their convictions. This was possible, in part, because of the antebellum expansion of the postal system and innovations in printing that historian John Tebbel has labeled "the golden age of magazine publication."[9]

---

[6]   Juliet H. Severance, "Farmers' Wives," *Transactions of the Wisconsin State Agricultural Society* 24 (1886), pp. 274–5.

[7]   For more on the history of the Hicksites as a schism within the Society of Friends, see Thomas D. Hamm, *The Quakers in America* (New York: Columbia University Press, 2003), pp. 39–46; and H. Larry Ingle, *Quakers in Conflict: The Hicksite Reformation* (Philadelphia: Pendle Hill, 1998). For a good overview of Seventh Day Baptist history, see Don A. Sanford, *A Choosing People: The history of Seventh Day Baptists* (Nashville: Broadman Press, 1992).

[8]   Nicholas Marshall, "The Rural Newspaper and the Circulation of Information and Culture in New York and the Antebellum North," *New York History* 88 (Spring 2007), p. 151.

[9]   John Tebbel and Mary Ellen Zuckerman, *The Magazine in America, 1740–1990* (New York: Oxford University Press, 1991).

When 13-year-old Juliet Worth enrolled in the DeRuyter Institute, a school established by the Seventh Day Baptists, she pursued a rigorous curriculum that included Latin, Greek, algebra, botany, and moral philosophy. After a religious revival swept through the Institute in the late 1840s, the birthright Quaker and a number of her classmates converted to the Seventh Day Baptist faith. Eager to put her newfound convictions to work, the zealous student donned the reform dress (a shortened skirt worn with pants) and began giving lectures on temperance, women's rights, and the abolition of slavery to classmates and neighbors. Naturally gifted in the art of oratory, she paid close attention to the style and content of other orators, for instance Sojourner Truth's famous "Ain't I a Woman Speech" delivered at an Akron, Ohio Women's Rights convention. By the time of her graduation in 1851, Juliet Worth had developed confidence, a questioning mind, a quick tongue, and a strong sense of individual agency unlimited by gender.[10]

Juliet Worth first learned of hydropathy, a system of healing more commonly known as the water cure, from a local physician who introduced her to the *Water-Cure Journal* in the 1850s. Like many other subscribers she devoured its pages in search of ways to improve her health and thus gain greater control of her life. Upon first glance, hydropathy appeared to be a system of water treatments— bathing, showering, douching, or wrapping with wet sheets—but further study of the movement's journals and books revealed a holistic approach to health that entailed exercise, vegetarian diet, and temperance. As historians Susan Cayleff and Jane Donegan reveal, thousands of Americans, including the author Harriet Beecher Stowe and suffragists Susan B. Anthony and Julia Ward Howe, viewed water cure as a form of empowerment because it taught individuals how to care for themselves and freed them from dependency upon drugs and doctors.[11]

Access to print culture ensured that marriage to John D. Stillman, motherhood, and migration to a Seventh Day Baptist colony in eastern Iowa did not deter Juliet Stillman's reform and career aspirations. One of approximately 50,000 subscribers to the *Water-Cure Journal*, she studied enough articles by hydropathist Russell Trall to know that she shared his reform-minded goals, which included the training of women and men to become water cure physicians and health reform lecturers. Unlike male-dominated "regular" medical schools, the only admission requirements for his Hygeio-Therapeutic College were "a common-school education, and the possession of common sense."[12] The hydropathic profession's receptiveness to

---

[10] *Catalogue of the Officers, Faculty, and Students of DeRuyter Institute, for the year ending November 29, 1848* (DeRuyter, NY: Cornelius B. Gould, 1848); "A Peculiar People," *St. Louis Globe-Democrat*, September 30, 1882, p. 11; "DeRuyter Institute— Exhibition," *Sabbath Recorder* 8 (10 July 1851), p. 14.

[11] Susan Cayleff, *Wash and Be Healed: The Water-Cure Movement and women's health* (Philadelphia: Temple University Press, 1987); Jane Donegan, *Hydropathic Highway to Health: Women and Water-Cure in antebellum America* (New York: Greenwood Press, 1986).

[12] "Hygeio-Therapeutic College," *Water-Cure Journal* 26 (July 1858), p. 12.

female practitioners meant that a married rural woman could gain access to medical education, which, in turn, offered the possibility of economic self-sufficiency. With the begrudging consent of her husband, she deposited her two young sons with a sister and traveled to New York City to enroll in Trall's school.

In the fall of 1857, New York City newspapers were filled with news of a nationwide financial panic caused, in part, by the declining value of western lands and railroad securities, in addition to the political uncertainty resulting from struggles between free soil and slavery forces fighting to determine the future of Kansas and Nebraska.[13] News of bank closings, business failures, massive unemployment, and civil unrest heightened Juliet Stillman's already keen interest in the social and economic inequities stemming from the modern industrial market economy. Because Trall viewed water cure as a holistic reform, he required students to read widely, attend lectures on current social and political events, and participate in debates on critical issues of the day.[14]

During the economic and social chaos of the late 1850s, Americans sought understanding in a variety of sources, among them a rapidly spreading belief system known as Spiritualism. The movement emerged in upstate New York in the 1840s and had thousands of devotees by the late1850s, among them author Harriet Beecher Stowe, bridge builder John A. Roebling, journalist Horace Greeley, and the abolitionist William Lloyd Garrison. More than a 100,000 women and men turned to such Spiritualist periodicals as *The Banner of Light* (Boston), *Mind and Matter* (Philadelphia), *Religio-Philosophical Journal* (Chicago), and *Spiritual Telegraph* (New York City).[15] Typically they featured letters from readers sharing their experiences at séances, messages conveyed to them from the departed, reactions to books and articles, and responses to other contributors' letters. Often, readers offered personal advice, as did A. Hillside to the woman who asked *The Banner of Light* readers for advice on how to keep her husband's affection. Readers, especially those isolated by geography or advocacy of marginalized causes, saw the depth and breadth of their communities confirmed on the pages of these publications, and, in time, their print-based conversations came to constitute what the scholar Benedict Anderson has labeled an "imagined community."[16] Many whose words appeared in these publications never met one another, and yet they felt an indelible kinship with those with whom they corresponded. Men and

---

[13] Charles W. Calomiris and Larry Schweikart, "The Panic of 1857: Origins, Transmission, and Containment," *Journal of Economic History* 51/4 (December 1991), pp. 811, 813, 816.

[14] Russell T. Trall, *The Illustrated Hydropathic Review* (New York: Fowler and Wells, 1855), p. 12; "Russell Trall," in *Appleton's Cyclopaedia of American Biography*, edited by Grant Wilson and John Fiske (1889), p. VI:154.

[15] Ann Braude, *Radical Spirits: Spiritualism and women's rights in nineteenth-century America* (Bloomington: Indiana University Press [second edition], 2001), pp. 25–31.

[16] A. Hillside, "The Unloved Wife," *The Banner of Light* 2 (February 13, 1858), p. 4; Benedict R. Anderson, *Imagined Communities: Reflections on the origin and spread of nationalism* (London: Verso, 1991), p. 224.

women found life partners through the *Water-Cure Journal*, solicited donations when they were in need, and offered words of comfort and counsel.

Juliet Stillman had read about the growing phenomenon of Spiritualism, but she did not become a believer until she attended her first séance in early 1858 and found the medium's "tests of the return of spirits ... strong and convincing." Highly receptive to the cause, she participated in a subsequent meeting of the medical school's debating society and attributed her powerfully persuasive rhetoric to the fact that she had been "positively controlled" by a spirit, stating, "I could hear what I said as if I had been a listener."[17] According to historian of Spiritualism Ann Braude, many female Spiritualists boldly uttered criticisms of such patriarchal institutions as marriage and then later attributed them to spirit control. That spring, for example, Juliet Stillman delivered a speech against marriage in which she argued that "mutual love and desire and not law" was the true basis of a "sex-relationship." Her words reached a much wider audience when the text of the speech appeared in *The Universe* under the title "Is the Present Marriage System a Failure?" more than a decade later.[18]

Upon earning her degree in April 1858, Juliet H. Stillman, M.D. returned to Iowa a changed woman, one who would soon surpass her husband when it came to influence, zeal, and economic power. First, however, she had to overcome the challenges of rural isolation, rejection by the all-male Clinton County [Iowa] Medical Society, and opposition from "drug killing, poison-peddlers, from old fogyism, [and] from nervous tea, coffee, and tobacco slaves."[19] Her understanding of monopolistic power had its roots in encounters with a medical monopoly that raised barriers to women's participation. In print venues she grounded her identity as a healer through carefully worded case studies that she published in health reform journals. When making bold pronouncements about the "hundreds, robbed of their birth-right, health, and then obliged to pay the robbers for doing the murderous deed," she intentionally signed her contributions with the gender-ambiguous "J. H. Stillman, M.D." Locally, Dr. Stillman built her practice by advertising in DeWitt's newspaper, giving free lectures about health, and treating charity cases and those deemed hopeless.[20]

When invitations to lecture arrived from those who read about Dr. Stillman in the reform press, a rapidly expanding network of railroads in the nation's heartland made it possible for her to carry the message throughout Iowa, Illinois, and Wisconsin.

---

[17] "Mrs. Juliet H. Severance, M.D., Milwaukee," *Facts* 1 (March and June 1882), pp. 10–11.

[18] Juliet H. Severance, [untitled letter], *American Journal of Eugenics* 1 (1907), p. 232; Juliet Stillman Severance, "Is the Present Marriage System a Failure," *Universe* (28 August 1869), p. 72.

[19] Juliet H. Stillman, "Hints to Reformers, *Water-Cure Journal* 26 (December 1858), p. 96.

[20] J.H. Stillman, M.D., "Experience in Hygeio-Therapeutics," *Water-Cure Journal* 29 (May 1860), p. 70; "Mrs. J.H. Stillman, M.D.," *Dewitt (Iowa) Standard* (16 January 1861), p. 1.

Serving as living proof of the lifestyle she endorsed, she wore the reform dress and maintained a vegetarian diet when delivering impassioned lectures on diet, dress reform, control of the passions, exercise, and hygiene to audiences struggling to navigate the chaos and confusion of the Civil War era. In her wake she left copies of publications and information about where more could be obtained. Unfortunately, her growing reputation meant that, even with the help of a servant, it was difficult to balance the competing demands of life on the lecture circuit, her growing medical practice, and family obligations, especially after the birth of a third child in 1860.[21] As a result of his dissatisfaction, Stillman deserted his wife and their children during the family's move from Iowa to Wisconsin in the fall of 1862. Departing the train in Chicago, he enrolled in the Rush Medical College and became a Civil War surgeon six weeks later. Unaware of his whereabouts, and left to fend for herself and three small children, Dr. Stillman settled in the agricultural community of Whitewater and immediately advertised her services as a hygeio-therapeutic physician in the local newspaper.[22] Given the community's excellent railroad connections and receptivity to Spiritualism, temperance, and dress reform, it was an ideal location to embark on a new phase of life, even for a soon-to-be-divorced woman.

Following the Civil War, American Spiritualists splintered into two major factions: those who viewed the movement as a religion, and those adherents who regarded it as a scientifically based social reform. Both relied on the press to convey their viewpoints. Women and men in the former category avoided such controversial issues as marriage reform and tended to publish accounts of spirit communications. Those in the latter group, including free lovers Victoria Woodhull and Moses Hull, championed such topics as women's social and sexual freedom and ultimately tested the limits of the Comstock Law (1873), which prohibited the dissemination of obscene material through the mail.

Skillful management of her public image in the press enabled Juliet Stillman to withstand efforts to demonize her as a free lover, while the controversy prompted by such accusations ensured that the words of this bold, frank, and confident champion of the oppressed would be heard. Her agnosticism, divorce, and happy remarriage to Whitewater Spiritualist and dancing teacher Anson B. Severance (just two weeks after his own divorce) placed her squarely among the radical Spiritualists. In addition to addressing inequalities inherent in the institution of marriage, she attacked the sexual double standard. After reading Lois Waisbrooker's *Helen Harlow's Vow*, a novel in which the title character is labeled by society as fallen, Severance declared in a published letter: "No woman is ruined until she thinks she is; until she accepts the condition."[23] Informed by her knowledge of medicine,

---

[21]   "Mrs. J. Dr. Juliet H. Severance," *Facts* 1 (March and June 1882), p. 386.

[22]   *Juliet H. Stillman v. J. Dwight Stillman*, case no. 3863, 18 June 1866, Circuit Court, Walworth County, Wisconsin; "Mrs. J.H. Stillman, M.D." [advertisement], *Whitewater Register*, 14 November 1862.

[23]   Juliet H. Severance, "Letter from Mrs. J.H. Stillman Severance," *Religio-Philosophical Journal* (20 August 1870), p. 2.

Spiritualism, and evolution (after reading Charles Darwin's *Origin of Species*), her writings also foreshadowed the turn-of-the-century eugenic movement when she argued that miss-mated husbands and wives produced children who were "not buds of promise ... but children of hate and disgust—the result of licentious gratification, doomed to suffer a lifetime." According to *Religio-Philosophical Journal* editor S.S. Jones, these and numerous other comments proved that she was a "practical" as well as a "theoretical" free lover.[24]

Juliet Severance's view of marriage as the foundation of society, the place where reformers could have the greatest impact, was remarkably similar to another Spiritualist whose name dominated the press during the early 1870s. Victoria Woodhull's meteoric rise on the American Spiritualist scene in the wake of the Civil War captivated thousands who subscribed to *Woodhull & Claflin's Weekly* so they could follow her adventures and read her words. Regarding Woodhull as a kindred spirit, Severance became a frequent contributor and her name, along with Woodhull's, became associated with the free-love wing of Spiritualism.[25] In May 1872 Juliet Severance endorsed Woodhull's nomination as Equal Rights Party candidate for president. Woodhull's candidacy was hopeless, but her demonization in the press contributed to Juliet Severance's further politicization. Indeed, as her published remarks delivered at an 1873 meeting of the Northern Illinois Spiritualist Association reveal, she viewed Woodhull's treatment by the press as "political efforts to suppress Spiritualism."[26] The only way to counter such oppression, she concluded, was by working for political solutions to the nation's social ills.

Like his wife, Anson Severance understood the value of the press in developing and sustaining one's identity as a reformer. In addition to advertising his psychometric readings (analysis of an individual's health, character, and future prospects by examining a lock of hair or autograph), he functioned as a public relations manager for his wife by keeping her name in print in the Spiritualist and freethought press. Coupling entertaining accounts of their travels with summaries of her speeches, he reminded readers of her availability to lecture, officiate at Spiritualist funerals, and heal the sick. In contrast with Anson's missives, which advertised and described, Juliet Severance's offered instruction and admonitions. Signing herself "yours for freedom and equality," she invoked all who read her impassioned essays on the failure of marriage or the flaws of the temperance movement to practice the principles they uttered and to join in raising "our voices

---

[24] Juliet H. Stillman, "The Social Question," *Religio-Philosophical Journal* (7 July 1866), p. 3; S.S. Jones, "Northern Illinois Association of Spiritualists," *Religio-Philosophical Journal* (25 October 1873), p. 4.

[25] S.B. McCracken, "Victoria C. Woodhull, Free Love, Spiritualism, and Several Other Things," *American Spiritualist* (13 April 1872), p. 4.

[26] "The Rockford Convention, Cont'd.," *Religio-Philosophical Journal* (12 July 1873), p. 8.

in thunder tones for *free speech and a free platform*."[27] Print offered an excellent platform from which to begin.

In the 1860s Juliet Severance's rural practice had opened her eyes to the plight of farmers, while her move with Anson Severance to Milwaukee in 1869 brought her into contact with iron molders and brewery workers. Outraged by the Social Darwinist tendency to blame the poor for their condition and galvanized by depressed conditions and unrest following the Panic of 1873, she signed on with Slayton's Lecture Bureau and embarked upon lecture engagements throughout the Midwest, Upper South, and Central Atlantic states. According to the Bureau's promotional material, "[h]er lectures show her to be a woman of unusual mental acumen, with a strong sympathy for the oppressed and the righting of all wrongs and social disorders in society and government."[28] As she traveled the country delivering lectures with such titles as "Strikes and the Commune, or the Industrial Revolution," her encounters with mineworkers, boot and shoe workers, and other workingmen and women informed her understanding of monopolies and led her to ponder the possibilities of political solutions to social and economic problems.

The growth of the American freethought movement in the late 1870s and early 1880s became possible because of its publications. Like Spiritualists, American freethinkers had a vibrant print-based community linked by the pages of the *Boston Investigator* (established in 1831), *The Index* (1870), *Truth Seeker* (1873), and *Liberty* (1881), as well as numerous other short-lived or local titles. The power of their combined voices fed Juliet Severance's hope that freethinkers could unite to exert political influence on behalf of the oppressed groups she had for so long championed. Aided by her connections to several freethinking Milwaukee Spiritualists, she rose to a leadership position in that city's local Liberal Club and joined the National Liberal League (NLL). As she had done within other movements, Severance used frequent and well-reasoned contributions in the form of letters to establish her authority within this male-dominated community. Her use of "J. H. Severance, M.D." for her signature may have been intentional, misleading some male correspondents who assumed that any doctor with whom they debated would be male.

Severance's advocacy of free love and free speech soon led to her alienation from the NLL's more conservative male leadership, and fireworks exploded at the League's 1880 Congress when the Severances and other "extremists" called for a repeal of the Comstock Act. "The difficulty with which the better class of Liberals have [sic] had to contend," argued League president and noted atheist orator Robert Ingersoll in a published response to Severance's request, "is with the faction of free lovers" who insisted on discussing such topics as abortion,

---

[27] "Letter from Dr. A.B. Severance," *Religio-Philosophical Journal* (7 October 1871), p. 2; "Letter from Juliet H. Stillman, M.D.," *Religio-Philosophical Journal* (11 August 1866), p. 3.

[28] "Juliet H. Severance," *Slayton's Season Circular, 1878–79* (Chicago: Slayton's 1878), p. 36.

marital sexual abuse, and prostitution. He wanted it understood that the Liberal League stood for separation of church and state, not for defending "all the slush that is written in this country." Ingersoll's resignation in protest provided Juliet Severance with an opportunity to fill a void in leadership, and for the next four years she worked tirelessly, albeit unsuccessfully, to establish a League-sponsored political party to work for repeal of the Comstock Act, enacted in 1873 to prohibit the circulation of obscene materials through the mail. She believed that male postal inspectors seized every opportunity to suppress circulation of publications conveying sexual knowledge that could, for instance, empower women to avoid unwanted pregnancies.[29]

Ultimately, Juliet Severance's quest for an arena in which she could lobby for legislation to alleviate the plight of oppressed groups, be they women in abusive marriages, editors and authors prosecuted under the Comstock Law, or oppressed workers, led her to Wisconsin's third-party political scene. She initially embraced the Greenback party, in large part because it had expanded from the cause of currency reform to include labor reform, social welfare legislation, and woman suffrage, but also because of her friendship with Spiritualist Greenback party members.[30] The latter, plus the force of her charisma and the power of her oratorical skills, created opportunities for her to bridge gendered barriers to female political participation, and in 1884 she was selected to serve as state secretary of the Wisconsin Greenback party and alternate delegate to the party's national convention. When the party's strength waned the following year, a politically adept Juliet Severance shifted her energies to the Knights of Labor, the first large national political organization to admit women on equal terms with men. Nationally the Knights claimed approximately 50,000 female members by 1886. Quickly rising to the fore, she became a Master Workman, chair of the Wisconsin state convention's by-laws committee, and one of 16 female delegates present at the 1886 national convention in Richmond, Virginia.[31]

As newspaper coverage reveals, Milwaukee had become a hotbed of labor activism by the spring of 1886, with the organization of an eight-hour league, a week-long boot and shoe workers strike, and the Bay View Riot on May 5, just one day after Chicago's Haymarket Riot. The death of eight men when the militia fired on a crowd of workers at the Bay View Iron Works reaffirmed Severance's conviction that the abusive power of monopolies must be curbed. Charges against Robert Schilling were dismissed, but when Milwaukee socialist and Central Labor Union leader Paul Grottkau stood trial, Severance joined him at the defense table each day in a show of solidarity, one of the few women present in the courtroom.[32]

---

[29]   "The Liberal League," *Cincinnati Daily Gazette* (20 September 1880), p. 2.

[30]   "Greenback Convention," *Milwaukee Sentinel* (25 May 1884).

[31]   Leon Fink, *Workingmen's Democracy: The Knights of Labor and American Politics* (Urbana: University of Illinois Press, 1983), p. 184.

[32]   Bayrd Still, *Milwaukee: The History of a City* (Madison: State Historical Society of Wisconsin, 1948), p. 285; "As Seen in Court," *Milwaukee Sentinel* (6 December 1886).

Relying upon the power of the pen to reach a wide audience, she monitored the *Milwaukee Sentinel*'s coverage of the case and sent the editor corrections when she detected errors in reporting or interpretation. Convinced that Milwaukee's labor agitation would lead to a "grand social revolution," Severance spoke frequently at meetings of labor assemblies and then peppered the liberal press with accounts of these events.[33]

When the Knights of Labor began to fade, Severance next joined forces with Schilling in the Union Labor Party (ULP), a coalition of members from the Farmers' Alliance, Greenback party, Grangers, and Knights of Labor. Once again her reputation as an orator propelled her to the front ranks, and newspapers of the state contributed to her influence by their thorough coverage of her speeches. In the fall of 1887 when the ULP held its state conference in Fond du Lac, for instance, she joined Congressman Henry Smith on the platform, the only female among 50 delegates present. In its coverage of the event, the *Milwaukee Sentinel* described how "Mrs. Dr. Severance" was invited to address the convention. "Evidently she was not taken by surprise, as she promptly came forward and spoke for an hour. The money power, she said, held the people by the throat. It was the business and duty of the union labor party to repeal class legislation and release the people from the poverty and want and woe which bear them down."[34] The following spring when Milwaukee supporters of the ULP assembled to discuss the upcoming municipal election, electricity filled the air when Juliet Severance stood to speak. Consistent to the core, she declared: "You have been told through the capitalistic press that this party is a class movement and that it is dangerous. The reverse is true. Class rule now exists and this movement is designed to repeal class laws ... . It's because the beggars and thieves have got so much that the laborers have so little."[35] Despite her tireless campaigning through speeches and in the press, the ULP lost momentum after the November 1888 elections, and she knew that it was time to reevaluate how she was spending her time and energy.

In Juliet Severance's mind, her lifelong dedication to health reform, labor activism, and advocacy of women's social, economic, and legal emancipation were seamlessly connected. "It is only through the enslavement of woman in marriage," she wrote, that "in this age, a race [of slaves] can be begotten that will submit to the fetters forged by church and state."[36] Her foray into organized politics, combined with her outrage at the execution of Chicago's Haymarket anarchists and the prosecution of two Kansas sex radicals who had entered into a free love marriage, left Dr. Severance with renewed determination to fight for the separation of church and state. The government, she argued, was trampling upon fundamental Constitutional rights "[w]ith obscenity laws, blasphemy laws, conspiracy laws;

---

[33] "A Woman Anarchist," *The [Oshkosh] Daily Northwestern* (2 December 1886), p. 1.

[34] "Labor Men Meet," *Milwaukee Sentinel* (18 November 1887); Alice Henry, *The Trade Union Woman* (New York: D. Appleton and Co., 1915).

[35] "Mrs. Severance's Harangue," *Milwaukee Sentinel* (21 March 1888), pp. 1–2.

[36] Juliet H. Severance, "The 'Lucifer Match,'" *Truth Seeker* (20 January 1887), p. 71.

with fines, imprisonment, and death as penalties; with Comstock the vicious to supervise the mails; with ignorant policemen to judge what is proper to be uttered at a public meeting ... with Pinkertons to protect the interests of the rich and shoot at their pleasure men, women, and children."[37] Always one to practice the principles she advocated, Severance left her husband of 22 years and in 1891 moved to Chicago to join a network of freethinkers, Spiritualists, health reformers, labor activists, and individualist anarchists who shared her sex radical views.

Over the span of a decade spent on the shores of Lake Michigan, Juliet Severance employed her pen and her voice to criticize monopolies—be they medical, marital, or industrial—and to champion such feminist goals as equality, reform of marriage laws, and repeal of the Comstock Act. She was especially incensed by the latter because it targeted sex radical publications and the authors, editors, and booksellers so vital to the causes she embraced. A visit to Joliet prison fueled her outrage over the 1893 conviction and imprisonment of Chicago agnostic bookseller and publisher George Wilson. No one, she argued, was safe from Comstock and his "assassins," all operating under the guise of fighting the vice of obscene literature. Indeed, she noted, two of the "condemned" books that Wilson sold could be found in the Chicago public library and "the other two are on sale at all of our prominent bookstores."[38] The federal indictments of author Ida Craddock (author of *The Wedding Night*) in 1899 and 1902 further angered Severance, who joined other freethinkers in blaming Comstock for Craddock's suicide just one day before she was to report to federal prison. Likewise, Severance attributed Moses Harman's death in 1910 to the long-term effects of Comstock's harassment and prosecution.[39]

In addition to waging a war of words with her nemesis Anthony Comstock, albeit words that never led to her arrest, Dr. Severance spent the 1890s until her death penning opinion pieces for such periodicals as the *American Journal of Eugenics*, the *Boston Investigator*, *Lucifer, the Light-Bearer*, and *Truth Seeker*. Readers grew accustomed to seeing her name regularly linked to the work of the American Secular Union, which, according to historian of American freethought Sidney Warren, had by the mid-1890s become virtually a paper organization with most of its advocacy occurring in print.[40] She also hosted receptions at her quarters on Warren Avenue in honor of such noted figures as anarchist Voltairine de Cleyre and *Lucifer, the Light-Bearer* editor Moses Harmon. By 1908, however, the woman who had written "On Life and Health, or, on How to Live a Century" was

---

[37]   Juliet H. Severance, "What Can Be Done," *Truth Seeker* (31 December 1887), p. 839.

[38]   Juliet H. Severance, "Shall Such Things Continue," *Truth Seeker* (11 February 1893), pp. 87–8.

[39]   William Lemore West, "The Moses Harman Story," *Kansas Historical Quarterly* 37/1 (Spring 1971), pp. 41–63; Juliet H. Severance, "Shall Such Things Continue," pp. 87–8.

[40]   Sidney Warren, *American Freethought, 1860–1914* (New York: Columbia University Press, 1943), p. 172.

feeling the effects of age. That winter a physical collapse prompted a final move to her daughter's home in New York City. Although her circle of coworkers in reform had diminished with the death of Ezra Heywood in 1893, Lois Waisbrooker in 1909, and Moses Harman in 1910, and several of the key publications that had for decades served as outlets for her voice ceased to exist, she nonetheless remained "as much interested in freedom as she was in her young days when her arguments for the abolition of Negro slavery were answered by brickbats."[41] An activist to the end, she died in 1919 while writing a letter (posthumously published) emphasizing the need for "more discussion of the vital questions of real life."[42]

* * *

Reading like a textbook on nineteenth-century social reform movements, Juliet H. Severance's life consisted of conscious choices, focused goals, and clear vision made possible by her participation within a network of social activists sustained by an abundant array of reform newspapers and periodicals. As Lynn Schofield Clark argues in *From Angels to Aliens*, "Identity construction is an ongoing process guided by the need each of us have to consciously make sense of our choices, and the often unconscious ways in which these choices create a form of social solidarity with (or distinction from) others."[43] Exposure to antebellum religious and reform movement publications and orators (most notably those of anti-slavery, dress reform, and water cure) during Severance's formative years awakened the rebel in this farmer's daughter and made it possible for radical ideas about women's mental independence, economic rights, and sexual freedom to take root. The practice of water cure provided economic self-sufficiency and credibility as an M.D., and Spiritualism freed her mind and offered further opportunities to share her words. Water cure and Spiritualism provided national outlets for disseminating ideas as well as print-based forums through which Severance could interact with like-minded women and men. A savvy political operative who was accustomed to outsider status because of her gender, religious views, and marital status, she pursued a singular goal: to overthrow the forces that perpetuated inequality, especially censorship, marriage laws, and monopolies. Her search for solutions led to the free-thought movement, third-party politics, and ultimately sex radicalism. Throughout her life she never abandoned or rejected a movement. She instead experienced it fully, absorbed the lessons it had to teach about power, and through print and the lecture circuit became an active part of its social and political network.

---

[41]   "Juliet H. Severance," *Medical Critic and Guide* 11 (1908), p. 276.

[42]   Juliet H. Severance, "An Important Question," *Truth Seeker* (11 October 1919), p. 655; "Juliet H Severance, M.D.," *The New York Times* (4 September 1919), p. 13.

[43]   Lynn Schofield Clark, *From Angels to Aliens: Teenagers, the media, and the supernatural* (New York: Oxford University Press, 2005), p. 11.

The rise of a modernist communications circuit that included advertising, reports of conventions and addresses delivered, news of speakers' travels, and readers' letters fostered the construction of sites in which late nineteenth-century sex radicals could coalesce and flourish despite legal constraints. According to Jurgen Habermas, the democratization of the press enabled a diverse array of people, including such marginalized groups as women and those who advocated socially marginalized causes, to join in "the struggle for freedom and public opinion."[44] Known for her persuasive and powerful oratory, Severance is a prime example of one whose speaking life became the platform that launched her into the print-based arena that facilitated the construction of her radical identity. The proliferation of newspapers and periodicals, along with improvements in transportation and mail delivery, enabled her words to transcend local boundaries and become a nationally recognized force. The controversy and hostility her activism engendered underscores the highly contested nature of the ideas she advocated and the power she sought to claim for herself and others who challenged the status quo in Gilded Age America.

---

[44] Jürgen Habermas, "The Public Sphere: An Encyclopedia Article," *New German Critique* 3 (Autumn 1974), p. 53.

Chapter 2
Changing Feelings:
Fallen Women, Sentimentality,
and the Activist Press

María Carla Sánchez

What did it mean to be female, at risk, and the subject of moral reform activism at the end of the nineteenth century? According to a writer for the organizational newspaper the *Advocate and Family Guardian*, it meant a sustained, detailed analysis of one's every word, look, and gesture. In an article entitled "A Plea for Some Girls," an author identified only by the initials "L.V.H." declares that "you and I know more than one girl who behaves 'so'":

> How does she behave? You know, for you saw her yesterday when she tried to catch the attention of that gentleman whom you passed in the street. You saw her last evening, and your blood boiled when she stood uncomfortably near that young man, and brushed a thread from his sleeve. She ran her fingers through his hair, but perhaps you didn't see that. She coaxed him to call; she asked him if she might take him driving in her pony-phaeton; in short, it was a clear case of the girl wooing. This is an extreme case![1]

"An extreme case" indeed, the severity of which is emphasized by the bluntness of the second person "you" and the twice-repeated insistence that "you know" what is at stake in this scenario. The narrator's direct address mirrors the directness of the "girl who behaves 'so,'" an aggressiveness evident in her physicality: she "[stands] uncomfortably near," touches an arm, moves "her fingers through his hair." She "makes your blood [boil]," a sensation that cannot be pleasant; after all, since the question remains unanswered of who, exactly, is made "uncomfortable" when she stands too close, it could very easily be "you." And it all unfolds in public, with men "whom you passed in the street," or out driving in the "pony-phaeton"; it's all on display, this usurpation of what, presumably, should be the young man's role in this scene. (Later in the article, the narrator confides that "I know a young man ... [who] has virtually refused" two young women who behave "so," but again, just the right amount of semantic imprecision leaves open an unspoken question. Exactly *what* has he "virtually refused," and what was "virtual" about that refusal?) One implication does seem disturbingly clear: that

---

[1]   L.V.H., "A Plea for Some Girls," *Advocate*, 16 July 1885, pp. 212–13.

"you" are a witness to this, and hence, "you know" things that you wish you didn't. "How does she behave?" You know, and yet none of this is mere rhetorical flourish. For the declaration that "this is an extreme case" is undercut by the previous assertion that "you and I know more than one girl" who acts this way. Extremity, then, does not entail rarity. Otherwise, why have this conversation at all?

What is the precise risk for "girls who behave 'so,'" according to the *Advocate*? The immediate peril is becoming "an old maid," unmarried, unmarriageable and aging, with "sharpness [that] will not leave their tones and that fretful expression" that mars a girl's face. In being marked in one's voice and one's mien, our narrator reveals that this unacceptable behavior not only consists of an excessive physicality, a disturbing embodiment, but its *remains* corporeal: a type of social failing turned into scar tissue. Embedded in fears of old maidenhood is a vision of futures disrupted, a putatively natural social cycle of marriage and motherhood that is torn apart by a brush of a man's sleeve. While this scenario inspires more rhetorical appeals from the narrator—"what can be the matter with them?" she asks plaintively—the answer is already clearly in view for "you and I" to see. "What does make these girls behave so?" she asks a final time. "Oh! mothers, mothers, what does make *you* behave so?"[2] And so we have our culprit.

Even if girls who behaved "so" were extreme, decidedly they were not uncommon, but rather a favorite subject of social commentary, political action, public health debate, legal machination, and of course literary endeavor from the mid-1880s through the early 1920s. As Mark Thomas Connelly has written, "It was hard for anyone, even the most naïve visitor from some provincial hamlet, to miss them" (3); sexually subversive women and their environments, both geographical and social, had become insistently visible in the public spaces of the United States. Girls behaving "so," "fallen women," prostitutes or whores: under these and other names, women beyond the strict boundaries of sexual propriety commandeered the attention of a wide spectrum of moral reformers at the turn of the century. These reformers, including those behind the *Advocate and Family Guardian*, attempted to discover why some girls behaved "so" and to alter the catalysts that allegedly drove them to it. In doing so they turned their attention to the role of popular print culture and sought to restore, and in some ways maintain, the sentimental ethos and narrative techniques of a previous generation. For these reformers the proper response to the end of one century and the birth of a new one, to a threatening modernist culture on the horizon and to a Progressive Era that promised to be too progressive, was to be sentimental. In this essay I examine late nineteenth- and early twentieth-century representations of fallen women from the *Advocate and Family Guardian*, a publication whose history makes it a compelling case study for understanding how activist, religious media approached the arrival of the new century and its changing roles for women.[3] In foregrounding the term "fallen women," I seek to illuminate

---

　　　[2]　　L.V.H., "A Plea," p. 213, emphasis mine.

　　　[3]　　The society that published the newspaper, the American Female Guardian Society, altered its title and their own organizational name several times over the course of their

the motif conjoining so many of the fears admitted by the *Advocate* writers and the reform community from which they emerged. For this community, women could be fallen in ways that were frightening, overwhelming, and almost always interconnected and conflated: morally, socially, and emotionally. A fall from grace, whether through a ride in a pony-phaeton or paid sex work, ejected women from the prescribed narratives of marriage and motherhood, which reformers understood as both natural and divinely ordained. For the reformers of the *Advocate*, a fall was always a disruption of stories that *should* unfold and thus a plot development to be forestalled by any means necessary. But preferably by sentimental means.

In what follows I analyze the *Advocate*'s efforts to combat fallenness and safeguard the women who composed their main constituency. I argue that the manner in which *Advocate* staff wrote about women—both the fallen and the thankfully saved—perpetuated a sentimental world view initially espoused by reformers half a century before them. That world view reified feminine familial relationships, particularly those of mothers and daughters. Thus responsibility for women's fallenness—as in "A Plea for Some Girls"—and credit for its avoidance were understood as belonging to mothers, whether biological or "maternal figures." The fidelity of moral reformers to philosophies, representations, and narratives past placed the *Advocate* in an intriguing position as glimpses of a transforming world became, in fact, a new, progressive, and modernist century. In studying the *Advocate*, then, I hope to raise questions about how writings that seem stubbornly, even wildly behind their times, might in fact uncannily fit them. Or in other words, in what sense might periodicals like the *Advocate* be modernist? What might modernism look like if religious, activist, and sentimental literature like this were factored into its equations?

When the first issue of the *Advocate* appeared, Andrew Jackson was president, the nation had fewer than 25 states, and no one yet knew of names like Poe, Stowe, or Melville. By the time of its final issue, slavery was long dead, women could vote, and airplanes perforated the skies. The country had fought Mexico, Spain, Germany, Austria-Hungary, and of course itself; six months after that last issue, Pearl Harbor would be bombed. While printing presses churned out the *Advocate*, the United States evolved from an uncouth former colony to a bona fide world power. The history behind the publication, both immediate and general, is genuinely vast. Yet as we have seen, at the end of the nineteenth century, with women making inroads in education and the political realm that would never be undone, the *Advocate* was worrying about girls touching sleeves and going for pony rides in the wrong company. To borrow one of their own phrases: what made them behave so?

---

century-long history. Throughout this paper I will refer to it as the *Advocate*. For complete publishing history, see Kathleen L. Endres and Therese L. Lueck, *Women's Periodicals in the United States: Social and Political Issues* (Westport, CT: Greenwood Press, 1996), pp. 1–11. For a history of the society see Flora L. Northrup, *The Record of a Century, 1834–1934* (New York: American Female Guardian Society, 1934); María Carla Sánchez, *Reforming the World: Social activism and the problem of fiction in nineteenth-century America* (Iowa City: University of Iowa Press, 2008); Barbara Meil Hobson, *Uneasy Virtue: The Politics of Prostitution and the American Reform Tradition* (New York: Basic Books, 1987).

* * *

The Advocate and Family Guardian was born out of the vibrant reform culture that took shape in the United States alongside the fervor of the Second Great Awakening and which metamorphosed at the end of the century into the Progressive Era. Prior to the Civil War, abolitionist activism dominated the attention of the citizenry and the press, while nascent women's suffrage and temperance movements attracted devoted adherents, laying the foundation for later expansion. The cause of moral reform was also born in the chaotic decades before the war, with its goal stated plainly in its name: to perfect the moral character of the nation, particularly as its sexual practices made themselves felt in the public arena. In the 1830s moral reform groups in New England and the mid-Atlantic states began organizing so as to combat the growing problem of prostitution, launching what some of its members called "a crusade ... in the press."[4] Out of this activism came a series of newspapers, including the *Advocate*, which began as the controversial print voice of the American Female Guardian Society. The publication commanded a small, mostly local distribution in New York City and its environs.[5] That city, in the words of Timothy Gilfoyle, "had become the carnal showcase of the Western world," young in comparison with London and Paris, but rapidly becoming their equal in terms of reputation and consternation about "women on the town."[6] Both the AFGS and its print organ grew, so that, even during the turbulent and financially constrained years of the Civil War, the paper boasted a national subscriber circulation of 41, 000 households.[7] In both its ante- and post-bellum forms, the *Advocate* ran news stories, short stories, and editorials documenting the progress of moral decay in northeastern cities. It also published poetry, correspondence, committee reports, and book reviews as testimonials to the fight against "the great sin."[8] As a financial success the paper was quite modest: certainly not in the same league as commercial, mass market media but beyond the immediate influence of most "niche" publications and also comparable to the most well-known periodicals springing from movements such as suffrage and temperance. Even so, the paper formed just one part of New York reformers' efforts to abolish prostitution, a plan that included the lobbying of political officials, harnessing of church-based social networks, maintenance of safe houses for vulnerable women, and, as the century wore on, alliances with like-minded activists in other arenas, especially temperance.[9] After the Civil War

---

4   Northrup, *Record*, p. 15.

5   See Northrup, *Record*, and Sánchez, *Reforming*.

6   Timothy J. Gilfoyle, *City of Eros: New York City, Prostitution, and the Commercialization of Sex, 1790–1920* (New York: W.W. Norton and Company, 1992), p. 29.

7   Endres and Lueck, *Women's Periodicals*, p. 11.

8   Northrup, *Record*, p. 15.

9   See Mary E. Odem, *Delinquent Daughters: Protecting and Policing Adolescent Female Sexuality in the United States, 1885–1920* (Chapel Hill: University of North Carolina Press, 1995).

the society's mission expanded to include the care of orphan children and the general moral safeguarding of all young women.[10] Despite the broad scope of these activities, the society and its paper remained a proudly all-female enterprise until well into the 1920s: women were approached, reproached, cajoled, harangued, exhorted, and morally swayed to help save their fellow women.[11]

The sisterhood desperately needed that help. According to the *Advocate*, as well as mainstream publications, fallenness was destroying the country: although it was "the chief bane of savages, [prostitution] is depopulating Christendom" averred the *New York Times* in 1858.[12] Fallen women were often portrayed as alluring temptresses in the popular literature of the day, but in the pages of moral reform publications that representation underwent a profound metamorphosis. Prior to and immediately after the Civil War, activist media like the *Advocate* represented fallen women as victims in need of sentimental sympathy, metaphorical identification, and, ultimately, of a salvation both literal and narrative. "Poor girl!" begins one article, reporting on the inmates of the group's newly established House of Industry. One of those inmates was "a young woman who had been ensnared by the tempter's wiles. She was thrown into circumstances of temptation where she least expected it—was intoxicated by flattery, and overcome by professions of attachment—the fatal net was spread, and her ruin was affected!"[13] Another young woman suffered what would now be termed date rape, "seduced" by a young man allowed to visit her at home: "She is a member of a virtuous and respectable, but poor family; and once had fair prospects. She is now an outcast from society, and finds it difficult to get opportunities to support ... herself and infant child."[14] Newcomers to the city asked the wrong person for directions, wandered on their own into the wrong neighborhood, fell into the wrong company due to lack of supervision; in situations too numerous to imagine, they were "seduced and abandoned," taken advantage of, victimized. In telling the stories of fallen women, the *Advocate* staff makes concerted efforts to belittle distinctions of class and

---

[10] By the 1870s the society listed its mission as the "rescue from degradation, physical and moral, [of] the children of want" first and foremost. Listed as third among its goals was "to afford a place and means of protection for destitute, respectable young women ... within the age and circumstances of temptation." Yet even with this ostensible alteration of mission, and the devotion of an ever greater share of the society's finances to the running of orphanages, as we shall see, the newspaper remained devoted to—not to say obsessed with—women, their vulnerability, and the prospects for their salvation. This mission statement remained unchanged until the end of the 1920s, and was reprinted in every issue of the paper.

[11] In the mid-1920s the AFGS began to use reprinted materials from other, like-minded sources to a greater extent than ever before. Bylines became common where they had once been uncommon, and male contributors or authors began to equal female. The reasons behind this change remain unknown.

[12] "Prostitution in New-York," *The New-York Times*, 10 November 1858.

[13] "Visiting Committee's Report," *Advocate*, 1 May 1849, p. 71.

[14] "Night-Sitting," *Advocate*, 1 December 1844, p. 356.

region, noting that in the US a fall from grace was appropriately democratic and a matter of equal opportunity. Thus the notice of a "$1000 Reward," offered by a Mr. Roy Marsh for the return of his 18-year-old daughter ("supposed to have been enticed away by some villain") marks the misery of the well-heeled, while "Adeline the Tailoress" conjures a distinctly different socio-economic environment.[15] A visit to the AFGS Nursing Home corroborates the egalitarian nature of women's victimization, for "ladies of birth, education and refinement, are found among" its inhabitants.[16] Occasionally the fallen are named, but more often they are not, rather faceless but tearful subjects of page after page. Even when they are named, Lizzie or Adeline, the details make for little distinction, as authors ask readers to focus on what their victimized girls have in common: their story. Similarly, an article or report's author might receive a "byline," but the majority of pieces are simply attributed "for the *Advocate*." The reading experience of the paper, then, is one of binary opposition writ large: a world populated only by victims and saviors. While details of setting and cause might differ—tending patrician on one page, alternately to the working poor on the next—the basic plot of the *Advocate*'s narrative never does. Woman is victimized by man. Woman falls. We, *women*, must do something to stop this.

These exhortations draw their emotional impact from the potent metaphorical identification with which they are wed. Such identifications figured fallen women invariably as daughters, sisters, and mothers, therefore deserving of the same care and protection as *your* daughter, sister, or mother. Men thus threatened to destroy not only individual women, but entire families: "You have coolly selected your victim in the bosom of some quiet happy family," stated one story, addressing its male antagonist directly. "Your victim ... but for you might have been the pride of the family ... *Your course is strewed with the sighs and tears and groans of widowed mothers who regret that their daughters had not died in their infancy.*"[17] *Advocate* writers obsessively detailed how such unlucky young women became "moral and physical wreck[s] ... a monument of God's hatred to sin," a living misery to their loving families.[18] Adeline, Roy Marsh's daughter, the young victim of date rape, the young woman "ensnared by the tempter's wiles": all are characterized as members of families, not as singular women now outside of proper social and sexual mores. Organizations similar to the American Female Guardian Society utilized the same metaphorical tools. The Philadelphia Magdalen Society, for instance, referred in a straightforward manner to women staying in

---

[15]   "$1000 Reward," *Advocate*, 15 January 1849, p. 11; H.C. Knight, "Adeline the Tailoress," *Advocate*, 16 April 1849, pp. 57–8.

[16]   "House Committee's Report," *Advocate*, 16 January 1872, p. 24.

[17]   Quoted in Carroll Smith-Rosenberg, "Misprisioning *Pamela*: Representations of Gender and Class in Nineteenth-Century America," *Michigan Quarterly Review*, 26/4 (1987): pp. 9–28.

[18]   "House Committee's Report," *Advocate*.

their sanctuary home as being "in the family."[19] Meanwhile, the Boston-based New England Female Moral Reform Society printed letters from former residents of their Temporary Home in their paper, addressed to the matron of that institution and all beginning "Dear Mother."[20] Such maternal worship was in keeping with the sacralization of women's traditional familial roles during the early and mid nineteenth century. The phenomenon that Barbara Welter long ago termed the "cult of true womanhood" found itself perfectly reflected in the writings of the AFGS, both as an articulated philosophy and through this activism's ideological contradictions. After all, the process of agitating on behalf of vulnerable women, in print and otherwise, required members of the AFGS to create a presence for themselves outside of the putative "woman's sphere" that they strove to protect. All this was performed in the name of saving sisters, daughters, and mothers. The New England reform group had perhaps summarized the moral reform maternal maxim most succinctly: "a generation of good mothers might do more than all the philanthropists, the missionaries, the reformers that have lived since the days of the apostles," they wrote. "Whereas bad mothers may do more harm than all the blood-thirsty conquerors, the tyrants, the despots, the cruel persecutors, that have ever cursed a dying world!"[21]

After the Civil War and as the turn of the century beckoned, the *Advocate* narrative remained very much the same: victims and saviors, imperiled mothers and daughters, a struggle between good and evil. And with a membership still overwhelmingly female, the potential victims represented in these narratives remained female, with one slight alteration: the threat of women's fallenness now seemed exponentially expanded in an exponentially enlarged nation. Thus in 1908 a reader could peruse "Forbid Them Not," a story about Lucy Ashton, a young girl whose "parents are very wicked and very poor."[22] A kind teacher attempts to bring her into the fold and thus into good company: "I felt that the only chance for the child was to get her interested in coming to Sabbath-school."[23] In this case the snobbery of the poor girl's fellow classmates prevents her assimilation. But when she dies, her death not only effects her own salvation from the hinted horrors of her home life, but also guarantees the conversion of her formerly aloof peers. The story closes with a quotation from Acts 11:7: "What God has cleansed, that call thou not common."[24] In 1887 readers could digest a similar tale, "Big Flat": a poor factory girl named Lizzie (same name, less money than her antebellum counterpart), mistreated by family, bosses, and the world, ending up alone in a

---

[19] John McDowall, *Magdalen Facts* (1832), p. 55.

[20] I discuss these letters and their import for metaphorical kinship at greater length in Chapter 3 of *Reforming the World*, especially pp. 126–9.

[21] "Some of the Consequences of Maternal Unfaithfulness," *The Friend of Virtue*, 15 July 1847, p. 221.

[22] "Forbid Them Not," *Advocate*, 15 August 1908, pp. 253–4.

[23] Ibid., p. 254.

[24] Ibid.

shabby rental over a saloon, listening to "the shrieks of beaten women, or the oaths and cries of a sudden fight."[25] Her suicide is halted by a good-hearted neighbor named the Widow Maloney who consoles Lizzie and takes her home.[26]

Where antebellum *Advocate* writers had imagined the destruction of matriarchal biological families, only offering AFGS personnel as replacement mother figures once ruin had already taken place, in the later part of the century, families seemed to have already come apart, and a mother's place needed to be supplied both in the home and in their stories. Thus the nonfiction story of Lucy Walton Fletcher ("A Beautiful Example"), a British fellow traveler, elaborated her own miraculous maternal performances. Showing interest in a Scottish infirmary patient with another troubling and unspoken history ("she's here for an ill cause … and she goes out to-morrow, and back to her ill ways, nae doot"), Fletcher speaks to her "with the greatest earnestness … she went down upon her knees, imploring [the girl] to give up her evil courses and go with her."[27] Though her pleas fail that day, they are ultimately proven efficacious: the young woman reforms and eventually finds "a respectable tradesman" with the help of Fletcher.[28] "They were married and went to London, where her husband engaged in a lucrative business, and Mrs. Fletcher saw her afterward, a happy wife and mother."[29] "Ill causes" and "ill ways"; "wicked parents" and haughty classmates; the shrieks of abused women resounding in a lonely hovel. At the turn of the century, the plight of fallen women and their at-risk sisters appears infinitely bleaker than that of their predecessors. These women depend upon the chance interventions of kindly neighbors or random visitors, rather than the efforts of loving mothers. Though only the resistant young woman of the Lucy Fletcher story is explicitly marked as a prostitute, fallenness or its possibility are implied for the others. Thus the perceived threats to these young women have blurred into innuendo and knowing winks. For example, in what ways exactly are poor Lucy Ashton's parents "wicked"? If she herself has yet to "fall," how do we explain the Acts quotation, which explicitly speaks of cleansing? At the same time, these shadowy threats have increased, no longer confined to the world of faithless men who will "seduce and abandon": in the modern world, parents, poverty, and indifferent peers all imperil a young woman's virtue. And let us not forget the young women with whose story we began, those "who behave so": they also suffer from failed mothering. Hence as time progressed in the pages of the *Advocate*, the need for "a generation of good mothers" transformed any woman—teacher, neighbor, concerned citizen—into that all-desired and ever-necessary maternal guide. If such women can be persuaded of their calling—and theoretically, such women are among the ranks of the *Advocate*'s readership—then stories can still unfold as they

---

25   Helen Campbell Stewart, "Big Flat," *Advocate*, 16 April 1887, p. 125.
26   Ibid.
27   "A Beautiful Example," *Advocate*, 15 March 1884, pp. 83–4.
28   Ibid., p. 84.
29   Ibid.

ought, as Fletcher's tale indeed makes evident. Salvation *is* possible; families can be rebuilt and reformed; women's fallenness literally can be undone.

For *Advocate* reformers working prior to the Civil War, telling sentimental stories about fallen women was key to furthering their cause, for the bluntest of reasons: Americans would do nothing about prostitution if they could not be taught to *care* about fallen women. Such had been the belief of one of the AFGS's influences, a New York-based Presbyterian minister named John McDowall. Attempting to work with prostitutes in the infamous Five Points neighborhood in the early 1830s, McDowall wrote:

> The pulpit and the press are the only sources through which the public mind can be enlightened. I have tried the former to as great an extent as the Providence of God prepared the way for me, and failed to get before the people. *On the press, then, hangs my last hope.*[30]

McDowall's Journal was a forerunner of the *Advocate*, and thus, one of the earliest examples of advocacy on behalf of fallen women.[31] In this aspect moral reformers found themselves presented with the same challenge of persuasion that faced other activists: what kinds of stories represented the best and most effective advocacy? The century's bestselling novel—also the bestselling abolitionist work of the era—perfected the narrative strategies employed by McDowall, the AFGS, and reformers of many stripes. *Uncle Tom's Cabin* (1852), like activist literature before and after it, emphasizes affective modes of reading and interpreting: foregrounding metaphorical likeness between readers and characters; featuring rhetorical appeals to readers' senses of justice, morality, and caring; encouraging the imagination of highly permeable boundaries between readers' lives and narrative worlds; and reifying feminine familial bonds, particularly those between mothers and children.[32] And unlike John McDowall, and to an extent truly enviable by other reformers, Harriet Beecher Stowe's novel "got before the people." Reading sentimental activist literature, then, one that nudged readers toward

---

[30] John McDowall, "The Last Hope," *McDowall's Journal*, January 1833, p. 1.

[31] I discuss the history of *McDowall's Journal* and its relation to the *Advocate* at length in *Reforming the World*, especially pp. 115–19.

[32] Several scholars discuss these aspects of sentimentality as they inform nineteenth- and early twentieth-century US literature. See Elizabeth Barnes, *States of Sympathy: Seduction and democracy in the American novel* (New York: Columbia University Press, 1997); Joanne Dobson, "Reclaiming Sentimental Literature," *American Literature* 69/2 (1997): pp. 263–88; Philip Fisher, *Hard Facts: Setting and Form in the American Novel* (New York: Oxford University Press, 1985); Glenn Hendler, *Public Sentiments: Structures of feeling in nineteenth-century American literature* (Chapel Hill: University of North Carolina Press, 2001). I discuss sentimentality in antebellum moral reform literature specifically in *Reforming the World*, Chapter 3. For the cultural impact of *Uncle Tom's Cabin* see Sarah Meer's *Uncle Tom Mania: Slavery, minstrelsy, and transatlantic culture in the 1850s* (Athens, GA: University of Georgia Press, 2005).

sympathetic emotional responses, formed an important aspect of reformers' missions. As the historical context changed from the Civil War to the Spanish-American War and then to World War I, this element of the mission never altered. Sentimentality and rhetorically charged storytelling remained the *Advocate*'s favored narrative choice. Thus in 1885 a contributor identified only as "C.P." declared that "I believe in the power of fiction to *instruct and elevate*. Ideal pictures of life may have an exalting, refining influence on character."[33] Or in other words: good stories would *do* good. Moral reformers, and many others, believed that reading about a poor slave named Tom had convinced many Americans to care about slavery. Well into the twentieth century, the reformers of the *Advocate* hoped that reading about Lucy and Lizzie and Adeline and their endless series of endangered girls would compel new generations of Americans to care about fallen women. That they clung to narrative styles popular in their parents' and grandparents' day tells us not only that moral reformers preferred a proven method of "getting before the people." It also reveals that while years and decades passed by, some social problems remained obstinately *there*, very much unwilling to be solved and slip away.

* * *

To read the *Advocate* throughout its century-long existence is in many ways to witness a demonstration of the power of the formulaic and the middle-brow and to watch the continued appeal of sentimental narrative. Nothing in the structures or vocabulary of their stories perplexed potential readers; simplistic and easily accessible, anyone possessed of a grade-school education could peruse them. Similarly, nothing about the imperiled women featured on *Advocate* pages stands out and indelibly individualizes them, sets them apart or makes them unusual. I've argued elsewhere that moral reform, foremost among social movements in the nineteenth century, founded its narratives upon a complex metaphorical endeavor whose goal was to (re)imbue disenfranchised women with social worth. They needn't be individualized to accomplish this; in fact, they should *not* be. It is difficult to distinguish one Lizzie or Lucy or Adeline from another—and this is the point. Saving fallen women necessitated likening them to other women, all women—in some cases, fictional constructs. It could happen to her; it could happen to your mother, sister, daughter; to your Sunday school student or your neighbor; it could happen to you. The passage of time does not alter the allure of the metaphor: the blur of stories and the starkness of categorical options (victim/savior, fallen/ virtuous) remain constant, faithful, *true* into the twentieth century. Thus, even as literary realism and then modernism emerged on the cultural stage, publications like the *Advocate* continued to tell stories as they always had. Certainly, it is a trademark of evangelical thought to stand outside of secular history and to reject

---

[33]   C.P., "About Reading Story Books," *Advocate*, 1 July 1885, pp. 196–7. Emphasis mine.

the purportedly historicizing and mundane for a teleology that exists outside of time. The staff of the *Advocate* understood themselves as doing God's work, an ethos evidenced not least by the scriptural quotation from Job that anchored their masthead: "I delivered the poor that cried, and the fatherless, and him that had none to help him … the cause that I knew not, I searched out."[34]

So even as traces of decades passing appeared in the paper, the main story, as it were, remained the same, new literary styles and movements be damned. The defining ethos of emerging modernist writing might be summarized by Ezra Pound's exhortation to "Make it new!" but such philosophies did not extend to those actively engaged in the work of trying to end prostitution.

Moral reform writing, as exemplified by the *Advocate*, reacted to the conditions of modernity in the 1890s and the 1920s in precisely the same ways as it reacted to the conditions of modernity in the 1830s. Which is not to say that moral reformers failed to understand what those conditions were. On the contrary, to read the *Advocate* from the 1880s through the 1920s is to follow a clear line of perceived threats to Christian belief, national morals, and the physical, emotional, and economic wellbeing of the nation's women. In this final section I turn to the most prominent of those threats, the pernicious influence of "bad" literature. It is an instance of the most elegantly simple logic: just as reformers believed that good stories could do good, they firmly held that bad stories would lead to misery. Saving women did not merely entail telling the right kind of stories about them. It also meant pointing out the wrong kind and thus acting as a type of literary adviser. Others in the United States might be concerned with the possibilities for technical innovation in literature, for playfulness with its language, or devotion to the furtherance of Art. The staff of the *Advocate* was more concerned with what literature could do *for* you or *to* you, and your ability to care, to act, and to help change the world.

The pages of the *Advocate* are permeated with articles on literature and proper reading. They outnumber articles on any other art form or cultural endeavor ten to one: to paraphrase John McDowall's pronouncement from the 1830s, "the pulpit and the press" were still the main organs through which the American public might be reached. Hence the products of that press retained primary importance over any other art. The anonymous author of a short piece entitled "Truth," from 1885, complains that "putting aside the bad books, which are working ruin and desolation, we see [the lack of truth] more and more in the daily newspaper records; the most of them give utterly false views of life."[35] Misrepresentation and outright lies are bad enough, but unrealistic expectations could be even worse: "And as a novel is hardly a novel, without a love story, there are the endless charges rung upon love. And the worst of it is the utterly false views they give."[36] While complaints about a lack of realism might seem ironic for the *Advocate*, they harken to past stories

---

[34]   Job 29:12, 16.

[35]   "Truth," *Advocate*, 1 December 1885, p. 358.

[36]   Ibid.

about "seduced and abandoned" young women who thought their real-life suitors would behave like novelistic heroes. This falsity and lack of realism give rise not only to a world in which young girls might become fallen women, but in which the very familial foundations of society crumble: "No wonder that young people, following such ideas, ... wake to find themselves unhappy. No wonder there are cases for the divorce court, no wonder there are suicides and miseries."[37] Bad stories create the wrong impressions, the wrong desires, give you the wrong idea—and we all pay the price.

Throughout the ensuing decades the newspaper sounded the same alarm: in 1925, for example, the article "Our Fiction Magazines" designated much of the current offerings as "border[ing] on a disguised pornography" certain to corrupt and harm.[38] Appealing to the parents among the faithful, its author suggests that "the checking of this flood of insidious and perverted story writing lies largely with the parental home."[39] A like-minded piece called "What People Like to Read" combined the visions of fiction-caused social chaos and the entreaty to familial guidance. "A campaign should be waged in every community with the end in view to improve the general taste in reading" the essay proclaims:

> We have gone movie mad and speed mad, and are leaving the training of our children and young people to the public schools, newspaper press and other public agencies. The voice of prayer at the family altar is a mere echo from former generations. The shrine at mother's knee has been exchanged for devotion to the funny paper and vapid pictures. Nothing can turn this tide except the restoration of religion in the home and the revival of a taste for god [sic] reading. These two things must go hand in hand.[40]

Reformers' repeated calls for an improved literature certainly accord with other expressions of discontent with early twentieth-century popular culture, and, in this last article's reference to film, one can see intimations of how that culture will change. The key terms "restoration" and "revival" speak directly to that which needs attention and signal reformers' values. In focusing upon literature, *Advocate* reformers paid respect to the then-prominent form of popular entertainment. They also pinpointed that element of popular culture already associated with women as both producers and consumers and which—prior to the conquest of film—still generated ideals of femininity. Or put another way: until Hollywood took over, popular literature was still where the fight was, as *Advocate* staff knew very well. And even in the heyday of Valentino and Mary Pickford, *Advocate* writers still believed, like their forebears, that the powers of literature followed clear patterns of cause and effect. Good literature, such as that found in their own pages, promoted good and led to happiness, safety, and sound morals. Bad literature resulted in

---

[37]   Ibid.
[38]   "Our Fiction Magazines," *Advocate*, May 1925, p. 66.
[39]   Ibid.
[40]   "What People Like to Read," *Advocate*, December 1925, p. 178.

"divorces," "suicides," "pornography," and the dissolution of the family (complete with a "shrine at mother's knee") as they knew it. For reformers such disasters all followed the same path. A divorced woman *was* a fallen woman to that era's devout Christians; a woman known to indulge in "pornographic" or suggestive literature was as tainted as the girls who brushed men's sleeves and asked them out in their pony-phaetons. The proper life stories which reformers understood as natural and divinely ordained—marriage, motherhood, and an implied faithful but uneventful existence—were potentially forestalled by improper stories printed on a page. (One might imagine a large, overarching implication across the decades of the *Advocate*'s storytelling: the saviors of their stories, like the kindly Widow Maloney or patient Mrs. Fletcher, definitely read the *right* kind of literature.) The stakes for virtuous and righteous storytelling, whether in 1830 or 1930, remained exorbitantly high.

In light of their fidelity to narrative strategies favored by generations past, it may be tempting to categorize activists like the American Female Guardian Society as woefully out of step and reactionary. In many ways, such characterizations would be true. As writers, they did not innovate or seek aesthetic excellence. As devout Christians, they distrusted much of the popular culture consumed by their neighbors. They proved singularly incapable of distinguishing between small infractions of social mores—brushing a sleeve, being "forward"—and the degradation that followed actual paid sex work in American cities and towns. Yet I would argue that in another sense, the women behind the *Advocate* were more in tune to their times than the more ambitious literary men and women who outshone them. In the 1920s and '30s as the publication entered its last phase of existence, fallen women fared little better than their ancestors had a hundred years earlier. The "purity campaigns," white slavery scares, and anti-vice movements of the turn of the century had resulted in increasing prostitution's presence within the mainstream media and the legal arena but had not lowered its perceived or documented rate of incidence.[41] The extraordinary growth of both the country's population and the urban areas that housed many Americans promoted a corollary expansion of women's sexualized labor: burlesque houses, taxi dance halls (where women danced with partners in exchange for cash), and speakeasies all joined the "traditional" brothel as locales where sexual gratification might be purchased.[42] Simultaneously, changing conceptions of what types of social behavior necessitated the involvement of political, legal, or criminal authorities, meant that women whose sexual behavior placed them outside of reigning norms risked state intervention into their lives to an extent their nineteenth-century counterparts could not

---

[41] Mark Thomas Connelly, *The Response to Prostitution in the Progressive Era* (Chapel Hill: University of North Carolina Press, 1980); Brian Donovan, *White Slave Crusades: Race, gender, and anti-vice activism, 1887–1917* (Urbana: University of Illinois Press, 2006); Odem, *Delinquent Daughters*.

[42] Elizabeth Alice Clement, *Love for Sale: Courting, treating, and prostitution in New York City, 1900–1945* (Chapel Hill: University of North Carolina Press, 2006).

have imagined.[43] Many aspects of society had "progressed" with the Progressive Era, but some things remained stubbornly the same, including the myriad ways in which women's sexual transgressions could cost them dearly. Being known as "fallen," loose, promiscuous, or a whore still damaged women. In maintaining their dedication to fallen women and to telling their stories sympathetically, *Advocate* writers showed themselves to be fully cognizant of what the twentieth century shared with the era before it. After all, the more things change … .

In this way, then, one might read moral reformers like the creators of the *Advocate* not as antithetical to modernism and a new, progressive century, but as the logical accompaniment to them: a reflection of, and self-identified voice for, all that carried over from the past. In the pages of this newspaper one can see the efforts of Americans utterly unconcerned with belletristic circles or artistic triumph nonetheless attempting to make narrative literally *work* for them. Their commitment to emotionally charged, sentimental, and highly rhetorical writing links them to early muckrakers as well as to later generations of proletarian authors. No less a kindred spirit than Jane Addams wrote in 1912 that "Sympathetic knowledge is the only way of approach to any human problem, and the line of least resistance into the jungle of human wretchedness must always be through that region which is most thoroughly explored … by sympathetic understanding."[44] Such understanding, and a demonstrable social change from it, is what *Advocate* writers sought. To include them in studies of the modernist moment is to see fully how activist and religious persons apprehended their culture and accordingly chose which elements to save, which to embrace, and which to fight. That fight, or "crusade in the press," ties them to others attempting to change their world, past, present, and future.

---

[43]   Mara L. Dodge, *"Whores and Thieves of the Worst Kind": A study of women, crime, and prisons, 1835–2000* (DeKalb: Northern Illinois University Press, 2002); Odem, *Delinquent Daughters*.

[44]   Jane Addams, *A New Conscience and an Ancient Evil* (New York: The Macmillan Company, 1912), p. 11.

Chapter 3

"She Will Spike War's Gun":
The Anti-War Graphic Satire of the
American Suffrage Press

Rachel Schreiber

A mother holds her baby in one arm and in the other a picket sign that reads, "There shall be no abridgement of the franchise because of sex" (Figure 3.1). A soldier, holding a bayoneted rifle, replies to her placard via the caption, stating "But madam, you cannot bear arms." To this the mother replies, "Nor can you, sir, bear armies." The two figures resemble each other visually, creating a symmetric balance. Both are tall and lean. While the soldier stands at attention, he nevertheless has a sway to his back that mirrors the curve of the suffragist/mother's hip. By creating a visual equivalence between the two figures, the artist places them on equal footing. Both are equally deserving of the franchise. The cartoon, drawn by (Annie) Lou Rogers and published in the suffragist publication *The Woman's Journal* in 1915, engages in World War I-era debates over suffrage that posited men's ability to defend the nation as central to their citizenship and their right to vote, by responding that women, too, participate in national defense via the (re)production of soldiers. During this period, these gendered ideas about citizenship fueled not only the arguments for women's enfranchisement, but also suffragists' relationship to the peace movement that opposed US entry into World War I. The woman's retort to the soldier eloquently inverts the rhetorical use of bearing arms as a benchmark of citizenship. While some argued that women should not vote because they do not fight wars, suffragists countered by claiming that women should indeed vote because they mother soldiers.

The suffrage movement was unified in its anti-war stance at the start of the Great War in Europe. On August 29, 1914, 1,500 women marched for peace in New York City, demonstrating broad-based support for pacifism.[1] In addition to arguing that women deserved the vote because they mother soldiers, suffragists also advocated for pacifism by claiming that women were in a unique position to oppose war because of their innate propensity for order. They believed

---

[1] The protest organizers had three stated goals: to express horror at war and sympathy for suffering in Europe, to urge President Wilson to attempt mediation, and to register women's unique objections to war, based on the moral outrage at violence and the endangerment of sons that only mothers could experience. See *New York Times*, 30 August 1914, II, 11:3.

Fig. 3.1   Lou Rogers, "Arms vs. Army," *The Woman's Journal,* March 20, 1915.

that women would help keep the nation out of wars propagated by men, who were inherently violent and militaristic. After 1914, as the war intensified and US intervention seemed imminent, the women's peace movements became increasingly radicalized, and the character of women's peace societies shifted. Its new members, versed in militant direct political action they had learned from British suffragists, began to question the passive tactics, such as peace marches, of the pre-war peace movements. Meanwhile, the conservative suffragists distanced themselves from the pacifists. They came to see in preparedness an opportunity for women to materially demonstrate their roles as active, respectable citizens who should be enfranchised, and they called for suffragists to abandon their initial anti-war position. The result, by 1917, was a splintering of the suffrage movement around the question of support for war versus pacifism and non-intervention.

Throughout this period suffragists relied on their journals as spaces for activism. In particular, the graphic satire of this press demonstrates the shifting, and at times contradictory, approaches these women took to potential US involvement in the First World War over the course of the decade. Analysis of the suffrage journal cartoons reveals nuances of how that press mobilized gendered notions of citizenship in order to make their cases for or against US involvement in the war in Europe. For a short number of years in the middle of the 1910s, the visual culture of the suffrage press imagined broadened possibilities for women's fulfillment of their roles as citizens. By 1917 the suffrage press would shift to more conventional representations of women, echoing the move among mainstream suffragists to support for preparedness and their call for US intervention in the Great War in Europe.

Suffrage journals played a key part in disseminating the message of the organizations that committed themselves to obtaining the vote for women. With over a dozen titles, these journals reached women in the urban centers as well as remote rural regions. The magazines featured articles on the efforts of suffragists, editorials, advertisements for suffrage paraphernalia, and graphic satire.[2] The latter images merit special consideration because they enable us to see the ways gender figured into this group's activism. Political cartoons are particularly useful to historians of gender since they almost always represent bodies. To emphasize their points, the cartoons often reveal (and betray) in a complex yet instant manner attitudes towards gender (as well as race, class, and ethnicity) to which written texts are oblivious, or which couldn't be communicated without endless verbiage. Further, political cartoons not only rely on readily recognizable figures, but they encapsulate with great efficiency a variety of political and social ideas, distilling them into one illustration with accompanying caption.

Another cartoon by Rogers exemplifies these characteristics of political cartoons, as well as the idea that voting women would help keep the nation out of conflict. Her striking cartoon titled "She Will Spike War's Gun," published in *Judge* on May 10, 1913, depicts a female figure, classically attired, using the "vote" as a tool to drive in a wedge that will dismantle the machinery of war (Figure 3.2). Her hammer signifies the power the vote will provide her to influence issues as important as war. But the woman is not the dowdy, old-fashioned suffragist of the nineteenth century. She is youthful and pretty at the same time as being muscular and powerful. Identified by her banner as a "new woman," she signifies a brand of modern femininity to which Rogers, and some other suffragists, subscribed.

As the years of the war wore on in Europe, it became increasingly clear that the United States would intervene. Given this inevitability, later cartoons demonstrate the ways that suffragists still used gendered arguments about the parity between women/mothers and men/soldiers to garner support for female suffrage. Relying on similar arguments to that of Rogers's "Arms vs. Army," Laura Foster's cartoon "Hand in Hand" posits that the vote would enable women to demonstrate their patriotism as equally as men did through soldiering (Figure 3.3). But unlike Rogers's cartoon that claims a special place for women as (re)producers of soldiers, Foster shows suffrage and soldiering as equal partners—a line of men and women walking in tandem. The men, though in business suits, hold their rifles at the ready. The first wears a sash that bears the word "patriotism." His female counterpart holds an American flag and wears a sash that reads "universal suffrage." The men

---

[2]   For an in-depth study of the various types of print and consumer goods produced in this era to promote suffrage, see Margaret Finnegan, *Selling Suffrage: Consumer Culture & Votes for Women* (New York: Columbia University Press, 1999).

Fig. 3.2   Lou Rogers, "She Will Spike War's Gun," *Judge*, September 14, 1912.

Fig. 3.3   Laura Foster, "Hand in Hand," *Judge*, June 30, 1917.

and women march forward very much in unison. Again here the male and female figures closely resemble one another. The representational strategy of depicting men and women as equals was one the suffrage press employed with some regularity. Yet, the heteronormativity of this pair assures us that suffrage will not completely undo familiar gender roles. Rather, Foster suggests that female patriots belong right beside the men who are ready to take up arms for their country. In fact, the desire to act patriotically and the desire for universal suffrage cannot be separated from one another, as Jane Addams and others posited.

Traditional roles for women were emphasized too in the regular alignment of patriotism and motherhood in this era. This was true in both the suffrage press as well as in conventional war propaganda. Images of mothers were used to extremely different ends—to address the need for women to remain in the home, taking care of children, or to argue for women's right to be involved in political decisions and public debate because of their maternal capacity. The latter approach can be seen in a cover drawn by James Montgomery Flagg for *The Woman Citizen* and published on October 27, 1917 (Figure 3.4). The cover appeared a little over a year after Flagg had published what would become his most famous image, in which Uncle Sam points to the viewer and states "I want YOU for US Army." Originally a cover for *Leslie's Weekly*, the "I want YOU" image was reprinted as a poster that has since become the most widely used recruitment image for the US Army to date.[3]

At the time, Flagg was better known for his prolific illustrations for women's magazines.[4] At the start of the war, Flagg joined the Committee on Public Information's Division of Pictorial Publicity, a voluntary organization comprised of the era's most commercially successful illustrators that produced drawings, posters, and other visual materials for the US government.[5] Charles Dana Gibson headed the organization's art department. Like Flagg, Gibson too was better known for his images of women. His "Gibson girl," a tall woman of Northern European descent with a small, upturned nose, rosebud lips, and a long fine neck, had quickly become known, since her initial appearances, as the quintessential "American ideal type" (Figure 3.5). Along with her successors, drawn by a number of illustrators including Howard Chandler Christy, Harrison Fisher, and Flagg, the Gibson girl was the exemplary "girl on the magazine cover" that instantiated some of the first, and most enduring, stereotypes of women in American mass print media.

---

[3]   The original date of publication as a cover for *Leslie's* was July 6, 1916. The image was reprinted as a recruitment poster in 1917. Source: <http://www.loc.gov/exhibits/treasures/trm015.html> (accessed 14 May 2012).

[4]   Carolyn Kitch, *The Girl on the Magazine Cover: The Origins of Visual Stereotypes in American Mass Media* (Chapel Hill: University of North Carolina Press, 2001), p. 102.

[5]   Susan E. Meyer, *James Montgomery Flagg* (New York: Watson Guptill Publications, 1974), p. 37.

Fig. 3.4   James Montgomery Flagg, cover for *The Woman Citizen*, October 27, 1917.

Fig. 3.5   Charles Dana Gibson, "Gibson Girl."

Though Flagg's cover for the *Woman Citizen* is done in a much simpler, pen-and-ink line drawing style than the Uncle Sam image, the heroic iconography of noble American patriotism is equally present here. The beautiful mother is young, and her facial features closely resemble the Gibson Girl. Her dress and hair, however, are traditional and connote her old-fashioned values, which might be contrasted to images of the independent New Woman also emerging at this time. Her body frames that of her baby, and mother and child gaze adoringly at one another. The caption reads, "Women bring all voters into the world. Let women vote." We thus recognize this woman as the mother of a *son*. The suffrage argument, reliant on the idea that all women are mothers, ties her right to vote to her male progeny's future as a soldier. Published in October of 1917, American readers would also have understood the image and caption to infer that mothers' sons grow up to fight for their country; therefore mothers should vote.

Motherhood was also invoked in pro-war propaganda, such as a Red Cross poster by Alonzo Earl Foringer (Figure 3.6). The triangular composition of mother and baby is classic and reminiscent of a Renaissance Pietà—a painting or sculpture of the Virgin Mary mourning over the body of her dead son Jesus. This composition was used often in mass media images of exalted mothers throughout the Progressive Era and connotes the mother's dedication to her son. In the poster, the Red Cross volunteer is seated and wears classical robes along with a Red Cross cap. She lovingly holds a wounded soldier, scaled down so that she is able to clasp his adult body to her bosom as a mother would a baby. The woman appears to be too young to be a soldier's mother, yet we are told by the title inscribed underneath her that she is "The Greatest Mother in the World." Is she his mother or his nurse? No matter. The maternal role played by the female war worker/nurse is a stand-in for all mothers who care for soldiers/sons. Women demonstrate their patriotism through this care. This figure's bodily pose and her facial expression reflect all the nurturing devotion to soldiers and dedication to the state that is expected of patriotic American women.

Women's positions as mothers and the equal roles women played in public life were themes invoked in the suffrage press to argue for enfranchisement and against war. But after the US entry into the war in 1917, the most common theme used in the suffrage press to argue for the vote built on the fact that, rhetoric aside, women's wartime roles, both at home and at the front, did sideline the tired dictum that enjoined women to remain in the home and obliged women to take over many male roles. In addition to the image of the war nurse who dedicated herself to the well-being of American troops, images of women filling men's places while they were across the ocean were used variously. Not only in the suffrage press, but also in the mainstream and socialist presses, these images were employed to support the need for women's access to the vote, to encourage preparedness and patriotism, or to argue against the war. One frequent trope found in 1910s visual culture was "the girl he left behind him." The differing iterations of this clichéd figure reveal her malleability—she could represent the cheerful "girl next door" who patriotically takes up shovel and hoe but is still in need of protection; she

Fig. 3.6   Alonzo Earl Foringer, "The Greatest Mother in the World," ca.
                1918.

could signify the financial desperation of those who attempted to fill in gaps in labor; she could symbolize new roles for women in American society; or she could symbolize a more ambiguous, confused response to the calamities of war.

The phrase "the girl he left behind him" had appeared in literature and popular culture since the Revolutionary War to refer not only to girls left behind by soldiers, but girls whose lovers left for extended journeys. A sentimental poem published by Edgar A. Guest in 1918 presents the standard World War I-era "girl left behind," who was specifically left behind by a soldier at war. Written from the point of view of the now-absent soldier's parents, the poem describes a girl who used to be "frivolous" and display "petty flaws," but who "blossomed into beauty" the day their son "bravely marched away." She is a girl-next-door type. Prior to their son's departure, the parents were a little jealous of his attention to her. But his volunteerism transforms her into a patriot who participates vicariously in the

Fig. 3.7   Guenther, "Get Behind ... ," ca. 1918. Image courtesy of the Library
                of Congress.

defense of the nation. Her very love for the American soldier shows that "she's no
longer young and flighty—she's the girl who loves our boy."[6]

The visual image of "the girl he left behind" appeared in a range of publications
during the 1910s. In a poster published by the New York Land Army Membership
Committee by an artist named Guenther, a young woman appears working in a
field (Figure 3.7). Ghosted behind her is the figure of a soldier, presumably he
who left her. Both figures are engaged in their respective tasks—she works a field,
and he lunges forward, emerging from behind her, bayonet at the ready. He is on
the battlefield—his posture is energetic and he looks beyond the frame, ostensibly
towards the enemy. By contrast, while she holds a farm implement and wears
appropriate farm-worker clothing, she seems to be posing for the image. She is not

---

    6   Edgar A. Guest, "The Girl He Left Behind," in *Over Here: War Time Rhymes*
(Chicago: The Reilly & Britton Company, 1918).

actively working the field, but appears coquettish and sweet. There is something askew about her image. Her overalls are a bit too big for her, implying that they belong to "him," and only the barest hint of a breast outline appears. Her body is somewhat androgynous. It is as if this illustrator could not fully image a woman performing this work, so that her face, which closely resembles idealized images of women appearing in magazines of this era, does not seem to belong on her body. Further, while she performs her absent lover's labor, he is still right behind her, signifying that his soldiering is performed in order to protect her. Overall, she communicates discomfort at finding herself in this (hopefully) temporary role, assuring viewers that she will gladly let him take over when he returns. The copy, addressed in second person, asks the viewer to "get behind" her, adding to the idea that, despite her new responsibilities, she still needs the support of others.

H.J. Glintenkamp offered a very different "girl he left behind" on the October 1914 cover of the socialist magazine the *Masses* (Figure 3.8). The *Masses* was staunch in its anti-war position, arguing that in war, the rich profit. They exhibit disregard for the lives of working-class soldiers, and are indifferent to increasing poverty at home. The woman in this image plows a field, but she overturns skulls and bones. The association between fall harvests and the reaping of soldiers was invoked in a range of radical anti-war literature of the time. Socialists were concerned about potential food shortages that could arise for the domestic working class as food would be exported abroad for both the military and as aid to European victims of war. Women, as traditional breadgivers, would be left to deal with the consequences.[7] In this way, the cartoon provides a powerful commentary on the vapid, cheerful girl usually depicted as the one left behind. Rather than depicting a girl who will bravely face the prospect of taking on work unfamiliar to her, Glintenkamp offers viewers a more critical look at the wartime challenges that women will face. As well, the woman imaged here is decidedly different from Guenther's female figure. This figure is quite unlike the typical magazine cover girl of the era. She is not thin and curvaceous, and her pose is not flirtatious. Her hair and the outline of her breast clearly mark her as a woman, although her body too is a bit androgynous. Unlike Guenther's, this woman's back is turned to the viewer so she cannot gaze at us alluringly. To some extent her body appears to be manly. In keeping with the ways that the socialist press tended to use normative gender roles in its arguments against capitalism, here we see a world turned upside down, where skeletons are reaped from the earth, and women must perform men's work.

Divergent images of "the girl he left behind" published in *The Woman Citizen* indicate the beginnings of the splitting of the suffrage movement's position on US intervention in the war. The latter of the two, published as an interior cartoon in the May 25, 1918 issue, was drawn by Clarence Daniel Batchelor, a popular women's magazine illustrator of the time, whose work resembles that of Charles Dana Gibson and James Montgomery Flagg (Figure 3.9). In this cartoon, Batchelor creates a play

---

[7]   Mark Van Wienen, "Poetics of the Frugal Housewife: A Modernist Narrative of the Great War and America," *American Literary History* 7, no. 1 (1995), p. 64.

Fig. 3.8   H.J. Glintenkamp, "The Girl He Left Behind Him," the *Masses*, October 1914.

on the "girl left behind" theme by drawing the same woman twice—the current "Louise," seen on the deck of a Red Cross ship wearing nurse's garb, reflects back on her pre-war self. Similarly to Guest's poem, Batchelor's cartoon, titled "The Girl She Left Behind Her" suggests that war transforms young girls into serious women, as evidenced by the old, pre-war Louise who was once a "leader of the younger set," seen in the inset in a parlor with a man's hand on her shoulder.[8] The style in which Nurse Louise is drawn will be repeated in *The Woman Citizen* during the war years, not only in interior cartoons but on covers as well, all drawn by Batchelor and all reminiscent of Gibson Girls. Louise portrays a positive image of women's wartime roles—roles that change their lives from frivolous to meaningful, all while maintaining their image as quintessential, all-American girls.

Less than one year earlier in August 1917, Lou Rogers published her version of the girl left behind on the cover of *The Woman Citizen*, a few months after the United States declared war on Germany (Figure 3.10). Rogers's image is

[8]   The man's presence in the image, along with the repetition of Louise's name in both depictions of her, might also serve to discourage a reading of this image as that of a woman who has left her female lover, a reading immediately available by the caption alone.

THE GIRL SHE LEFT BEHIND HER

Fig. 3.9   C.D. Batchelor, "The Girl She Left Behind Her," *The Woman Citizen*, May 25, 1918.

far more ambiguous than the Guenther girl, the Glintenkamp, or the Batchelor. A bewildered young woman stands on a pedestal amidst the maelstrom of war. As the waves that lap at her feet describe, she represents the girl he left behind him "in factory," "in field," and "in home." Across the ocean, the storm that is making "the world safe for democracy" rages on. What are we to make of her? Unlike the Guenther girl, she is not coquettish. Unlike both the Guenther and Glintenkamp images, she is not seen working in a field, and unlike Batchelor's figure, she does not occupy an active wartime role. Rather, she appears out of any context, standing at the edge of the nation. She wears a dress and perhaps an apron, signifiers of femininity, yet her fist is clenched in an expression of physical resolve. She is neither the "New Woman" that Rogers designated in an earlier cartoon, nor the typical girl on a magazine cover. She seems ordinary, an average woman trying to make sense of conflicting roles.

By August of 1917 the American suffrage organizations and the women's peace parties had become deeply divided. As the eventuality of war approached, these women's groups faced decisions regarding the agendas of their organizations

The Girl He Left Behind Him

Fig. 3.10   Lou Rogers, "The Girl He Left Behind Him," *The Woman Citizen*,
August 25, 1917.

and the future focus of their efforts. On the one hand, militant suffragists insisted
that suffrage remain their front and center issue, and that they not get involved in
the question of whether to go to war. They warned in their journal *The Suffragist*
"that the National Association [of Woman Suffrage, or NAWSA] was inviting a
recurrence of the tragedy of the 1860s, when woman suffrage had stood aside for
the war and the Negro," as C. Roland Marchand describes.[9] Further, these militants

---

[9]   The reference here is to the fact that the abolition and suffrage movements were
initially one and the same, but female suffrage was ultimately dropped from the agenda.
When the Fifteenth Amendment was added to the Constitution guaranteeing the vote to
freed male slaves, woman suffragists pushed for the amendment to include women, but they
were shot down by the claim that such an addition would impede passage of the amendment.
See Roland C. Marchand. *The American Peace Movement and Social Reform, 1898–1918*
(Princeton, NJ: Princeton University Press, 1972), p. 215.

would not support women's war work. Under the direction of Crystal Eastman, active member of the New York branch of the NAWSA and the Executive Director of the American Union Against Militarism, the New York branch broke away from the NAWSA and commenced publication of its own journal, *Four Lights: An Adventure in Internationalism*. The journal ran for only a few short months before it was shut down under the US Espionage Act, which forbade speech that might interfere with the success of the military effort abroad.[10] Conversely, the NAWSA, under the leadership of Carrie Chapman Catt, had begun to argue that women's war work would provide a material demonstration of women's patriotism, show them to be necessary citizens, and therefore worthy of the vote.[11]

The editors of the Washington, DC-based journal *The Suffragist* and other militants who remained anti-war claimed that women did not need to prove their worth by volunteering for the war effort and should remain true to their anti-war position, stating: "Before the war women were only the mothers of men. They have now risen to the dizzy heights of makers of machine guns."[12] Is this the height on which stands Rogers's "girl he left behind him?" Published on the cover of the "official organ" of the NAWSA, Rogers seems to be responding not only to the crisis that women faced by the impending war, but the crises within the organization as well. The claim that women are mothers first reiterates the suffrage organization's appeal to motherhood as the unifying identity for all women. The statement is sarcastic in its claim that being a "maker of machine guns"—that is, a producer for the military economy—would be valued more highly than motherhood. It also alludes to the idea that mothering should be fulfillment enough of women's war obligation to warrant their enfranchisement.

The Rogers cover would be one of the very last she would complete for the publication. Although there is no way to know for certain, we might surmise that within the factions that developed among the NAWSA, she did not support the idea of women becoming involved in war work and preparedness as a way to promote suffrage. This conclusion is based on the fact that, while Rogers had been an extremely regular contributor to the magazine until the US entry into the war, after June 1917 her contributions to the magazine were clearly diminished.[13] The direction of the magazine shifted considerably too. The organization's decision to support women's war work as a means to gain respectability for the cause of suffrage is clearly evidenced in the shift in cover illustrations in the months following the US entry into the war, including the Flagg cover discussed earlier in

---

[10]   The *Masses* was also shut down under this act. Crystal Eastman's brother, Max Eastman, was one of the *Masses* editors.

[11]   Crystal Eastman attempted, but failed, to stop Carrie Catt from leaving the New York branch, which was increasingly distancing itself from the policies of other NAWSA branches. See Marchand, *The American Peace Movement*, p. 216.

[12]   As quoted in Marchand, *The American Peace Movement*, p. 216.

[13]   During the year 1917, Rogers illustrated eight covers, which included the majority of the issues published between June and December.

Fig. 3.11   C.D. Batchelor, "Behind the Man Behind the Gun," *The Woman Citizen*, October 6, 1917.

this chapter. On October 6, 1917, several weeks before the Flagg cover appeared, *The Woman Citizen* published another iteration of the "girl he left behind" theme, this one also by Batchelor (Figure 3.11).

This Batchelor cover is also a precursor to a series of covers he would complete for the magazine in the coming months that focuses more explicitly on women's wartime roles. For the October 1917 cover, Batchelor produced a dynamic composition that sets a soldier in the midst of battle in a visual comparison with a female munitions worker—a "maker of machine guns." He is drawn in a circular frame, bayoneted-rifle in hand, heading out of the frame to the left. Another circular frame is inset, in which appears a woman sitting at some sort of munitions-making machinery. In the mirrored layout, she faces away from the center of the frame to the right. This munitions worker is not overly feminine—but for her curls emerging from under her hat, and the context of the illustration, we would not necessarily be able to clearly identify her as a woman. Both the munitions worker

Fig. 3.12   C.D. Batchelor, "Win-the-War Women: The Munition Worker," *The Woman Citizen*, April 13, 1918.

and the soldier wear uniforms and hats and seem intent and occupied with their purpose, their squarely set jaws held in solemn attention to their given task. The title, "Behind the Man Behind the Gun," does not signify that the girl left behind pines away for her lover, nor that she fills in the gaps in his labor as best she can, but that each figure is equally essential to the success of the war.

The Woman Citizen's shift towards conventional magazine covers represented by Batchelor's October 1917 cover continued in the following months. The illustrations on the ensuing covers signal a change. On April 13, 1918 the magazine began running a series of cover illustrations devoted to "win-the-war women"—that is, women performing a variety of jobs in support of the war effort.[14] This series, also illustrated by Batchelor, exemplifies the ways in which

---

[14]   Batchelor produced eight covers in this series. They were published sporadically from April 13, 1918 to October 5, 1918.

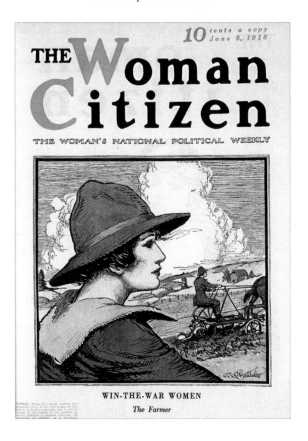

Fig. 3.13   C.D. Batchelor, "Win-the-War Women: The Farmer," *The Woman Citizen*, October 6, 1917.

many organizations that had espoused an anti-war stance prior to the US entry into the war shifted their positions dramatically by the end of 1917. Batchelor's "win-the-war women" are patriotic, and they become more attractive—much like Nurse Louise. Batchelor's munitions worker reappears on the cover that initiates the series (Figure 3.12). Same circular frame, same hat and uniform, same square jaw, but this time we can clearly see her face, featuring a delicate nose and pouty, lipsticked mouth. Similarly, Batchelor's win-the-war woman farmer displays ideal features and gazes ahead seriously, preoccupied perhaps with the tasks that await her (Figure 3.13). How different indeed from the farmer on the *Masses* cover who reaps dead soldiers from the earth!

Over time, Batchelor's win-the-war women become increasingly feminine and even seductive. Perhaps the most provocative win-the-war woman of all is the "Speaker," "selling," we are told, "for Uncle Sam" (Figure 3.14). Selling what?

Fig. 3.14   C.D. Batchelor, "Win-the-War Women Selling for Uncle Sam: The Speaker," *The Woman Citizen*, June 29, 1918.

Ostensibly, she is selling the liberty bonds and war savings stamps advertised behind her. With her low-cut dress, New Woman style, Gibson-girl good looks, and parted lips, she is more of a seductress than any of the others. Admittedly, the image is an antidote to the usual ponderous treatment of women who speak in public. Nevertheless, it marks a clear turn for the suffrage magazine to sexualized covers, in keeping with mainstream magazines of the era.

But it is Batchelor's win-the-war "Knitter" who most clearly mimics the prevailing image of a woman on a magazine cover—she is nearly identical to covers done by Charles Dana Gibson and other male illustrators of the time (Figure 3.15). Additionally, "The Knitter" stakes the journal's position in debates regarding women's wartime roles and the contribution offered by their domestic production. Pro-war suffragists argued that domestic labor, such as knitting, would be a significant way for women to contribute to the war effort and demonstrate their patriotism. These women argued that domestic work such as knitting not

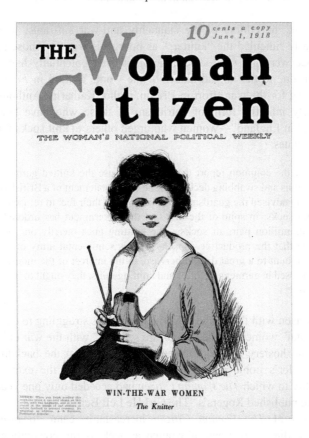

Fig. 3.15　　C.D. Batchelor, "Win-the-War Women: The Knitter," *The Woman Citizen*, June 1, 1918.

only provided material support to soldiers through skills that women alone possessed, but proved their deep commitment—physical and psychological—to the war effort. Just as soldiers put their bodies on the line for their country, knitting provided women a somatic level of involvement with the war. As one writer stated in *The Woman Citizen* on April 13, 1918: "We eat, sleep and drink the purposes of this war. No more than the men can we women keep the subject from our lips. Our hands are sentient with it as we knit and knit."[15] Clearly, by spring of 1918 *The Woman Citizen* had embraced women's participation in the war effort, its editors' language emphatic in its insistence on women's bodily engagement—experienced here through their knitting fingers—with war.

---

[15]　Editors, "An Open Letter to Women in War Time," *The Woman Citizen*, 13 April 1918.

By contrast, the editors of the staunchly anti-war suffragist journal *Four Lights* regularly ridiculed the "knitters" as bourgeois women whose attempts at war assistance were not only superfluous, but even potentially harmful to the labor market, due to the unpaid nature of the work. Writing in *Four Lights* of women knitting for the war effort in Britain, author Katharine Anthony belittled the "peculiarly infantile form of patriotism of those who have been dubbed 'Sister Susies' in England"—women who urged others to knit socks for soldiers. Anthony continues:

> In spite of the common report that the sailors use the knitted garments for cleaning guns and swabbing decks; in spite of the statement of a British officer who openly advised the guardsmen for the good of their feet to refuse to wear home-knit socks; in spite of the fact that the government has ordered three and a half million pairs of socks;—the knitting goes merrily on. One can only hope that the productive capacity of this sentimental army of knitters will not amount to a great deal; otherwise, in the interest of the thousands of women massed in garment factories and knitting mills, they ought to be legally restrained.[16]

Set in comparison with the image of garment workers struggling to earn a living, the "sentimental" women whose "hands are sentient" with the war effort as they knit inessential hosiery appear hopelessly naïve. Against the backdrop of this debate, Batchelor's noble and beautiful knitter confirms the extreme gender conventionality to which *The Woman Citizen* had acceded only one year after the magazine had published Rogers's "The Girl He Left Behind" cover.

The covers of *The Woman Citizen* increasingly came to resemble the mainstream media's depictions of women as well as the conventional gender images in the recruiting posters from World War I. This was a significant departure from the covers of the Rogers era. Like many other groups who had espoused anti-war positions earlier in the decade, by April 1917 *The Woman Citizen* had shifted from a position of peace and non-intervention to one of support for preparedness and American victory. Scholar Carolyn Kitch notes the ways in which, by the time of US involvement in World War I, suffrage imagery increasingly resembled mainstream representations of women: "it was crucial to the broad communicative power of such images in 1917 and 1918 that the threat [of woman suffrage and militancy] be tempered by the women's beauty, and these women bore a striking resemblance to Gibson Girls."[17] Before 1917, in what we might describe as the Rogers era, the character of the covers of *The Woman Citizen* did not conform to

---

[16] Katharine Anthony, "The 'Sister Susie' Peril," *Four Lights: An Adventure in Internationalism* (July 14, 1917).

[17] Kitch, *The Girl on the Magazine Cover*, 78. While Kitch notes the use of conventional gender images in the suffrage imagery published during the war, she does not identify this as a shift from a different, pre-war iconography.

prevailing gender norms.[18] Did the editorial board consciously promote this shift, encouraging the use of more mainstream visual gender codes in order to temper aspects of the magazine that might be considered as a "threat"? It is quite possible that, faced with the passage of the US Espionage Act, the publication's support for the war was a compromise that enabled them to continue publication, a concession that the artists and editors of *Four Lights* refused to make.

The "win-the-war women" series of *The Woman Citizen* reveals other features of gendered understandings of citizenship in the years of the First World War. The series presents an aporia. On the one hand, the images propose numerous roles for women, many of which had before the war been reserved for men only. On the other hand, the series does so through stereotypical representations of gender. In some ways the very conventionality of these images anticipates American women's eventual return to previous roles—their forays into jobs in manufacturing and agriculture would only be temporary, as they would be sent back to the home once the soldiers returned from war.

Ultimately we might ask, what did American suffragists who came to advocate preparedness gain from such support? Did women's wartime roles and their climb aboard the preparedness bandwagon "win" them the vote? The Nineteenth Amendment would not pass until a few years after the end of World War I. Suffrage scholars now generally agree that there was no direct correlation between women's war work and the eventual passing of suffrage. We might conclude that suffragists' eagerness to demonstrate their capacity for patriotism and citizenship led them to represent themselves in ways that limited the possibilities for American women's futures. Further, women's enfranchisement in 1920 would not serve to expand women's choices. In fact, in many ways the passing of the Nineteenth Amendment signaled the endpoint of accord within the American woman's movement, as beyond the desire for suffrage American women could not establish common goals.[19] Perhaps the post-1920 disunity in the American woman's movement had its roots in the splintering of the suffrage parties and women's peace movements as the United States entered World War I.

For a few short years before US entry into the war, the suffrage press published cartoons that were diverse stylistically as well as in the topics they addressed. Lou Rogers's graphic satire, in particular, appeared to broaden gender possibilities and envision meaningful social roles for American women. As the decade wore on and US involvement in the Great War seemed more imminent, the mainstream suffrage movement eschewed radical anti-war positions in the belief that some degree of respectable reputation was necessary in order to exercise influence.

---

[18] During this period, Rogers drew the majority of covers. The ones she did not draw more closely resembled her own than those done by Batchelor. Many of the covers not done by Rogers before 1917 were also drawn by female illustrators, including Laura Foster and others.

[19] See for example Nancy Cott, *The Grounding of Modern Feminism* (New Haven: Yale University Press, 1987).

While some suffragists did hold firmly to their anti-war stance and accepted the label of radicalism, the preponderance of voices from the suffrage movement had come, by April 1917, to not only support the war but also to rely increasingly on predictable ideas about gender in this support. After 1917 the visual culture of *The Woman Citizen* took a decidedly conservative turn, mirroring the shift in the suffrage movement's position on the war and also providing evidence of the ways in which the magazine came to rely on emergent "girl-on-the-magazine-cover" illustrations. In the end, the suffrage movement's dependence upon conventional ideas about women's roles in relation to citizenship and war (including the supposition that women's primary social role was motherhood) presaged the inability of suffrage's passing to bring true gender equality to American women. Initially the suffrage press claimed to envision a radically different society. By the decade's end, the gender conventions of American pre-war society were reinscribed in their pages.

Chapter 4

Publishing a "Fighting Spirit": Marianne Moore in the Little Magazines During WWI

Nikolaus Wasmoen[1]

> There are two things that I have always been disappointed not to be able to put into my work—a sense of the sea and a fighting spirit, and it delights me that anything I have written should remind you of the sea or seem to you to set itself in opposition to mediocrity and the spirit of compromise.
> —Marianne Moore, letter to H.D., August 9, 1916[2]

Marianne Moore, in the letter quoted above, responds to the first published review of her work in the August 1916 number of *The Egoist*. Moore writes that she is "delighted" to be acknowledged by H.D. as "a fighting spirit ... in opposition to mediocrity and the spirit of compromise." But "mediocrity" and "compromise" of what exactly? For what is Moore "fighting" in her early work?

This paper examines Moore's early publications in three little magazines during the First World War—*The Egoist: An Individualist Review* published in London, *Poetry: A Magazine of Verse* in Chicago, and *Others* in New York. The distinct oeuvres of Moore's poetry represented in these periodicals reflect alternative conceptions of the relationship between poetry and other fields of communicative action, differences that I discuss in relation to these periodicals' editorial responses to the sweeping political event of the First World War and the particular efforts of a young woman to launch herself as a recognized poet and critic.[3] Moore put these publications to different kinds of work; reflexively, these

---

[1] Permission for the use of the lines from "The Fish," as found in folder I:02:04 of the Marianne Moore Collection, located at the Rosenbach Museum and Library, is granted by David M. Moore, Esquire, Administrator of the Literary Estate of Marianne Moore. All rights reserved. Unpublished letters by Hilda Doolittle (H.D.): Copyright 2012 by The Schaffner Family Foundation. Used by permission.

[2] Marianne Moore, *The Selected Letters of Marianne Moore*, edited by Bonnie Costello, Celeste Goodridge, and Cristanne Miller (New York: Knopf, 1997), p. 113. Cited hereafter *SL*.

[3] See Georgina Taylor, *H.D. and the Public Sphere of Modernist Women Writers, 1913–1946* (New York: Oxford University Press, 2001) for an extensive application of Habermas's theories of "communicative action" and the "public sphere" to the wider network of female contributors and editors around H.D.; Jürgen Habermas, *The Theory of*

publications shaped Moore's early public appearances as an American poet at home and abroad. Foregrounding the textual and editorial construction of her early published poems addressing war and militarism reveals how Moore critiqued and negotiated the boundaries between poetics and politics as a relatively unknown female poet in the United States during the 1910s.[4]

Mark Morrisson has argued that by continuing the general editorial practices of its more explicitly feminist precursors, *Freewoman* (1911–1912) and *New Freewoman* (1913) even while it introduced more poetry and literature into its pages, *The Egoist* (1914–1919) facilitated a "counter-public sphere" that allowed for a broadly based discursive community linking artistic work to social and political activity.[5] By reading the public and private networks of critical exchange between Moore and her wartime editors at *The Egoist*, especially H.D., I model how such a counter-public sphere might be made to work critically in relation to Moore's early poems and her intertextual, conversational poetics.[6] The significance of the bibliographic and editorial encodings of a little magazine as a site for discursive interaction between poetics and politics is further established in Moore's unhappy engagement with Harriet Monroe's *Poetry* and the aesthetic glosses it lent to the materials it published.[7] In the final section, I turn to the

---

Communicative Action Volume 1: Reason and the Rationalization of Society, translated by Thomas McCarthy (Boston: Beacon Press, 1984).

[4]   See also George Bornstein, *Material Modernism: The Politics of the Page* (Cambridge: Cambridge University Press, 2001), p. 115: "The diachronic textual and political complexities of Moore's verse make clear that to read or to edit merely the linguistic codes of Moore's poems diminishes them. It strips off the gender coding of the network of modernist women editors and publishers, as well as of Moore's insistence that cooperation and antagonism could operate both across and within gender, as well as across or within racial groups. It denudes the poems, too, of their rich social and political context."

[5]   For a discussion of the development of the *Freewoman/New Freewoman/Egoist* and the editorial work of Dora Marsden and Harriet Shaw Weaver see Mark S. Morrisson, *The Public Face of Modernism: Little Magazines, Audiences, and Reception, 1905–1920* (Madison: University of Wisconsin Press, 2001), pp. 84–132; and Bruce Clark, "Suffragism, Imagism, and the 'Cosmic Poet': Scientism and Spirituality in *The Freewoman* and *The Egoist*," in *Little Magazines & Modernism: New Approaches*, edited by Suzanne W. Churchill and Adam McKible (Aldershot, UK and Burlington, VT: Ashgate, 2007), pp. 119–32. The entire runs of *The Freewoman, The New Freewoman, The Egoist, Others*, and *Poetry* (to December 1922) have been published online by The Modernist Journals Project: <http://dl.lib.brown.edu/mjp>.

[6]   For a complete listing of Moore's publications from 1907–1924 and "A Publication Biography" of all 12 periodicals in which her work appeared up to 1924, see: Marianne Moore, *Becoming Marianne Moore*, edited by Robin Schulze (Berkeley: University of California Press, 2002). Cited hereafter *BMM*.

[7]   Standard references for *Poetry* under Harriet Monroe's editorship include: her autobiography, *A Poet's Life: Seventy Years in a Changing World* (New York: Macmillan, 1938); and biography, Daniel J. Cahill, *Harriet Monroe* (New York: Twayne, 1973). Jayne Marek devotes a chapter to Monroe's editorship, including the years addressed here, in: Jayne Marek, *Women Editing Modernism* (Lexington: University of Kentucky Press, 1995).

visually spare but socially hospitable pages of *Others*—and its circle in New York and New Jersey—to examine Moore's exemplary status in this American counter-public sphere.[8] More than any other domestic publication during the decade before Moore became *The Dial*'s editor in the mid-1920s, *Others* extended Moore's remote presence in the influential *Egoist* closer to home. Such early transatlantic, cooperative oppositions eventually established Moore as both the "poet's poet" of Anglo-American modernism and, later in her life, as one of its most publicly visible figures.[9] This made Moore's one of the most influential voices to emerge from modernism's early days in the continued conversations about the personal and public responsibilities of art and artists from the 1920s to the present day.

In 1915—the year in which Moore first published outside of the undergraduate and alumni publications of Bryn Mawr, her alma mater—*activism* did not yet mean what it does today. During the early years of what was then still the "European War," to be an *activist* meant to advocate or support Germany in the war.[10] Moore was never such an "activist," but it is telling that her first public appearances in print roughly coincide with this first usage of *activism* as a political term, denoting the taking of a specific side in what would become the First World War.[11] Moore's transatlantic publications during the war present a broader sense of social and political responsibility on the part of the poet than merely taking a side.

Moore read the magazines to which she submitted very carefully in terms of the social, political, and aesthetic engagements that they might represent for her work, occasionally withholding future contributions from a magazine when she discovered herself at odds with what she perceived as its "approach to art."[12] Her correspondence and contributions to *The Egoist*, *Poetry*, and *Others* show that Moore identified these organs with distinct, and sometimes changing, ends.

---

[8]   The fullest account of *Others* and its transformations during the 1910s under Alfred Kreymborg is Suzanne W. Churchill, *The Little Magazine "Others" and the Renovation of Modern American Poetry* (Aldershot, UK and Burlington, VT: Ashgate, 2006).

[9]   For an overview of the reception of Moore's work, see Linda Leavell, Cristanne Miller, and Robin G. Schulze, preface to *Critics and Poets on Marianne Moore: "A Right Good Salvo of Barks"* (Lewisburg, PA: Bucknell University Press, 2005), pp. 12–13: "Poets have always figured prominently among Moore's advocates ... she has sometimes been dubbed a poet's poet." On Moore's later WWII poems and criticism see: Susan Schweik, "Writing War Poetry Like a Woman," *Critical Inquiry* 13 (1987), pp. 532–56.

[10]   "activism, n.," *OED Online*, March 2011 (Oxford University Press) <http://www.oed.com/viewdictionaryentry/Entry/1957> (accessed 18 May 2011).

[11]   On Moore's activity in what we might now call suffragist "activism," see: Linda Leavell, "Marianne Moore and Georgia O'Keeffe: The Feelings of a Mother—A Woman Or A Cat," in *Marianne Moore: Woman and Poet*, edited by Patricia C. Willis (Orono, ME: National Poetry Foundation, 1990), p. 300; *SL*, p. 65, p. 77, p. 99; Charles Molesworth, *Marianne Moore: A Literary Life* (New York: Atheneum, 1990), pp. 90–91, pp. 116–17.

[12]   Moore to Harriet Monroe, May 10, 1918, *SL*, 115: "*Poetry's* approach to art is different from my own."

As Cristanne Miller finds in her analysis of Moore's early war poetry, Moore's texts "assert structures of interaction."[13] Moore's various published texts were not just passive mediums for expression or communication with an audience; they embedded significant assertions about the way that textual interactions between her work and its public audience might be, or should be, structured. *Marianne Moore and the Cultures of Modernity* by Victoria Bazin, the most recent book-length study of Moore, argues that Moore's texts assert her "poem's immersion in rather than its detachment from the textual debris of modernity."[14] As Bazin's analysis suggests elsewhere, we ought to follow the implications of textual "immersion" yet further. The extensive and careful attention Moore gave to her publications suggests she did not prioritize poems (content) over their material textualizations (medium).[15]

As an undergraduate and alumna Moore published regularly in the Bryn Mawr student journal, *Typn O'Bob*, and alumni magazine, *The Lantern*.[16] Around the time of her graduation in 1909, Moore had begun to openly consider herself a professional writer, and over the next five years she continued to submit poems to prominent periodicals including *Book News*, *The Smart Set*, and *The Masses* without success.[17] *The Egoist* became the first periodical to publish Moore outside of Bryn Mawr when its literary editor, Richard Aldington, included two poems in the April 1915 number: "To A Man Working His Way Through The Crowd," addressed to theater critic Gordon Craig; and "To the Soul of 'Progress.'"[18] These titles are indicative of two forms of pseudo-lyrical address Moore used frequently during this period to evoke the object and tone of her poems while avoiding the disclosure of any definite lyrical or rhetorical subject.

The first type, including "To A Man Working His Way Through The Crowd / To Gordon Craig," addresses a prominent literary or artistic figure with more-or-less praiseful observations (such as in Moore's similar poems "To Browning" and "To William Butler Yeats On Tagore").[19] The final stanza of "To A Man ..." finds:

---

[13]   Cristanne Miller, "'What is War For?': Moore's Development of an Ethical Poetry," in *Critics and Poets on Marianne Moore*, edited by Leavell, Miller, and Schultze, p. 58. Miller makes this point in regard to "written text," as she focuses on the mostly unpublished work by Moore from 1909 to 1914, but it describes Moore's subsequent published texts as well.

[14]   Victoria Bazin, *Marianne Moore and the Cultures of Modernity* (Aldershot, UK and Burlington, VT: Ashgate, 2010), p. 36.

[15]   For an account of Moore's well-acknowledged interest in the "art of the printed word," rare books and prints see Molesworth, p. 420.

[16]   *BMM*, p. 495.

[17]   *SL*, p. 75.

[18]   *The Egoist* 4:2 (April 1, 1915), p. 62; reproduced in *BMM*, p. 188. Aldington also accepted "To William Butler Yeats on Tagore," which he included in the May 1, 1915, "imagist" number of *The Egoist*; reproduced in *BMM*, p. 357.

[19]   "To Browning," *The Egoist* 8:2 (2 August 1915), p. 126; reproduced in *BMM*, p. 174.

Undoubtedly you overbear,
But one must do that to come where
There is a space, a fit gymnasium for action. (ll. 10–12)

The context of this poem's publication in *The Egoist*, where it shares the page with Madame Ciolkowska's serial war correspondence from France titled "Fighting Paris," alters the significance of its quest "Through The Crowd" for "a space, a fit gymnasium for action." The poem's purely linguistic content would imply that extremity, "overbear," works to separate the critic from "The Crowd" as a preliminary to "action." However, the actual "space" of the poem's public interaction in *The Egoist* suggests that its valorization of social marginalization is itself an affinitive gesture, editorially and bibliographically connecting the quest for "a space ... for action" to the wartime politics of *The Egoist*'s first-person "Fighting Paris." [20]

This connection is further strengthened by Moore's "To the Soul of 'Progress,'" which Aldington also placed on the same page. "To the Soul of 'Progress'" represents a different form of address used to dissect or critique an abstract noun (such as in Moore's "To Statecraft Embalmed" and "To a Steam Roller") or title (such as in "Cisar, or / Caesar, or / Kaiser").[21] "To The Soul of 'Progress'" addresses a mock idealization, "The Soul of 'Progress,'" which Moore excoriates as "a mill stone":

You use your mind
Like a mill stone to grind
Chaff. (ll. 1–3)

Under the influence of "Progress," "War" (with a capital W) denies transcendence to the soldiers dismembered in the poem.[22] In this address to false consciousness,

---

[20] See *BMM*, p. 442: "Even as the *Freewoman/New Freewoman/Egoist* became increasingly devoted to the arts, it maintained the format and layout of an overtly political paper ... [similar to] other serious 'journals of opinion' like the *New Statesman* or ... the *New Age*. The compressed format suggested that the literary content of the *Egoist* was the equivalent, in its way, of important social commentary." For a recent discussion of modernism and social commentary in the *New Age* see: Robert Scholes and Clifford Wulfman, *Modernism in the Magazines: An Introduction* (New Haven: Yale University Press, 2010).

[21] "To Statecraft Embalmed," *Others* 1:6 (December 1915), p. 104; reproduced in *BMM*, p. 203. "To a Steam Roller," *The Egoist* 10:2 (1 October 1915), p. 158; reproduced in *BMM*, p. 190. "Cisar, or / Caesar, or / Kaiser" is an unpublished manuscript in folder I:04:25, Marianne Moore Collection, Rosenbach Museum and Library, Philadelphia. Cited hereafter as RML.

[22] In an unpublished typescript, I:04:57, RML, Moore titled/addressed an almost identical version of this poem "To Art Wishing for a Fortress into Which / She may Flee from her Prosecutors, in- / stead of Looking for a Jail in Which to / Confine Them." As in her famous "Poetry," which asserts in an early version "I too dislike it" and "enigmas are

Moore takes the watchwords of patriotic fervor (soul, progress) and places them in the poem's own verse machinery of diction, rhythms, and rhymes to strip their euphemistic glosses—"Grind," "twisted," "torso, / Prostrate," "Black," "lost / Head," "Red." Moore's "To The Soul of 'Progress'" presents no orator with whom one can meaningfully agree or disagree. By refraining from the presentation of any such *ethos*, on which persuasive appeals must ultimately depend, Moore forces the reader to feel the weight of the poem's statement as a willful articulation that forgoes winning or losing minds to a cause. Observation and representation are presented as the basis for a community of writers and readers gathered by their contingent affinities, rather than prescriptive national or racial identities. Charles Altieri argues that "[T]he test of will" for Moore "was to make one's individual concerns patent within the most unrelenting social conditions."[23] Moore sought a poetry that did not, on the one hand, offer the poet as a vicarious "stand patter"; but did not, on the other hand, revoke her access to the kind of individual concerns huge movements like the war effort subsumed.[24]

With its feminist and internationalist politics rubbing shoulders with imagist poetry and avant-garde fiction, *The Egoist* in 1915 had come to represent what Mark Morrisson has defined as "a broad-based counterpublic sphere," which set itself "in opposition to bourgeois social norms, liberal and statist politics, and, above all ... bourgeois literary taste."[25] Such a print community sought to cultivate what Miller identifies as Moore's own discursive goal: "a communally focused authority" that stressed the participation of individuals in the processes of judgment and decision-making, while maintaining the capacity of those individuals to participate across and within different configurations of genre, gender, racial, political, and social affiliations.[26]

H.D. would recognize Moore's critical sense of difference in her introductory review including three of Moore's poems ("To A Screen-Maker," "Feed Me, Also, River God," and "Talisman"), which she published in the August 1916 *Egoist*

---

not poetry," Moore finds little to redeem in abstractions, whether "Progress" or "Art." For her 1924 collection *Observations* published by the Dial Press in New York, Moore retitles "To the Soul of 'Progress'" to "To Military Progress."

[23] Charles Altieri, *The Art of Twentieth-Century American Poetry: Modernism and After* (Oxford: Blackwell, 2006), p. 53: Altieri's quoted claim regards Moore and Mina Loy together in the wider context of the source chapter.

[24] "To the Stand Patter" is a rejected title to Moore's "To Be Liked By You Would Be A Calamity" published in her family friend William Rose Benét's short-lived *The Chimaera* 1:2 (July 1916), p. 56; reproduced in *BMM*, p. 218. "Stand-patter" also appears in the review that provoked Moore's "To A Steam Roller," quoted in *BMM*, p. 191. For an analysis of the impact of Liberal discourse about the war on modernist literature in London see: Vincent Sherry, *The Great War and the Language of Modernism* (New York: Oxford University Press, 2003).

[25] Morrisson, p. 86.

[26] Cristanne Miller, *Marianne Moore: Questions of authority* (Cambridge, MA: Harvard University Press, 1995), p. vii.

shortly after taking over the magazine's literary desk from her husband Aldington, who had enlisted to avoid conscription.[27] H.D. addresses "readers of *The Egoist*," the audience she imagines for Moore at the time, who have "read Miss Marianne Moore's poems again and again, and questioned, half in despair—is this a mere word-puzzle, or does it mean something?" H.D., at least, thinks "it does," particularly in relation to the First World War.

Alluding to the speaker in T.S. Eliot's "The Love Song of J. Alfred Prufrock" (published the previous June in *Poetry*) who lamented, "It is impossible to say just what I mean!" H.D. attributes to Moore a hypothetical quotation: "see, you cannot know what I mean—exactly what I mean ... and I do not intend that you shall know ... ."[28] If the speaker of Eliot's poem evoked frustration over an inability to make known "just what I mean," H.D. suggests that Moore obversely reproaches any tacit expectancy for disclosure. "Yet," H.D. finds:

> we are not always baffled. Miss Moore turns her perfect craft as the perfect craftsman must inevitably do, to some direct presentation of beauty, clear, cut in flowing lines, but so delicately that the very screen she carves seems meant to stand only in that serene palace of her own world of inspiration—frail, yet as all beautiful things are, absolutely hard—and destined to endure longer, far longer than the toppling sky-scrapers, and the world of shrapnel and machine-guns in which we live.

H.D. appeals to the apparent contradiction of "perfect craft" and "the world of shrapnel and machine-guns" to identify Moore as a potential model for endurance.[29] The resistance to transparent rhetoric described by H.D. evokes, at once, the artificial frailty that removes the poet's utterance from the center of power, and at the same time, the absolute hardness that resists the people and parts of the world that share a rhetorical understanding with power. Within a "world of shrapnel and machine-guns," endurance is measured, H.D. suggests, by the collaborative work of reading and rereading undertaken through the little magazine.

In *The Political Aesthetic of Yeats, Eliot, and Pound* Michael North argues that "Modern poetry transcends the opposition between individual and community not through harmony but rather through discord, because that discord is a common condition suffered by all ... . Individuals are related in such works not by similarity but by their lack of similarity, by the suffering they endure in the absence of

---

[27]   H.D., "Marianne Moore," *The Egoist* 8:3 (August 1916), pp. 118–19; entire review reproduced in *BMM*, pp. 367–8. For a recent history of propaganda, conscription, and conscientious objectors to the First World War in the United States see: Christopher Capozzola, *Uncle Sam Wants You: WWI and the making of the modern American citizen*, (Oxford: Oxford University Press, 2008).

[28]   T.S. Eliot, "The Love Song of J. Alfred Prufrock," *Poetry: A Magazine of Verse* 6:3 (June 1915), pp. 130–35.

[29]   H.D.'s language suggests she may have seen Moore's rejected title, "To Art ... ," for "To The Soul of 'Progress,'" cf. note 22.

genuine community."[30] The community-building power of a perceived "common condition," however negative, is not a mere abstraction. Through her submissions to and correspondence with the editors of *The Egoist*, Moore participated in this "discord" as a "common condition" within the transatlantic conversation of literary modernism. She contributed poems that de-falsify and expose, rather than replace or restore, the insubstantial foundations of a nationalist cause for war. In an effusive letter of August 21, 1915 from London, H.D. promises Moore that "there are others like us!" while encouraging her to visit "Perhaps next summer," by which time she hoped the fighting might be over.[31] In such a light, we can see the social and political commitments underwriting Moore's contributions to *The Egoist* that placed her discovery and introduction to the public at the heart of *The Egoist*'s editorial mission and the influential version of modernism represented in its pages.

Nevertheless, not all of Moore's submissions to *The Egoist* were entirely new to the war years in which she published there. H.D.'s review includes two poems revised from earlier versions published at Bryn Mawr. The longer of these two was winnowed from her 1909 "To A Screen-Maker" into "He Made This Screen." As it appears in full in *The Egoist*, one hears the increased cutting power of Moore's poetry:

He Made This Screen

Not of silver nor of coral,
But of weatherbeaten laurel.

Here, he introduced a sea
Uniform like tapestry;

Here, a fig-tree; there, a face;
There, a dragon circling space—

Designating here, a bower;
There, a pointed passion-flower.

H.D. situates this poem in her review to reinforce her sense of Moore's "perfect craft" as an escape from the gritty, ruinous world without. After surveying the depressing, visceral wastes in "To The Soul of 'Progress,'" however, a reader and re-reader of *The Egoist* might suspect the sacrosanctity of "This Screen." We notice, following H.D.'s further suggestion, the emergence of "sea-change," an

---

[30] Michael North, *The Political Aesthetic of Yeats, Eliot, and Pound* (Cambridge: Cambridge University Press, 1991), p. 19.

[31] Hilda Doolittle autograph letter signed to Marianne Moore, London, August 21, 1915, V:23:32, RML.

element lacking in the previous versions of this poem, which do not include the line "he introduced a sea."[32]

In the addition of "a sea," Moore allows greater rein to her figurations than in earlier versions. "[A] sea" disrupts the measured space that "he" carves in the plastic screen, imbuing motion in the stationary and disrupting its static serenity. We are asked to see in the tissue of the poem something "uniform like tapestry" in the clear-cut lines of verse and, at the same time, the textural instabilities "he introduced." This shift would not be noteworthy except for the poem's deictic insistence on its superficies, that it shows "*This* Screen." But, how can we see the screen that the poem prods us to see when any sense of whose eyes we are looking through is withheld? What, then, is the poem, situated within H.D.'s review, asking us to see or do?

To answer such questions, a reader of *The Egoist* in the summer of 1916 might have relied on their literary editor for support. H.D. placed an excerpt from Ezra Pound's translation of the *Dialogues of Fontenelle* to begin on the same page on which her introduction to "Marianne Moore" ended. This excerpt features an exchange between "Homer and Aesop" over their dissimilar designs on readers.

> Aesop: You must have been very daring to leave your readers to put the allegories into your poems! Where would you have been had they taken them in a flat literal sense?
>
> Homer: If they had! It would have incommoded me little.
>
> Aesop: What! The gods mangling each other ... would all this have been good without allegory?
>
> Homer: Why not? ...[33]

---

[32] Several early versions of "He Made This Screen" exist. In a letter home from Bryn Mawr in December 1908, Moore included two rejected versions of the poem, titled "To an Artificer" and "To a Screen-Maker," reprinted in *SL*, pp. 52–3. Kirstin Hotelling Zona suggests that "To An Artificer" and "To A Screen-Maker" comprise a single poem, but the letter in which they appear describes two "versions" and numbers them separately. See: Kirstin Hotelling Zona, *Marianne Moore, Elizabeth Bishop, and May Swenson: The feminist poetics of self-restraint* (Ann Arbor: University of Michigan Press, 2002), p. 19. Moore eventually published a third version, titled "To A Screen-Maker," in the *Tipyn O'Bob* 6 (January 1909), pp. 2–3; reproduced in *BMM*, p. 335. Jeanne Heuving quotes an additional version of "To A Screen-Maker" from an unpublished letter of 4 February 1909, in VI:15a:03, RML. See: Jeanne Heuving, *Omissions are not Accidents: Gender in the Art of Marianne Moore* (Detroit: Wayne State University Press, 1992), p. 56.

[33] In the version of this translation by Pound in *Pavannes and Divisions* (New York: Knopf, 1918), p. 60, Homer's second sentence reads "It would have incommoded me a little." The earlier printing in *The Egoist* reading "incommoded me little" better matches the sense of Homer's other statements, suggesting the *Pavannes and Divisions* reading is a misprint.

In translating Fontenelle's—comically Socratic—Homeric dialogue, Pound refurbishes for a modern audience its challenge to poets: "leave the readers to put the allegories into your poems!" Moore takes up a form of this challenge. She presents her artifice without attaching it to a meaning that we can confidently claim to share by identifying with the screen-maker or the speaker of the poem. We come upon the screen, as it were, on our own, in the absence of an epistemological model, and faced with the work of making something of it ourselves. H.D.'s canny editorial practice recalls such individualist reading subjects to their participation in the community connected through the little magazine.

Moore would submit two final poems to *The Egoist* in 1918, after the literary desk had been transferred to T.S. Eliot. The first of these, "Reinforcements," appeared as American deployment to Europe hit full swing, including Moore's brother Warner who sailed as a chaplain aboard the USS *Rhode Island*.[34] The poem's first two lines take the air out of civility: "The vestibule to experience is not to / Be exalted into epic grandeur." The poem is not so yielding "to experience" as the presence of a vestibule might prepare us to expect. This passage "to experience" leads only to an equivocal sense of "advancing," which reduces men to "fish":

> ... These men are going
> To their work with this idea, advancing like a school of fish through
>
> Still water—waiting to change the course or dismiss
> The idea of movement, till forced to. (ll. 2–5)

Dissension, to "change the course or dismiss / The idea," is postponed indefinitely in anticipation of unknown external force. Unlike sheep that are taught to recognize their shepherd, "Reinforcements" are denied knowledge of the "force" that gives them their identity, the force that is the root of their name. The build-up of "Reinforcements" seems as much the cause as the effect of the violence they would oppose. Moore's "Reinforcements" emphasizes the difficulties of representing the enormity of what she sees without participating in its reinforcement herself: "... The words of the Greeks / Ring in our ears, but they are vain in comparison with a sight like this" (ll. 5–6). Unable to discern the advance of all these men's work, the poem excuses itself from simile for fear that even to compare the military's deployments to restive fish may, nonetheless, exalt "a sight like this." Thus primed to resist the vagaries of figural speech, the poem's final stanza turns to the prepositional phrase and adjective to modify, rather than compare, "this" or "it":

> The pulse of intention does not move so that one
> Can see it, and moral machinery is not labeled, but
> The future of time is determined by the power of volition. (ll. 7–9)

---

[34] "Reinforcements," *The Egoist* 6:5 (June–July 1918), p. 21; reproduced in *BMM*, p. 232. "The Fish," *The Egoist* 7:5 (August 1918), p. 95; reproduced in *BMM*, p. 234. On John Warner Moore's enlistment see *SL*, p. 77.

Moore refashions the materials of the war by remaking them verbally to give her "volition" power. By the artificer's manipulation of her medium, "Intention" is given to, not likened to, a "pulse"; "machinery" is plucked of its "label[s]" to become "moral"; and "The future" is given, not compared to, "time." The power this enacts is not persuasive. Its artist's hand "does not move so that one / Can see it." Moore's appeal against reinforcement extends her sense of what can be accomplished within the semi-private, undisclosed confines of her poems without recourse to the terms of a public, "epic grandeur."

Moore's second 1918 *Egoist* poem, "The Fish," references the "school of fish" in "Reinforcements."[35] The movement away from simile and figural comparison in the final stanza of "Reinforcements" provides an immediate context for unpacking the significance of Moore's technical virtuosity in "The Fish." As Moore originally submitted it to *The Egoist*, "The Fish" comprises eight regular quatrains. This conventional arrangement, like later and more famous syllabic versions published after the war, runs its title into its first line:

The Fish

Wade through black jade.
Of the crow-blue mussel-shells, one
Keeps adjusting the ash-heaps;
Opening and shutting itself like
An injured fan. (ll. 1–5)

Moore picks up in "The Fish" where she left off in "Reinforcements": the fish do not wade through something "like" black jade, they "Wade through black jade." The water the fish wade through has itself been constructed by the mollusks beneath it. Amid this scene of mineral transformation and "the fish" it contains, our attention is brought to "one" within the group of "mussel-shells," who seems to participate in the sea-change of "black jade" by "adjusting the ash-heaps." The poem, however, is shunted, forebodingly, from transformation to mere comparison in describing "a sight like this" with a simile: "like / An injured fan." It continues:

The barnacles undermine the
Side of the wave—trained to hide
There—but the submerged shafts of the

---

[35] John M. Slatin is the first critic to read "Reinforcements" and "The Fish" together as I do here, but Slatin draws on different later syllabic arrangements of "The Fish" published in *Poems* (1921) and *Observations* (1924). See: John M. Slatin, *The Savage's Romance* (University Park: Pennsylvania State University Press, 1986), pp. 69–77. For an analysis of the multiple revisions and later publications of "The Fish" see Bornstein, *Material Modernism*, p. 117.

Sun, split like spun
Glass, move themselves with spotlight swift-
Ness into the crevices—
In and out, illuminating

The turquoise sea
Of bodies. ... (ll. 6–14)

When day breaks, it comes upon the scene not as natural light, but "with spotlight swift- / Ness" divulging "the bodies" which the "black jade" of the mussels obscured by their dark making. Contrary to expectations, the "Sun" in this poem and its spin of simile occlude, rather than illuminate, the bodies they ought to literally and metaphorically bring to light. What this suggests, and what I think we need to take seriously, is that Moore is not presenting a delayed revelatory moment by withholding and enjambing "The turquoise sea / Of bodies" until a moment of light or illumination. What she presents is an interruption of a more disturbing, unheroic poetic work that does not claim to illuminate anything. If anything it makes its objects less alive by "adjusting" them to its, and not God's or Reason's, peculiar pattern. Its "adjusting" is bound up with its injury, the trauma of a "sight like this."

The slimy, tentacled, inter-contaminated miscreation that follows could not occur in the hard, cold surface of "black jade" that opens the poem. That stone sheaf is punctured, liquefied by the recognition of its scene of death—perhaps by the running of tears in anger or anguish. Only in "The water" that is not jaded or held fleetingly by enjambment as "turquoise sea," could one write of the disaster wrought by a torpedo:

... The water drives a
Wedge of iron into the edge
Of the cliff, whereupon the stars,

Pink rice grains, ink
Bespattered jelly-fish, crabs like
Green lilies and submarine
Toadstools, slide each on the other. (ll. 14–20)

Moore here has come, in the year of her own pious brother's deployment, to the limit of her poetic vocation as counter-public speech. What can be said after the clear-cut stars of the night sky have been spotlighted as grainy starfish lasciviously sliding in a mangled submarine mass? How can it be said?

Moore picks up with an austere survey of "the edge / Of the cliff" in the wake of "a / Wedge of iron:"

All external
Marks of abuse are present on
This defiant edifice—
All the physical features of

Accident—lack
Of cornice, dynamite grooves, burns
And hatchet strokes, these things stand
Out on it; the chasm side is

Dead. Repeated
Evidence has proved that it can
Live on what cannot revive
Its youth. The sea grows old in it. (ll. 21–32)

Against the double speak of heroic destruction that occludes a "sight like this," Moore presents a "defiant edifice." This "defiant edifice," like the poem that makes it so, makes present "All external / Marks of abuse," but does not assuage these wounds with rhetorical flourish, semantic depth, or allegory. The poem discovers "Accident" propagating the death and violence it witnesses. Moore will no more claim to change what "Repeated / Evidence has proved" in "The Fish," than she will leave the "vestibule to experience" in "Reinforcements." The poem ultimately returns to what it needs to continue. The poem implies it can subsist on an experience unworthy of aggrandizement or diminishment: "it can / Live on what cannot revive / Its youth." The sea, which had been a technical watershed in 1916, now "grows old in it." Moore leaves her readers to put the allegories into her poems, as the Homeric charge against political allegory in Pound's translation suggests they ought to be.

H.D. assumed the role of a sponsor for Moore in her early efforts in the little magazines, but she also helped to make the London counter-public sphere in and around *The Egoist* a personal concern to her friend across the Atlantic by interpreting her work as a response to shared challenges and ambitions. In H.D.'s letter of 15 April 1916 to Moore, we overhear the expatriate mingling the language she used in the publication with a more personal response: "I am … too happy I almost think!—Perhaps it is the background of misery that is partly responsible: … friends lost, dear friends, 'at the front' or else in prison … I [am] hopeless facing the year—alive with daffodils—but somehow the great current is there— … deep, deep and the daffodils & the poetry are the scattered froth above shipwreck & innumerable deaths!"[36]

One might hear resonances with "The Fish" in "the scattered froth above shipwreck & innumerable deaths!" but, as we have seen, courage can provide, by 1918, only hardness and defiance. There are no Wordsworthian daffodils floating along "The turquoise sea / Of bodies" by the last years of the war. In a 1917 draft of "The Fish," though, Moore inserts in brackets an aside that helps one see how her polished poems arise from the challenges and opportunities she discovered in *The Egoist*. Moore considered adding at line 14: One may guage [sic] / Sincerity of edge, in / Such recesses of the mind, we / Find flowers

---

[36] Hilda Doolittle autograph letter signed to Marianne Moore, London, April 15, 1916, V:23:32, RML.

entwined / With bodies there."[37] The insertion would not have fit the scrupulous diction of the rest of the poem. However, it reminds us that Moore's "defiant edifice" was fashioned for the specific demands she faced during wartime when "in ... recesses of the mind, we," like H.D. in her distraught letter, "Find flowers entwined / With bodies there." As I hope to have shown, *The Egoist* and its imbrications of the social, political, and aesthetic fields within its pages gave Moore's "sense of the sea and a fighting spirit" purchase on modernism and its transatlantic sphere.[38]

The Egoist was of course not the only magazine available to Moore at the time, nor was it the first little magazine she approached. She had submitted a group of poems to Harriet Monroe's *Poetry* as early as July 1914. Moore's interactions with Monroe contrasted markedly with the mutual appreciations she exchanged with Aldington, H.D., and Eliot. Monroe's correspondence regarding Moore's 1914 submission is now lost, but it was apparently quite critical of the young poet's work, as Robin Schulze deduces from Moore's extant replies.[39] Thanking Monroe for "suggestions as to title" for the five-poem series Monroe had selected from the group Moore had submitted and expressing gratitude "for criticism, even adverse," Moore proposed calling the group "Tumblers, Pouters and Fantails."[40] Monroe shortened Moore's title to "Pouters and Fantails" when she published the group in May 1915, including "That Harp You Play So Well," "To An Intra-Mural Rat," "Counseil To A Bachelor," "Appelate Jurisdiction," and "The Wizard in Words."[41]

---

[37]   Marianne Moore, "The Fish," 1917. I:02:04, RML; this draft includes "U.S.A." in the address written on the top of the page, suggesting that Moore may have intended, at some point, to submit this version in England, although I am not aware of any record to confirm this.

[38]   Despite the creative attempts to resurrect the little magazine's readership after the end of WWI described in Morrisson, 458–60, "*The Egoist* folded at the end of 1919 to allow the Egoist Press to concentrate on book publication," especially James Joyce's *Ulysses*, whose rejection by Weaver's printers contributed to her closing of the magazine. The Egoist Press went on to publish the unauthorized first collection of Moore's poetry, *Poems* (1921), edited by H.D. and Bryher (Winifred Ellerman). In 1924 Moore published her first authorized collected volume, *Observations* with the New York Dial Press, for which she won the prestigious Dial Award, and, eventually, the editorship of the *Dial* magazine until it closed in 1929. On Moore's editorship see: Jayne E. Marek, "The Ironic 'Editorial We': Marianne Moore at the *Dial*," in *Women Editing Modernism: 'Little' Magazines and Literary History* (Lexington: University Press of Kentucky, 1995), pp. 138–68; William Wasserstrom, *The Time of The Dial* (Syracuse, NY: Syracuse University Press, 1963); Nicholas Joost, *Scofield Thayer and The Dial: An illustrated history* (Carbondale: Southern Illinois University Press, 1964).

[39]   *BMM*, pp. 481–4.

[40]   Moore to Harriet Monroe, April 8, 1915, *SL*, p. 97.

[41]   *BMM*, pp. 479–84. Moore, "Pouters and Fantails," *Poetry* 6:2 (May 1915), pp. 70–72.

The bibliographic coding of *Poetry* presented Moore's poetry in a very different aspect than her publications in *The Egoist*. Famously launched in 1912 with funds secured through five-year subscriptions from Chicago businessmen, Monroe's *Poetry: A Magazine of Verse* aimed to elevate poetry as an art by isolating it from other kinds of writing in a magazine devoted wholly to verse and literary criticism.[42] Even its book reviews and literary essays were relegated to a separate section at the back of the book, along with its few pages of advertising.[43] Like the editorial cordons around its poems, the physical format of the magazine— well-margined 5½ x 8-inch single-column pages bound in fine covers ornamented with an iconic Pegasus—announced its separation from the journalistic and popular press periodicals of its day, which favored cheaply printed large sheets packed tightly and less discriminately across multiple columns (see Figure 4.1). Instead of the visually compacted dialogue constructed in the pages of *The Egoist*, *Poetry* sought to connect poet and reader by narrowing the focus of their interaction in a cleaner, more iconic page. This bibliographic and aesthetic straitening of poetry worked against the often-cited Whitmanian motto Monroe printed on the back of every issue: "To have great poets there must be great audiences too." Monroe expressed her editorial idealism more fully in a note in the October 1914 number: "Art is not an isolated phenomenon of genius, but the expression of a reciprocal relation between the artist and his public. Like perfect love, it can be supreme only when the relation is complete."[44] Monroe's idea of "supreme" Art, "Like perfect love," involved clean, white sheets uncluttered by the outside pressures of the day.

---

[42] On modernism's economics see Lawrence Rainey, *Institutions of Modernism: Literary Elites and Public Culture* (New Haven: Yale University Press, 2005); and "The Cultural Economy of Modernism," in *Cambridge Companion to Modernism*, edited by Michael Harry Levenson (Cambridge: Cambridge University Press, 1999), p. 44.

[43] As Sean Latham, Robert Scholes and Clifford Wulfman have argued, periodical advertising can be as critically revealing as any other content. See: Sean Latham and Robert Scholes, "The Changing Profession: The Rise Of Periodical Studies," *PMLA* 121 (March 2006), pp. 517–31; Scholes and Wulfman, *Modernism in the Magazines*. For example *Poetry* (May 1915) includes ads for "Bound Volumes of poetry" and books such as Houghton Mifflin's The New Poetry Series, including *Some Imagists Poets: An Anthology* and *Laurence Binyon's The Winnowing Fan: Poems on the Great War*, and Ezra Pound's books published by Elkin Matthews in London (sold in the US through *Poetry*'s office). A full-page ad for *The Egoist*'s "Special Imagist Number" names Moore as part "of the young Anglo-American group of poets, known as 'THE IMAGISTS.'" *The Egoist* and *Poetry* often traded such advertising, like many little magazines. See Morrisson, pp. 54–83, on the running "Art of Versification" ads in *Poetry*.

[44] Harriet Monroe, "The Audience—II," *Poetry* 5:1 (October 1914), pp. 31–2. Monroe's comment was part of an open forum and was preceded by Ezra Pound, "The Audience—I," *Poetry* 5:1 (October 1914), pp. 29–30. Over what he perceived as Monroe's submission to tired democratic proprieties, Pound provocatively counter-argued "the artist is not dependent upon his audience" in his opening salvo.

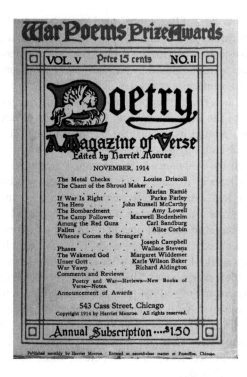

Fig. 4.1   *Poetry: A Magazine of Verse*, vol. 5, no. 2, November 1914. Image
              courtesy of the Modernist Journals Project.

I am not aware of any record of which poems Moore sent to Monroe, but the
pre-war compositions published in "Pouters and Fantails" present a playful, almost
frivolous diction far removed from the scrupulous social and ethical critiques
Moore developed in her revised and new poems following 1914.[45] "Counseil
To A Bachelor," for instance, presents an "Elizabethan Trencher Motto," which
Moore claimed to have discovered in the Bodleian Library.[46] The slight wit of
this peculiar "found" poem seems to depend upon a broad allusion to the *Aeneid*
in placing its maxim to "marie not yett" and "no wyfe get" on a trencher. In the
Aeneid, Aeneas is warned against marrying his own premature love, Dido, whom
he must desert to fulfill his destiny of founding Rome. In the third book of the
Aeneid in Dryden's translation, Aeneas recounts another prophecy of Celaeno,

---

[45]   Moore was also apparently not pleased with her *Poetry* grouping, including only
"To an Intra-Mural Rat" and "The Wizard in Words," retitled "Reticence and Volubility," in
her 1924 *Observations*. Reproduced in *BMM*, pp. 51–2.

[46]   A previous version of this poem titled "Councell to a Bachelor" was printed in *The
Lantern* 21 (Spring 1913), p. 106; reproduced in *BMM*, p. 349.

leader of the harpies, that he will also not found Rome until he and his men "By famine forc'd, your trenchers you shall eat" (III:209–77).[47] Such diverting bric-a-brac appears relatively sterile next to Moore's later compositions from the 1910s and '20s, which sterility only seems to be reinforced by their embedding in *A Magazine of Verse* whose bibliographic aesthetic discourages the inter-textual and inter-genre reading on which Moore's poetic so much depends.

Poetry was not impervious to the war, but it couched its explicit responses to the war in a rhetoric of exception that reasserted the separateness of art even as it admitted extra-literary concerns and material. In the November 1914 special war issue, Monroe's magazine recovers its vision of poetry as an isolate of the social and political world by stressing its academic selection process for its "War Poems Prize Awards." An editorial note promoted the special war issue's "assemblage of widely varying ideas" among its selections from "over seven hundred" American and British submissions (among them "War Yawp" by Richard Aldington and "Phases" by Wallace Stevens). However, this note also promoted *Poetry*'s method of selection in terms of a personally disinterested, socially-blind process for its pseudo-academic prizes: "Each poem submitted was read and decided upon before the envelope containing the poet's true name was opened."[48]

In another issue of war poetry in October 1918, to which Moore contributed a review of Yeats's *Wild Swans At Coole*, Monroe gives prominence to the work of "Miss Eloise Robinson of Cincinnati, who is now doing canteen work in France [and] is becoming widely known as a poet," placing her poem "Fatherland" first in the volume.[49] Again, however, *Poetry* seems to make a point of justifying these intrusions of the war with the ultimate effect of neutralizing them as exceptions. Excerpts printed from Robinson's war correspondence are pardoned with another editor's note: "We cannot forbear quoting for the benefit of our readers portions of recent letters from poets at the front."[50] The prominent placement of Robinson's poem and the repeated emphasis on her status as a "poet" in the editor's notes bespeak Monroe's perception that such incursions into the realm of *Poetry* require special sanction.

---

[47]   Moore's "Elizabethan Trencher" might also obliquely reference the banquet scene in *The Tempest*. See William Shakespeare, *The Tempest*, edited by Virginia Mason Vaughan and Alden T. Vaughan (London: Arden Shakespeare, 1999), p. 238 n.52.1. The prophecy is fulfilled in the seventh book of Virgil's poem.

[48]   "Notes," *Poetry* 5:2 (November 1914), pp. 96–7. For a discussion of publishers' prizes in the commercial press in this period see: Ellen Gruber Garvey, *The Adman in the Parlor: Magazines and the gendering of consumer culture, 1880s to 1910s* (Oxford: Oxford University Press, 1996). As Garvey shows, reader submission prizes had developed into one of the main promotional tools for periodicals in the early 1900s. The swell of submissions and interest in *Poetry* resulting from its War Poems Prize Awards participates in this broader print marketing trend through its layered appeals to "subscribers, and the public in general."

[49]   *Poetry* 8.1 (October 1918), p. 58.

[50]   Ibid., p. 55.

The academic and isolating editorial visions outlined in these wartime numbers of *Poetry* contributed to the growing fault lines between Moore and Monroe, as summed up in Moore's first letter to Ezra Pound in 1919, in which she compares her publications in *Poetry* unfavorably to those in *The Egoist*: "My first work to appear outside of college was a poem … [in] *The Egoist* in 1915 and shortly afterward, four or five poems of mine were published by *Poetry*, a fact which pleased me at the time, but one's feeling changes and not long ago when Miss Monroe invited me to contribute, I was not willing to."[51]

Others, an irregular periodical and related poetry anthology series operated by Alfred Kreymborg out of New York, offered Moore a space for experimental intertextual poetics during the 1910s. Including revisions and reprints of poems first published elsewhere, she published relatively extensively in Kreymborg's organs from 1915–1920.[52] Moore's association with *Others* also connected her and her work to an active and influential social group (including William Carlos Williams, Wallace Stevens, Man Ray, and others) surrounding Kreymborg's enterprises, especially after she moved to New York with her mother following her brother's enlistment. In the January 1919 letter to Pound quoted above, Moore continued: "Alfred Kreymborg has been hospitable and does not now shut the door on me." However, she further claimed at the time to "grow less and less desirous of being published, produce less and have a strong feeling for letting alone what little I do produce." Nevertheless, in New York "the amount of steady co-operation that is to be counted on in the interest of getting things launched, is an amazement to me." Humility kept Moore from saying so, but among the most notable "things" thus being "launched" was her distinctive poetic, which, as we've seen, bears the marks of its cooperative roots most clearly in the context of her early publications.

Already a veteran of the short-lived little magazine *Glebe*, Kreymborg founded *Others* in 1915 with the support of wealthy patron Walter Arensberg, who funded the first year of publication. With the lone exception of a yellow cover in homage to Aubrey Beardsley's notorious *Yellow Book*, Kreymborg kept to his belief that *Others* "was to be a thing with a physical ideal as austere as the one which must govern the choice of manuscripts."[53] *Others* included no editorial comments, correspondence, or contributor biographies (unlike most of its peer publications). Its reader was implicitly directed to pay attention to the verse it contained, and only the verse (see Figure 4.2). At the same time the magazine

---

[51]   Moore to Ezra Pound, January 9, 1919, *SL*, p. 123. Moore contributed only three prose pieces to *Poetry* after "Pouters and Fantails" (until much later in 1932): "A Note on T.S. Eliot's Book [*Prufrock*]" and "Jean De Bosschére's Poems" in *Poetry* 12:1 (April 1918), pp. 36–7, pp. 48–51; and "Wild Swans," a review of Yeats's *The Wild Swans at Coole* (Dundrum: Cuala Press, 1918) in *Poetry* 8:1 (October 1918), pp. 42–4.

[52]   Churchill, p. 135 n.3; *BMM*, p. 467.

[53]   Alfred Kreymborg, *Troubadour: An American Autobiography by Alfred Kreymborg* (New York: Sagamore Press, 1925), p. 172; quoted in *BMM*, p. 468.

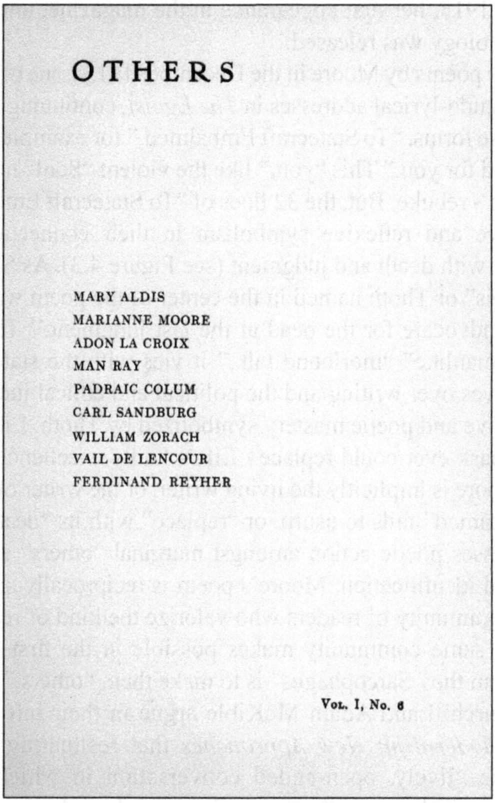
OTHERS

MARY ALDIS
MARIANNE MOORE
ADON LA CROIX
MAN RAY
PADRAIC COLUM
CARL SANDBURG
WILLIAM ZORACH
VAIL DE LENCOUR
FERDINAND REYHER

VOL. I, No. 6

Fig. 4.2 *Others*, vol. 1, no. 6, December 1915. Image courtesy of the Modernist Journals Project.

embedded its "austere" ideals within an overtly social gesture encapsulated in its title: to appear in *Others* without any immediate contextualizing information, except what might be gleaned from an author's name, stressed the magazine itself as a social grouping. Bibliographically stripped of the professional, class, national, racial, ethnic, and other affiliations that would otherwise distinguish them in various manners and degrees, these "others" were presented in a closer, narrower collaborative allegiance than contributors to *Poetry* or *The Egoist* ever were.[54] This radical gesture of prioritizing poetical affiliation engendered a "fit gymnasium" for much of Moore's most experimental and outspoken work in print

[54] See also Churchill, p. 136: "[I]n the social context of *Others* … [Moore] works to invent a discourse that defines individuals not by preconceived gender categories, but by principles of equality and difference."

from December 1915, her first appearance in the magazine, until 1920, when the final *Others* anthology was released.

All five of the poems by Moore in the December 1915 issue of *Others* follow the pattern of her pseudo-lyrical addresses in *The Egoist*, continuing and extending her range within these forms. "To Statecraft Embalmed," for example, begins, "There is nothing to be said for you." This "you," like the violent "Soul" in her *Egoist* poem, occasions Moore's rebuke. But, the 32 lines of "To Statecraft Embalmed" elaborate a more extensive and reflexive symbolism in their connection of militaristic political rhetoric with death and judgment (see Figure 4.3). As Schulze points out, the Egyptian "Ibis" or Thoth named in the center of the poem was both the god of writing and the advocate for the dead at the last judgment.[55] The poem not only critiques "statesmanlike" "moribund talk," it vies with the statecraft it embalms for the prerogatives over writing and the political and ethical judgment that attend upon the discursive and poetic mastery symbolized by Thoth. Lines 22–3 exclaim, "As if a death mask ever could replace / Life's faulty excellence!" As the accuser of these lines Moore is implicitly the living writer, or the writer of the living, which "Statecraft Embalmed" fails to usurp, or "replace" with its "death mask." Set in a volume that stresses poetic action amongst marginal "others" as a rival to given political or social identification, Moore's poem is reciprocally sanctioned through its appeal to a community of readers who valorize the kind of reading and writing which that very same community makes possible in the first place. To win its readers over "from the / Sarcophagus" is to make them "others," too.

Suzanne Churchill and Adam McKible argue in their introduction to *Little Magazines & Modernism: New Approaches* that resituating modernists such as Moore in the "lively, open-ended conversation in which they were first conceived and read" by contributors, editors, and readers connected through publications like *Others*, suggests a "conversational model for modernism."[56] I have suggested earlier in this paper that we recall the historical sense of "activism" to keep the historical specificity of Moore's communicative actions in the wartime little magazines in dialogue with contemporary criticism's own social and political inflections. Perhaps we would do well to make the same gesture with the "conversation" of modernism.[57] The earliest sense of *converse* in fourteenth-century English meant "to live with," and did not imply "to speak with" until the time of Shakespeare: the accident of living together in historical "conversation" took two centuries of usage to acquire the modern sense of "conversation" as a dialogue.[58]

---

[55]   *BMM*, p. 204.

[56]   Churchill and McKible, p. 12.

[57]   See also the related application of Moore's neologism "conversity" in Bazin: passim.

[58]   "converse, v." *OED Online*. March 2011 (Oxford University Press), <http://www.oed.com/view/Entry/40763> (accessed 18 May 2011).

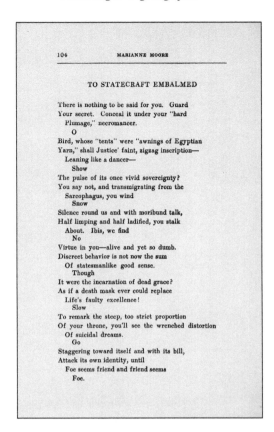

Fig. 4.3   Marianne Moore, "To Statecraft Embalmed," *Others*, vol. 1, no. 6, December 1915. Image courtesy of the Modernist Journals Project.

Discursive action, even for people who find themselves in the same place and time, has never been automatic in language or in life, and modernism was no exception. However, the reconstructive reading of little magazines we have undertaken shows how a socially engaged conversation nevertheless happened between different kinds of writers and different kinds of work in the transatlantic spheres of Anglo-American modernism during the war. It may be impossible to say just what Moore's "fighting spirit" means, but by reconsidering her works in the multiple contexts of their publication, we're not always baffled, and we will continue to be less so as we read more deeply into the textual records of the critical conversation of modernism at the dawn of the age of World War.

Chapter 5
Holiday Activism:
Good Housekeeping and the
Meaning of Mother's Day

Katharine Antolini

On May 10, 1934, Dr. Howard Haggard, an associate professor of Physiology at Yale University, opened as the first featured speaker at the Maternity Center Association's Fourth Annual Mother's Day luncheon in New York City. To an audience of over 300 guests seated in the Grand Ball Room at the Waldorf-Astoria, Dr. Haggard demanded an answer to why an estimated 10,000 women died in childbirth each year. "Who is to blame?" he implored. "Who is accountable?" In a search for those responsible, the professor requested all present at the society luncheon to serve as the jury for an impromptu inquest.[1]

In his mock inquest Dr. Haggard cross-examined five witnesses: the physician unable to provide quality obstetric care; the educator and elder mother who ill-prepared the nation's youth for the demands of parentage; "Mr. Everyman" who remained indifferent to the plight of women and children; and, finally, the publisher who faltered in his obligation to shape public awareness. Of the publisher, he enquired whether or not an American mother deliberately killed by an alien government would be considered newsworthy. To which his fictional publisher answered, "Yes, of course it would be news." If such acts of murder were repeated many times, continued Dr. Haggard, could not public opinion be stirred to the point of declaring war to defend American mothers? Again, the publisher agreed it was possible. "Why, then, if this is the case, do not the needless deaths of three mothers a day, 10,000 a year, similarly arouse the American public to rise to concerted action to end this atrocity? Why are not these deaths publicized as would be deaths at the hands of an alien government?" he beseeched. "Because they are not news," answered the publisher, "the public is not interested in them, does not want to hear about them, read about them; in short, is largely indifferent to them." As Dr. Haggard ended his interrogation, he assured the luncheon jury that there was still hope that apathetic publishers could themselves be inspired to lead rather than follow public interest. "The educational example set by the Maternity Center Association is gradually penetrating public consciousness—

---

[1]   Dr. Howard W. Haggard, Speech presented at the Fourth Annual Mother's Day Luncheon, 10 May 1934, Maternity Center Association Papers, Archives and Special Collections, A.C. Long Health Sciences Library, Columbia University Medical Center, New York.

shaping public opinion," he stressed. "The tragedy is that while the shaping goes on, so do the deaths."[2]

The Maternity Center Association (MCA), located in New York City, had been dedicated to the cause of maternal and infant health since its founding in 1918. Complications resulting from childbirth were a leading cause of death for women between the ages of 15 and 44 in the early twentieth century, second only to tuberculosis nationwide. Unless an emergency required earlier attention, expectant mothers did not routinely seek medical care until late in their pregnancies; consequently, the United States' maternal mortality rate of 62 per 10,000 live births ranked the nation 14th among 16 western countries in its ability to provide safe maternity care.[3] To combat the crisis in New York, the MCA promoted the need for quality prepartum and postpartum medical care through its center on Manhattan's East Side (see Figure 5.1). In an area where 4,000 babies on average were born each year, the association conducted prenatal and postnatal clinics, supplemented hospital nursing services, provided 24-hour nursing supervision for home births, and conducted a series of educational courses for expectant mothers (and eventually "stag classes" for expectant fathers) through this single center. The MCA also gained a national reputation as a training center for public health nurses and professional nurse-midwives.[4]

As revealed in Dr. Haggard's mock inquest, the Maternity Center Association and its supporters identified an array of factors contributing to the country's disgraceful maternal mortality rates—chief among them, of course, being the unremitting public apathy. Although increased community awareness had lessened the public

---

[2]　Ibid.

[3]　Kriste Lindenmeyer, *"A Right to Childhood:" The U.S. Children's Bureau and Child Welfare 1912–46* (Urbana: University of Illinois Press, 1997), p. 65; The Maternity Center Association, *Six Years in Review 1930–1935* (1935), p. 5; Richard A. Meckel, *Save the Babies: American public health reform and prevention of infant mortality, 1850–1929* (Ann Arbor: University of Michigan Press, 1990), pp. 202–4; Genevieve Parkhurst, "Every Baby Needs a Mother," *Good Housekeeping* (February 1934), p. 27; Rebecca Jo Plant, *MOM: The transformation of motherhood in modern America* (Chicago: University of Chicago Press, 2010), pp. 120–30.

[4]　The MCA originally administered a network of clinics throughout New York City with other public health organizations but decided to centralize its work to a single center in 1921. By 1929, requests by public health nurses to study at the MCA's field clinic outgrew the physical capacity of the center, prompting the association to send its nurses throughout the country to lead training seminars. The MCA opened the Loberstine Midwifery Clinic and the Loberstine Midwifery School in the early 1930s. The organization still operates in New York City under the name Childbirth Connections, adopted in 2008. Laura E. Ettinger, *Nurse-Midwifery: The birth of a new American profession* (Columbus: Ohio State University Press, 2006), pp. 72–95; Esme J. Howard, "Navigating the Stormy Sea: The Maternity Center Association and the Development of Prenatal Care 1900–1930" (master's thesis: Yale University School of Nursing, 1994), p. 29, pp. 28–43, pp. 74–8; The Maternity Center Association, *Maternity Center Association Log, 1915–1975* (1975), pp. 7–11; Sarah Twerdon, "The Maternity Center Association as a Vehicle for the Education of Motherhood" (master's thesis: Columbia University, 1947), pp. 5–11, p. 44.

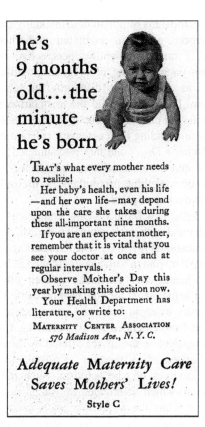

he's
9 months
old...the
minute
he's born

THAT's what every mother needs
to realize!
   Her baby's health, even his life
—and her own life—may depend
upon the care she takes during
these all-important nine months.
   If you are an expectant mother,
remember that it is vital that you
see your doctor at once and at
regular intervals.
   Observe Mother's Day this
year by making this decision now.
   Your Health Department has
literature, or write to:
MATERNITY CENTER ASSOCIATION
   576 *Madison Ave., N. Y. C.*

**Adequate Maternity Care
Saves Mothers' Lives!**

Style C

Fig. 5.1   Maternity Center Association, "he's 9 months ... ," 1931. © Childbirth
                Connection. Used with permission.

health threats levied by diphtheria, typhoid fever, smallpox, and even tuberculosis
by mid-century, the maternal death rate continued unabated; nothing would change,
according to the MCA, while American men and women remained ignorant of the
crisis. This lack of general concern inspired the association's national Mother's
Day educational campaigns throughout the 1930s, trusting that an enlightened
public would subsequently demand adequate maternity care for every woman.[5]

---

[5]   The Maternity Center Association, "Radio Talk Suggestion for Mother's Day,"
Publicity Kit for Mother's Day, May 10, 1931 (1931), pp. 4–5, Maternity Center Association
Papers; The Maternity Center Association, *Six Years in Review 1930–1935*, pp. 2–6; Dr.
Thomas Parran Jr., New York State Commissioner of Health, "Why Our Lack of Progress
in Preventing Maternal Deaths," speech presented at the Fourth Annual Mother's Day
Luncheon, 10 May 1934, Maternity Center Association Papers.

The MCA's holiday campaigns sought to fundamentally change how American society viewed, experienced, and even celebrated motherhood. The association aggressively advanced a modern scientific perspective of motherhood that challenged the common understanding of pregnancy and childbirth as purely natural events, as well as attempted to dismantle the taboos surrounding the topic's public discussion. But not only did the association strive to strip away the euphemisms hindering the candid discourse of reproduction, it hoped to strip away the mawkishness surrounding the customary celebration of Mother's Day. It promoted a "new Mother's Day," one that re-channeled the sentimentality of the holiday observance into a constructive social service to mothers. "Instead of arousing ourselves to do something for mothers," criticized the MCA, "we as a people prefer to give them a potted plant."[6]

The success of the 1930s "new Mother's Day" campaigns relied heavily on the cooperation of the media and with each campaign the MCA sought the broadest possible reach for its educational literature. The association especially recognized the potential role that popular women's magazines played in exposing a substantial number of women to a health crisis particular to their life experiences. Many women turned to a favorite magazine for guidance on domestic issues throughout the early twentieth century as rapid industrial and urban expansion physically isolated more Americans from extended family networks. Loyal readers thereby became increasingly dependent on the advice offered by the publication's staff of specialists and medical experts. It is, therefore, a mistake to discount traditional women's magazines as sources of true activism. Such publications offered a "respectable" avenue from which to broaden the social discussion of women's domestic and civic roles. Thus the MCA was understandably eager to utilize the genre's established reputation as a trusted source of general maternity and childcare information in order to reach a vast female audience.

Yet the annual campaign's call for comprehensive obstetric care and its harsh critique of the traditional Mother's Day celebration met with mixed reactions from the editors of the era's most popular women's magazines. Editors of these multimillion-circulation publications recognized the precarious balance they had to maintain between following and shaping public opinion. Described as "a reading supermarket" by one twentieth-century editor, women's magazines endeavored to "cheer a little, inform a little" and "challenge a little."[7] Thus editors disagreed on exactly how far to push their more conservative female readers by championing social causes, including the seemingly relevant cause of maternal health.

---

6 Maternity Center Association, *The Story of the New Mother's Day* (1935); Hazel Corbin, General Director of the Maternity Center Association, "Make Maternity Safe," Radio address from the Fourth Annual Mother's Day Luncheon, May 10, 1934, Maternity Center Association Papers.

7 Herbert R Mayes, *The Magazine Maze: A prejudiced perspective* (Garden City, NY: Doubleday and Company, Inc., 1980), p. 91. Mayes succeeded Bigelow as the editor of *Good Housekeeping*.

By attempting to lead public opinion, an editor risked the real danger of straying too far ahead of the magazine's readership.[8]

In 1934, *Good Housekeeping* formally joined the MCA's Mother's Day campaign—but with some reservations. A survey of editorial columns, articles, and fictional stories featured in *Good Housekeeping*'s May issues reveals the magazine's struggle to reconcile a public commitment to progressive social action on behalf of mothers and children with the MCA's call to abandon the sentimental celebration of Mother's Day. The ambivalence expressed within its pages reflected a larger social ambivalence surrounding competing models of American motherhood and the role of women's magazines in advancing new maternal standards in the early twentieth century.

"Let's Make this Mother's Day Mean a Better Chance for Mothers Everywhere" (1931 MCA Campaign Slogan)

The Maternity Center Association was not the only organization to appropriate the celebration of Mother's Day in the 1930s. In 1933 Congress amended the original 1914 Mother's Day Flag Resolution that first designated the second Sunday in May a federal holiday. In addition to the customary display of the national flag and presenting tokens of affection to mothers, the new resolution asked the American people to observe Mother's Day by contributing to charitable agencies providing relief for families victimized by the economic recession, especially the country's "unprecedented large numbers" of mothers and children suffering from the chronic unemployment or death of a male wage earner.[9] The amended Mother's Day Resolution immediately bolstered the work of benevolent organizations hoping to extend the holiday's celebration into month-long campaigns for individual causes.[10] Nor was the MCA the first organization to court the endorsement of popular women's magazines in its attempt to change the celebration of Mother's Day. Throughout the 1920s and 1930s, a New York philanthropist led a movement to officially rename the maternal holiday

---

[8]   Ibid.; Bruce Gould and Beatrice Blackman Gould, *American Story: Memories and reflections of Bruce Gould and Beatrice Blackman Gould* (New York: Harper and Row Publishers, 1968), pp. 172–3; Kim Chuppa-Cornell, "Filling a Vacuum: Women's Health Information in *Good Housekeeping's* Articles and Advertisements, 1920–1965," *Historian* 3 (2005), pp. 454–73; Mary Ellen Zuckerman, *A History of Popular Women's Magazines in the U.S., 1792–1995* (Westport, CT: Greenwood Press, 1998), p. 143.

[9]   *Mother's Day*, SR. 16, 73rd Congress, 1st session, *Congressional Record* 77 (1 May 1933), p. 2615.

[10]   For a larger discussion of other organizations that used Mother's Day in their charitable promotions in the early twentieth century see, Katharine Antolini, "Memorializing Motherhood: Anna Jarvis and the Struggle for Control of Mother's Day" (dissertation, West Virginia University, 2009), pp. 120–267.

Parents' Day. George Hecht, the notable publisher of *Parents' Magazine*, nationally endorsed the Parents' Day movement until 1941.[11]

The MCA's holiday educational campaigns, however, were serious undertakings for an organization with limited access to public funds after the failed renewal of the Sheppard-Towner Act (also known as the Maternity and Infancy Act) in 1927. Private donations underwrote the annual campaigns ranging from $2,000 to $6,000 in total expenses—equivalent to an estimated $32,000 to $78,000 today.[12] Its primary expense was the elaborate publicity kit sent free to hundreds of health organizations, churches, women's clubs, civic groups, and to thousands of media sources across the country. The MCA's full publicity kit included nine separate sections and measured close to 100 pages in length. The kit was designed to provide ready-made Mother's Day campaigns for any community hoping to improve maternal health services in their area. It offered detailed advice on how to stir public awareness and provided outlines for local meetings, forms for holiday proclamations by state governors and city mayors, and formats for church bulletins and sample sermons. Moreover, the kit included prepared promotional advertisements and standard speeches on maternity care, as well as a series of feature stories and radio talks that varied by length. With its first national campaign in 1931, the MCA fulfilled 700 requests for its publicity kit; five years later the number of requests grew to over 2,000.[13]

In addition to its standard publicity kit, the MCA designed a 12-page illustrated pamphlet specifically tailored to the needs of publishers, entitled, "If the Public Only Knew! Editors Can Help Mothers on Mother's Day" (see Figure 5.2). Over 4,000 magazines and 2,000 daily and weekly newspapers received the pamphlet in the 1931 inaugural campaign. In it the MCA offered ten individual stories and articles, varying in length from 350 to 1,200 words, with recommendations on the type of periodical for which each article was best suited, such as for general use or specifically for use in women's or men's publications. Topics included descriptions of the maternal health crisis and the solution of proper prenatal and postnatal care. But the articles also urged the public to join the MCA's new celebration of Mother's Day, insisting that no real honor could be paid to mothers until public-spirited men and women joined the concerted effort of the nation's health providers and civic organizations.

---

[11]   Ibid., pp. 146–63; Ralph LaRossa and Jaimie Ann Carboy, "A Kiss for Mother, a Hug for Dad," *Fathering* 6.3 (Fall 2008), pp. 249–65.

[12]   The Maternity Center Association, *Six Years in Review*, p. 13, p. 12, p. 22. "Measuring Worth," <http://www.measuringworth.com>.

[13]   See The Maternity Center Association, *Campaign Suggestions for Mother's Day, May 12, 1935* (1935); The Maternity Center Association, *Report of the Mother's Day Educational Activities, Maternity Center Association 1936* (1936), section II, p. 3, Maternity Center Association Papers; The Maternity Center Association, *Publicity Kit for Mother's Day, May 10, 1931*, Maternity Center Association Papers; The Maternity Center Association, *The Story of the New Mother's Day*.

"The American nation honors motherhood, yet—" charged one article, "we have the highest maternal death rate of any civilized nation in the world!"[14]

In addition to the feature stories and articles, editors could select eight promotional advertisements from the media pamphlet. The prestigious marketing firm J. Walter Thompson Company prepared the electrotypes for the holiday campaigns which included a promotional cartoon crafted by Pulitzer Prize Winner Charles R. Macauley. Entitled, "Facing Facts on Mother's Day," the cartoon featured Uncle Sam rocking a recently orphaned baby. With both his hands on a cradle, he looks solemnly at a sign exposing the United States' disgraceful maternal health record in comparison to other western countries. "Uncle Sam is troubled—16,000 mothers every year fail to answer roll call on

---

[14]   Ibid., p. 4, p. 10; see also, The Maternity Center Association, *Publicity Kit for Mother's Day, May 10, 1931.*

Mother's Day," grimly notes the caption. "They die having babies. Of these 10,000 could be saved, if people knew the importance of adequate maternity care."[15]

During a time when most media sources deemed the frank scientific discussion of maternity as indecent, the holiday campaigns succeeded in exposing a national audience to information that had never before appeared in popular print. The immediate response was overwhelming. In the wake of the first campaign, over 3,000 expectant mothers wrote the MCA to request its educational literature, and civic organizations around the country promised to incorporate the issue of maternal and infant care into their community service. The popularity of the 1931 campaign thoroughly convinced the association of the nation's eagerness for a new celebration of Mother's Day.[16] By the decade's end, the MCA marveled at the progress it had made in combating the ignorance that had caused such indifference to the health crisis in the past.[17] Yet it was more than just the novelty of seeing the word "pregnancy" in print outside of medical journals or being permitted to mention the measurement of the female pelvis on the radio; no longer were editors simply satisfied with sanitized discussion of maternal deaths or only willing to cover events if prominent socialites or political figures were featured speakers. "They say 'Give us a solution,'" reported the MCA. "Tell us what is necessary to protect mothers and babies. Provide us with stories of real families. We don't want to skim the surface, we want the facts."[18]

The MCA heralded the 1936 holiday campaign as its most successful. That May both the National Broadcasting Company (NBC) and the Mutual Broadcasting Company (MBC) aired special programs on maternity care, while the Columbia Broadcasting System (CBS) covered the Sixth Annual Mother's Day Luncheon at the Waldorf-Astoria. In addition, five nationwide newspaper syndicates published

---

[15]   The Maternity Center Association, "If the Public Only Knew!" p. 1, Maternity Center Association Papers.

[16]   The Maternity Center Association, *Maternity Center Association Log, 1918–1943* (1943), p. 11; "The Mother's Day Campaign," *American Journal of Nursing* 31.7 (July 1931), p. 839.

[17]   The MCA was not successful in overcoming all taboos. The New York State Board of Regents censored the association's motion picture, "The Birth of a Baby." The Board deemed it indecent, immoral, and corruptive of public morals. Not every state censored the motion picture, however. According to Maternity Center Association President Mrs. Shepard Krech, for example, 15,000 people attended the first day of showing in Minneapolis, Minnesota in 1938. Mrs. Shepard Krech to Mr. Davidson n.d. (circa 1939), Maternity Center Association Papers.

[18]   Margaret Cuthbert, Director of Women's Activities of the National Broadcasting Company, Inc, to Shepard Krech, April 27, 1938, Maternity Center Association Papers; Miss Hazel Corbin, Maternity Center Association General Director to Dr. Howard Haggard, April 5, 1938, Maternity Center Association Papers; Mrs. Shepard Krech to Mr. Davidson (May1838?), Maternity Center Association Papers.

articles related to the holiday campaign.[19] First Lady Eleanor Roosevelt, a long-time supporter of the association, encouraged public support for the "New Mother's Day" in her syndicated column "My Day." "I have been wondering if in addition to sending flowers and cards to our mothers, we might not as a nation, devote a little more time to the study of the real conditions confronting mothers in these United States," she wrote.[20]

The MCA eventually realized that a "one size fits all" educational campaign would fail to reach the largest possible audience, especially in regards to courting the support of traditional women's magazines. The association had to accept and accommodate, however reluctantly, the boundaries that *Good Housekeeping*'s endorsement placed on its campaigns, not just in the soft censorship of the campaign's candid discussion of maternity, but also with its sometimes uncompromising assault on the traditional Mother's Day celebration. Within medical journals, such as the *American Journal of Nursing*, the MCA freely criticized the "wholesale Mother's Day propaganda" of greeting cards, flowers, and idle words of appreciation; medical professionals echoed the association's denouncement of such holiday rituals as "vacuous sentimentality," even "sacrilegious," given the nation's abhorrent maternal mortality record.[21] In contrast, editor-in-chief William Bigelow insisted on a holiday campaign better suited to *Good Housekeeping*'s mainstream female readership, one which offered a varied discussion, portrayal, and celebration of motherhood.

"A Day for Mothers"

William Frederick Bigelow devoted his 1940 May editorial to the evolution of the Mother's Day holiday. He recognized the competing celebratory models surrounding the day's annual observance. Many still chose to honor their mothers in the sentimental style first established by the holiday's founder, Anna Jarvis, who envisioned a day commemorating the boundless love and selfless care that mothers provided their families. Bigelow agreed that the sentimental celebration had certainly succeeded in its purpose to increase the "telling of love" between mother and child. His editorial also congratulated the work of the Maternity Center Association. Its annual campaign had effectively lowered the maternal death rate over the last ten years. Thanks to the association's efforts, he enthused, "Mothers' Day this year will be a happy day in tens of thousands of homes that

---

[19] Maternity Center Association, *Report of the Mother's Day Educational Activities, Maternity Center Association 1936*, section I, pp. 2–6.

[20] Eleanor Roosevelt, "My Day," 20 May 1936, Eleanor Roosevelt Papers Project, <http://www.gwu.edu /~erpapers/>.

[21] "The Mother's Day Campaign," p. 839; "Saving Mothers from Unnecessary Deaths," *American Journal of Nursing* 34.3 (March 1934), p. 272; "Nurses and Safe Maternity," *American Journal of Nursing* 37.4 (April 1937), pp. 392–3.

would otherwise have had no mother." But there was more to the celebration of Mother's Day than the example set by Jarvis or even the MCA, warned Bigelow:

> On Mothers' Day mothers should dominate our hearts because they are *good mothers*, not just the physical means of bringing our lives into the world. Love and respect, even filial love and respect, *must be earned, must be deserved* ... . *If she meets the true requirements of motherhood*, she can face Mother's Day, or any day, with a smile in her heart if not on her lips.[22]

To help illustrate his point, the same issue included a one-page article with the ominous title, "Mother's Day—of Reckoning." The article presented four cartoon vignettes featuring women making the most common of mothering mistakes, ones that were sure to lead to regular visits with a child psychiatrist. For mothers breaking up a scuffle between two boys by fighting themselves, the catchy caption cautioned, "Nice of you to take his strife—Can you do it through his life?" Worst of all, it warned, were the "doting others," "Why can't we have bashful mothers?"[23]

By the end of Bigelow's tenure at *Good Housekeeping* in 1942, the magazine was fully immersed in the timely discussion on what made a "good mother," specifically one worthy of praise on Mother's Day. The editor's unapologetic measure of maternal worth echoed a larger mid-century trend of "antimaternalism" or "mother-blaming" that has been well documented by recent historians.[24] Modern critics attacked the Victorian image and sentimental celebration of "natural" motherhood—defined as the inherent capacity of all women to be good mothers by virtue of their maternal instincts or all-encompassing "Mother Love." According to twentieth-century public health reformers and doctors specializing in the new fields of obstetrics and pediatrics, the requirements of motherhood had fundamentally changed since the nineteenth century. Modern women were expected to rise to the new maternal standards for their own sake and the sake of their children, which meant relying on the proper guidance of experts. A woman's maternal instinct was no longer enough to ensure the successful rearing of her children.[25] As early as

---

[22] William Frederick Bigelow, "A Day for Mothers," *Good Housekeeping* (May 1940), p. 4. Emphasis added.

[23] Kay Riley, "Mother's Day—of Reckoning," *Good Housekeeping* (May 1940), p. 18.

[24] For an overview of the historical trends in the discourse of motherhood in the twentieth century see: Sharon Hays, *The Cultural Contradictions of Motherhood* (New Haven: Yale University Press, 1996); Maxine Margolis, *Mothers and Such: Views of American women and why they changed* (Berkeley: University of California Press, 1985); Plant, *MOM*; Barbara Beatty, Emily D. Cahan and Julia Grant, eds., *When Science Encounters the Child: Education, Parenting, and Child Welfare in 20th-Century America* (New York: Teachers College Press, 2006).

[25] Lindenmeyer, *"A Right to Childhood,"* p. 64, p. 72; Alisa Klaus, *Every Child a Lion: The Origins of Maternal and Infant Health Policy in the United States and France, 1890–1920* (Ithaca: Cornell University Press, 1993), p. 15, p. 51; Meckel, *Save the Babies*, p. 122, p. 201.

1911, *Good Housekeeping* had joined the discussion with an anonymously authored article suggesting that a singular trust in the maternal instinct was responsible for the nation's high infant mortality rates: "This fearful death rate will be reduced only by trained mothers, hospitals, specialists, and trained nurses. We survived our babyhood and youth because we were hard to kill, and that is the only reason any child survives untrained, unrestrained maternal instinct."[26]

This new and powerful assault on motherhood did not completely dismantle the traditional or over-romanticized portrayal of Victorian motherhood. For twentieth-century traditionalists, motherhood was still a sacred calling. They believed in the power of Mother Love and its transformative capacity, explains historian Rebecca Jo Plant. Mother Love "could turn a shallow and vapid woman into a noble character; it could recall a wayward son or daughter to the path of virtue; it could mold a poor and scrawny boy into a great and powerful leader." Traditionalists continued to define American motherhood as a "fundamental pillar of the nation's social and political order" and were prepared to protect this maternal institution from its new vocal detractors.[27] And in the midst of the conflicting public discourse over the standards of true motherhood, people still celebrated Mother's Day each year. The holiday's cultural representation throughout the era exposed the ongoing struggle between the traditionalists and the champions of modern motherhood, as both sides used the holiday to define the intrinsic value of motherhood in American society.

Even Bigelow hesitated to completely abandon the traditional celebration of Mother's Day in the 1930s despite his, and the magazine's, past advocacy of improved maternal and infant health care. Prior to World War I, the leading women's magazine considered the promotion of Progressive reforms as good business, but only *Good Housekeeping* sustained its social crusading throughout the early twentieth century. Bigelow ran in-depth articles on a range of social causes, including schooling for poor Appalachian children, Indian affairs, and the exploitative conditions of female workers. Moreover, *Good Housekeeping* offered one of the strongest endorsements of the Sheppard-Towner Act in the 1920s.[28] The magazine closely followed the debates surrounding the bill's passage in 1921, wanting to increase the public pressure in its favor. Bigelow unabashedly chastised the politicians who feared the "ghost of socialized medicine" with the federal funding of prenatal clinics and public health professionals.[29] Nine years later, he lamented Congress's final move to stop funding the health programs established under the Sheppard-Towner Act. It was disgraceful, he insisted, for a government to show a greater interest in subsidizing the raising of corn or hogs than lowering the nation's maternal and infant mortality rate.[30]

---

26   "Maternal Instinct Run Riot," *Good Housekeeping* (March 1911), p. 245.

27   Plant, *MOM*, p. 5.

28   Zuckerman, *A History of Popular Women's Magazines*, p. 130, pp. 183–6.

29   Bigelow, "What the Editor has to Say," *Good Housekeeping* (March 1921), p. 6.

30   Bigelow, "Fighting the Good Fight Again," *Good Housekeeping* (May 1930), p. 4. Other featured stories supporting the Sheppard-Towner Act: Frances Parkinson Keyes,

As part of Bigelow's advocacy for the Sheppard-Towner Act, *Good Housekeeping* featured full-length articles about the Maternity Center Association and its success in lowering the death rates for mothers in New York City. Coincidently, these articles mainly appeared in the magazine's May issues. It was reasonable then for the MCA to assume the magazine's immediate endorsement of its educational campaigns given Bigelow's past support for its cause. Yet that was not the case. Neither Bigelow, nor (presumably) the magazine's female readership, was ready to suddenly alter the fundamental meaning and celebration of Mother's Day stipulated by the campaign. "We have been reading a lot in the papers lately about reforming Mother's Day and a lot of it we don't like," admitted Bigelow in his May 1931 editorial. The following spring he wrote again of the MCA's request for the magazine to join its effort to "make Mother's Day significant" and his decision to turn down that request; he simply believed the time was not right for such a bold campaign.[31] Even after Bigelow officially endorsed the annual holiday campaign two years later, *Good Housekeeping*'s selection of featured articles and stories continued to send mixed messages over the true meaning of Mother's Day and the image of motherhood it commemorated.

The popular celebration of Mother's Day did not begin with the day's official designation as a national holiday in 1914. The federal government simply offered a formal recognition of a holiday already being observed in every state in the country. It was Anna Jarvis who led the successful movement to reserve a day in commemoration of American mothers beginning in 1908.[32] The following year, *Good Housekeeping* endorsed the new holiday by formally introducing Jarvis and the meaning of her Mother's Day observance to its readers. The day was meant to "make us better children by getting us closer to the hearts of our good mothers," the article emphasized, a day to "brighten the lives" of all mothers who selflessly served their families. The magazine also introduced the holiday's official emblem,

---

"Letters From a Senator's Wife," *Good Housekeeping* (March 1921), p. 12; Anne Shannon Monroe, "Adventuring in Motherhood," *Good Housekeeping* (May 1920), p. 28; Katherine Glover, "Making America Safe for Mothers," *Good Housekeeping* (May 1926), p. 98.

[31] Bigelow allowed Metropolitan Life Insurance Company to purchase advertising space to promote the MCA's campaign, however. Bigelow, "Mothers' Day," *Good Housekeeping* (May 1931), p. 4; Metropolitan Life Insurance Company Advertisement, *Good Housekeeping* (May 1931), p. 126; Bigelow, "Two Big Days," *Good Housekeeping* (May 1932), p. 8.

[32] Jarvis organized the country's first official Mother's Day services in both her hometown of Grafton, West Virginia, and her adoptive hometown of Philadelphia on May 10, 1908. Mother's Day International Association, *The Mother's Day Movement* [1912?], p. 3, Mother's Day Archives, International Mother's Day Shrine, Grafton, West Virginia; Howard Wolfe, *Behold Thy Mother: Mother's Day and the Mother's Day Church* (Kingsport, TN: Kingsport Press, 1962), pp. 192–5. Others have claimed to be the original founder of Mother's Day in the United States. For a larger discussion of the holiday's history see, Antolini, "Memorializing Motherhood," pp. 20–119.

the white carnation, a flower meant to symbolize the purity, faithfulness, charity, beauty, and love of a mother's care.[33]

Under Jarvis's sentimental model of motherhood, *all mothers were good mothers*. A woman's maternal worth was to be honored on Mother's Day—never questioned or demeaned; thus her holiday celebration effectively reinforced the popular image of motherhood as a sacred calling. *Good Housekeeping*'s editorial staff and readers initially responded to the holiday's maternal message. In 1910 editor-in-chief James Eaton Tower (Bigelow took over the position in 1913) felt that a day honoring Mother Love was "doing no harm, as far as we can see" and that the holiday was certainly "richly worth the thought and the time required, just for the sweet influence of the memory of the mothers gone."[34] Readers also contributed stories expressing their appreciation of the small, yet special, gestures offered to them on Mother's Day, such as an eight-year-old daughter wanting to prepare the family dinner.[35]

The selection of fiction printed in the May issues throughout the 1920s further strengthened the holiday's original sentimental message. The stories touted the transformative nature of Mother Love. Through these stories, readers experienced the pain of widowed mothers neglected by the very children they had lovingly reared and then shared in the redemption of those ungrateful children as they earned their mothers' forgiveness.[36] One told the tale of a policeman, "with no use for the sentimentality of Mother's Day," who follows a vagrant through town, convinced that he was sure to commit a crime. He watches as the man uses the last of his money to buy and mail a greeting card to his dear mother. The policeman eventually realizes the vagrant was actually his long-lost brother and is shamed into sending his own message home.[37]

By the 1930s, however, more articles that expressed the anti-maternalist trend tentatively found their way into *Good Housekeeping*'s May issues. The magazine's editorial staff recognized the risk of alienating its female audience by appearing to openly attack the maternal worth of American women on Mother's Day. In the April 1930 issue, the magazine even prepared its readers for the forthcoming article written by Kathleen Norris, entitled "If You Are the Right Kind of Mother, You Will Not Be Looking for Back Pay on Mother's Day." The preemptive editorial cautioned readers

---

[33] "Mother's Day," *Good Housekeeping* (May 1909), p. 645.

[34] "Mother Love," *Good Housekeeping* (May 1910), p. 628.

[35] "To Help Mother," *Good Housekeeping* (May 1915), p. 607.

[36] Juliet Wilbur Tomkins, "A Submerged Mother: A Tale for Mother's Day," *Good Housekeeping* (May 1911), pp. 547–54; Gertrude Brooke Hamilton, "Where is Your Mother?" *Good Housekeeping* (May 1920), pp. 47–8, p. 188, pp. 190–96.

[37] Octavus Roy Cohen, "Mothers' Day," *Good Housekeeping* (May 1926), pp. 78–80, pp. 121–2; In contrast to the majority of Mother's Day stories, Dorothy Dix occasionally used her "Mirandy" series to challenge the sentimental holiday model. Dorothy Dix, "Mirandy on Mothers," *Good Housekeeping* (May 1918), p. 42, p. 96; Dorothy Dix, "Mirandy on the Mothers' Union," *Good Housekeeping* (May 1919), p. 42, p. 149.

to approach the article with an open mind, so as not to be offended, and to remember that when Mrs. Norris criticized the women she calls "octopus mothers" (defined as a mother "who tightens her tentacles about her daughter or son and drains all the beauty and possibility out of that child's life forever") she spoke as a mother herself.[38]

Despite the willingness to publish potentially controversial articles on motherhood, Bigelow held to an early reluctance to join any Mother's Day campaign designed to turn a day of love and homage for one's mother into another day of almsgiving. Like Jarvis who resented the charitable campaigns that reduced mothers to objects of pity on Mother's Day, Bigelow too wondered what was a better tribute to a mother on her special day—a picture postcard from an errant son, or a basket of food from another mother's son? He believed the former would better feed a mother's heart. Although "no true son or daughter of a good mother will ever turn a deaf ear to another mother's appeal for help," he knew there were other ways to advocate for the nation's mothers besides tarnishing the beautiful symbol of the maternal holiday. No one should be made to feel guilty for putting his own mother first, especially on Mother's Day.[39]

Furthermore, the morbid tone of the MCA's holiday campaigns did not initially appeal to Bigelow either. The association relied heavily on scare tactics in its early publicity. Promotional ads described the "pathetic life" of thousands of babies left motherless each year, forced to turn to foster-mothers, orphanages, and relatives as poor substitutes. "The tragedy, the waste, the heartbreak is immeasurable."[40] Campaign literature frequently altered the holiday's white carnation emblem from its intended symbol of Mother Love to a graphic symbol of death, with 16,000 white carnations representing the 16,000 mothers who annually perished in childbirth (see Figure 5.3).[41] Although such shocking imagery never completely left its promotional repertoire, the MCA ultimately recognized that such descriptions created needless dread about maternity and chose to soften its rhetoric in later campaigns. "Merely deploring this condition will not change it," the association admitted.[42]

---

[38]   "Our Own Four Walls: Where *Good Housekeeping* Readers, Writers and Editors Can Talk to One Another as Members of the Family," *Good Housekeeping* (April 1930), p. 98; Kathleen Norris, "If You Are the Right Kind of Mothers, You Will Not Be Looking for Back Pay on Mothers' Day," *Good Housekeeping* (May 1930), p. 28. Although the labeling of mothers who became too involved in their children's lives as "octopus mothers" directly criticized American mothers, the larger article attempted to provide a more positive message. Norris encouraged women to find outside interests of their own, separate from their children's, in order to develop a separate identity.

[39]   Antolini, "Memorializing Motherhood," pp. 164–267; Bigelow, "Mothers' Day," p. 4.

[40]   "A Pink Carnation—or a Life on Mother's Day?" *The New York Times* (12 May 1929).

[41]   The Maternity Center Association, "If the Public Only Knew!" p. 5.

[42]   Although the positive aspects of maternity care were not the "headline catchers," admitted the MCA, in the long run they achieved "sounder educational and more constructive action on the part of mothers, fathers, and community leaders." Maternity

Fig. 5.3   Maternity Center Association, "16,000 White Carnations," 1931.
© Childbirth Connection. Used with permission.

The MCA finally earned *Good Housekeeping*'s official endorsement, therefore, when it changed its publicity strategy and offered a more positive or constructive educational campaign beginning in 1934. "WE YEILD—or does one say bow?— to the inevitable," proclaimed Bigelow. "Mothers' Day is going off the sentimental standard."[43] He approved the new direction in which the MCA was taking its campaign. Instead of simply alarming the public about the extent of the maternal crisis, the MCA made a better effort to educate the public on how to improve the care of mothers and children in their communities. *Good Housekeeping* featured

Center Association, *Maternity Center Association Log, 1918–1943*, p. 13; Maternity Center Association, *The Story of the New Mother's Day*, p. 12.

[43]   Bigelow, "Get Ready For Mothers' Day," *Good Housekeeping* (April 1934), p. 4.

a seven-page article championing the association's work in its May issue to officially show its support. "You'll do your part if you read this article and follow its suggestions for community service," promised the magazine.[44] Evidently, Bigelow saw nothing threatening to the original purpose of Mother's Day in the 1934 campaign. "Just the opposite," he insisted. "If it succeeds, there will be more mothers for sons and daughters to love and honor as the years go by."[45] The MCA campaign appeared to make space for the sentimental and modern celebration of motherhood, according to Bigelow's interpretation, which was exactly what *Good Housekeeping* attempted to do within its own pages.

Earning the endorsement of one of the era's most respected and profitable women's magazines was certainly a huge advantage for the MCA's holiday campaign and its effort to spread its modern view of maternity. As a self-defined "trade journal for women," *Good Housekeeping*'s readership was already receptive of expert advice on all domestic topics, and by the 1930s, it had its own staff of resident medical experts who wrote monthly advice columns related to motherhood and childrearing.[46] Dr. Josephine H. Kenyon advised readers for over 25 years as the director of *Good Housekeeping*'s "Health and Happiness Club" specifically designed for mothers. She too praised the advantages of prenatal and postnatal care for all prospective mothers. In her May 1938 column, Dr. Kenyon directly cited the MCA's success in lowering the death rate of mothers and infants under its clinic's care as clear evidence for the need of medical supervision.[47] Thus when Bigelow endorsed the MCA's educational campaign, he certainly recognized its synchronicity with the established views of the magazine's trusted corps of experts.

Nonetheless, the promotion of a scientific model of motherhood was not without its critics in both the larger social arena and within the pages of popular women's magazines. Many questioned the assumption that modern medical care was synonymous with progress. The traditionalist defenders of motherhood as a sacred calling feared the damage brought by the intrusion of medical experts and public health programs on the lives of mothers and children. They insisted that government meddling could not replace Mother Love nor the wisdom gained from maternal experience.[48] Recent historians have voiced similar

---

[44]   Rita S. Halle, "Make Motherhood Safe; It Can Be Done!" *Good Housekeeping* (May 1934), p. 90.

[45]   Bigelow, "Get Ready For Mothers' Day," p. 4.

[46]   Chuppa-Cornell, "Filling a Vacuum," pp. 455–7; Frank Luther Mott, *A History of American Magazines* (Cambridge, MA: Harvard University Press, 1968), vol. 5, pp. 136–7; Zuckerman, *A History of Popular Women's Magazines*, p. 129.

[47]   Christopher Brooks, "She Helped to Raise a Million Babies," *Good Housekeeping* (May 1940), p. 17; Dr. Josephine H. Kenyon, "A Message to Prospective Mothers," *Good Housekeeping* (May 1938), p. 83.

[48]   Kristen Barker, "Birthing and Bureaucratic Women: Needs Talk and the Definitional Legacy of the Sheppard-Towner Act," *Feminist Studies* 29.2 (Summer 2003), pp. 333–5; Lindenmeyer, *"A Right to Childhood,"* pp. 85–8.

criticisms, documenting the hidden costs of women's adherence to a maternal model that defined maternity as an "illness of nine months"; such costs included the undermining of women's maternal confidence and autonomy, as well as the erosion of trust in informal female support networks.[49]

Even *Good Housekeeping* refused to *fully* resign itself to weighing a mother's worth solely against the new expert opinions on Mother's Day. Although noticeably scaled down since the 1920s, there was still space for the sentimental celebration of motherhood in its May issues. Amidst the editorials, advice columns, or articles about "octopus mothers," were full-length stories idealizing the mother-son relationships of seven American presidents (including Sara Delano Roosevelt and her son, of course) and poems and parables dedicated to Mother Love.[50] In 1936, the same year that the MCA hailed as its most successful holiday campaign, author and journalist Margaret E. Sangster openly worried about the "Victorian softness" lost to a new generation of mothers. "The modern mother understands the psychology that dictates the actions and the reactions of the young mind, but can she always grasp, as my mother did, the craving for affections that is based on a child's unreasonable demands?" she wondered. She perceived today's children as very much like the children of yesterday, in that they simply desired "a mother who was the feminine counterpart to God—save only that she was nearer and warmer."[51] Clearly, Sangster praised the natural grace and value of an emotionally involved mother over that of a detached scientific observer.

"Make Motherhood Safe for Mothers" (1933 MCA Campaign Slogan)

The Maternity Center Association ceased its national Mother's Day campaigns in the 1940s, although it continued to serve as an important advocate for quality maternity care and the training of professional nurse-midwives. The MCA

---

[49] "Asks Nation to Curb Maternity Deaths," *The New York Times*, May 4, 1931, p. 21. Historians date the emergence of the scientific model of motherhood to the late nineteenth century. Throughout the twentieth century, the model underwent different modulations or "schools of thought." What remained constant throughout the model's evolution, however, was the belief that women needed expert guidance to properly raise children. For a deeper discussion see, Rima Apple, "Constructing Mothers: Scientific Motherhood in the Nineteenth and Twentieth Centuries," in *Mothers and Motherhood: Readings in American history*, edited by Rima Apple and Janet Golden (Columbus: Ohio State University Press, 1997), pp. 90–110; Julia Grant, *Raising Baby by the Book: Education of American mothers* (New Haven: Yale University Press, 1998), pp. 137–60; Hays, *The Cultural Contradictions of Motherhood*, pp. 19–50, p. 44; Margolis, *Mothers and Such*, pp. 11–107.

[50] Temple Bailey, "A Little Parable for Mothers," *Good Housekeeping* (May 1933), p. 19; Rose Darrough, "To My Mother," *Good Housekeeping* (May 1935), p. 19; Rite Halle Kleeman, "Seven Proud Women," *Good Housekeeping* (May 1937), pp. 28–9, pp. 187–200; June Kelly, "Mother Love," *Good Housekeeping* (May 1939), p. 162.

[51] Margaret E. Sangster, "Mother Memories: Is Today's Child Missing Something that Yesterday's Child Holds Dear?" *Good Housekeeping* (May 1936), p. 25.

certainly deserves acknowledgment for helping to shape women's understanding and acceptance of formal prenatal and postnatal care, as well as raising their expectations in regards to the quality of that medical care. Popular women's magazines deserve a share of that recognition as well. The genre was among the leading proponents of the scientific model of motherhood. The magazines' cadres of experts devoted more time to the topic of general prenatal care, for example, than any other women's health issue in this period.[52] In 1937 *Good Housekeeping* even endorsed the practice of twilight sleep to erase the "mental scar of remembered pain" of childbirth; no longer should modern mothers suffer the "demoralizing terror," and "depleting exhaustion" of a natural delivery, insisted the article.[53] Thus popular women's magazines (even those that never officially endorsed the MCA's educational campaigns) joined the larger movement to professionalize the fields of obstetrics and pediatrics. Above all, the magazines helped transform the public discourse of maternal and infant mortality by portraying such deaths as indefensible travesties rather than the inevitable realities of women's often tragic reproductive lives.

In comparison to the MCA's promotion of quality maternal and infant healthcare, however, the association's campaign to design a "new Mother's Day" was not as successful. Many Americans may have willingly (or grudgingly) accepted the new scientific dictates measuring a mother's worth in the early twentieth century, but apparently only 364 days out of the year. Even as *Good Housekeeping* entered further into the debate over the modern requirements of motherhood, it remained attuned to the social ambivalence surrounding the changing perceptions of women's maternal roles. It could not completely dismiss the traditional appeal of the original Mother's Day message for its female readers and, perhaps more importantly, its commercial sponsors. The sentimental celebration glorified women as natural caretakers and praised the power of Mother Love, while the MCA's "new Mother's Day" observance (whether intentionally or unintentionally) appeared to chide mothers who did not know enough, or care enough, to seek proper medical supervision for themselves and their children. Moreover, it effectively attempted to shame the American public for wanting to show their appreciation for individual mothers with flowers and greeting cards instead of supporting community activism in the name of all mothers. When given the choice, most Americans in the 1930s chose to see all mothers as good mothers deserving of unconditional praise and special tokens of affection—at least on the second Sunday of May.

---

[52] Apple, "Constructing Mothers," p. 96; Chuppa-Cornell, "Filling a Vacuum," p. 457; Plant, *MOM*, pp. 118–35.

[53] Constance L. Todd, "Babies Without Pain," *Good Housekeeping* (November 1937), p. 78.

Chapter 6

"Give this copy of the *Kourier* magazine to your friend. You will help him. You will also help society": 1920s KKK Print, Propaganda, and Publicity

Craig Fox

The Ku Klux Klan that surfaced all over the United States in the early 1920s enjoyed a phenomenal degree of mainstream popularity. Central to the hooded organization's ascendancy, and playing a number of vital roles in its spectacular success, was its abundant print culture.

The KKK endeavored to construct itself as a positive force in American national life and skilfully utilized print media to this end. Taking immigration restriction and prohibition enforcement as its chief political and moral causes, Klan propaganda created a graphic and unambiguous world of Good versus Evil, of morality versus degeneracy, the echoes of which resonated throughout its many publications and fed into active participation in the movement. Klan print rallied the order's huge band of followers around the collective imagery of "100% Americanism," providing a common identity and unified front from which to battle the alleged and unthinkable encroachments of the nation's one true enemy: the shadowy "un-American."

Geographically, Klan print took the organization's influence well beyond its southern roots. Facilitated by the establishment of an official KKK press which operated as a thoroughly modern and financially efficient business operation, its distribution network was wide-reaching and its commercial instincts sharp. Engaging the nation in printed debate via a plethora of affiliated publications, the Klan strove for attention and social relevance. As the movement began reaching far larger and more general audiences than ever before, it emerged from the margins—a scenario reflected in the staggering uptake in membership which confirmed it as perhaps the most significant social movement of its era.

Authors and editors of KKK literature encouraged readers to bring the movement into their religious, social, and business lives, often in ways deliberately invisible to the outside world. Conversely, Klan publications were also deeply hungry to showcase the movement's prodigious growth and tangibly demonstrate its unified strength and positivity. As well as directly soliciting readers' presence en masse at huge regional parades, they also—by publicizing the KKK's growing range of alternative, and very visible, institutions—bolstered the notion of a far-reaching, highly active, and plainly inclusive Klan community. In the process, KKK organs not only courted their ultimate goal of mainstream respectability, but also helped facilitate, for all the members of disparate local branches, a sense of solidarity with a far larger, nationwide Klan network of which they could justifiably feel a part.

The most immediately striking function of Klan print was its propagandistic power. Pro-Klan writers, print editors, and pamphleteers during the 1920s primarily concerned themselves with constructing a positive public identity for the secret order: a heroic and reassuring image defined in binary opposition to their simultaneous constructions of a monstrous national enemy. Their vivid propaganda creations—aimed in equal measure at smearing the Catholic Church and exalting its Protestant counterpart—were designed to cause widespread moral outrage at the corrupting advances of "foreign doctrines," and to inspire in response an army of patriotic, Protestant citizens to join the KKK in necessary defense of the American realm.

The starting point for Klan propagandists was to anchor the movement in issues of real, widespread political and societal concern, identifying and interpreting America's major social ills, and offering up the KKK as a viable solution to all of them. In a postwar environment awash with anxious public perceptions of rising crime rates, declining standards of morality, and endemic political corruption, Klan tracts typically attacked the non-Protestant immigrant, focusing particularly upon the dire threat imported with "Romanism." Huddling in city enclaves, printing own-language newspapers, and resisting integration, the international Catholic—and the corrupt political "machine" that represented him—was portrayed as a moral menace. "The majority of our unassimilated aliens are Roman Catholics," wrote Klan Imperial Wizard Hiram Evans, "often not able to speak English … all are 'wet'; almost all are in the 'foreign' colonies of the alienized cities, and completely controlled by the vicious bosses who are the greatest disgrace of American politics."[1]

Klan print not only explicitly linked immigrants to crooked politics and the illegal liquor trade, but also blamed them for soaring levels of vice, prostitution, and sexual immorality in American towns and cities, as well as for labor union disruption and the teaching of seditious religious doctrine in American schools. "If you believe in the preservation of American ideals, the enforcement of law, the ascendancy of the white race, the separation of church and state, the perpetuation of the free public schools, and the Christian religion, join the Klan," wrote one prominent KKK essayist. "Otherwise, line up with crooks, lawbreakers, moral reprobates, non-Christians and those who do not owe their first allegiance to the United States."[2]

---

[1]   Hiram Wesley Evans, "The Ballots behind the Ku Klux Klan," *World's Work* 55 (1927), p. 250.

[2]   Knights of the Ku Klux Klan, *Papers Read at the Meeting of Grand Dragons, Knights of the Ku Klux Klan at Their First Annual Meeting Held at Asheville, North Carolina, July 1923; Together with other articles of interest to Klansmen* (Atlanta: Knights of the Ku Klux Klan, 1923).

Bundling all of these issues together, other tracts went further still, capitalizing on the contemporary popularity of Eugenic theory to claim not just a religious, but also a genetic basis for America's woes.[3] According to Evans's nativist line, not only had the porosity of US immigration policy already surrendered up the nation to becoming "overrun with undesirables ... a veritable melting pot for the scum of the earth," but the country's imperiled state, left unchecked, would deteriorate much further and fast. "The Nordic American today," he claimed, "is a stranger in large parts of the land his fathers gave him ... even our unborn children are being crowded out of their birthright!" Foreign influences, furthermore, "dominate our government," and have "stacked the cards of success and prosperity against us." At the present birth-rate, the Imperial Wizard warned, "the Nordic stock will have become a hopeless minority within fifty years."

Cautioning readers against "the clamor of the alien and the alien-minded liberal," Evans demanded "a return of power into the hands of the everyday, not highly cultured, not overly intellectualized, but entirely unspoiled and not de-Americanized, average citizen of the old stock." As a vehicle for such a power shift, he advocated membership in his growing Klan organization, classifying it as a movement "of the plain people" and a "protest movement—protesting about being robbed." The hooded order's solution, he said, would be "a sane and progressive conservatism along national lines," aimed at creating "a growing sentiment against radicalism, cosmopolitanism, and alienism of all kinds."[4]

Having courted the public by rooting its crusade in pressing social issues, Klan print propagandists' imagery would move away from reality, into the realms of the fantastic, the gratuitous, and the voyeuristic in order to present an obvious, clearly defined enemy figure against which the Klan's sense of self would appear all the more coherent. As Michael Rogin has noted in his work on the long tradition of American "countersubversive" movements, "the alien comes to birth as the American's dark double, the imaginary twin who sustains his brother's identity. Taken inside, the subversive would obliterate the American; driven outside, the subversive becomes an alien who serves as repository for the disowned, negative American self." In this light, Klan anti-Catholic propaganda becomes less a concern with reality than an exercise in

---

[3]   Madison Grant's *The Passing of the Great Race; or the Racial Basis of European History* (New York: C. Scribner's Sons, 1921) is often credited as the "scientific" basis for the 1924 National Origins Act. The Act established a draconian nation-specific quota system of immigration, severely limiting the total annual number of new arrivals to the United States.

[4]   Hiram Wesley Evans, "The Klan's Fight for Americanism," *North American Review* 223 (Spring 1926), pp. 33–63. Along similar lines, and perhaps the most prominent example of Klan thinking on immigration restriction was Evans's lengthy essay *The Menace of Modern Immigration* (Atlanta: Knights of the Ku Klux Klan, 1924).

self-definition, a ritual of separation from all undesirable "others" on the American political and social landscape.[5]

In casting its enemies in the role of subversive alien foe, KKK propaganda transformed the pluralities and nuances of its ethnic and political surroundings into a fantasy struggle between just two sides: the forces of good and a looming empire of degradation and evil. The yardstick of self-definition in this era of social flux was a simple, yet unquantifiable measure: "Americanism." As served up by Klan literature, the immigrant, and more particularly the Catholic, became a sinister embodiment of the ultimate un-American, set in absolute opposition to the Klan's proud, self-declared community of "100% Americans." The perceived existence, real or imagined, of such an adversary served to more sharply define the Klansman's role and the legitimacy of his claims. Having lined up in no uncertain terms with the patriotic cause, the KKK dealt in absolutes. The nation, its publications told the reading public, was in the midst of an apocalyptic battle between dark and light, with no middle ground. To declare against the Klan was to declare against America itself.

A glut of laudatory literature portrayed the KKK as noble, righteous, and self-sacrificing—a band of proud Protestant crusader-Knights dedicated to defending the United States and its elevated ideals of freedom and democracy. The typical Klansman presented a picture of rugged masculinity: chivalrous, decisive, and heroic protector of family, home, and "pure American womanhood." His associations were entirely wholesome, and his love of flag, Constitution, and Christian Bible unconditional. Crucially, his concerns—paying lip service to "law and order," to free public schools, to regular church attendance, to patriotic duty, and to "old-time" morality—aligned with the traditional conservative values of white Protestant America. Countless sentimental portrayals tangled KKK origins indelibly with the "spirit" of America's founders, and appropriated the images of Washington and Lincoln, along with those of Uncle Sam and Christ himself, for the Klan cause.[6]

The heroic Klan identity was further reinforced by its fictionalization, in novels and magazine serializations, which adopted popular romantic conventions. *Knight Vale of the KKK*, for example, a story "of love, patriotism, intrigue and

---

[5]   See Michael Rogin, *Ronald Reagan, the Movie and Other Episodes in Political Demonology* (Berkeley: University of California Press, 1987), p. 50, p. 275, p. 284.

[6]   Hiram Wesley Evans, "The Klan: Defender of Americanism," *Forum* 74 (December 1925), pp. 801–14; "The Spirit of the Fathers," *Kourier* magazine, February 1927, pp. 12–13. The Klan even claimed Imperial Wizard Evans to be Lincoln's reincarnation, "come back to Earth, to finish his mission." See *Kourier* magazine, February 1926, pp. 8–12, pp. 16–17, p. 29, p. 32; September 1926, pp. 2–4; October 1926, p. 1, pp. 6–7. The most prominent example of the Christ link is E.F. Stanton, *Christ and Other Klansmen, or Lives of Love: The Cream of the Bible Spread upon Klanism* (Kansas City, MO: Stanton & Harper, 1924). Also see the elaborately illustrated pro-Klan tracts of Bishop Alma White: *The Ku Klux Klan in Prophecy* (Zarephath, NJ: The Good Citizen, 1925); *Klansmen: Guardians of Liberty* (Zarephath, NJ: The Good Citizen, 1926); and *Heroes of the Fiery Cross* (Zarephath, NJ: The Good Citizen, 1928).

adventure," mingled Protestant righteousness, romance, and an all-conquering American spirit, placing a dashing, clean-cut Klansman in the mantle of hero. Similarly, *Harold the Klansman* promised not only "a wholesome love story," but was also aimed at "making plain the real purpose and practices of the Ku Klux Klan." Indeed, this was a tale for which there were high expectations in the Klan community, one reviewer even claiming that "*Harold* ... is a great social novel destined to make its impress on the thought of America, and in years to come it will be one of the great historical novels of this generation."[7]

As a counterpoint, KKK print editors delighted in the creation of a demonic, un-American opposite number. Aiming to shock morally upstanding patriots into supporting the Klan, portrayals of the "enemy" brimmed with salacious detail of both sexual depravity and nation-threatening political conspiracy.[8] KKK publications routinely caricatured the Catholic priest as a scheming deviant seeking to undermine America's manhood and corrupt its womanhood via the confessional box, lecherously extracting "inmost secrets ... sexual procedures and techniques" and encouraging "extra-marital activities, masturbation, homosexuality, and unnatural fornication."[9] Meanwhile, the hugely popular autobiography of infamous "ex-nun" Helen Jackson, often promoted in Klan organ *Dawn*, detailed at length the catalogue of outrageous tortures and humiliations she had allegedly suffered at the hands of sadistic nuns in one of "Rome's slave pens" in Detroit. Teaming up with celebrated "ex-Romanist" L.J. King, Jackson took her crowd-pleasing anti-Catholic peepshow on the road, selling literature and promoting the KKK's image-building efforts with high-profile public lectures all over the Midwest.[10]

---

[7] A. Saxon, *Knight Vale of the KKK: A Fiction Story of Love, Patriotism, Intrigue and Adventure* (Columbus, OH: Patriot, 1924); George Alfred Brown, *Harold the Klansman* (Kansas City, MO: Western Baptist, 1923). Other examples include Egbert Brown, *The Final Awakening: A Story of the Ku Klux Klan* (Brunswick, GA: Overstreet & Co, 1923).

[8] Accusations of this nature were certainly not new, and voyeuristic diatribes charging a widespread sexual depravity within the Roman church were popularized throughout the 1910s, notably in the pages of *The Jeffersonian* magazine. Tom Watson, its editor, had also produced titles as suggestive as *The Inevitable Crimes of Celibacy* and *What Goes on in Nunneries*. For a wide-ranging history and analysis of anti-Catholic propaganda into the early twentieth century, see Michael Williams, *The Shadow of the Pope: The Story of the Anti-Catholic Movement in America* (New York: Whittlesey House, McGraw-Hill, 1932).

[9] See, in particular, William Lloyd Clark, *The Devil's Prayer Book, or an Exposure of Auricular Confession as Practiced by the Roman Catholic Church: An Eye-Opener for Husbands, Fathers and Brothers* (Milan, IL: Rail Splitter Press, 1922). Prolific as anyone in this line of imagery, Clark made a cottage industry out of the Klan's literature war against the Roman church. He advertised his diatribes regularly in the KKK organ *Dawn*, as well as promoting subscriptions to his own monthly publication *The Rail Splitter*, the self-proclaimed "greatest anti-Catholic monthly paper on the American continent."

[10] Helen Jackson, *Convent Cruelties or My Life in the Convent: Awful Revelations* (Toledo, OH: Helen Jackson, 1919). King was a veteran campaigner, having edited and published an annual compendium of all things anti-papal since 1911. His *Converted*

Reinforcing Klan-endorsed fantasies, the pair regaled large and enthusiastic audiences with titillating, highly sexualized stories of Catholic perversion behind the bolted gates of convent prisons, in a world where fornication, mutilation, rape, abortion, and infanticide were commonplace.[11]

Of more pressing political concern, however, were the images conjured by Klan print of its enemies as anti-American conspirators. Concentrating first and foremost upon the threat from Rome, Klan propagandists attacked the international Catholic Church with the same vehemence with which Henry Ford's *Dearborn Independent* assailed the "International Jew."[12] Drawing heavily upon the anti-papal creations of the "Know-Nothings" of the 1850s and American Protective Association of the 1890s,[13] monolithic conspiracy tales abound in Klan literature, and anti-Catholic headlines dominated every issue of the KKK weeklies. "In brief," Imperial Wizard Evans warned his readers, "the Pope has ordered American Catholics ... to bring the American government under his control."[14] At the heart of the Klan's concern was Catholic fraternal order the Knights of Columbus, who supposedly outnumbered the US army five-to-one, stockpiled weapons in church basements nationwide, and prepared for a violent and impending religious battle.

Catholic and Protestant Missionary Annual continued production well into the 1920s, embracing and actively championing the re-emergent Klan, as well as advertising hundreds of other anti-Catholic tracts and authors.

[11]   The focus in Klan propaganda literature on sexual and moral degeneracy, and particularly upon taboo-breaking perversions, incest, and sadism, is entirely in keeping with imagery found in a number of other historic "anti-" movements. See, for instance, David Brion Davis, "Some Themes of Counter-subversion: An analysis of Anti-Masonic, Anti-Catholic and Anti-Mormon literature," *Mississippi Valley Historical Review* 47 (1960), pp. 205–24.

[12]   Complementing Klan propaganda, Ford's *Dearborn Independent* was published and distributed through, amongst other channels, his thousands of car dealerships. During the early 1920s, the magazine notoriously featured many anti-Semitic articles, later compiled and published in their own right, outlining the dangers of the profit-hungry "International Jew." Though in much of the United States the Jew was very much a secondary Klan target behind the Roman Catholic, numerous KKK pamphlets did circulate nationally, warning, for instance, of the "libertine Jew," an immoral and predatory "moral leper" who was implicated in all manner of organized crime, sexual degeneracy, and corruption of wholesome American youth. See: Sam H. Campbell, *The Jewish Problem in the United States* (Atlanta: Knights of the Ku Klux Klan, 1923). While the KKK did not abandon completely the familiar ground of the "race problem," African Americans, perceived as a much less imminent threat to the national status quo, received relatively little attention in this period.

[13]   Humphrey J. Desmond, *The Know-Nothing Party* (New York: Arno Press [reprint], 1969); Williams, *The Shadow of the Pope*.

[14]   *Dawn*, 21 October 1922, p. 3; *Kourier* magazine, August 1926, pp. 13–20; April 1927, p. 20; March 1925, pp. 14–17; *Michigan Kourier*, 21 November 1924, p. 1; Hiram Wesley Evans, *The Attitude of the Ku Klux Klan toward the Roman Catholic Hierarchy* (Atlanta: Knights of the Ku Klux Klan, 1927), p. 5.

As "evidence" of the foul plot, the KKK printed and distributed copies of the notorious *Bloody Oath*. Claiming to represent a strict pact signed by all "K of C" recruits, it included promises to "burn, hang, waste, boil, flay, strangle and bury alive" all Protestants and Masons, to "rip up the stomachs and wombs of the women," and "crush their infants' heads against the walls."[15]

The repellent identity created by Klan print propagandists for the un-American Catholic may have been essentially a caricature, but it was certainly effective in creating active involvement in the movement. Recalling his use of the "bogus" oath, one former Klan recruiter later claimed that it "was accepted as genuine, and was the means of securing a large number of members for Ku Kluxism."[16] Everywhere that the Klan circulated tracts, concerned citizens internalized and reacted to the tales and images they saw in print. Clear, too, from the numerous existing accounts of those who lived through them, is that such colorful rumors of an appalling Roman revolution percolated easily down from the literature to become the paranoid gossip of the towns and villages of Protestant Middle America.[17] Recounting the KKK days in small-town Michigan, the following description is typical:

> The Ku Klux Klan created quite a stir in our area in the years between 1921 and 1925 ... there were no Negroes in our area, but it isn't difficult to create a villain and the Pope and the Catholics became the rallying point for the Klan ... The lure of the masses to the Klan was being told the Catholics were going to take over the country and the Pope would be installed as the King. The Klan was recruiting with fervour. Stupid people joining?? No, not at all. Two or three people can fuel the fires of hate if reason leaves the mind. It could happen again.[18]

Conducting interviews in Indiana in the 1980s, Kathleen Blee found that "memories of the sexual tales spread by the Klan," even some sixty years on, "are still fresh in the minds of former Klansmembers and contemporaries" of the movement.[19] Also apparent from almost every modern study of the Jazz Age Klan is the credibility

---

[15]   George Estes, *The Roman Katholic Kingdom and the Ku Klux Klan* (Portland, Oregon: Empire, 1923), pp. 7–12. The *Alleged Oath* was a scurrilous document, many versions of which had long circulated in anti-Catholic circles. This passage is taken from a version printed in *Congressional Record*, 15 February 1913 (3rd session), vol. 49, part 4, pp. 3216–17.

[16]   Henry Peck Fry, *The Modern Ku Klux Klan* (Boston: Small, Maynard, 1922), pp. 113–14.

[17]   See, for example, Robert Coughlan, "Konklave in Kokomo," in *The Aspirin Age: 1919–1941*, edited by Isabel Leighton (New York: Simon and Schuster, 1949), pp. 105–29; Robert S. Lynd and Helen M. Lynd, *Middletown: A Study in Contemporary American Culture* (London: Constable, 1929), p. 482; Kathleen M. Blee, *Women of the Klan: Racism and Gender in the 1920s* (Berkeley: University of California Press, 1991), pp. 92–3.

[18]   Don Bollman, *Run for the Roses: A 50 Year Memoir* (Mecosta, MI: Canadian Lakes, 1975), p. 18.

[19]   Blee, *Women of the Klan*, pp. 86–91.

given to its print propaganda claims, in the initial years at least, to be a positive force for solving America's social problems. In local case study after local case study, the organization appears to have consistently attracted swathes of ordinary, law-abiding citizens from all socio-economic backgrounds, invariably impressed that "the best people," in terms of local respectability and moral standing—the Masons, civic activists, boosters, Protestant ministers, and other pillars of the community—were flocking to join.[20] Clearly, KKK image-building had struck a chord with a large portion of American citizenry, who were only too ready to identify with "100% Americanism" and join together to rally for its cause. In the words of one of Blee's informants, the "store owners, teachers, farmers ... the good people all belonged to the Klan ... They were going to clean up the government, and they were going to improve the school books [that] were loaded with Catholicism."[21]

Dramatizing sentiments already well supported in mainstream politics and social life—a moral justification for Prohibition enforcement and a Eugenics-driven crusade for immigration restriction which would produce the National Origins Act of 1924—the ideology expressed in Klan literature stood "as a particularly important example of white Protestant attitudes, not a deviant exception to mainstream thinking."[22] Importantly, then, Klan strength was not just to be located in the ranks of its burgeoning membership, but also in the much larger contingent of approving (if not joining) onlookers who found themselves in broad agreement with its print propagandists' calls to activism. As sociologist Guy Johnson observed as the Klan spread like wildfire in 1923, "it is not enough to say that the great body of uninitiated Klansmen are merely in sympathy with the movement. *They are the movement!*"[23]

As an organization, the 1920s KKK was nothing if not commercially minded, and the technical efficiency of its print empire would aid the spread of its influence immeasurably. Openly operating as "the Knights of the Ku Klux Klan Incorporated" (a brand under which it would legally protect its ever-growing output of official regalia and printed matter), these were, in the words of the *Washington Post*, the order's "halcyon days," during which it became "the world's most high-powered 'racket' ... one of the biggest money makers of all time, a shining example of big business in a big way."[24]

---

[20]   For a representative selection of the "Populist-Civic" interpretation of the 1920s Klan, see: Shawn Lay, ed., *The Invisible Empire in the West: Toward a new historical appraisal of the Ku Klux Klan of the 1920s* (Urbana: University of Illinois Press, 1992); Craig Fox, *Everyday Klansfolk: White Protestant life and the KKK in 1920s Michigan* (East Lansing: Michigan State University Press, 2011).

[21]   Blee, *Women of the Klan*, p. 2.

[22]   See, for example, "Keep on Guarding the Gates," *Current Opinion* (June 1923), pp. 652–4; and "Guarding the Gates Against Undesirables," *Current Opinion* (April 1924), pp. 400–401. Quote from Leonard J. Moore, *Citizen Klansmen: The Ku Klux Klan in Indiana, 1921–1928* (Chapel Hill: University of North Carolina Press, 1991), p. 31.

[23]   Guy B. Johnson, "A Sociological Interpretation of the New Ku Klux Movement," *Journal of Social Forces* 1 (May 1923), p. 445.

[24]   *Washington Post*, 2 November 1930, p. 1.

By mid-1923, Klan leadership had established the official Ku Klux Klan Press as a purpose-designed propaganda unit. Eyeing increasingly lucrative economies of scale, Imperial Wizard Evans then set about combining the national movement's merchandizing and dissemination operations. Trading out of Buckhead, Georgia, near to his "Imperial Palace" headquarters, a modern regalia factory and printing plant opened its doors in September 1923, mass-producing robes and literature under the same roof. According to Evans, "the investment in the printing plant from the treasury of the Knights of the Ku Klux Klan will be approximately $20,000, and it is estimated that this sum will be saved to the Klansmen of the country during the first year." Furthermore, whereas "printing had been done formerly by a private firm," the new plant employed around forty "skilled workers, all Klansmen," using "the latest improved technology" in automatic printing machinery, "purchased most advantageously."

Such was the demand from the thousands regularly joining the Klan that within months the Buckhead plant had to be expanded further, with a new three-story construction supplementing the existing premises. Adding "general offices, [a] shipping department, and storage for paper and cloth" to a substantially enlarged Klan press and robe manufacturing concern, in-house KKK operations now totalled some "25,000 square feet of manufacturing space." This resulted in what postal authorities called "one of the most efficient and expert shipping departments in the south," and in the opinion of its promoters served as "an example of the perfect co-ordination of effort that has made the Klan the most talked-of organization of all time."[25]

The official press churned out every item of Klan-endorsed literature to be disseminated to local units throughout the United States. Most significant of these was national KKK organ the *Imperial Night-Hawk*, which debuted in March 1923, stating its intentions in no uncertain terms:

> This publication ... aims to carry a weekly message from the Imperial Palace to every Klansman in America ... the name NIGHT HAWK, courier to the Exalted Cyclops and messenger to the Klans, indicates the mission of this magazine ... to keep Klansmen informed of activities at the Imperial Palace in their behalf and of the progress and advancement of the Knights of the Ku Klux Klan throughout the nation. The magazine will be published once each week and will be made available to every Klansman at his Klavern.[26]

---

[25] *Imperial Night-Hawk*, 15 August 1923, pp. 6–7; 12 September 1923, p. 8; 2 April 1924, p. 8; 28 May 1924, p. 8; *Dawn*, 28 July 1923, p. 9. Though this was the first time KKK print was fully centralized, the order's first national leader, William J. Simmons, had made earlier attempts at founding a press. He formed the Atlanta-based Searchlight Publishing Company in early 1922, which produced the first, if short-lived, official Klan organ *The Searchlight*.

[26] *Imperial Night-Hawk*, 28 March 1923, p. 4.

Subsequently altering its newspaper format to become *Kourier* magazine,[27] the official publication was a constant throughout the life of the "popular" Klan organization, and would run continuously for almost 14 years.

While maintaining its own status as the authoritative voice of the KKK, the official press happily supported other publications which shared its mission. It was particularly enthusiastic in its endorsement of a lively and growing print culture amongst regional Klan branches. The *Hawkeye Independent*, "a weekly newspaper devoted to the interests of the Ku Klux Klan in the state of Iowa," was singled out for praise, as was *Arizona Klankraft*, which "already ... has an established circulation of several thousand." Amongst others given a glowing mention were Seattle's *Watcher on the Tower*, Alabama's *TWK Monthly*, Tennessee's *Klan Krusader*, Minnesota's *Call of the North*, and the *Firefly* of Illinois.

Numerous state and city editions of KKK broadsheets proliferated, too, including titles such as *Klan Kourier* and the *Night-Hawk*. Typical of these was *Fiery Cross*, available in various regional versions, and described by the official press as "a live wire publication which preaches the principles of the Klan for the benefit of all who may read." Though later taken under central Klan direction, the *Fiery Cross* newspaper first operated out of Indianapolis. Boasting some 200,000 paid-up subscribers by September 1923, the weekly publication regularly pointed to evidence of its own growing popularity. Citing ever-rising circulation figures, its pages also claimed that newsboys' stocks, hawked at Klan events, were regularly exhausted amid flurries of great excitement within moments of going on sale.[28]

Trading out of Chicago and heavily plugging the Klan cause, meanwhile, was the particularly prominent *Dawn*, "a journal for true American patriots," while the anti-Catholic fraternal organ *Fellowship Forum*, published in Washington, DC, often carried favorable reports of Klan news and events nationwide. In April 1923, the *Imperial Night-Hawk* proudly declared that "there are now a score or more weekly papers, whose mission it is to uphold Klan principles, prospering in widely scattered sections of the United States." This was a rapidly shifting figure, very much on an upward trajectory.[29]

The sheer popularity of the movement made it an issue of huge public interest. With the eyes of America upon it, the Klan had as many fierce opponents who charged its members with ignorance and religious bigotry as it had vocal converts drawn in by the hooded order's talk of moral reform, "law and order," and prohibition enforcement. The attention devoted to it in print, positive and negative alike, highlighted the organization's status as the hottest debate topic of the times, and in doing so fed directly into further public interest and continued growth in membership.

---

[27]   The monthly *Kourier* magazine replaced the *Imperial Night-Hawk* in December 1924. See the notice to this effect in *Imperial Night-Hawk*, 12 November 1924, p. 7.

[28]   Countless examples include *Fiery Cross (Michigan State Edition)*, 28 September 1923, p. 1, p. 8, p. 13; 21 December 1923, p. 1; 21 March 1924, p. 7.

[29]   *Imperial Night-Hawk*, 18 April 1923, p. 5.

Back in 1921 the *New York World* had run a sweeping month-long exposé campaign, using a series of articles to allege Klan involvement in corruption and masked violence in the southern states. Syndicated in 18 of the nation's newspapers, the antagonism of papers hostile to the Klan not only brought the organization notoriety, but also resulted in an official Congressional hearing. During two full days of testimony before a House Committee, however, Klan founder William Simmons had emerged utterly triumphant, apparently appearing both eloquent and convincing, and winning over an audience which by the end of the hearing had "stood in ovation." Ultimately failing to uncover any crime with which to charge the organization, the entire exercise served merely to help introduce new and broader audiences to the Invisible Empire through extensive nationwide press coverage. "We have been given," boasted Simmons afterward, "fifty million dollars worth of free advertising by the newspapers."[30]

As its ominous presence in American society grew, public curiosity meant a ready market for pamphleteers and self-appointed authorities on the Klan. Such tracts outlined, for example, the *Faults and virtues of the KKK*, explored *The Challenge of the Klan*, or asked, simply, *Does the USA need the KKK?* Others took an overtly religious tack, outlining *Catholic, Jew, KKK: What they believe, where they conflict*, while the Klan's Imperial Wizard even went head-to-head in print with prominent Jewish intellectual Israel Zangwill in the pages of joint publication *Is the KKK Constructive or Destructive?: A Debate.*[31] That these and similar questions were pondered so widely and taken so seriously in a national arena says one thing above all others—that the KKK during its remarkable "popular" phase could be attacked, but it could not be ignored.

Compelled by the obvious level of interest, the editors of mainstream publications effectively aided the Klan's crusade for relevance and audience, rendering its existence anything but marginal. Allowing representatives of the Invisible Empire to address broad, nationwide readerships through their pages, a number of popular magazines devoted generous space to the Klan issue throughout the 1920s, giving liberal rein to both pro- and anti- arguments. *Literary Digest*, for example, outlined the case "For and Against the KKK," while the *Forum* asked "Is the KKK Un-American?" *McClure's* magazine, meanwhile, ran articles

---

[30] New York World, *The Facts about the Ku Klux Klan* (New York: The World, 1921). Philip Dray, *At the Hands of Persons Unknown: The lynching of Black America* (New York: Random House, 2002), pp. 278–9.

[31] Frank P. Ball, *Faults and Virtues of the Ku Klux Klan* (Brooklyn, NY: F.P. Ball, 1927); Stanley Frost, *The Challenge of the Klan* (Indianapolis: Bobbs-Merrill Company, 1924); Fred Bair, *Does the USA need the KKK?* (Girard, KS: Haldeman-Julius, 1928); George S. Clason, ed., *Catholic, Jew, Ku Klux Klan: What they believe, where they conflict* (Chicago: Nutshell, 1924); Edward P. Bell, *Is the Ku Klux Klan Constructive or Destructive? A debate between Imperial Wizard Evans, Israel Zangwill and others* (Girard, KS: Haldeman-Julius, 1924); Blaine Mast, *KKK Friend or Foe: Which?* (Kittanning, PA: Herbrick & Held, 1924). These few titles represent a mere sample of a much larger body of debate in the local and national press during the 1920s.

contrasting the Klan experience in the North and the South, while *Current History*, *Colliers* magazine, *Outlook*, and *World's Work*, amongst others, all maintained a running interest in the Klan issue, with each at one time or another featuring interviews with or articles penned by Klan leaders.[32]

Even the most vocal of opponents were forced to concede the remarkable effect upon the public imagination. "When a man joins the Ku Klux Klan," lamented anti-Klan print publicist Aldrich Blake, a sensation seems to come over him as definite as falling in love. He simply drops out of society and enters a new world."[33] Looking back over the Klan's "juggernaut" phase, the *Washington Post* quoted national membership figures of almost nine million at the organization's 1925 high-water mark. Not only were "funds of over $100,000,000" supposedly collected from paying members in the few short years of its life, the secret order had successfully "exploited its mythical political power to limits now seen as ridiculous." The movement, too, had very definitely gone nationwide, with the *Post* reporting a Klan presence in every single state of the union, with its greatest areas of strength very much in the North, the Midwest, and the West, rather than in its Southern birthplace.[34]

The Invisible Empire's printed output performed an important function in terms of reinforcing the idea of a wide, active, and inclusive Klan community. Movement literature provided constant practical direction, while periodicals reported extensively on Klan-building efforts across the nation, all of which helped coalesce the vast network of individuals in the KKK constituency. In this sense, it is possible to view the identity- and community-building activities of the 1920s KKK in terms of the emergence of a counterpublic of sorts. Just as Mark Morrisson has described marginalized groups on the political left as counterpublics which created their own "institutions of publicity—papers, meetings, book shops,

---

[32] "For and Against the Ku Klux Klan," *Literary Digest*, September 24, 1921, pp. 34–40; William R. Pattangall, "Is the Ku Klux Klan Un-American?" *Forum* 74 (September 1925), pp. 321–32; Max Bentley, "The Ku Klux Klan in Indiana" and "The Ku Klux Klan in Texas," *McClure's Magazine* 57 (May 1924), pp. 11–21; pp. 23–33; Hiram Wesley Evans, "The Catholic Question as viewed by the Ku Klux Klan," *Current History* (July 1927), pp. 563–8; William G. Shepard, "Ku Klux Koin," *Collier's National Weekly*, 21 July 1928, pp. 38–9; "How I Put Over the Klan," *Collier's National Weekly*, 14 July 1928, pp. 5–7; and "The Fiery Double-Cross," *Collier's National Weekly*, 28 July 1928, pp. 8–9; Stanley Frost, "When the Klan Rules: The Crusade of the Fiery Cross," *Outlook* 136 (January 1924), pp. 20–24; Evans, "The Ballots behind the Ku Klux Klan," pp. 243–52.

[33] Aldrich Blake, *The Ku Klux Kraze* (Oklahoma City: Blake, 1924), p. 17. Muckraking exposés from alleged ex-Klan officers inevitably emerged, too, a couple of the more well-circulated being Lem A. Dever, *Masks Off! Confessions of an Imperial Klansman* (Portland, OR: Dever, 1925) and Marion Monteval, *The Klan Inside Out* (Claremore, OK: Monarch, 1924).

[34] *Washington Post*, 2 November 1930, p. 1, p. 4. Representing one of the highest estimates to come from a non-Klan source, the *Post* put nationwide membership in 1925 at 8,904,871. Amongst the strongest Klan states, it contended, were Michigan, New Jersey, Ohio, and California, alongside more traditional KKK strongholds such as Texas.

publishers, street-selling, spectacles, and parades,"[35] so too, in each of these respects, did the Ku Klux Klan, with the ultimate aim of becoming influential enough to enter the dominant public sphere in a meaningful way.

The first and best-established of the KKK's alternative institutions of publicity was the Klan press itself, erected as an independently inspired mass publishing enterprise in opposition to the mainstream newspaper presses. Acting as instruments of communication and solidarity for a geographically vast movement, national Klan periodicals helped spread the hooded order's influence throughout the United States, bringing wider context and allowing even the smallest, most isolated provincial unit to experience a sense of connection to a greater, like-minded social network. Packed with snippets, reports, photographs, opinion, and editorials on current events "throughout Klandom," they provided a site of information and interaction, allowing members to compare progress, to share news, and even indulge in friendly intra-Klan competition. As well as being mouthpieces and newsletters of the order, these publications served as the most direct of recruitment tools. "Give this copy of the *Kourier* magazine to your friend," implored editors of the Klan monthly. "You will help him. You will also help society."[36] Readers of the *Imperial Night-Hawk* were similarly urged to "put it where it will do the most good for Klankraft … Give it to some loyal American who should be with us in the fight we are making."[37]

Though most copy was taken up with sermons, lectures, and reports of Klan-building activity in the regions, the movement's periodicals served, to an extent, as interactive public forums, with editors inviting correspondence, and dedicating space to "news and views by readers," satirical cartoons, and pages "for poets and their verses."[38] In practice, what was actually published here was a hand-picked collection of letters and personal tributes in praise of the organization. Featuring most commonly were morale-boosting poems from readers, often set to familiar tunes and invariably with patriotic themes, reflecting entirely the kinds of identity-confirming imagery that Klan propaganda had been working to convey. Replete, too, with the elaborate trappings of an exclusive fraternal order, the pages of Klan publications were used to disseminate a secretive ceremonial language of passwords, greetings, and warning signals.[39] Showcasing the more intriguing

---

[35]　Mark Morrisson, *The Public Face of Modernism: Little Magazines, Audiences, and Reception 1905–1920* (Madison: University of Wisconsin Press, 2001), pp. 11–12.

[36]　*Kourier* magazine, November 1927, p. 27.

[37]　*Imperial Night-Hawk*, 11 July 1923, p. 4.

[38]　See for example: *Dawn*, 20 January 1923, p. 4; 17 March 1923, p. 5; 18 August 1923, p. 8; 3 November 1923, p. 26.

[39]　Knights of the Ku Klux Klan: *Kloran* (Atlanta: Knights of the Ku Klux Klan, n.d.); *Klan Building* (Atlanta: Knights of the Ku Klux Klan, n.d.); *Klansman's Manual* (Atlanta: Buckhead, 1924). Also see Coughlan, "Konklave in Kokomo," p. 119 and David M. Chalmers, *Hooded Americanism: The history of the Ku Klux Klan* (New York: Franklin Watts [second edition], 1976), p. 117.

ritual elements of Klan membership—the thrilling pretensions of secrecy and exclusivity—organizational magazines set about exploiting the fact that its attraction, for many, "lay not in its creed but in its excitement and its in-group fraternalism." In joining, any white American-born Protestant could "participate in the sacred ritual that connected him with millions of others in fraternity and mystic power."[40] Klavern ritual was not only a social leveler, but a means of entry into an invisible and rapidly expanding national kinship network. Armed with signals and passwords learned in the order's literature, the new KKK initiate received "an automatic circle of friendship ... a support system."[41]

The pages of Klan publications also became powerful advertisers, creating a highly commercial niche Klan economy as an alternative to the mainstream one. As the movement's public profile expanded, so too did ads for affiliated lines of Klan-themed merchandise, from propaganda tracts from specialist publishers, to printed Klan satire, sheet and recorded music, as well as Klan-based theater and film productions, radio broadcasts, mail-order novelties, and even all-Klan leisure resorts.[42] More surreptitiously, and particularly common in all forms of Klan print, were explicit instructions for the active practice of "vocational Klanishness," with members urged to "always favour a Klansman in the commercial world, whether it be in buying, selling, advertising, employment, political, social or in any way wherein a Klansman is affected."[43] In practice, this provided financial advantages for tight-knit circles of Klan business owners and (despite denials from national leadership) effectively constituted economic boycott of local non-Klan business, with particularly harmful consequences for Catholic- and Jewish-owned stores.[44]

With Klan print imagery focusing on upstanding Protestantism, perhaps the most logical and active avenues of KKK recruitment were local community churches, and the movement's periodicals played a key role in facilitating this. Protestant ministers were typically amongst the very first to be approached by Klan recruiters in a new locale and, in return for preaching a pro-Klan message to their flocks, were offered free memberships and complimentary subscriptions to the leading Klan organs. Editors, meanwhile, encouraged readers simply to "Go to Church

---

[40]   Chalmers, *Hooded Americanism*, p. 115, p. 118.

[41]   Blee, *Women of the Klan*, p. 164.

[42]   On Klan commercial culture, see Fox, *Everyday Klansfolk*, pp. 19–31, pp. 184–5.

[43]   *Imperial Night-Hawk*, 7 November 1923, p. 3; Knights of the Ku Klux Klan, *The Practice of Klanishness* (Atlanta: Knights of the Ku Klux Klan, 1924), pp. 2–4. The Klan press typically featured large numbers of KKK-themed adverts from local businesses hoping to increase trade on the strength of obvious affiliations. Serving almost as de facto employment agencies, they also carried adverts from companies looking exclusively for "100 percent American employees."

[44]   Knights of the Ku Klux Klan, *Thirty-Three Questions Answered* (Atlanta: Knights of the Ku Klux Klan, n.d.), pp. 18–19. The Klan merchant community in Indiana, for instance, were issued with "TWK" placards ("Trade With a Klansman") to display in their store windows and had their businesses registered in their local unit's directory of approved, Klan-owned traders. See Blee, *Women of the Klan*, pp. 147–51.

Sunday," and regularly featured a wide-ranging, cross-denominational directory of local churches which might favorably be attended.[45] Eventually, however, the KKK replicated the functions of the mainstream Protestant churches to such a degree as to become in many ways its own religious institution and a viable replacement for them. Visible evidence of this was ensured extensive coverage via the many reports and photographs published in its own press pages. The periodicals featured not only the sermonizing efforts of Klan religious leaders, but also innumerable accounts of KKK-fronted charity drives, civic activism, municipal improvement, and educational good works from across the nation. Amongst literally hundreds of similar stories featured in the Klan press, readers were regaled with details and images of Klan Christmas basket deliveries, donations to the YMCA and Red Cross, support for sick or orphaned babies, efforts at "cleaning up the movies," the building of Klan hospitals, Klan flood relief funds, mass presentations of Bibles to public schools, and Klan-funded Protestant refuges for reformed prostitutes.[46]

Even more eye-catching was the Klan performance—and of course its press reportage of—traditional rite-of-passage rituals, which the order had wholly appropriated from the churches. Accounts of elaborate, fully-robed Klannish weddings, funeral parades, even mass open-air baby christenings regularly peppered the pages of Klan organs, becoming high-profile, if outlandish, social events, as opposed to private ceremonies.[47] Not only did these events bring the organization somewhat noisily into the public domain, the fact that every stage of life could be publicly dramatized and celebrated within the bounds of KKK membership "solidified a sense of the totality of the Klan world." From the inclusive safety of a united Klan community, robed and hooded white Protestant Americans "could be married, celebrate the birth of children, and mourn the departed" before huge, encouraging, and often curious crowds.[48]

The Klan press built community spirit by energetically advertising the vibrancy and vitality of the organization nationwide, and encouraging engagement. Extensive coverage of KKK institutions both reflected and fed into an undoubted public fascination with all things Klan and helped the order along in its quest for mainstream respectability and acceptance. So too did claims to have converts on university campuses as prestigious as Harvard and Princeton,[49] as well as efforts

---

[45]   *Imperial Night-Hawk*, 18 April 1923, p. 5; 19 March 1924, p. 4; *Dawn*, 21 October 1922, p. 13; 28 October 1922, p. 13; and 4 November 1922, p. 13.

[46]   This is just a small, representative selection of examples taken from the *Imperial Night-Hawk*: 28 March 1923, p. 2; 9 May 1923, p. 2; 23 May 1923, p. 8; 6 June 1923, p. 4; 27 June 1923, p. 3; 3 October 1923, p. 3; 28 November 1923, p. 8; 9 January 1924, p. 3; 23 January 1924, p. 8.

[47]   Countless reports on all of these types of ceremonies can be found in almost any edition of the regional or local Klan press. See, for example, the mass Klan christening in Stamford, Connecticut, reported in the *Michigan Kourier*, 8 August 1924, p. 6.

[48]   Blee, *Women of the Klan*, p. 163.

[49]   The Klan made its presence felt on many a university campus during the 1920s. See, for example, *Dawn*, 20 January 1923, p. 11; 21 July 1923, p. 16; 15 December 1923,

to get involved constructively with the nation's younger generation. Promoting the Klan's youth movement as an alternative to the Boy Scouts, KKK organs published clip-and-return membership subscription forms alongside adverts for the *Junior Klansman*, "little brother to the *Fiery Cross*," featuring an array of "news items, sketches, drawings, [and] cartoons" contributed by the nation's junior Klansmen.[50]

In terms of publicity it was the colorful mass parades and public pageants which the Klan press sponsored and reported so extensively upon that were its most effective form of alternative institution. Despite a stated predilection for "invisibility," the 1920s KKK had an exhibitionist flair for pageantry, and took to the streets in spectacular fashion both openly and often. Presenting the most common avenue for the average member to feel involved in the movement, Klan newspapers directly solicited readers to become active participants at huge regional parades, gatherings, and patriotic celebrations. Taking place typically in commemoration of distinctly American holidays, these vast carnivals brought the Klan directly to the city sidewalks and public fairgrounds, and featured an intoxicating mix of KKK floats, marchers, barbecues, live music, patriotic speeches, initiations, cross-burnings, religious services, extravagant fireworks shows, and all manner of related grandstanding.

Preparing for such events the Klan weeklies focused upon the opportunity to showcase the geographical unity and sheer numerical strength of the hooded order. Eye-catching multi-page promotional spreads advertising a "Kolossal Klan Karnival" or a "Ku Klux Home Koming" were a common feature in the pages of *Dawn* and were clearly an effective draw, judging by later reports of attendances numbering sometimes into the hundreds of thousands. Providing an accessible space for members of scattered regional Klans to regularly come together in open celebration of their common affiliation and white Protestant American identity, the carnivals helped foster a sense of solidarity and group belonging—a belonging that the Klan press endeavored to extend to sympathetic, and possibly recruitable, outsiders. The "Great Mid-West Pageant of Klankraft," boasted *Dawn* in September 1923, "will bring together in a wonderful assemblage all the Klansmen of Michigan, Indiana, Illinois,

---

p. 19; Kenneth T. Jackson, *The Ku Klux Klan in the City, 1915–1930* (Chicago: Ivan R. Dee [second edition], 1992), p. 170; Timothy Messer-Kruse, "Memories of the Ku Klux Klan Honorary Society at the University of Wisconsin," *The Journal of Blacks in Higher Education* 23 (Spring 1999), pp. 83–93; *Imperial Night-Hawk*, 1 October 1924, p. 8. Serious attempts, both ultimately unsuccessful, were also made by national Klan leaders to purchase Valparaiso and Lanier Universities, with the intention of operating them as training grounds in complete accordance with Klan principles. See *Dawn*, 2 June 1923, p. 4; 29 September 1923, p. 9; 11 November 1923, p. 3; Jackson, *Klan in the City*, p. 36; Fry, *The Modern Ku Klux Klan*, p. 21, p. 31.

[50] *Fellowship Forum*, 25 July 1925, pp. 5–6; *Fiery Cross (Indiana State Edition)*, 17 August 1923, p. 1; *National Kourier*, 3 July 1925, p. 1; Blee, *Women of the Klan*, pp. 157–62. Attacking the competition, one Klan paper also claimed that "the Roman Catholic hierarchy has taken over the Boy Scouts of America, lock, stock and barrel," leaving the Junior Klan as the "only remaining boy's organization free of papal influence."

Iowa and Wisconsin in a showing of strength that will stagger the nation." In support of the event, not only were readers urged to take the opportunity to come and hear the Imperial Wizard himself speak, but also to "bring your family" and "as many eligible friends and their families" as possible because "we want them to see our work."[51]

* * *

If respectable status, a widespread audience, and entry into the mainstream public sphere were indeed the ultimate goals of KKK leaders, then they were goals clearly accomplished, if briefly, in the interwar years. Looking back retrospectively over the Klan's "popular" phase, editors of the movement's periodicals, certainly, were in little doubt of their own influential hand:

> The *Kourier* has found recognition among America's best libraries. A complete file of its entire twelve volumes can be found in the Congressional Library at Washington, where it was placed by request. It can be found monthly in many city public libraries ... During the twelve years of its publication, it has gone into every state in the union and into the far-flung outposts of civilization. Through the mails, it has reached every English speaking country, and regularly penetrated the most isolated sections of the more backward continents. It has ridden the waves of a hundred battle wagons, and broken the monotony of far-flung army posts. It has graced the table of European government officials as an accurate interpretation of the stream of American life ... [and] had a conspicuous part in arousing and mobilizing contemporary popular opinion.

In reality, the *Kourier* editor's pride in what he considered his magazine's enduring achievement could not mask the fact that the Klan was on its way out almost as quickly as it had come to the fore. Amidst fractured leadership, political and financial squabbling, and moral scandal, the heady days of the Invisible Empire had passed even before the end of 1925, and neither the organization nor the press which supported it would ever enjoy anything approaching their like again. Even so, while the numerical strength of the Klan would wane dramatically as the depression years approached, its official organ remained the most consistent and most visible working remnant of the hooded order's glory days, continuing to be "published without a single break in monthly issue" until late 1936, in effect outlasting the movement itself.[52]

In its prime, the "second" Ku Klux Klan had enjoyed huge mainstream success, set apart from other historical incarnations by wide-ranging popular appeals

---

[51] For examples of promotional copy for the huge Klan festivals, see *Dawn*, 12 May 1923, p. 10; 25 August 1923, pp. 12–13; 1 September 1923, pp. 5–6; 23 September 1923, pp. 5–6; 13 October 1923, pp. 12–13. For accounts of the effectiveness and staggering scale of such events, see Coughlan, "Konklave in Kokomo"; and Fox, *Everyday Klansfolk*, pp. 187–97.

[52] *Kourier* magazine, November 1936, pp. 20–22. This was the closing message from the final issue, marking the point at which it was forced to reluctantly cease production "because the income from subscribers does not equal the cost of publication."

to Protestant morality, prohibition, and law enforcement, rather than an overt reliance upon vigilantism. Its magazines and newspapers provided sites for the expression of impassioned viewpoints, sites which its spokesmen utilized to root the movement's rhetoric in pressing social issues, intending ultimately to inspire readers to activism in correcting America's problems. Using print as a vehicle, the Klan's abundant propaganda imagery was stark and uncompromising, firmly aligning the Invisible Empire with every stock symbol of American Protestantism and attacking the caricatured specter of an invading, Catholic, and deeply foreign foe. Rallying followers around a unified, collective (in fact, "100 percent") American identity, Klan print was able to successfully present the movement, albeit for an ultimately short-lived period, as a positive force in national life.

The Klan was not only a looming presence in contemporary printed debate of all kinds, but also the mass-producer of its own self-sustaining print culture. Aided by a financial capacity and technical efficiency which allowed it to spread the Klan message geographically far and wide, the organization's ability to capture the attention of mainstream audiences brought focus to what might ordinarily have been a marginal position. With recruits numbering well into the millions by the mid-twenties, the Jazz Age Klan transcended the borders of the old South for the first time, and its organs could count themselves successful in helping build a truly national presence.

Giving practical direction to readers trying to integrate the movement into their own social realities, Klan publications helped coalesce the KKK network and create a sense of Klan community. In providing a media platform to the gamut of KKK institutions, events, and advertisers nationwide, they continually encouraged participation in a movement which appeared both energetic and inclusive. Ever eager to influence the dominant public sphere, Klan organs also solicited direct action, particularly at the mass gatherings that they promoted and reported upon. Providing huge, participatory celebrations of white Protestant culture as interpreted by the KKK, such gatherings served as both an outward demonstration of the apparent potency of the Klan as a societal force, and as a cohesive source of solidarity and camaraderie for its members. Effectively coordinated by the movement's press, they presented opportunities for socialization and networking between otherwise unrelated units and individuals and reconfirmed the relevance of grass-roots activists across the regions through collective celebration of their binding national mission—the preservation of "Americanism."

Chapter 7

Productive Fiction and Propaganda: The Development and Uses of Communist Party Pamphlet Literature

Trevor Joy Sangrey

On March 25, 1931 nine young black men, ages 13 to 20, were pulled from a train and arrested for fighting with white men (and winning). The young white men, having jumped the train after the fight and walked to the nearest town, told the authorities an exaggerated story of black men armed with guns and knives. This account quickly led to a crowd gathering at the next train stop, Paint Rock, Alabama, where the authorities and the crowd pulled many young people off the train, youths who were "hoboing" along the rails looking for work. Two young white women, dressed in overalls, were also taken from the train and tried to run, but were caught and brought back to the commotion at the platform. Either at the behest of their arrestors or on their own volition, the young women, Victoria Price and Ruby Bates, accused the young black men pulled from the train of gang rape.[1]

Facing the Southern justice system for a crime against white women's purity, these young men, Charlie Weems, Ozie Powell, Clarence Norris, Olen Montgomery, Willie Roberson, Haywood Patterson, and Andy and Roy Wright, made famous around the world as the Scottsboro "Boys,"[2] were rushed to trial on April 6, 1931 in the small town of Scottsboro in Jackson County, Alabama. The trial was set for Fair Day or Horse Trading Day, when thousands of people

---

[1] For more on the Scottsboro arrest and trial, including detailed accounts of the different versions of the arrest drama, see: James Allen, *Organizing in the Depression South: A Communist's Memoir* (Minneapolis: MEP Publications, 2001); Dan Carter, *Scottsboro: A tragedy of the American South* (Baton Rouge: Louisiana State University Press, 1979); Glenda Gilmore, *Defying Dixie: The radical roots of Civil Rights, 1910–1950* (New York: W.W. Norton & Co., 2008); James Goodman, *Stories of Scottsboro* (New York: Pantheon Books, 1994); Walter Howard, *Black Communists Speak on Scottsboro: A documentary history* (Philadelphia: Temple University Press, 2008); and Robin D.G. Kelley, *Hammer and Hoe: Alabama Communists during the Great Depression* (Chapel Hill: University of North Carolina Press, 1990).

[2] Following Gilmore, I use this formulation to both acknowledge the popular way the trial was referred to while also recognizing the very racialized logics at work in the naming of the young black defendants as "boys," so often a term used pejoratively for black men of any age.

from the surrounding area were in town for market and entertainment.[3] The trials were swift, each lasting on average a few hours. By April 9 Judge E.A. Hawkins sentenced eight of the nine to death in the electric chair. Roy Wright's case ended in a mistrial, as the jury could not agree upon death or life imprisonment for the 13-year-old defendant.

After the April 9 sentencing, the International Labor Defense (ILD), a legal defense organization associated with the Communist Party (CPUSA) and the US section of International Red Aid approached the families of the defendants offering free legal representation for appeals to the Scottsboro rulings. Members of the Nine faced a jury up to four more times, seven of them receiving at least three death sentences. Aspects of the case were brought before the US Supreme Court twice: once on account of the poor representation the defendants were given at the first trial and secondly because black people were systematically excluded from the jury selection. Trial theatrics included Ruby Bates's dramatic reversal of her testimony and appearance in court on behalf of the defense and Judge Horton's dismissal of the Haywood Patterson's fourth guilty verdict because it did not correspond to the testimony given at the trial. The trial was covered internationally in newspapers, radio programs, and small-press literature, especially pamphlets.

The pamphlet coverage was not unique to this trial, as many important and current issues were discussed at the time in small booklets, as well as the more common journalistic forms such as newspapers, journals, and weekly, biweekly, or quarterly magazines. Pamphlets, small publications often put out by social movements or protest groups, offered a more sustained critique, being usually longer than articles, with a more considered and complete analysis of contemporary issues and debates. Pamphlets vary from ten to upwards of 60 pages, and are often a single signature, sheets of paper folded in half, and bound in paper with simple staple, tied, or glued spines. The majority of the CPUSA pamphlets of the early half-century are around 40 pages, printed in black and white, on standard bond paper. Pamphlets were useful for Party activists for a trial such as Scottsboro since they enabled the author to present more information about the trial and the political backdrop of the situation. Similarly, pamphlets could reach people of varying literacy levels, telling stories through pictures to engage illiterate or semi-literate audiences. Anecdotal stories describe black Southern communities reading pamphlets aloud to each other at community meetings and using pamphlets to begin discussions about important local topics.[4] Furthermore, since pamphlets offered more information and context to a situation, activists could and did use them not just to present new ideas, but also to open up spaces to imagine new and radical futures.

---

[3]   Scottsboro Defense Committee, *Scottsboro: The shame of America* (New York: Scottsboro Defense Committee, 1936), p. 11.

[4]   Kelley, *Hammer and Hoe*, p. 94. Kelley also notes that few households had radios, suggesting the importance of text- and image-based media.

This essay tells the story of Scottsboro pamphlets as well as pamphlets organized around the call for self-determination for black people in the Black Belt, a move later called the Black Nation Thesis. These pamphlets, produced by the CPUSA between 1928 and 1937, are a significant part of the Party's work with black people in the Southern United States, pointedly discussing the various ways that social movements challenge cultural norms and impact political discourse. Specifically, this essay offers the idea of *productive fiction* to examine how pamphlets enabled social movement activists, leaders, and rank-and-file members of the Party to reflect on cultural and economic conventions and to imagine possible futures that included radical social change, specifically to the ways that race and racism structured daily life. The term "productive fiction" suggests that the Party did not think that the Black Nation as imagined in the Resolution on the Negro Question[5] would come to pass soon, or perhaps ever, rather that it was an important, even vital, political idea, at least on paper.

The pamphlets also illustrate two different functions of CPUSA small-press literature: pamphlets that function as *internal pedagogical tools* to ruminate on social movement goals and dreams and those that were used as *propaganda* to increase membership, educate the masses, sway political opinion, and motivate concrete action. Analyzing these two aspects of pamphlet literature demonstrates how activists were struggling with the debates around race, economic inequality, and sexuality in both internal and outwardly focused political work. The pamphlet form specifically opens up speculative conversations about race and class and highlights these struggles for the CPUSA. This essay opens with a discussion of the history of the CPUSA and CPUSA pamphlets framed within the context of race discourse in the 1930s. The argument about the importance of CPUSA pamphlets unfolds through two examples: the first, the outwardly focused Scottsboro Trial pamphlets, which function as propaganda for the CPUSA; and the second, internally focused pamphlets that highlight the speculative form of Party pedagogy around race and class.

Simmering racial tensions, reorganized after Reconstruction, pitted working-class white people against working-class black people. Wealthy and powerful white people used white supremacy to enlist the support of poor whites, often through appeals to white purity, and manufactured stories of black men as predators on white women. As many authors have noted, most notably Ida B. Wells Barnett in her pamphlet *Southern Horrors: Lynch Law in All Its Phases* published in 1892, lynching often drew on and exacerbated tensions around race, class, and sexuality.[6]

---

5   The Colonial Commission, at the Sixth Congress of the Communist International, Comintern, passed the Resolution on the Negro Question in 1928. The Resolution detailed that black people had the rights to self-determination because they were an oppressed nation, which, in the United States, included the right to secede from the union.

6   Ida B. Wells-Barnett, *Southern Horrors: Lynch law in all its phases* (New York: The New York Age Print, 1892). For more on class, sexuality, and lynching see: Bettina Aptheker, ed., *Lynching and Rape: an exchange of views by Jane Addams and Ida B. Wells*

Stories like Scottsboro, where black men were accused of raping white women, were not uncommon and often led to a local white mob, with the tacit or explicit support of local (white) law enforcement, hanging or burning the accused without a trial. Indeed, as Robin D.G. Kelley notes, such events were "public spectacles intended to punish and terrorize the entire black community."[7]

In order to mount a successful activist campaign in response to the Scottsboro verdicts, the CPUSA needed to challenge the conventional discourses on race, sexuality, and class upheld through lynching and terror-style "justice" in the South. To do this, the CPUSA and ILD focused on offering a new way of thinking about race as wedded to a class analysis.[8] Glenda Gilmore, in her study of the radical roots of civil rights, notes that Communists themselves were discussing these issues:

> A Communist [Paul Crouch] argued that the greatest value of Scottsboro could be found in this connection of race and class: "We had hundreds of such cases [rape charges] ... but they were not considered problems of labor movements ... [With Scottsboro we] demonstrated in practice what was before theory ... that the struggle of the Negro masses was part and parcel of the struggle of the American working class."[9]

Often the CPUSA and the ILD pamphlets were much stronger in their wording, showing how the low wages for white workers were maintained because black workers could not unionize. Indeed, the ILD and the CPUSA pamphlets demonstrate that the tensions around race, class, and sexuality were high, and in 1931 the courtroom in Scottsboro became the political stage for such conversations.

The CPUSA used the Scottsboro case, especially the trial itself, to wage a huge public campaign to raise awareness, especially in the North, of black issues in the South. The campaign also publicized the Party's newly minted Black Nation Thesis and directly challenged the legal system of Alabama and the US Supreme Court. Many have argued that Scottsboro was a major turning point in the CPUSA's work with black people, bringing in members and publicizing the Party and its

---

(New York: American Institute for Marxist Studies, 1982); Hazel Carby, "On the Threshold of the Women's Era," in *Dangerous Liaisons*, edited by Ann McClintock, Aamir Mufti and Ella Shohat (Minneapolis: University of Minnesota Press, 1997); Angela Davis, *Women, Race & Class* (New York: Vintage Books, 1983); Jacquelyn Dowd Hall, *Revolt against chivalry: Jessie Daniel Ames and the women's campaign against lynching* (New York: Columbia University Press, 1993); and Robyn Wiegman, "The Anatomy of Lynching," *Journal of the History of Sexuality* vol. 3, no. 3 (1993), pp. 445–67.

[7]   Robin D.G. Kelley, "Foreword," in *Scottsboro Alabama: A story in linoleum cuts*, edited by Andrew Lee (New York: New York University Press, 2008), p. viii.

[8]   Du Bois's *Black Reconstruction*, published in 1935, does similar work but has a different audience and scope. W.E.B. Du Bois, *Black Reconstruction in America* (New York: The Free Press, 1935 [1998]).

[9]   Paul Crouch to Earl Browder, quoted in Gilmore, p. 127.

organizational platform.[10] Walter Howard, in his book on black Communists' work on the Scottsboro Case, notes that black membership in the CPUSA "mushroomed from two hundred members in 1930, less than 3 percent of the total, to seven thousand in 1938, over 9 percent."[11] To understand the impacts of the Scottsboro Nine trial, it is important to note the Party's history working with black organizers and on issues centered on black communities.

The CPUSA grew out of two separate organizations in 1919, with potentially one black member at one of its founding conferences.[12] Early on the Communist Party had few black members but worked, sometimes antagonistically, with other leftist organizations focusing on and working more explicitly with black people, especially in Harlem.[13] One such organization was the African Blood Brotherhood, a radical black organization founded in 1919 by Cyril Briggs, which eventually fed many radical black activists into the CPUSA.[14] By the middle of the 1920s, the CPUSA counted among its members a small group of black activists who were active in the Party apparatus, many traveling to Russia to attend the training schools for organizers and influencing larger Party direction at the Comintern conventions.

Many of these prominent black activists from the United States were part of the conversation at the Sixth Convention of the Comintern in 1928, which finally passed a "Resolution on the Negro Question."[15] This resolution, though vaguely worded and not taken up immediately in any national Party subsidiary groups, eventually became the call for Self-Determination for Black People in the Black Belt, a move later known as "The Black Nation Thesis." The specifics of the resolution were nebulous. Generally the argument was that black people were an oppressed national minority group and, using Stalin's definition of a nation, were

---

[10] For a thorough discussion of the CPUSA's role in black radical organizing see: Allen, *Organizing*; Gilmore, *Dixie*, Howard, *Black Communists*; and Kelley, *Hammer and Hoe*.

[11] Howard, p. 9.

[12] Gilmore argues that Lovett Fort Whiteman claims that he was at the founding conference of the CPA, but there is some evidence that he was actually in the South, see Gilmore, p. 36. Also, though I use CPUSA throughout, the Communists originally formed two parties, the Communist Party of America and the Communist Labor Party, which were united by 1929.

[13] See Mark Naison, *Communists in Harlem During the Depression* (Chicago: University of Illinois Press, 1983).

[14] For more on the African Blood Brotherhood see: Naison, *Harlem*; and Mark Solomon, *The Cry was Unity: Communists and African Americans 1917–1936* (Jackson: University of Mississippi Press, 1998).

[15] The Comintern, also written as COMINTERN, was the acronym for the Third International or the Communist International of 1919. For more on black people from the United States working with the Comintern, please see: Harry Haywood, *Black Bolshevik* (Chicago: Liberator Press, 1978); Gilmore, *Dixie*; Kelley, *Hammer and Hoe*; Naison, *Harlem*; and Solomon, *Unity*.

therefore entitled to "self-determination."[16] Self-determination, in this instance, was understood as the right to more or less secede from the United States, with the area of the South called the Black Belt becoming the national space of these black people.[17]

The resolution from 1928 was poorly received in the United States and not very well publicized. Indeed, the first public airing of the tenets of the Black Nation Thesis in the United States was the 1931 pamphlet covering the "trial" of August Yokinen. This pamphlet, *Race Hatred On Trial*, asserted that racism and "white chauvinism" were best understood alongside a clear analysis of class and anti-imperialist struggle.[18] By 1932 an entire series of pamphlets dealing with the Black Nation Thesis and the call for self-determination was printed and distributed, including Harry Haywood and M. Howard's *Lynching*, John Spivak's *On the Chain Gang*, and *The American Negro* by James S. Allen.[19] In addition, Party members, both black and white, were busy including the call for self-determination in their campaigns for office, in speeches for Party conventions, in the various Party news outlets, and in the Party pamphlets.[20]

Many of the pamphlets produced around the Black Nation Thesis were direct reprints of speeches given at Party conventions or for election rallies, such as William Foster and James Ford's 1932 presidential campaign material, *Foster and Ford for Food and Freedom*. However, the pamphlets engaged in this essay are more considered pieces, obviously meant as study or discussion guides.

---

[16]   Stalin had defined a nation as "A historically evolved, historical community of language, territory, economic life, and psychological make-up manifested in a community of culture." For more on Stalin and the National Question see Cedric J. Robinson, *Black Marxism: The making of the Black radical tradition* (Chapel Hill: University of North Carolina Press, 1983 [2000]), p. 63.

[17]   James R. Forman carefully outlines the importance of the CPUSA's formulation on self-determination, see: James Forman, *Self-Determination and the African-American People* (Seattle: Open Hand Publications, 1981).

[18]   This was a Party "trial," similar in scope to the show trials becoming popular in the Soviet Union, but with fewer political teeth. This trial of a Finnish party member, August Yokinen, was one of the first places that the CPUSA put into practice the aims and goals of the Black Nation Thesis. The workers' jury found Yokinen guilty of "white chauvinism" for not allowing blacks to come to a dance at the Finnish Worker's Hall. For more on this trial see: Solomon, *Unity*, pp. 139–42; and CPUSA, *Race Hatred on Trial* (New York: Workers Library Publishers, 1931).

[19]   M. Howard was the Party name for Milton Halpern, and James S. Allen was the Party name for Sol Auerbach, both Jewish Party members originally from New York City. Harry Haywood, a black man from Chicago, had been involved in the writing of the Resolution on the Negro Question, see his autobiography for more information: Haywood, *Bolshevik*.

[20]   For examples see: Earl Browder, *The Communist Party and the Emancipation of the Negro People* (New York: Harlem Section of the Communist Party, 1934); William Foster, *Ford and Foster for Food and Freedom* (New York: Communist Party National Campaign, 1932); and League of Struggle for Negro Rights, *Equality, Land and Freedom: a Program for Negro Liberation* (New York: League of Struggle for Negro Rights, 1933).

Indeed, many pamphlets were directly referred to and referenced in the discussion material and questions provided by the Party Agit-Prop and/or Education Departments.[21] Though not archived together, the educational materials suggest that pamphlets were regularly used by individual chapters to both learn the Party line and new initiatives, but also to think about the larger impacts and ideology of Party rhetoric. These pamphlets were designed to engage Party members politically by presenting new information and insights, distilling Party doctrine, and opening a space for imagining various politically informed futures.

In these goals and uses, the pamphlets draw on a long and varied history of political pamphleteering in both the United States and Europe. Pamphlets, first widely popular in seventeenth-century England, were also regularly used in the Revolutionary War, the US Civil War, and by countless religious, political, and civil groups. Political pamphlets in particular shed light on the nuances of political debate and the many sides of political argument.[22] Richard Newman, Patrick Rael, and Philip Lapsansky, building off the foundational work of Dorothy Porter, archive many works of early African American pamphleteers and note the importance of the pamphlet as a form for early black protest.[23] Though little has been written about radical pamphleteering after the First World War, activist groups across the political spectrum published pamphlets in the turbulent inter-war years, including many from leftist groups such as the CPUSA. The CPUSA produced countless pamphlets on an international, national, and local level; in the United States alone, there were multiple Party presses and many pamphlet series numbering in the hundreds.

There are no records of how many pamphlets were printed or their distribution by the CPUSA in the 1930s; however, it is clear that there were different intended audiences for various pamphlets and that many pamphlets enjoyed second and third printings.[24] Pamphlets produced for Party members and progressive allies relied on language and examples that would have been unfamiliar and awkward for a general audience, often offering up anecdotes about the Russian revolution, language steeped in communist rhetoric, or long-winded explanations of intricate Party decision-making details.[25] In contrast, pamphlets distributed to a wider

---

[21] "Communist Party Papers." Printed Ephemera Collection. PE 031, Box 1, folder "Courses and Curriculum" 1934–undated. Tamiment Library, New York University.

[22] J. Michael Hayden, writing about political pamphlets in France in 1614–1615, notes that pamphlets can, indeed, be used "to reveal concrete and abstract trends" in political life. Hayden, "The Uses of Political Pamphlets: The example of 1614–1615 in France," *Canadian Journal of History* 21 (August 1986), p. 159.

[23] See: Richard Newman, Patrick Rael, and Philip Lapsansky, eds., *Pamphlets of Protest* (London: Routledge, 2001).

[24] The University of Michigan Labadie Collection of Communist Party Pamphlets includes 1,245 titles but does not claim to be exhaustive.

[25] George Orwell, in an essay from 1944, notes that this obtuse form was common for English-language leftist political work. See: George Orwell, "Propaganda and Demonic Speech," in *All Art is Propaganda: Critical essays* (Boston: Mariner Books, 2009).

audience, such as those produced around the Scottsboro case, refrained from Party-specific rhetoric, took pains to use accessible language, and often included many provocative images to support their larger argument.

Although the audience and goals differed for pamphlets produced as propaganda for the Scottsboro campaign and those written as internal pedagogical tools for the CPUSA, these pamphlets all imagined a different organization of race, class, gender, and sexuality, and, as such, functioned as key activist spaces. Specifically, this essay frames these pamphlets as productive fiction because they suggest a radical, if sometimes impossible, vision of the future and, through this suggestion, allow for broader social movement imagination around issues of race, class, and justice.

Scottsboro Pamphlets: Propaganda of the ILD

The widely distributed *They Shall Not Die! The Story of Scottsboro in Pictures* is a perfect example of a more broadly positioned booklet (see Figure 7.1). This pamphlet, printed multiple times in 1932, tells the story of the Scottsboro "Boys" with a simple and engaging story by Elizabeth Lawson and poignant drawings by A. (Anton) Refregier.[26] Like other ILD pamphlets, such as *On the Chain Gang* by the journalist John Spivak, this pamphlet is less a policy debate or a clarification of Party principles than a story meant to publicize the case and win support for the International Labor Defense. Unlike later ones, this pamphlet did not include a plea for funds or letters to the mayor or other elected officials; the only advertisement was the ubiquitous call to read other CPUSA publications on the back page, sporting *The Liberator* and a list of CP pamphlets on the "Negro Question."

The "Story in Pictures" also demonstrates the much broader range of literacies addressed by this and other Scottsboro pamphlets. Lawson's pamphlet, published in New York City, uses simple speech to accompany Refregier's allegorical drawings, such as the cover illustration to *They Shall Not Die!* Refregier's sketch of two workingmen cutting down a lynching tree in Scottsboro illustrates the tagline. Without any text, the image—the court-house in the background, the ropes dangling ominously from the unseen branches, the wood-chips flying from the axes—enables easy identification with the CPUSA's claim that the legal systems is going to "legally lynch" the young Scottsboro defendants.

---

[26] Lawson, Elizabeth, D.B. Amis, and League of Struggle for Negro Rights. *They Shall Not Die! The Story of Scottsboro in Pictures* (New York: League of Struggle for Negro Rights by Workers' Library Publishers, 1932). B.D. Amis, a prominent black Party member, identifies Elizabeth Lawson in his introduction to the pamphlet as the Managing Editor of *The Liberator*, the journal published by the League of Struggle for Negro Rights. Refregier was an "artist-worker" and member of the John-Reed Club. Refregier, a Russian immigrant, would go on to make a name for himself as a prominent muralist, working up from the Worker's Progress Administration rolls to paint the famous Rincon Post Office mural in San Francisco.

Fig. 7.1   A. Refregier. Cover art, *They Shall Not Die! Story of Scottsboro in Pictures*, 1932. Used with the generous permission of Walter Goldwater Radical Pamphlet Collection, African American History Collection, D-207, Special Collections, University of California Library, Davis.

Images on every page of the pamphlet further elucidate the story and allow for stark illustration of the political aims. As they first emerge in the text, Ruby Bates and Victoria Price, the white women accusers, are pictured as just like the "Boys" in torn overalls, being egged on by a well-dressed authority figure.[27] Later in the story, the judge looms large between the defendants and the electric chair, visually eliminating the need for a jury or a trial to condemn the young defendants to death (see Figures 7.2 and 7.3).[28]

---

[27]   Lawson, *They Shall Not Die!*, p. 8.
[28]   Ibid., p. 10.

Fig. 7.2   A. Refregier. "Inside the Court," *They Shall Not Die! Story of Scottsboro in Pictures*, 1932. Used with the generous permission of Walter Goldwater Radical Pamphlet Collection, African American History Collection, D-207, Special Collections, University of California Library, Davis.

Other Scottsboro pamphlets follow this model of evocative images and simple, persuasive text free of many direct references to Party politics. In this the Scottsboro pamphlets follow a line of CPUSA pamphlets geared to a broader audience, with provocative images and an accessible, direct message. *Death Penalty! The Case of Georgia Against Negro and White Workers*, a pamphlet from 1930, uses many of the same tropes to protest against the trials of M.H. Powers and Joe Carr, two young white Communist organizers who were arrested in Georgia for "inciting to insurrection." The charges against Powers and Carr, the ILD maintains, stem from the distribution of a leaflet for a meeting of workers in Atlanta. Under the heading of "An Appeal to Southern Young Workers" the leaflet shows a black worker and a white worker shaking hands. The ILD argues that this call for solidarity challenges the long-standing color line that upholds black workers' oppression. Thus the authors argue that the leaflet and the challenge to white supremacy suggested in the image were the real threat to the white capitalist bosses and the reason for the invocation of "capitalist justice" in the form of the death penalty. The pamphlet serves both as publicity for the trial as well as a call for funds for the ILD, complete with a contribution form on the back cover. The pamphlet agitates for the freedom of multiple prisoners, "Newton, Burlak,

Fig. 7.3   A. Refregier. "The Two White Prostitutes," *They Shall Not Die! Story of Scottsboro in Pictures*, 1932. Used with the generous permission of Walter Goldwater Radical Pamphlet Collection, African American History Collection, D-207, Special Collections, University of California Library, Davis.

Story, Dalton, Powers, Carr" are all listed on the back, and it follows many of the same patterns of argument employed in later trial publicity pamphlets, including a summary and refutation of the alleged crimes, an overview of the case and trial, and, finally, an analysis of this case as part of a system-wide problem with roots in capitalism. The pamphlet specifically takes on the death penalty and rings with the refrain of the prosecuting attorney: "Your Honor, we ask for the death penalty in these capital cases," but also centrally concerns the oppression of black people in the South, including an indictment of the working conditions for black people, lynch law, and the chain gang. The cover of the pamphlet communicates many of these ideas. The skull on the Statue of Liberty holding the electric chair instead of a torch suggests the death of the ideals of liberty as linked to the death sentences for Communist organizers. This pamphlet does not specifically take up the arguments or rhetoric of the Black Nation Thesis, lacking any calls for "self-determination" or "the Negro Nation." Rather, and similar to *They Shall Not Die!*, the pamphlet targets a readership outside of Party circles and works to educate the masses about the issues facing oppressed workers, pushing for concrete actions and increased political awareness.

In both scope and content this pamphlet is easily situated in the history of propaganda, highlighting the early definition of the term to mean education and persuasion, rather than the later turn to indicate deceit and manipulation. The history of propaganda is long and complex, but most discussions trace contemporary US understandings of the term to the First World War and the propaganda campaigns of President Woodrow Wilson.[29] Definitions of propaganda from the 1930s, for example in the works of Lasswell and Blumenstock, differentiate propaganda from education and highlight systems of control.[30] In contrast, the CPUSA pamphlets highlight the similarity of the aims of education and propaganda, especially around the Scottsboro Trials. In these pamphlets the simple text and message, accessible language and metaphor, and the evocative images work together to both inform the public about the case and to subtly suggest the correctness and value of the Communist line.

The portrayal of women in the Scottsboro pamphlets demonstrates another aspect of propaganda: the accessible messaging builds off accepted tropes of womanhood to communicate challenges to systems of race and class. Women were, obviously, central to the case against the Scottsboro defendants though they show up rarely in the pamphlets concerning the trial. Early pamphlets by the ILD often barely mention the young women on the train, sometimes noting they had been "forced into prostitution by low wages and lack of work" but not suggesting much about their motivations and lives or livelihoods.[31] Other pamphlets focus extensively on the mothers of the Scottsboro Boys, allowing these black women to show on the pages often to elicit support and sympathy from the readers. The mothers are portrayed as tired but resilient, traveling all over the world to publicize the case and get their sons out of jail.[32] Here black women function as ciphers for the troubles of the working class, characters

---

[29]   Noam Chomsky, *Media Control: Spectacular achievements of propaganda* (New York: Seven Stories, 1991 [2002]), p. 11. For more on the history of propaganda see: Leonard Doob, *Propaganda: Its Psychology and Technique* (New York: Henry Holt and Company, 1935); Gareth Jowett and Victoria O'Donnell, *Propaganda and Persuasion* (London: Sage Publications [third edition], 1999); Harold Lasswell and Dorothy Blumenstock, *World Revolutionary Propaganda: A Chicago study* (New York: Alfred A. Knopf, 1939); and Steven Seidman, *Posters, Propaganda, and Persuasion in Election Campaigns Around the World and Through History* (New York: Peter Lang, 2008). It is also important to note that many of the academic works on propaganda are ardently anti-Communist and use Communism and the USSR to discuss the negative understandings of propaganda, focusing on deception and manipulation. The prime example of this trend is John Clews, *Communist Propaganda Techniques* (New York: Frederick A. Praeger, 1964).

[30]   As Lasswell and Blumenstock note, in a discussion of revolutionary propaganda, "propaganda is the manipulation of symbols to control controversial attitudes; education is the manipulation of symbols (and of other means) to transmit accepted attitudes (and skills)," p. 10. See also, Doob, *Propaganda*, p. 89. For a more contemporary definition, see Jowett and O'Donnell, *Propaganda and Persuasion*.

[31]   Lawson, *They Shall Not Die!*, p. 2.

[32]   International Labor Defense, *The Story of Scottsboro* (New York: International Labor Defense, 1931).

but not actors in the drama. Perhaps neither the Scottsboro Defense Committee, the coalition charged with the Nine's defense after 1934, nor the ILD were willing to clearly take on the complex ways that the women were instrumentalized in the trial, as both groups glorified Ruby Bates as young, beautiful, and pure-of-heart, contrasting her with the old, ugly, conniving, and manipulative Victoria Price. The pamphlets slip into accepted tropes of womanhood, portraying women as stock characters but never fleshing out their experiences or the impact the trial would have had on their lives.

Though this stereotypical portrayal of women is not uncommon for the CPUSA, at the same time other activists were keenly aware of the important aspects of gender oppression. For example, the 1935 pamphlet *The Position of Negro Women*, by Eugene Gordon and Cyril Briggs, highlights the economic exploitation of black women. This work builds off of the work of other prominent Communist women, both black and white, who were struggling to bring women's issues to the forefront of the Party platform; women such as Maude White, Claudia Jones, and Louise Thompson Patterson, who were involved in high levels of communist work, and the large numbers of black women in the rank-and-file membership of the Southern CPUSA.[33] The propaganda-style pamphlets of the Scottsboro trial, however, did not take on these critiques, but rather built their analysis on quick, stereotypical portrayals of women. Perhaps some of the pamphlets' authors did not think gender issues were important to the Scottsboro case. In other work, however, Lawson discusses women's issues and supported women publishing and participating in public discourse. Though there are no records of such a discussion, it is likely the Scottsboro pamphlet authors were trying to appeal to the largest possible audience and sacrificing women's issues to reach a broader base, appealing to familiar tropes of gender to communicate new ideas about race and class.

The Scottsboro pamphlets, similar to many other pamphlets produced by the ILD, were written for propaganda purposes, with the aim of increasing membership, educating the public, and motivating concrete political action. Within these pedestrian goals, however, the pamphlets challenged long-held beliefs about the justice system, the place of black people in US civil life, and the possibilities of overturning lynch-justice. This challenge was very much an example of productive fiction; it was a leap of faith to think that the race relations that had structured US sociality for over a century would change, that the Scottsboro Nine could escape lynching. Other CPUSA pamphlets of the time, however, targeted Party members and allies and employed more considered rhetorical strategies, relying less on images and foregrounding political and economic analysis. These pamphlets served as internal pedagogical tools and worked to create a space for collective imagining and as such were also productive fictions. Specifically, they offered the speculation of a "Negro Nation," which was fertile ground for reconceptualizing the ideas of race, class, and, eventually, gender.

---

[33] For more on black women in the CPUSA, see: Erik McDuffie, *Sojourning for Freedom: Black women, American Communism, and the making of Black left feminism* (Chapel Hill: Duke University Press, 2011).

Self-Determination: Productive Fiction of the CPUSA

Many authors have argued that the Black Nation Thesis is a prime example of the failure and ridiculousness of the CP platform during the Third Period,[34] while former Party members and others claimed that in the Black Nation Thesis the CPUSA was reaching too far and misrepresenting the desires and needs of black people.[35] In contrast, this essay suggests a more nuanced analysis of the rhetorical choices of the Black Nation Thesis, noting how the Thesis opened up important conversations on race, class, and, by the 1940s, gender. This work was most readily accomplished through the calls for "self-determination," a phrase that pointed to the Party's key theoretical work on race.

Although some Party members were supportive of all of the claims of the Black Nation Thesis for decades to come, not all of the CPUSA was sympathetic to the Thesis in any of its incarnations.[36] Again, the term "productive fiction" signals the important, innovative, and imaginative aspects of the Thesis, and also recognizes that perhaps many of the activists and organizers in the Party did not think a "Negro Nation" would really come to exist. In both language and scope, the Thesis was out of step with the rhetoric of the United States since it used ideas of nation in ways unfamiliar to the US context and was particularly fuzzy on the distinct ways that race and nation might work, both separately and in conjunction with each other.[37] However, such critiques of Comintern policy were not welcome in the 1930s, and explicit dismissal was not possible while maintaining Party membership.[38]

---

[34]   For sympathetic, but critical, reviews of the Black Nation Thesis see: Philip S. Foner, *American Socialism and Black Americans: From the age of Jackson to World War II* (Westport, CT: Greenwood Press, 1977); William Z. Foster, *History of the Communist Party in the United States* (New York: Greenwood Press, 1968); and Earl Ofari Hutchinson, *Blacks and Reds: Race and class in conflict 1919–1990* (East Lansing: Michigan State University Press, 1995).

[35]   For examples see: Harold Cruse, *The Crisis of the Negro Intellectual* (New York: William Morrow & Company, 1967); Manning Johnson, *Color, Communism, and Common Sense* (Belmont, MA: American Opinion, 1963); The Racism Research Project, *Critique of the Black Nation Thesis* (Berkeley: Racism Research Project, 1975).

[36]   Harry Haywood, for example, in his much later autobiography, *Black Bolshevik*, is unapologetically supportive of the Black Nation Thesis in its many forms, while the four years it took for the CPUSA to publish any meaningful work on the "Negro Question" also speaks to ambivalence in the Central Committee.

[37]   In my other work on the Black Nation Thesis, I argue that the nationalism expressed in the CPUSA pamphlets was unique, combining legacies of Soviet nationality policy, ideas of the Western nation state, and Garvey and the Universal Negro Improvement Association's arguments about Black Nationalism and racial uplift. See: Trevor Joy Sangrey, "'Put One More "S" in the USA': Pamphlet Literature and the Productive Fiction of the Black Nation Thesis" (dissertation, University of California, Santa Cruz, June 2012), Chapter 4.

[38]   The relationship between member Parties and the Comintern was mostly one-way; an individual Party subsidiary could not flout the dictates of the Comintern, though everyone was invited to participate in drafting and passing resolutions.

The CPUSA had to work with the articulation of the "Resolution on the Negro Question," all the more so after the 1930 rearticulation of the resolution,[39] in part because it was a dictate from the Comintern and also because of the particular history of the CP in the United States and its relationship to the Comintern.[40] However, it should again be noted, that the Resolution was passed with significant US input from prominent CPUSA members both black and white.[41]

In the late 1920s Party organizing with black people had been centered in Chicago and Harlem under the auspices of the American Negro Labor Congress, the Sanhedrin conference, and other activities of Lovett Fort-Whiteman, Cyril Briggs, Otto Huiswoud, and brothers Otto Hall and Harry Haywood. With the Black Nation Thesis, and the CPUSA-organized League of Struggle for Negro Rights, much of the organizing refocused on the South, especially in Alabama and Georgia, at first with textile workers and later with sharecroppers and the unemployed. In these later organizing drives, the Black Nation Thesis provided key background and conceptual frameworks for the Party but was not the focus of the on-the-ground organizing. As discussed above, some authors produced pamphlets to bring Southern people into the struggles supported by the CUPSA; even more so, the journal *The Southern Worker*, edited by James Allen, was useful to develop Southern Party platforms and issues. The Black Nation Thesis pamphlets, however, focused on Party members and other progressives as their main audience and worked with the ideas of the Black Nation Thesis to develop Party conversations on race and nationality.

Two key pamphlets, *The American Negro* by James Allen and *The Negroes in a Soviet America* by Allen and James Ford, demonstrate how these more conceptual and theoretical pamphlets create speculative spaces—productive fictions—in their approach to the Black Nation Thesis. The first pamphlet, published in 1932, lays the groundwork for the analysis of race while not elaborating on the ideas of self-determination. The second pamphlet, published in 1935, delves further into the potentials opened up by the Black Nation Thesis, offering real alternatives and imaginative spaces for Party members to think about the liberation of black workers. Together, these two pieces demonstrate how CPUSA pamphlets produced around the Black Nation Thesis provided spaces for the Party to imagine different

---

[39] The first draft of the Resolution on the Negro Question was confusing for many and the Comintern passed an addendum in 1930, see: Communist International, "The Negro Question in the United States Resolution of the Communist International," *The Communist International Journal* 8 (1931).

[40] "American Exceptionalism" had been the call phrase of Jay Lovestone as General Secretary of the CPUSA. Lovestone and his supporters had been very publicly ousted from the Party in 1929. Thus any calls for "it's different in America" would have been met with suspicion and resistance. See: Foster, *History*, p. 272.

[41] Involved in the discussion on the Negro Question were Harry Haywood, Otto Hall, Lovett Fort-Whiteman, Charles Nasanov, Samuel Adams Darcy, Bertram Wolfe, and Sen Kayama, though by no means was everyone in agreement. For more on the politics of passing the 1928 Resolution see: Gilmore, *Dixie*, pp. 62–4; and Solomon, *Unity*, pp. 70–77.

possibilities in terms of race and class. Neither of these pamphlets tackles issues of gender; it would not be for another few years that Cyril Briggs, Claudia Jones, and others would use the apparatus of the Black Nation Thesis to think about the super-exploitation of black women. However, as productive fictions these pamphlets provided an important rallying point around the call for self-determination and allowed the Party to build deeper conversations about race in the United States.

James S. Allen's *The American Negro*, number 18 in the International Pamphlet series, was the first CPUSA pamphlet fully devoted to looking at the situation of black people in the United States. This pamphlet was revised by the author to reflect "important changes in the United States and the world situation" and republished in 1938 under the title *Negro Liberation*.[42] Party education materials regularly refer to both editions of this pamphlet as part of the theoretical backbone of the CPUSA work with black people. Allen's pamphlet consists primarily of a careful compilation of statistical and 1930s census data to note the widespread economic exploitation of black workers and to make a "map showing a continuous stretch of dense Negro population in the South—the Black Belt."[43] The Black Belt was useful as the location of struggle for a black nation; other pamphlets highlight the concrete importance of the land and black workers' claims to the land based on generations of tilling the soil.[44] Specifically, the pamphlet uses the Black Belt to highlight the position of black people in the United States including an analysis of tenant farming, migration, and industrial labor and labor unions.

In line with other more insular pamphlets, *The American Negro* is sectarian, attacking what Allen calls the "race leaders" or middle-class black people who work with the NAACP, the black church, and institutions of higher learning such as Howard University. He continues noting how specifically the capitalist system, and the white capitalists who run the state and through it both the army and courts, are at the root of the oppression of black people. The end of the pamphlet is therefore dedicated to an investigation of these issues and the Communist solution, self-determination for black people in the Black Belt.

This early pamphlet offers only a brief sketch of the CPUSA program of self-determination. Allen glancingly notes an idea of nationalism, stating: "Negroes, who suffer super-exploitation and persecution as an oppressed people or nationality, can only attain full equality with other people of the world by a struggle against the white ruling class, against which the white workers are also struggling."[45] Allen does comment that self-determination is the only way for black people in the South to achieve full equality, but he only begins to suggest what this might mean, offering ideas and statistics that are too vague to be meaningful. He states that black people in the Black Belt should be able

---

[42]   James Allen, *Negro Liberation* (New York: International Publishers, 1938), p. 2.

[43]   James Allen, *The American Negro* (New York: International Publishers, 1932), p. 5.

[44]   For examples of this argument see: League of Struggle for Negro Rights, *Equality, Land and Freedom*.

[45]   Allen, *American Negro*, p. 29.

to exercise governmental authority over this entire territory and determine their relationship to other governments, especially the United States government, including the right of separation if so desired. This necessarily includes the demand for the withdrawal of the armed forces of American imperialism from this territory.[46]

Allen links the struggles of black people in the United States to other anti-imperialist struggles and to struggles of liberation around the world, suggesting a deep critique of imperialist capitalism and a figure of occupation to illustrate the historical, economic, and legal oppression of black people but not offering any concrete solutions. At this point the call for self-determination stands in as a catch phrase with little meaning or substance, as a reference point for a larger conversation on developing an understanding of race that takes into account imperialism, historical economic and geographic subjugation, and the continuing practice of pitting white and black workers against each other. This piece does not, however, offer much in terms of creating a space for internal party dialogue about race, though it gives the building blocks for such a conversation. Concrete ideas of nationalism, a complete reckoning of self-determination, and a more developed relationship between the struggles of black people in the United States with world-wide colonial struggles will enable Allen, in his later revision of this pamphlet, *Negro Liberation*, to suggest alternative programs for black Communists interested in working toward liberation.

But it is *The Negroes in a Soviet America*, James Allen and James Ford's collaborative work published in 1935 by the Workers Library Publishers, which most specifically lays out the imagined promise of the Black Nation Thesis. This promise is blatantly Soviet in both content and form, as easily evidenced by the title of the pamphlet as well as its cover art (see Figure 7.4). The smiling face of a young black man looks out from the cover, offering the promise of a new hope. Flanking him are small vignettes of industrialization on the left and a small rural farm on the right, images of what the pamphlet promises the South would look like after a Soviet Revolution. The image of the young black man, wanting for nothing and enjoying life, suggests prosperity under socialism—a sharp contrast to images of wretched workers struggling under capitalism that graced so many other pamphlet covers. This pamphlet offers the clearest articulation of the Black Nation Thesis, and opens a space to imagine different race relations through an explicitly fictional picture of a "Soviet America" that will alleviate the ills of racism.

It would be possible to read this pamphlet as advocating for a communist revolution in the United States that would create a society duplicating the USSR.[47]

---

46   Ibid., p. 30.

47   Readings like this are especially prominent in right-wing publications over the past five decades or so. The pamphlet was even reprinted by the National Economic Council in 1945 and then by the conservative John Birch Society in 1956. More recently David Allan Rivera offers a similar reading of the pamphlet, using it as a backdrop to the communist conspiracy from the 1920s through the civil rights movement. See: David Allan Rivera's *Final Warning: A history of the new world order* (Oakland, CA: Conspiracy Books, 1984 [2004]).

Fig. 7.4   Cover art, *The Negroes in a Soviet America*, 1935. Used with generous permission from the collection of Saul Zalesch, <http://www.ephemerastudies.org>.

Such a reading would of course run into problems because the social and economic situation in the United States was not comparable to the USSR in many ways, quite a few of which are outlined in the pamphlet's discussion of the development of capitalism in the United States. Reading the pamphlet as a fiction, rather than a blueprint for the revolution, opens up a space for activism that works toward a different imagining of life for black workers. The pamphlet opens an imaginative, speculative space, in line with other pieces issued as part of the *In a Soviet America* series, texts proclaiming the potential benefits of sovietization for minors, youth, seamen, and professionals. The *Negroes in a Soviet America* is an enticement to think about the possibilities of revolution and a call to arms against the rampant oppression of black people. Indeed, most of the pamphlet, as is common with CPUSA booklets, details the economic and social oppression faced in the United States, offering a refrain of "in a Soviet America" to highlight the ills of the United States by proposing an alternative.

In subsections labeled the "Soviet United States" and the "Soviet Negro Republic," dreams of a new world include redresses to current problems. The claims are as simple as: "The horrors of segregated, over-crowded ghettos will disappear. All residential sections of the city will be opened to the Negro."[48] Or as grandiose as proposing that black "farm families would now have the possibilities of leisure and peace, plenty and abundance, education and culture."[49] Still further, black people, after a revolutionary overthrow of the current system, could set up any kind of government, nation, or state that they might want to best meet their needs and desires.[50] Ford and Allen, obviously, imagine a Soviet state for the "New Negro Republic" but carefully demonstrate that the reorganization of wealth and power that this transition would entail would echo the historical period of Reconstruction. "We have somewhat of a similar situation in our own history. In the years 1867–1877, a revolutionary dictatorship ruled the South. The purpose of this dictatorship was to prevent the former slaveowners from returning to power."[51]

The suggestions of a "Soviet America" are wonderful dreams for black working and unemployed people who materially had nothing and had even fewer prospects for making a good life. In 1935 the US Congress passed relief measures, but little money was coming down to sharecroppers and unemployed people in the South. The "Soviet America," the idea of a space, a land, for black people to live and prosper, was the most spectacular kind of fiction. But it was also a productive one, a suggestion of something better that pointed to the real problems that black people faced in their everyday lives.

For the authors of the pamphlet, the Black Nation Thesis and the "Soviet America" were useful fictions, offering examples of how things could be different for struggling farmers, sharecroppers, and others who were nominally part of the Communist Party. Especially in the work with sharecroppers in Alabama, a pamphlet that outlined different ways to collectively farm and organize labor was a great boon.[52] For other readers of the pamphlet, the stories of a "Soviet America" highlighted the huge economic, social, and cultural disadvantages

---

[48] James Ford and James Allen, *Negroes in a Soviet America* (New York: Workers' Library Publishers, 1935), p. 38.

[49] Ibid., p. 44.

[50] Ibid., p. 39.

[51] Ibid., p. 41.

[52] For more on sharecropping practices see: Kelley, *Hammer and Hoe*. Importantly, the Soviet American the pamphlet suggests was fiction, but even more so was the Soviet reality the pamphlet supposedly builds upon. Though perhaps the US authors of the piece were not aware, the Soviet's forced collectivization of farmland, especially in the Ukraine, lead to widespread famine in 1932–1933 and the death by starvation of between 6 and 8 million. See: Timothy Snyder, *Bloodlands: Europe between Hitler and Stalin* (New York: Basic Books, 2010).

black people faced. Rather than the Scottsboro pamphlets that focused on legal issues and nine particular cases, the allegory of the "Soviet America" could speak to many and offered a long-term engagement of problems plaguing black people in the South.

Particularly interesting is the way the pamphlet uses the history of a betrayed Reconstruction to suggest a "Soviet America." By drawing upon the specifically US history of Reconstruction, by showing the promise of the decade and the collapse of that promise at the hands of greedy business owners and thus the unequal development of the North and the South, Allen and Ford use the "Soviet America" to illustrate the long history of Southern exploitation and offer a return to what is imagined as a utopian moment of US history. Looking closely at sharecropping, textile mills, and chain gangs, the authors unpack the economic exploitation. They also address social issues, citing the "diseases of poverty [that] will for the first time meet a stronger foe" in a "Soviet America."[53] Finally, they grandly suggest: "President Roosevelt's present estate in Georgia and the other resorts of the millionaires can be turned into sanatoria, hospitals, clubs, etc. Palm Beach can become the haven of tired workers and toiling farmers."[54] The dreams were large; the promise of a "Soviet America" was only "a mere peep into the vistas of a glorious future for the masses" as pictured on the cover of the pamphlet.[55] But this glimpse was an important one, and one that worried the Communists' critics because it inspired the organizers, allies, and the central committee to do important work with black people in the Southern United States.

In the 1930s, notions of race were greatly in flux, with white supremacist and fascist organizations, liberals and progressives, and radical organizing groups all articulating a different rhetoric about race. Most prominent depictions of race focused on sexuality and often used sexuality to drum up racist fears, as was so apparent in the Scottsboro case.[56] The pamphlets discussed here sharply contrast this representation of race, thinking about the impacts of class on racist violence and the ways that race and class implicated each other in the lives of poor black southerners.[57] Though these pamphlets are not the only place where race and

---

53   Ford and Allen, *Soviet America*, pp. 46–7.

54   Ibid., p. 47.

55   Ibid.

56   See "Myth of the Black Rapist" in Angela Davis, *Women, Race, and Class*; and Paula J. Giddings, *Ida: A Sword Among Lions: Ida B. Wells and the campaign against lynching* (New York: Amistad, 2008).

57   By the 1940s Claudia Jones's pamphlet and editorial work would also take gender into account, talking about the "super exploitation of Black Women." This work was building off of earlier, but not as widely read, declarations of "super exploitation" by Maude White and other Party activists. For more on black women in the Party, Jones and White in particular, see and Carol Boyce Davies, *Left of Karl Marx: The political life of Black Communist Claudia Jones* (Durham, NC: Duke University Press, 2007) and McDuffie, *Sojourning for Freedom*.

class were being knitted together,[58] the CPUSA pamphlets brought this discussion to the public through an organized, influential, and growing social movement. Specifically, the pamphlets' function and form enabled Communist Party activists to not only spread the word about CPUSA activities and values, but also to discuss and disseminate material that suggested a different kind of future. *The Negroes in a Soviet America* and *The American Negro* demonstrate the early work of the Black Nation Thesis as a productive fiction for the Party and allies to speculate and reconceptualize race and class.

The Scottsboro pamphlets also rely on a spectacular imagination of freedom and equality but do not engender the same kind of considered discussion of Party politics or economic and cultural revolution. These pamphlets, produced for a wider audience and employing a variety of strategies to reach people with varying literacy and who were not familiar with Party rhetoric, did not employ fictions to engage their readers in a larger speculation about race relations, rather they were much more traditionally styled as propaganda pushing for the freedom of the Scottsboro Nine, through direct action and raising money for the defense work. However, these pamphlets still built on a dream of freedom and equality for black people, as of yet unrealized in the early 1930s.

Both sets of pamphlets, the propaganda the CPUSA produced around the Scottsboro Nine trial and the more theoretical pieces written for an activist audience, demonstrate the important space of the pamphlets in social movement small-press literature. The CPUSA used the longer pamphlet form, as well as the positioning of pamphlets as more accessible than books but more in-depth than news or journal articles, to open up speculative conversations about race, class, nation, and, eventually, gender. As productive fictions these pamphlets functioned as essential tools for the CPUSA to challenge the prevailing attitudes on race, class, and gender that would have impact on decades of activism to come.

---

[58] Du Bois's seminal work *Black Reconstruction* was also published in 1935.

Chapter 8
Containment Culture:
The Cold War in the *Ladies' Home Journal*, 1946–1959

Diana Cucuz

> Confronted as we are by a relentless attack upon our institutions by the
> communists, the all important thing is that we preserve the morale, the spirit and
> the hopefulness of the democratic tradition. Only time will tell us whether or not
> it is a fortunate coincidence that the most critical period in our history arrives
> just as the census reveals that women now outnumber the men in our nation ...
> The women now have the opportunity and the power to bring our democratic
> system through its greatest test.[1]

These were the words of Arkansas Senator William J. Fulbright in a 1951 *Ladies'
Home Journal* article urging female readers to do their part in containing the
communist forces that threatened Cold War America. By nature, he argued, women
had an instinctive concern for the preservation of the race, and as such, faced a
responsibility they could not escape.[2] This call to action may seem unusual during
a period long remembered for its zealous commitment to the family, the home,
and domesticity. Public memory views the complacent "happy housewife heroine"
as an image that permeated Cold War discourse. In this nostalgic portrayal,
women were relegated to the home, where they created a loving and stable family
life that could provide the safety that was needed in a world characterized by
an aggressive Soviet expansionism. Purveyors of American culture, it was
argued, promoted a discourse that left little option for women but to conform
to this white, middle-class ideal of domesticity. One of these purveyors was the
mass-circulation monthly magazine specifically geared towards women. The
messages of these magazines were especially important because they were easily
accessible and were read by millions of women each month. As a result, they
became easy targets of criticism from journalists such as Betty Friedan, who in her
seminal work, *The Feminine Mystique*, condemned them for their abandonment of
the independent, career-driven heroines that characterized the Great Depression
and World War II. However, the above quotation reveals that while a discourse of

---

[1]   W.J. Fulbright, "How to Get Better Men Elected," *Ladies' Home Journal*
(November 1951), p. 218.

[2]   Ibid., p. 52.

domesticity existed within the content of postwar women's magazines, it was not the *only* discourse that existed. Rather, postwar women's magazines were largely shaped by the experiences of the Cold War and the threat of Soviet communism, and as such, contained multiple and often contradictory messages.

In the years between 1946 and 1959, arguably the height of the Cold War, the *Ladies' Home Journal* promoted a discourse of domesticity to its readers that was closely intertwined with the ideology of the Cold War, particularly the American foreign policy doctrine of "containment." Alan Nadel, in *Containment Culture*, argues that containment was first used in 1946 to suggest that "the power of the Soviet Union would not endanger security if it could be contained within a clearly defined sphere of influence."[3] Elaine Tyler May, in *Homeward Bound*, writes on the relationship between domestic ideology and Cold War politics. May argues that while these visions are not traditionally connected, private life is deeply connected to political ideology and public policy.[4] Typically viewed as a foreign policy doctrine, containment also describes the extent to which numerous venues in American life contributed to a culture that sought to curb communism at home.[5] In this domestic version of containment, the home became the "sphere of influence." It was purchased by the successful breadwinner and could contain potentially dangerous social forces, but if properly managed by the skillful housewife, the home could contribute to the secure and fulfilling life to which Americans aspired.[6] Domestic containment blurred the lines between the public and the private and became a way for women, particularly housewives, to demonstrate their loyalty and patriotism to their country. It has been well documented that throughout American history, in spite of popular perceptions, "private" women have been active in the public sphere in various shapes and forms, particularly during times of upheaval.[7] The Cold War was no different.

In the postwar period, the *Ladies' Home Journal* regularly contained articles that reflected the politics of the era. While the magazine reflected and promoted the ideals of a white, middle-class, and heterosexual culture, the *Ladies' Home Journal* still became the most popular women's magazine of the period. By the mid-1950s it had reached 5 million readers on a monthly basis, many of whom, regardless of their differences, undoubtedly strove to achieve the vision of the American Dream that permeated US culture. While many articles promoted a discourse of domesticity, others reflected the circumstances of the Cold War period, encouraging women, and even children, to take active roles in containing the Soviet threat. These roles called on them to be good wives, mothers, *and*

---

[3]   Alan Nadel, *Containment Culture: American narrative, postmodernism and the atomic age* (Durham, NC: Duke University Press, 1995), pp. 2–3.

[4]   Elaine Tyler May, *Homeward Bound: American families in the Cold War era* (New York: Basic Books, 1988), p. 10.

[5]   Nadel, *Containment Culture*, pp. 2–3.

[6]   May, *Homeward Bound*, p. 14.

[7]   See Mary P. Ryan, *Women in Public: Between banners and ballots, 1825–1880* (Baltimore: Johns Hopkins University Press, 1992).

citizens in the public sphere. Every person in the postwar home could do their part in containing communism. Many of these articles came from renowned journalist Dorothy Thompson, who wrote a monthly column for the *Journal*. While the *Journal* was known to contain its share of fluffy pieces, Thompson often wrote on civic and political issues. In August 1950 she wrote "A Primer on the 'Cold War,'" which defined the term Cold War for *Ladies' Home Journal* readers. It defined it as a condition in which "opponents are struggling with each other by every means except an armed clash, each meanwhile arming with ever more powerful weapons in anticipation of an attack from the other, and in the hope of deterring through fear, such an attack."[8] The article made the intended ideological position of the *Ladies' Home Journal*, and its readers, clear. It argued that the Cold War was justifiable because communists, by nature of their theoretical principles, would not feel secure as long as any world power was capitalist. Americans, therefore, were unwillingly forced into a Cold War by a Soviet Union which felt compelled to indulge in a perpetual struggle with the noncommunist world.[9] The threat of Russian expansionism became a common theme in the *Ladies' Home Journal*. An April 1948 article entitled "The Economical Man is the Patriot" argued that communism has become an "instrument of the perennial Russian world conquest dream. It is compatible with Russian nationalism and no other."[10] Communism, according to the article, depended on the breakdown of the established order, an order that threatened sacred American institutions such as "churches, moralities, traditions, education, industrial leaders, noncommunist labor leaders, and the popular bodies of the state."[11] A February 1952 article entitled "To Protect Civil Liberties" stated that communism worked to break down faith and tradition. Communists, it stated, decry Christianity as a myth, history as a lie, national heroes as scoundrels, and patriots as bigots. The criminal is a victim, parental influence is despotism, classical education is reactionism, and order is tyranny.[12]

This theme dominated well into the 1950s, in spite of the death of Soviet leader Josef Stalin and the thaw in relations between the two countries. A 1958 article entitled "What Price Liberty?" compared the West to ancient Rome, arguing that modern Western civilization was as challenged as the great civilization of Rome immediately before its decline and fall. It condemned the American government and its people for their poor response to this challenge. While we have extolled the "virtues of liberty, the superiority of the American and Western standard of living, pointed out the vices and failures of the Communist regimes, and kept this

---

8 Dorothy Thompson, "A Primer on the Cold War," *Ladies' Home Journal* (August 1950), p. 11.

9 Ibid.

10 Dorothy Thompson, "The Economical Man is the Patriot," *Ladies' Home Journal* (April 1948), p. 11.

11 Ibid., p. 12.

12 Dorothy Thompson, "To Protect Civil Liberties," *Ladies' Home Journal* (February 1952), p. 12.

country ... in a formidable military posture," we have not clearly analyzed the challenge.[13] It was safe to assume, according to the article, that Soviet leaders would not launch a nuclear war, but it was not safe to assume that they had abandoned their intention of becoming the most powerful nation in the world.[14] The article argued that the Soviet Union had many advantages. For example, it was easily able to appeal to Asian and African nations that were resentful over years of Western colonial rule. The solution, therefore, was for the West to further expand its influence into these areas. Rather dramatically, the article argued that "it would be history's most ironic jest if the Communists proved themselves abler capitalists and traders than capitalist lands."[15] According to the article, there was no reason for this to happen except for "public and congressional apathy, indolence and indecision ... . The issue must be settled in the present Congress, on a bipartisan basis. Otherwise we may lose the world of freedom ... in this generation."[16] The *Ladies' Home Journal* presented a grave picture of the international world, emphasizing the threat of communism to sacred American institutions and to the established world order.

Foreign policy was connected to the home front, in that the successful defeat of communism, according to *Ladies' Home Journal* rhetoric, depended not necessarily on Eastern Europeans and Russians themselves, but on the government and the American people to do their part to help.[17] In a regular column entitled "If You Ask Me," readers wrote in to ask former First Lady Eleanor Roosevelt for advice on matters of a personal, professional, and often political nature. In one response to a question regarding the necessity of FBI loyalty tests, Roosevelt responded that she hoped the FBI "would not do more than it is now doing about communism in this country," and in fact, she would prefer to see it do less and American citizens do more.[18] Indeed, so that they knew exactly what it was and how to fight it, the *Ladies' Home Journal* defined the American communist for its readers. A January 1953 "Report on the American Communist" depicted a communist as a native-born, white American who grew up in the lap of urban luxury and received an excellent education. He or she was young, timid, lonely, spiritually and emotionally frustrated, and the product of a broken home. Somewhat condescendingly, he or she could easily be described as "a long hair individual who lives in a world of books, but never did an honest day's work with his hands."[19]

American women were encouraged to identify threats to the established order and do their part in containing communism by taking an active role in civic life in the postwar years. During this period female involvement in local communities

---

[13]   Dorothy Thompson, "What Price Liberty?" *Ladies' Home Journal* (May 1958), p. 11.

[14]   Ibid., p. 14.

[15]   Ibid.

[16]   Ibid.

[17]   Thompson, "The Economical Man is the Patriot," p. 12.

[18]   Eleanor Roosevelt, "If You Ask Me," *Ladies' Home Journal* (April 1948), p. 77.

[19]   Dorothy Thompson, "Report on the American Communist," *Ladies' Home Journal* (January 1953), p. 12.

and governments served dual purposes. It reinforced the discourse of domesticity by arguing that political participation could be seen as an extension of the female role within the home, while simultaneously reinforcing a discourse of containment by promoting active citizenship for women who were concerned about upholding white middle-class values that were antithetical to communism. Appeals to readers became fiercely patriotic. A February 1952 article entitled "No Place for a Woman?" encouraged women to exercise their right to vote because failure to do so was "un-American." Not exercising one's right to vote was a refusal to "fight for and protect the American way of life, the American home and the American family." [20] The article explained that the rise of Adolf Hitler, Benito Mussolini, and Josef Stalin was due to the apathy of citizens. The author urged the reader to review what indifference to voting did in other countries. "It has produced evil dictators' intent upon enslaving the world and destroying the United States."[21] A September 1952 article entitled "The Eyes of the World are Upon Us" encouraged *Ladies' Home Journal* readers to vote in the next election by pointing out that the number of Americans who had voted at the national level had been on a steady decline since 1880, culminating in a new low of 42 percent in 1950.[22] Yet, the article argued, we "are the country which is 'selling' democracy to the world. We are ... trying to persuade Asia, the Middle East, Africa, the South America dictatorships that the right of the people to rule their own destinies is the most precious political heritage men can have."[23] The article went on to salute eight women who were persuaded to take political action by the fact that their most valuable contribution to their country, aside from their family, was active political participation. The *Ladies' Home Journal* incorporated women's public participation as "part of a positive image of the modern American woman in the postwar world."[24] Articles such as "14 Points for Beginners in Politics" instructed women to register and vote, research candidates, attend meetings, join organizations and parties, and volunteer for political tasks. With this easy to follow advice, women could keep both their homes and countries safe from communism.[25]

Election years were particularly important in the *Ladies' Home Journal*. The desire to enlist women in the fight against communism took on a more urgent tone. A January 1952 article called "It's Time Women Took Direct Action" told women that the United States was entering an election year facing a crisis. "Shocked by revelations of corruption and moral callousness in public life, challenged by communism to prove that free government can work," the article asked

---

[20] Margaret Chase Smith, "No Place for a Woman?" *Ladies' Home Journal* (February 1952), p. 50.

[21] Ibid.

[22] "The Eyes of the World are Upon Us," *Ladies' Home Journal* (September 1952), p. 51.

[23] Ibid.

[24] Joanne Meyerowitz, "Beyond the Feminine Mystique: A Reassessment of Postwar Mass Culture, 1946–1958," *Journal of American History* 79 (March 1993), p. 1469.

[25] Margaret Hickey, "14 Points for Beginners in Politics," *Ladies' Home Journal* (February 1952), p. 49.

"what can American women do about it?"[26] Articles assured women that political involvement would be a simple extension of family life. One, entitled "You Can Ask Questions," told women that a home could not be divorced from its community. Political leaders made decisions that affected the lives of women and their families on a daily basis. As such, women should ask questions of their local candidates in order to make informed decisions on Election Day. It encouraged women to use their leisure time toward the "common good" because as a good citizen democracy is not just something you discuss, it is "something you do."[27] Another, entitled "What's the U.S. to You?" advocated the goals of national organizations such as the League of Women Voters and urged women to become members of the party of their choice. They could even start at the bottom by addressing envelopes, ringing door bells, making telephone calls, or baby-sitting for other mothers who were involved. It warned women to get involved immediately, as "delay could mean trouble for your community or your nation."[28] Women were told to make politics their business. "Voting, holding office, and raising your voice for new and better laws are just as important to your home and your family as the evening meal or spring house cleaning."[29] Election-year messages, such as this one, were a far cry from the messages of female complacency that are commonly associated with the postwar period.

By associating women's activism with domesticity, the *Journal* attempted to debunk the myth that the world of politics was strictly male. Women could get involved by extending their domestic talents to the political realm. For example, women could advocate for traditionally "female" issues such as improved health care and education, municipal reform, and neighborhood beautification. Men, in turn, could support their wives' endeavors because their new positions would simply be an extension of their traditional, more feminine roles. An August 1952 article entitled "Women's Place in Politics" stated that the average man, while recognizing the right of women to vote, believed that politics, unlike housekeeping, was not the place for women. "So many women seem to agree," the article stated, but "nothing could be farther from the truth. The fact is that many public problems are quite similar to housekeeping problems and the housekeeper's viewpoint is essential to their solution."[30] While not depreciating the possibilities open to women in state and national politics, the article argued that local government was a natural expression of female interest and power. It grimly warned that democracy is engaged in a "struggle for survival ... . If we fail to govern our home localities

---

[26] Erwin D. Canham, "It's Time Women Took Direct Action," *Ladies' Home Journal* (January 1952), p. 18.

[27] "You Can Ask Questions," *Ladies' Home Journal* (March 1952), p. 165.

[28] Margaret Hickey, "What's the U.S. to You?" *Ladies' Home Journal* (April 1950), p. 23.

[29] Ibid.

[30] Harold W. Dodds, "Women's Place in Politics," *Ladies' Home Journal* (August 1952), p. 47.

well, popular government will collapse all along the line. If we succeed at home, we shall similarly succeed at Washington."[31]

In October 1951, the *Journal*'s editors began a monthly column called "Political Pilgrim's Progress." Its first column argued that the greatest danger posed to democratic society was not a military attack, but rather America's "do-nothing" citizens, who had become apathetic and lazy. In order to encourage political involvement, the column showcased "average" women who made democracy integral to their lives by becoming active within their communities.[32] Throughout the postwar period, the *Journal* frequently invoked examples of these types of women. For example, January 1952's "It's Time Women Took Direct Action" depicted two politically active women, Mrs. Dorothy McCullough Lee, the first female mayor of Portland, Oregon, and Mrs. N, the state chairman of a women's organization that had created better schools, parks, sewage plants, and assembly halls.[33] In November 1954, the *Ladies' Home Journal* devoted an article to Estes Kefauver's senatorial campaign in Tennessee. The lengthy piece focused on Edna Jamison, a woman who worked tirelessly as a manager for Kefauver's campaign. Jamison was chosen primarily for her political activity in her hometown of Jackson, Tennessee, which included her prominent role in her church, in education reform, and in establishing the town's first League of Women Voters. Rather humbly, she declared that her main motivation, aside from her son in service was, like mothers everywhere, her deep concern for the frightening state of the world. She believed it was more important than ever to send to Washington the best the country had to offer.[34] In February 1952 an article entitled "Women Like You and Me in Politics" depicted the stories of 13 "normal" women in public office, all chosen because of their appeal to the average *Ladies' Home Journal* reader.[35] Dorothy Davis, for example, was elected mayor of the small town of Washington, Virginia. With the help of her all-woman council, she was able to use her domestic skills to institute the most efficient system of "town housekeeping" that Washington had ever seen, all with its first-ever surplus of $300.[36] The remainder of the article told the stories of 12 other "average" women, who were in reality rather remarkable, but who, according to the article, easily and effectively ascended to political office. A 1953 article entitled "They Say it with Action" stated that more than 2,000 women serve in US city, state, and national government positions. It offered an intimate look at nine of them in order to inspire more women to action. The nine included Los Angeles city councilor Rosalind Weiner. At 24, she was the youngest woman ever

---

[31] Ibid.

[32] The Editors, "Who Cares?" *Ladies' Home Journal* (October 1951), pp. 46–7.

[33] Erwin D. Canham, "It's Time Women Took Direct Action," *Ladies' Home Journal* (January 1952), p. 18.

[34] Rosemary Jones, "Kefauver's Secret Weapon," *Ladies' Home Journal* (November 1954), p. 208.

[35] "Women Like You and Me in Politics," *Ladies' Home Journal* (February 1952), p. 48.

[36] Ibid.

elected to council. She was recently married and worked to successfully combine a career with marriage. Another was Katherine Elkus White, the mayor, or "city mother" as she called herself, of Red Bank, New Jersey. She was the married mother of two who prided herself on her ability to bake a "mean cake."[37] Finally, there was Mrs. John B. Sullivan. As Missouri's first congresswoman, she ran in 1952 after her late husband's sudden death and won. When voters complained that a woman's place was in the kitchen, she agreed, but explained that certain circumstances sometimes forced a woman to earn a living. She was also, of course, a great cook.[38] "Political Pilgrim's Progress" impacted *Journal* readers a great deal, as can be evidenced in the examples given above. The September 1952 issue featured eight women, each one crediting the column for somehow instigating their civic participation, whether it encompassed writing letters, canvassing, creating women's organizations, or even running for Congress.[39] The *Journal* walked a fine line by letting its readers know that women should and could be politically active, while simultaneously fulfilling their traditional roles as wives and mothers.

Descriptions and images of women's political participation did not go unnoticed by *Ladies' Home Journal* readers, many of whom wrote in to voice their opinions on the topic. In February 1952, one young reader criticized an American society that made it "almost impossible for anyone under the voting age to do anything in the field. The political parties are interested only in voters."[40] Articles, however, encouraged not only women of voting age, but also teenagers and children to become involved in the political process. Although teens were not yet eligible to vote, one article wrote, they could hand out information on candidates and polling places, vote reminders, or baby-sit for mothers.[41] Another wrote that children could join organizations such as the Girl Scouts, where, through a project of practical citizenship, they could study firsthand the duties and obligations of American citizens and earn a "government badge."[42] American youth and their education became an increasingly important discursive topic in the postwar period. Aside from the interest in children that generally accompanies a magazine geared towards women and the family, this interest was partly derived from the fact that by the mid-1950s Russia had made extraordinary leaps in scientific and technological achievement, particularly in nuclear weaponry and aerospace engineering. American concerns over Soviet advancement by the mid-1950s incited many lengthy articles during that period that compared the education systems of the two countries. In a May 1956 article entitled "The Challenge of a Soviet Education," Thompson praised the strong Soviet education system, which in one generation, she claimed, had turned a nation with a 90 percent illiteracy rate

---

[37]   "They Say it with Action," *Ladies' Home Journal* (February 1953), p. 149.

[38]   Ibid., p. 150.

[39]   "The Eyes of the World are Upon Us," pp. 50–51.

[40]   Myrna Leventhal, "Letter to the Editor," *Ladies' Home Journal* (February 1952), p. 5.

[41]   Margaret Hickey, "Teen-Age Citizens," *Ladies' Home Journal* (February 1956), p. 61.

[42]   Margaret Hickey, "Never Too Young," *Ladies' Home Journal* (November 1954), p. 37.

into one with 100 percent literacy.[43] Comparing curriculums, she argued that there was not one high school in America in which students would get the preparation in science and mathematics they would get in Soviet schools. A February 1958 article by Thompson entitled "Do American Educators Know What They Are Up To?" outlined the purpose of the Soviet education system, which according to an American report issued by The Office of Education in the Federal Government, was to train the youth to be an "obedient, industrious, enthusiastic and highly competent servant of the state, thoroughly prepared to perform the functions required by a state bent on stepping forward as the premier industrial and military power of the world."[44] While Thompson made it clear that she was not advocating a Soviet style of education, she did argue that the Soviets were more successful because they at least had goals that defined their education system. Instead, The Office of Education vaguely defined American education as a system designed to promote "freedom, peace and the fullest development of the individual."[45] This was not good enough for Thompson. According to her, Americans needed to abandon their "easygoing" education system which encouraged selfishness and neglected patriotism.[46] It was essential to create an education system that would suit the talents and abilities of top students, ensure that they remain in school, and, perhaps most importantly, remain competitive against Soviet students.

Curiosity about the threat of communism created a demand for information about life in the Soviet Union. Since only a small number of Americans had the knowledge to speak on the subject, the *Ladies' Home Journal* invoked women, typically the wives of foreign correspondents and members of the Foreign Service, as well as famous faces, to describe life in the Soviet Union, a common theme throughout the postwar period. *Ladies' Home Journal* letters, as well as articles, described the repressive conditions of the country. In February 1958 one reader wrote that she and her husband, a radio-television correspondent, lived in the National Hotel directly across the street from the Kremlin. Every floor, she wrote, contained portraits of Soviet leaders Lenin and Stalin, who "seem to examine everyone who gets off the little elevator."[47] John Steinbeck's August 1946 account of his trip to the Soviet Union stated that there was nothing in the Soviet Union that goes on outside the vision of Stalin. "His portrait hangs in every room of every museum. His bust is in front of all airports, railroad stations, bus stations. His picture in needlework is undertaken by the students of schools. Every house

---

[43] Dorothy Thompson, "The Challenge of a Soviet Education," *Ladies' Home Journal* (May 1956), p. 11.

[44] Dorothy Thompson, "Do American Educators Know What They Are Up To?" *Ladies' Home Journal* (February 1958), p. 11.

[45] Ibid., p. 12.

[46] Dorothy Thompson, "The Soviet School Child," *Ladies' Home Journal* (February 1956), p. 25.

[47] Nancy Jones Levine, "Letter to the Editor," *Ladies' Home Journal* (February 1958), p. 4.

has at least one picture of him. He is everywhere."[48] In April 1952 the *Ladies'* *Home Journal* published a series called "Letters from Russia." Written by the wife of the former ambassador to Russia, Lydia Kirk's entries showed the difficulty Americans faced while living in Russia. On July 27, 1950, after writing that her husband's authorization to visit Germany came through, she wrote that it would be "hard to … come back after a sight of the outside world. More and more we seem cut off from all contact and communications with these people. The gulf of ideas, of taste, of sympathy even, grows deeper and deeper."[49] Her letters detailed the rigidities of the Soviet system, such as the difficulty American Embassy employees had in obtaining visas and the frequency with which they were sent home for no apparent reason; the Soviet stranglehold on culture, which included the blacking out of English language radio broadcasts; and grim events, such as seeing a dead man dragged along the streets of Moscow, the closing of the Catholic Church she attended, and the general inability to forge relationships with Russians who feared the consequences of an American friendship. Historian Joanne Meyerowitz has pointed out that a common approach in encouraging women's political participation in the postwar period was to contrast the "freedoms" and "liberties" that characterized America with the oppression that characterized Russia.[50] In the *Ladies' Home Journal*, descriptions of women were most frequently invoked to show the differences between the two countries, as well as the possible ramifications of communism on any given society.

As early as November 1946, Joseph Phillips, a foreign affairs columnist for *Newsweek*, argued that in order to fully understand the Russian people, special attention needed to be paid to the "character and habits of Russian women" who experienced a "special hardship" under communism.[51] This sentiment was eagerly embraced by *Ladies' Home Journal* editors. In 1946 Steinbeck spent two months in Russia, entering the homes and lives of women and children, for the purpose of writing an article showing that "Russians are people too."[52] The resulting "Women and Children in the U.S.S.R.," depicted the different lives that Russian and American women led. According to Steinbeck, Russian women neither had the pay nor the opportunity to purchase the consumer goods that were available in America. Russian women had a desire to consume, but clothing, makeup, and perfume were scarce and expensive.[53] A June 1955 article entitled "They Let Us Talk to the Russians" reaffirmed that the Russian eagerness to consume was not always satiated. It told the story of four Columbia University students who

---

[48]   John Steinbeck, "Women and Children in the USSR," *Ladies' Home Journal* (August 1946), p. 45.

[49]   Lydia Kirk, "Letters from Moscow," *Ladies' Home Journal* (April 1952), p. 132.

[50]   Meyerowitz, "Beyond the Feminine Mystique," p. 1469.

[51]   J.B. Phillips, "Typical Woman of Postwar Moscow," *Newsweek* 28 (November 4, 1946), p. 52.

[52]   Steinbeck, "Women and Children in the USSR," p. 44.

[53]   Ibid, pp. 48–9.

travelled to Russia. Their visit to Moscow's largest department store showed them that although stores were crowded with people, they lacked the abundance and variety of consumer goods that were available in America.[54] Russian women faced a particularly daunting task. Encouraged to procreate for the sake of the nation, they lacked the consumer goods necessary to attract men. Articles like these articulated the inadequacies of a Soviet system that deprived its women of the makeup, perfume, and clothes they eagerly desired. The American capitalist system, in contrast, created a marketplace in which women could enjoy a wide variety of goods at low prices. Indeed, an abundance of resources was one of the things that for Americans set them apart from Soviets. A December 1946 article entitled "America's Greatest Problem" stated that the greatest problem facing postwar America was "that of maintaining the uninterrupted production of abundant goods of all kinds." A serious crisis in production would not only affect the happiness of Americans, but also "adversely influence the whole world."[55] More than ever before, during the Cold War American capitalism became associated with consumption and therefore happiness. *Ladies' Home Journal* editors intended their readers to recognize this and sympathize with the deprived women of Russia.

The inadequacies of the Soviet system were also highlighted in the extent to which women worked. On the farms they visited, Steinbeck wrote that "women ran the house, did the cooking, took care of the chickens, pigs, goats and cows. They traded, and bought and sold."[56] Young women also worked long hours in the fields. They "come home, eat, rest for an hour, bathe, put on clean clothes and go to their clubs to dance violently until one o'clock in the morning. We do not know when they slept."[57] In spite of the fact that these articles described what was perceived to be a sad existence under communism, Steinbeck concluded that the Russian people lived on the hope that tomorrow would be a better day. "The women we met were poor, industrious and hospitable ... . They want to raise fine children and to educate them. They want to live better and more comfortable lives. They work incredibly hard to that end."[58] Bruce and Beatrice Gould, in their 1955 account of their visit to Russia, described Russians as a "busy, determined, and stolid people engaged in an enormous enterprise." However, they also led "grim" lives.[59] These grim but hopeful lives were not foreign to American women, many of whom had lived during the Great Depression and World War II and had dreamed of a better life for themselves and their children. A March 1952 article by Thompson

---

[54] The Editors, "They Let Us Talk to the Russians," *Ladies' Home Journal* (June 1955), p. 152.

[55] Dorothy Thompson, "America's Greatest Problem," *Ladies' Home Journal* (December 1946), p. 6.

[56] Steinbeck, "Women and Children in the USSR," p. 51.

[57] Ibid.

[58] Ibid., p. 59.

[59] The Editors, "We Saw How Russians Live," *Ladies' Home Journal* (February 1955), p. 59.

entitled "I Write of Russian Women" also contrasted the working experiences of Russian and American woman but was more critical of the communist regime. She claimed that while communism had proclaimed the emancipation of women, Russian women were expected to work from the age of 18 to 55 and were the most "exploited toilers" in the country.[60] She described the working conditions of women in both the factory and the farm, all of them overworked, underpaid, and saddled with the burden of the double day. According to Thompson, these were the wives of men who "aren't helping with the dishes at night. That's beneath the dignity of the Russian male ... . They're probably drowning the cares of the day in vodka—while mamma mends their socks."[61] Of course their circumstances were meant to differ from those of American women, whose lives were unburdened by heavy work, relieved by the advances of modern capitalism, and rewarded with loving husbands who actually helped with the dishes. Aside from a privileged few who were highly educated with important jobs, Thompson wrote, she did not believe that "Russian women liked the regime." Her "woman's eye" noticed that "Russian women, as a whole, look unhappy."[62]

Descriptions of communist conditions in the *Ladies' Home Journal* did not solely encompass American accounts of their experiences in Russia but also the stories of individuals who had experienced communism firsthand and migrated to America. These were stories of a grateful people who embraced their new country and did their own part in promoting its values. *Ladies' Home Journal* readers could see that domestic containment, in small but important ways, could be practiced by everyone, even by former Soviets themselves. The April 1952 article "Escape to Freedom" told the dramatic journey of the Kutvirts, husband Otakar, wife Duda, and their two sons Tommy and Daniel. Native Czechs, the couple had traveled to Czechoslovakia from Rochester, New York to visit family after the war. Family illness and a communist coup in 1948 forced them to remain in the country for three long years under a repressive regime that made it difficult to escape to freedom. With one small son and another on the way, they were forced to flee by foot from the Czech mountains into Germany, but no risk, according to the article, "was too great to escape."[63] Their lengthy ordeal in communist Czechoslovakia taught the Kutvirts to cherish democracy. After returning to America, Otakar began teaching economics at the University of Rochester, often condemning communism in his lectures, and Duda began giving speeches on living conditions under communism, an act which she believed was her duty as an American. As a result of their ordeal and their disdain for the communist system that had drastically altered their beloved homeland, the family embraced their new cultural surroundings.

---

[60]   Dorothy Thompson, "I Write of Russian Women," *Ladies' Home Journal* (March 1952), p. 11.

[61]   Ibid., p. 12.

[62]   Ibid.

[63]   Dorothy Cameron Disney, "Escape to Freedom," *Ladies' Home Journal* (April 1952), p. 181.

The Czech language was no longer spoken in their household, Czech holidays were no longer observed, and, according to them, their children would "inherit a proud heritage. Tommy and Dandy are going to have no other loyalties. They are to be middle-class Americans, and we intend them to know it."[64] The message was simple, the gift of freedom was priceless, and a middle-class existence was ideal and attainable for anyone living in America. The example of the Kutvirts, however, showed that in order to achieve this dream one had to abandon his or her European roots and fully embrace American democratic values.

Ladies' Home Journal articles were clearly intended to appeal to the emotions of its female readers. They capitalized on the common bonds that existed between American and Soviet women in order to encourage the former to take a stand against communism. These common bonds included the ability to participate in the joys of consumption, to stay at home and raise her family without being burdened by outside work, and to practice Christianity freely and openly. Articles emphasizing the Christian roots of Soviet women encouraged Americans to connect with them on a spiritual level. A 1953 article entitled "The Great Affirmative" warned *Journal* readers that under communism Christians were in danger. While churches still existed, and people still attended, the state intended to exterminate every faith other than Marxism.[65] An October 1956 article entitled "Women Versus the Kremlin" showed that, during these difficult times, women sustained Christianity because they insisted on keeping it alive within their homes.[66] Soviet leaders, such as Nikita Khrushchev, however, believed that, with the help of carefully orchestrated atheistic propaganda, Christians would eventually "free themselves from their religious delusions."[67] While the article described the Sunday crowds in the few churches that still existed (the majority were taken over by the state and turned into museums), it also showed that those in attendance were primarily women. Formal Christianity, through the institution of the Russian Orthodox Church and its clergy, would play no role in the lives of its children. Sunday schools were banned, as the government reserved the right to educate and train all the nation's children under 18. According to Khrushchev, a communist education, based entirely on a scientific world outlook, was ideal. If children were to be educated in Christian values, the responsibility rested primarily on parents and families to maintain Christianity within a communist system that tolerated the existence of religion but made it clear that it hoped to eventually destroy it. The article alarmingly quoted Khrushchev as declaring Soviet socialism triumphant in undermining the social roots of religion and destroying the base of the church.[68] Historians have analyzed

---

64   Ibid, p. 197.

65   Dorothy Thompson, "The Great Affirmative," *Ladies' Home Journal* (November 1953), p. 14.

66   Charles C. Parlin, "Women Versus the Kremlin," *Ladies' Home Journal* (October 1956), p. 46.

67   Ibid.

68   Ibid., p. 50.

the relationship between Christianity and anticommunism in the postwar period. Stephen J. Whitfield in *The Culture of the Cold War* has argued that in the postwar period, America was unique because unlike any other country it experienced a dramatic upsurge of piety and church affiliation. Religious adherence and church membership became a way of affirming the American way of life during the Cold War, "especially since the Soviet Union and its allies officially subscribed to atheism."[69] The importance of battling communism with piety became an important theme for public figures, both political and religious. Wisconsin Senator Joseph McCarthy, for example, declared in his famous Wheeling, West Virginia speech that the war was on in the "final all out battle between Communistic atheism and Christianity."[70] The Reverend Billy Graham also argued that communism had "declared war against God, against Christ, against the Bible, and against all religion."[71] During the Cold War the connection between politics and religion was reinforced, and it was continuously articulated in *Ladies' Home Journal* articles. Readers could empathize with Soviet women and contain communism simply by practicing their Christian faith and encouraging fellow Americans to do the same.

In the postwar period Russian women in the *Ladies' Home Journal* were depicted as doing it all, mainly because the repressive regime under which they lived gave them no other choice. Given a choice, however, at least in the context of these articles, they would certainly choose to live under a system of American capitalism. The Goulds, for example, during their 1955 visit to Russia, described the interest of young people in learning about American life. Mrs. Gould's copy of the *Ladies' Home Journal* was so popular, among women *and* men, that she often found it difficult to hold onto. According to her, the articles that most fascinated women were pictures of homes, kitchens, and fashion.[72] The hope among Americans was that increased exposure to the outside world, even if only through a women's magazine, would lead to an increase of political, economic, social, and religious freedom in Russia. Descriptions of Russian women in the *Ladies' Home Journal* were important in that they showed how and to what extent communism affected the human soul. The accuracy of these representations was further reinforced by the fact that they came from the seemingly objective observations of average people, traveling to the Soviet Union, who did not have an overt political agenda. They depicted a superior American way of life, contrasted with a Soviet one in which women were unfeminine, unfulfilled, and unhappy, all of which were evidence of the potential dangers of communism to the social order and to the privileged position of American women. It was assumed that femininity, fulfillment, and happiness were derived from the home, family, material prosperity, and religious freedom that were made available to American

---

[69] Stephen J. Whitfield, *The Culture of the Cold War* (Baltimore: Johns Hopkins University Press, 1991), p. 83.

[70] Ibid.

[71] Ibid.

[72] The Editors, "We Saw How Russians Live," p. 187.

women through democracy and capitalism. In reading the repressive conditions of a proud Russian people, American women could sympathize and recognize that by "containing" communism at home, or even doing something as small as handing over an issue of the *Ladies' Home Journal*, they could perhaps one day alter the wretched circumstances of Russian women.

An analysis of domestic containment in the *Ladies' Home Journal* shows that politics can be greatly enriched through analyses of culture and vice versa. Historians such as Emily Rosenberg have argued that examining the significance of policy discourses means moving beyond conventional sources and making uses of those approaches more associated with cultural studies.[73] In intertwining the seemingly separate realms of politics and culture, our understanding of the place of women in a given society can be deepened. During the Cold War, mass-circulation monthly magazines geared towards women, particularly the *Ladies' Home Journal*, contained multiple and contradictory messages. While promoting a discourse of domesticity that at times relegated women to the home, the *Ladies' Home Journal* also promoted a discourse that put them implicitly, and at times explicitly, on the front lines in upholding white, middle-class American values and, thus, containing domestic communism and the Soviet threat. These discourses complicated the role of Cold War-era women and encouraged them to expand their horizons beyond the complacent "happy housewife heroine" that Friedan described. *Ladies' Home Journal* articles indicate that "average" American women *did* listen to these calls to action and *were* politically active during the Cold War in many ways, small and large. Readers believed that these acts contained communism and protected American democracy. Journalists like Friedan, therefore, were not wrong in their belief in the existence of a discourse of domesticity in the postwar period, but that interpretation has been expanded to suggest that multiple, often contradictory discourses, existed in that period. With the widespread fear that domestic communism and Soviet expansionism could threaten the established political, economic, and social order, it would have been impossible, and perhaps irresponsible, for women's magazines like the *Ladies' Home Journal* to ignore the political potential of its readers.

---

[73] Emily S. Rosenberg, "Foreign Affairs After World War II: Connecting Sexual and International Politics," *Diplomatic History* 18.1 (January 1994), p. 70.

Chapter 9
Challenging the Anti-Pleasure League: *Physique Pictorial* and the Cultivation of Gay Politics

Whitney Strub

Male physique magazines populated the racks at urban newsstands across the nation in cold war America, circulating too through the mails, sometimes openly, sometimes in plain brown wrappers. In an age of heightened national anxiety over bodies, desires, and the national project, nobody embraced the magazines. To the authorities they were often obscene representations of a threatening and deviant homosexual underworld, to be suppressed at all costs; to the burgeoning homophile movement, they were an unseemly blemish invoking too many lurid stereotypes about gay identity at a time when the movement's primary goal was respectability.

Nobody embraced the physique magazines, but readers by the thousands bought them. Circulation figures can only be given in estimates, but historians agree the beefcake photos of physique culture drew many times more purchasers and readers than the political discourse of the early homophile publications, disseminating tens of thousands of magazines. Nonetheless, from the emergence of the homophile movement through the Stonewall rebellion of June 1969, physique magazines remained excluded from the institutional auspices of the formal gay rights movement. This exclusion in turn cast a historiographical shadow, whereby LGBT historians often inherited from the homophile movement a distinction between political activism and disreputable cultural activity.

Yet physique culture provided a venue for a collective expression of gay desire that was inherently political in the context of Cold War America and became self-consciously so under the auspices of such publishers as Bob Mizer, founder and editor of *Physique Pictorial* (see Figure 9.1). In foregrounding images while complementing them with an editorial voice at least as, if not more, politicized than that of contemporaneous homophile publications, Mizer and *Physique* accomplished two important tasks. First, Mizer cultivated a politically conscious gay counterpublic; in contrast to homophile magazines, presumably read by those already motivated to think politically, physique readers did not come to the publications for primarily political reasons.[1] Mizer, though, refused to let

---

[1] Michael Warner defines counterpublics as communities crafted through the reflexive circulation of texts, which "can work to elaborate new worlds of culture and social relations" and "make possible new forms of gendered or sexual citizenship." See Michael Warner, *Publics and Counterpublics* (New York: Zone Books, 2005), p. 57.

Fig. 9.1   *Physique Pictorial*, vol. 5, no. 1 (Spring 1955). Used with permission of the Bob Mizer Foundation.

them enjoy the visual splendors of the male body without acknowledging the political dimensions of doing so in a violently homophobic society. His editorials persistently directed readers toward homophile organizations; even if not all readers pursued these suggestions, few could come away from *Physique* without some sense of themselves as participating in social contests over sexuality and the public sphere. Second, while serving as silent partner to an unresponsive homophile movement, *Physique* and its kin crafted a more expansive sense of gay politics—one that encompassed homophile calls for civil liberties but also, through both its discursive articulation and the very nature of its graphic design, which juxtaposed sensual depictions of the male body against vigorous assertions of political rights, staked a claim to a legitimization of gay pleasures quite absent from homophile platforms.

This defense of a gay pleasure culture, even if textual rather than sexual per se, not only took place in the unprecedentedly public space of commercial print media, but was even collectively negotiated in reader letters to the editor—a crucial infrastructural act of community-building outside the realm of conventional notions of the political sphere, but critical nonetheless in the formation of a collective, if always contested, gay community imaginary. Recent scholarship in LGBT history has striven to provide a corrective to institution-centric conceptualizations of activism, given that the sheer act of public visibility, much less expression of desire, is always already a political act under conditions of heteronormativity.[2] Examining *Physique Pictorial* through that lens supports this project and supplements David Johnson's recent assertion that, while scholars often position activism and consumerism as antagonists, it was in fact "the very rise of a gay consumer market that helped provide the rhetoric and construct the networks that fostered gay political activism."[3] *Physique Pictorial*'s politics of resistance and desire constitute one significant example of this dynamic in action.

While scholars of the queer past have not entirely ignored physique magazines, they have often examined them according to a logic somewhat inherited from the homophile era, rarely integrating such cultural activism as *Physique Pictorial* into the early gay rights movement. Even as the narrativization of gay history began to emphasize the place of physique magazines, Richard Meyer wrote in 2006, "the scholarship on radical gay politics to date has almost entirely ignored questions of visual representation, while art historians have narrated the period of the late 1960s and early 1970s without reference to gay politics."[4]

Further, even as physique culture and other erotic media have been recuperated into a more expansive historical vision of gay history, the analytical primacy of the visual has superseded other important aspects that might forge closer links between seemingly polarized camps in gay print media. Thomas Waugh's magnificent study of gay male visual erotic culture, *Hard to Imagine*, rightly credits the purchasing, sharing, and appreciating of photographs with forging gay sensibilities, desires, and communities, but only briefly acknowledges the editorial content of physique magazines. Other historical accounts likewise collapse physique culture into the strictly visual without further examination.[5]

Such scholarship, while richly analytic on matters visual, and crucial in demanding recognition of erotic and pornographic representation as central to queer history, nonetheless inadvertently reinscribes a bifurcated narrative of "respectable" political activism and the sexual politics of visual and erotic pleasure as separate and distinct. In fact, physique magazines were

---

[2]   Anne Enke, *Finding the Movement: Sexuality, Contested Space, and Feminist Activism* (Durham, NC: Duke University Press, 2007). For the classic expression of this analysis in lesbian history, see Elizabeth Lapovsky Kennedy and Madeline Davis, *Boots of Leather, Slippers of Gold: The history of a lesbian community* (New York: Routledge, 1993).

[3]   David Johnson, "Physique Pioneers: The Politics of 1960s Gay Consumer Culture," *Journal of Social History* 43.4 (2010), p. 870.

[4]   Richard Meyer, "Gay Power Circa 1970: Visual Strategies for Sexual Revolution," *GLQ: A Journal of Lesbian and Gay Studies* 12.3 (2006), p. 441.

[5]   Thomas Waugh, *Hard to Imagine: Gay male eroticism in photography and film from their beginnings to Stonewall* (New York: Columbia University Press, 1996), p. 217; Jeffrey Escoffier, *Bigger Than Life: The history of gay porn cinema from beefcake to hardcore* (Philadelphia: Running Dog Press, 2009), p. 16; Lillian Faderman and Stuart Timmons, *Gay L.A.: A history of sexual outlaws, power politics and lipstick lesbians* (New York: Basic Books, 2006), pp. 74–5.

intimately linked to the homophile movement, despite the movement's refusal to acknowledge, much less embrace, the fact. An examination of *Physique Pictorial*, arguably the most important physique magazine, reflects these links. Generally remembered and examined on a primarily visual plane, *Physique* editor Bob Mizer also developed a sophisticated, politically minded editorial voice during the formative years of the homophile movement in the 1950s. Combining erotic imagery with political commentary in unprecedented ways, *Physique* cultivated an erotic politics hinging on imagery, words, and the textual interplay of the two on the page. Mizer frequently used the resultant voice to coax readers into recognizing the political valences of their consumption of the contested magazine (see Figure 9.2).[6]

While the social meaning of homophile respectability has been debated by historians, its ubiquity has not. The first sustained gay rights group, the Mattachine Society, was established at the turn of the 1950s at the height of a "lavender scare" that saw exacerbated police surveillance and persecution, psychiatric castigation of homosexuality as deviant and psychotic, and media imagery of shadowy perverts and child molesters, all accomplished with the belligerent state sponsorship of a federal government committed to purging its ranks of homosexuals, down to the lowliest federal job. Homophile groups responded to these attacks with an assimilationist, even patriotic effort premised on attempting to integrate homosexuals into the national body politic. Respectability, as historian Martin Meeker notes, thus became a "deliberate, strategic move" designed to dismantle homophobic stereotypes and allow for greater public visibility and acceptance.[7]

Homophile respectability necessitated a disavowal of the disreputable, reflected in a 1965 set of regulations for picketing issued by the Mattachine Society of Washington. "People are much more likely to listen to, to examine, and hopefully, to accept new, controversial, unconventional, or unorthodox ideas and positions," the MSW contended, "if these are presented to them from sources bearing the symbols of acceptability, conventionality, and respectability, as arbitrary as those symbols may be." For pickets and public protests, this meant

---

6   On *Physique Pictorial*—which awaits definitive scholarly treatment—see Dian Hanson, *Bob's World: The Life and Boys of AMG's Bob Mizer* (Koln, Germany: Taschen, 2009); F. Valentine Hooven, *Beefcake: The muscle magazines of America: 1950–1970* (Koln, Germany: Taschen, 1995); and Winston Leyland, ed., *Physique: A pictorial history of the athletic model guild* (San Francisco: Gay Sunshine Press, 1982). The best treatment remains Waugh's in *Hard to Imagine*, pp. 209–83.

7   John D'Emilio, *Sexual Politics, Sexual Communities: The making of a homosexual minority in the United States, 1940–1970* (Chicago: University of Chicago Press, 1983), pp. 75–91; David Johnson, *The Lavender Scare: The Cold War persecution of gays and lesbians in the federal government* (Chicago: University of Chicago Press, 2004); Martin Meeker, "Behind the Mask of Respectability: Reconsidering the Mattachine Society and Male Homophile Practice, 1950s and 1960s," *Journal of the History of Sexuality* 10.1 (2001), pp. 78–116, p. 90.

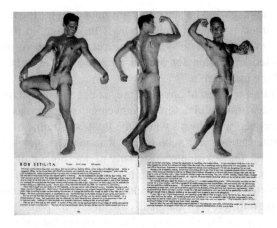

Fig. 9.2   *Physique Pictorial*, vol., 5, no. 1 (Spring 1955). Used with permission of the Bob Mizer Foundation.

homophile self-presentation was sharply regulated; "Dress and appearance will be conservative and conventional," the MSW insisted.[8] Indeed, the very name of the movement deliberately desexualized homosexuality, pinning its public image to the more ennobled ancient Greek connotations of *philo*, the higher sort of love etymologically unmoored to troublesome sexuality.

The ramifications of this respectability extended into numerous realms of homosexual public visibility, but erotic materials proved a particularly sensitive spot for homophile groups. With beefcake-driven physique magazines cited as "evidence" of homosexual perversity by such antigay agencies as the Florida Legislative Investigation Committee, whose 1964 expose *Homosexuality and Citizenship in Florida* deployed sensationalist "exposes" as stigmatizing devices, homophile groups found it necessary to distinguish themselves from this cultural terrain.[9]

In addition to this hypersexualized stigmatization, homophile publications faced the constant threat of obscenity charges no matter how far they removed themselves from the erotic world of smut or beefcake photos. For instance, *ONE*, a pioneering homophile magazine that faced scrutiny and suppression from postal authorities from its inception in 1953, ultimately spent most of the latter half of the decade defending itself in court from obscenity charges designed to keep its serious, non-erotic contents from circulating in the mails. In defending

---

[8]   Mattachine Society of Washington, "Regulations for Picketing" (29 May 1965), Craig Rodwell Papers, box 2, folder: 1965, International Gay Information Center Collection, New York Public Library.

[9]   Florida Legislative Investigation Committee, *Homosexuality and Citizenship in Florida* (Tallahassee, 1964), n.p.

itself, though, the magazine bolstered certain boundaries: "It can be agreed that being 'against smut' is entirely praiseworthy." In shoring up its own unsmutty respectability, *ONE* declined to defend prurience on its own merits.[10] As the Mattachine Society of Washington argued, "a distinction must be made between the serious and the pleasurable."[11]

This deliberate exclusion of physique magazines and other erotically charged material from the "official" homophile movement operated according to clear and logical directives, and always within the tight constraints of state-sponsored violence, criminalization, and subjugation that marked gay life in the Cold War era. Certainly the revisionist historians of the homophile movement are correct to refocus primary culpability on the various legal, cultural, and political mechanisms of heteronormativity that mandated a sexually desiccated vision of gay self-identity as the only one even marginally tolerable in the public sphere (salacious representations of queer life always remained available for sensationalized—and antigay—media discourse).

Yet even with that severe imbalance of power noted, homophile anti-eroticism sacrificed a great deal of gay interest and activity at the altar of respectability. Not only were physique magazines a booming site of gay cultural production and consumption at mid-century, but they often espoused an unacknowledged politics complementary to the homophile agenda. Bob Mizer's *Physique Pictorial*, in many ways the flagship enterprise of physique culture, embodied this; its readers might be considered the silent gay majority of the homophile era—at least, silent to the ears of the Mattachine. In fact, they had a great deal to say, and Mizer provided them a frequent forum to express it.

Begun in Los Angeles almost concurrently with the Mattachine Society, *Physique Pictorial* devoted its first several years to photographs of scantily clad men, generally in athletic poses that provided erotic stimulation alongside the social alibi of bodily self-improvement. Publisher Bob Mizer had begun even earlier, founding the Athletic Model Guild (AMG) in 1945 to distribute his photographs. Governmental persecution resulted in a half-year 1947 federal prison sentence for the youthful Mizer (born in 1922) for sending obscene pictures through the mails. Undaunted, Mizer reconfigured his work into a magazine, *Physique Pictorial*, in 1951. While kept separate from the homophile movement, *Physique* nonetheless took on the role of feeder, routing its readers toward gay rights activism despite the absence of expressed appreciation from the organs of the movement. Over time, *Physique Pictorial* would move beyond this silent-partner role to develop a significant voice of its own, presented collectively through both Mizer's editorials and its printed reader letters.

In its first few years, *Physique* existed primarily as a bound version of the work already undertaken by AMG, simply compiling attractive, enticing photographs

---

10   William Lambert, "Editorial," *ONE* (April 1958), pp. 4–5.

11   Mattachine Society of Washington, "Washington Section," *Eastern Mattachine Magazine*, November–December 1965, n.p.

with minimal verbal editorial intervention. Based out of the modest house just outside downtown Los Angeles on West 11th Street where his widowed mother had raised him and his brother, Mizer did not garnish *Physique Pictorial* in lavish graphic design, utilizing a spartan aesthetic of several dozen small, black and white pages. Photographs of loincloth-clad men wrestling and posing, with nudity limited to backside shots, and scattered sketch-art representations of similar scenarios, dominated its pages. What seems to have shifted this framework toward greater verbal content was yet another homophobic set of obscenity charges against Mizer. By 1954, heterosexual magazines like *Playboy* graced the magazine-rack landscape everywhere, legitimizing eroticized nudity to an unprecedented level. This failed to prevent Los Angeles authorities, spurred on by such feverishly antigay fear-mongering as that of *Mirror* newspaper columnist Paul Coates's repeated attacks, from arresting Mizer for the depictions of the male body offered by *Physique*.[12]

The week of Mizer's arrest, "that lusty Busty Brown," also known as "Miss Anatomy," was advertised performing her "big strip-a-thon" burlesque show at Strip City on Western and Pico, not far from Mizer's own studio.[13] The double standard could hardly be more blatant, and Mizer's trial was even worse, a sham in which the city displayed nude photographs not properly filed as exhibitions nor actually found in Mizer's possession and described his wrestling photographs as "scenes of brutality and torture" to secure a conviction. While Mizer managed to have the conviction (and two-month jail sentence) overturned on appeal, the episode politicized him, as would be reflected in *Physique*'s pages, where he provided the sole editorial voice.[14] Meanwhile, homophile venue *ONE*, facing its own postal obscenity charges during Mizer's ordeal, engaged in extensive polemics against ideologically motivated obscenity charges but avoided comment on Mizer's case. While the Mattachine had in large part built its reputation in gay circles through its legal defense of member Dale Jennings after his arrest for cruising in a park, it made no discernible effort to provide Mizer assistance or highlight his case as similar in nature.[15]

Into this discursive void, Mizer launched a newly impassioned *Physique Pictorial*. Beginning in the spring 1955 edition—volume five—the photographic content held steady, but the editorial voice rose in volume. "In California private homes are searched (without warrants), and it is held by some courts that mere possession of a nude photograph is a crime," Mizer's unsigned editorial declared

---

[12]   For Coates columns that directly called for action against Mizer in the days before his arrest, see Coates's "Well, Medium, and RARE" column, *Mirror* (4 May 1954 and 18 May 1954).

[13]   Strip City advertisement, *Los Angeles Examiner* (20 May 1954).

[14]   Respondent's Brief, *People v. Mizer* case file, Municipal Court of Los Angeles No. 23722 (1954), Los Angeles County Record Center.

[15]   C. Todd White, *Pre-Gay L.A.: A social history of the movement for homosexual rights* (Urbana: University of Illinois Press, 2009), pp. 23–7.

before delivering an inflammatory comparison to Nazi Germany.[16] If the parallel was a bit facile, the anger was evident and well earned. Not only did Mizer posit the publishing of the magazine as an act of political resistance, but he also solicited readers to understand themselves as linked in a quasi-criminal underground simply by virtue of their consumer choices. In this, the circulation of *Physique* culled a gay counterpublic into being.

Mizer proved capable of redirecting oppressive tropes against themselves. While the conflation of homosexuality and communism as entwined attacks on the American family was a core organizing principle of Cold War discourse, Mizer in 1960 wondered instead, "Is the So-Called 'Anti-Smut' Campaign Communist Inspired?"[17] Turning the tables on those who smeared homosexuality with unflattering but ostensibly descriptive terms, Mizer also claimed "Perverts and Degenerates are Often Severely Critical of Physical Culture Magazines," a theme he would often return to in suggesting it was those who so relentlessly persecuted benign bodily celebration who harbored the truly perverse sexual obsessions.[18] Mizer could be quite sly in these tactics, in 1959 responding to hate mail that condemned the "sexual overtones" of the magazine by suggesting "the letter-writer may have a problem similar to that of the minister in the Sommerset-Maughm [sic] story 'Rain,'" the reference presumably intended to slip past uninformed readers but wink to knowing gay ones.[19]

In the absence of an organized homophile voice of protest against police attacks on physique culture, *Physique* meticulously documented the recurring persecution from the LAPD against itself and physique readers, which ranged from low-intensity casual harassment of the AMG studio to allegedly warrantless home invasions in which the police stormed into a private 1961 house party "like a bunch of cockroaches," arrested everyone, and searched the house for nude photographs.[20] *Physique* also provided an important service in reporting obscenity

---

[16] Editorial, *Physique Pictorial*, Spring 1955, p. 2. Mizer's editorials remained unsigned because, as he explained, "*Physique Pictorial*'s editor has no intention of being a martyr and hasn't the finances for an armored car and bodyguard." Editor's note, *Physique Pictorial* (Spring 1958), p. 7.

[17] "Is the So-Called 'Anti-Smut' Campaign Communist Inspired?" *Physique Pictorial* (August 1960), p. 18.

[18] "Perverts and Degenerates are Often Severely Critical of Physical Culture Magazines," *Physique Pictorial* (November 1961), p. 7.

[19] Letter and Editor's response, *Physique Pictorial* (Spring 1959), p. 9. W. Somerset Maugham was already understood by the reading public—and especially by gay circles— as a problematic but quite homosexually inclined author by the 1950s. While not gay in nature, his story "Rain" involved a missionary whose efforts at morally policing others masked repressed prurient interests of his own. On Maugham's place in mid-century culture, see Michael Sherry, *Gay Artists in Modern American Culture: An imagined conspiracy* (Durham: Duke University Press, 2007), p. 53.

[20] "How 'Safe' is Your Photo Collection?" *Physique Pictorial* (Fall 1958), p. 19; "Los Angeles Police Claim You May Not Have a Collection of Nude Photographs in Your Private Home," *Physique Pictorial* (August 1961), p. 3.

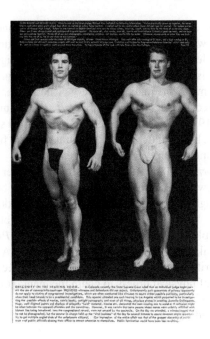

Fig. 9.3   *Physique Pictorial*, vol. 6, no. 1 (Spring 1956). Used with permission of the Bob Mizer Foundation.

campaigns against other physique distributors, like the travails of New York photographer Al Urban, also generally omitted from the homophile press, again presumably for reasons of respectability.[21] The anger of Mizer's prose, evident even in these brief examples, differed from the more conciliatory homophile style, but reflected an awareness of the sheer homophobic brutality that was unlikely to allow social space for a civil dialogue (see Figure 9.3).

The cost of Mizer's outspokenness was an avoidance of direct acknowledgment of homosexuality. The combination of open homosexuality and eroticism remained de facto illegal in the heteronormative legal strictures of postwar obscenity law, a threat very tangible to Mizer after the repeated criminalizations of his work.[22] It was a mutually exclusive binary in the 1950s. While the homophile movement had chosen open, if desexualized, homosexuality, Mizer, precluded from embracing both aspects, of necessity swerved away from ever addressing the seemingly obvious.

[21]   "Photographer Seeks Financial Aid to Appeal Unjust New York Conviction," *Physique Pictorial* (January 1961), p. 12; "New York Photographer Wins Appeals Case on Nudes," *Physique Pictorial* (March 1962), p. 2.

[22]   Whitney Strub, "The Clearly Obscene and the Queerly Obscene: Heteronormativity and Obscenity in Cold War Los Angeles," *American Quarterly* 60.2 (2008): pp. 373–98.

In its approach to coating homosexuality with the thinnest veneer available, *Physique Periodical* went beyond most of its peer publications. *Adonis*, a Jersey City magazine founded in 1954, opted for coded language of a meeker sort, beginning its second issue with a statement of purpose vaguely explaining, "It is not easy to publish a magazine that delves into uncharted seas of public opinion." "Pensiveness" emerged as a recurring motif in *Adonis*'s picture captions of moody muscularity, and by 1957 the magazine delicately broached subculturally specific language in calling its bodybuilder subjects "debutants who first 'came out' in this magazine" before launching into even greater renown.[23]

Meanwhile, *Tomorrow's Man*, which began near-concurrently in Chicago before shortly moving to New York, adopted more circumlocutory tactics, insinuating its heterosexuality through recurring invocations of bodybuilders' allure to women and the invigorating "sight of a pretty girl."[24] Another approach to situating physique culture, employed by the Ridgefield, New Jersey *Physique World* in the early 1960s, was to link it to Cold War nationalism; with the American body politic identified with the virile masculinity of President John F. Kennedy, the magazine cited his celebration of physical fitness to claim the mantle of Americanism. "The entire physique field wishes to thank the President," it proclaimed, "for telling the nation that taking good care and being proud of one's body isn't anything to be ashamed of."[25]

While the nature of these alibis varied, all included at least some subtle nod toward gay readers; if *Adonis* took the most obvious (or clumsy) approach, *Tomorrow's Man*'s near-obsessive referencing of the Kinsey reports and the harmlessness of masturbation obliquely hinted at the varieties of sexual desire and expression located beyond the admired and admiring women of its surface rhetoric. Given Kinsey's notoriety for documenting the widespread homoerotic activities of American men, the mere celebratory citation of his reports in the charged erotic context of a physique magazine could itself serve as a queer signifier.[26] Even in positioning itself alongside the supremely hetero-phallic JFK, *Physique World*

---

[23] "Foreword," *Adonis*, issue 2 (n.d., 1954), p. 3; "The Pleasure is Requested," *Adonis* (March 1957), p. 4. For "pensive" captions, see "The Moody Pensiveness of Steve is Reflected Here," *Adonis* (April 1956), p. 6; "The Deep Pensiveness of Youth," *Adonis* (May 1957), p. 15.

[24] David Huntly, "Your Sex Personality," *Adonis* (March 1959), p. 7; Lou Sand, "Females Prefer He-Males," *Tomorrow's Man* (June 1956), pp. 6–7.

[25] Untitled statement inside front cover, *Physique World*, no. 2 (n.d., c.1961).

[26] For *Tomorrow's Man* masturbation and Kinsey discussion, see: Geo. MacGregor, M.D., "Three Vital Sex Questions," *Tomorrow's Man* (April 1953), pp. 26–9; "Those Kinsey Reports," *Tomorrow's Man* cover (March 1954); Lou Sand, "The Truth About Masturbation," *Tomorrow's Man* (May 1956), pp. 6–8, p. 22; David Huntley, "Looking at Masturbation Sensibly," *Tomorrow's Man* (January 1958), pp. 6–7, p. 38. On Kinsey's media circulation and cultural meaning, see Miriam Reumann, *American Sexual Character: Sex, gender, and national identity in the Kinsey Reports* (Berkeley: University of California Press, 2005).

nodded to more hostile times, reminding readers that "during some harassing periods *one* institution, like a voice in the wilderness, has carried on a strong and often lonely battle to fight physical decay." The nature of that harassment went unarticulated but was presumptively transparent.

While also availing itself of some necessary alibis and evasions, *Physique Pictorial* went beyond many of its peers in its rhetorical engagements with homosexuality. Unable to simply declare its own origins, *Physique* made a point of taking a nonjudgmental stance that, in the context of the 1950s, was itself deeply counternormative. When magazine *Iron Man* "sounded the alarm that homosexuals are invading the bodybuilding field" in 1956, *Physique* responded not with direct denial, but with an interrogation of the allegation's significance. "We wonder," Mizer wrote, "if really good people show prejudice against any minority group." Employing a set of comparisons directly informed by Mattachine founder Harry Hay's trailblazing analysis of homosexuals as a distinct, oppressed social minority, Mizer's essay mused, "What difference does it make if a bodybuilder is Catholic or Protestant, white or black, Republican or Democrat, homosexual or heterosexual." A follow-up letter from a mother of four bodybuilding sons, three happily married and one homosexual, went beyond even toleration to recommend affirmation: after her son confessed to her, "Mrs. RT" wrote, she took him to a psychiatrist, who instead of trying to rehabilitate his sexuality (the prevailing practice of the time), "told us it would be impossible to change the boy's nature" and instead advocated accepting his condition. "At first I was heartbroken but am now reconciled. John lives with another young man who shares his interests, both are highly successful in films ... and I am now as proud of Dick as any of my other children. Thanks for your own sympathetic attitude" she concluded—a striking tale to reach print in such a fraught context.[27]

Mizer's response to the *Iron Man* attack concluded by suggesting, "We understand that those who want factual information about the so-called homosexual problem can get free literature without their name going on a mailing list," and gave the addresses of One, Inc. and the *Mattachine Review*.[28] Indeed, despite the movement's disregard and even hostility toward his work, Mizer deliberately crafted *Physique Pictorial* as a router to send readers toward homophile groups. The magazine's strong defense of civil liberties included numerous urgings to donate to such groups as the American Civil Liberties Union, but Mizer also frequently encouraged support for the Mattachine Society, One, Inc., and other homophile groups. When the San Francisco homophile group League for Civil Education was founded in the early 1960s, Mizer quickly highlighted it and wrote,

---

[27] "Homosexuality and Bodybuilding," *Physique Pictorial* (Fall 1956), p. 17; Mrs. RT, letter, *Physique Pictorial* (Spring 1957), p. 4. It is impossible to verify the accuracy of the letter, and most of the magazine's correspondence files were lost after Mizer's 1992 death. Most important was the sheer fact of the letter's printing. Author correspondence with Dennis Bell, Owner, Athletic Model Guild, 24 May 2011.

[28] "Homosexuality and Bodybuilding."

"the publisher of the paper is a real fighter."[29] While it remains impossible to quantify the number of readers Mizer directed toward homophile groups, there is no reason to doubt his effect in both encouraging political consciousness and making readers aware of the institutional topography of the movement.

Undergirding much of *Physique Pictorial*'s political project was an endorsement, albeit often tacitly rendered, of pleasure—sexual, bodily, spectatorial, and otherwise—as a legitimate end in itself. This complemented its visual celebration of the male body and periodically floated near the rhetorical surface as well. In a typical 1957 rant against suppressive "police goon squads," Mizer bemoaned that Big Brother "quite decidedly dictates your sex life, and wants to imprison you if you don't accept his limitations on art censorship."[30] The implicit defense of pleasure—by negative example—was even more pronounced in a satirical call for recruits to join the "Anti-Pleasure League": "To be a member you must be willing to find an evil interpretation in everything people do which causes them happiness. A prime target of course is the joyous jubilation found in physical culture and the graphic presentation of beautiful bodies."[31] In this phrasing, Mizer dispensed with the Cold War-hopping alibis and simply suggested the sheer sensuous pleasure of his text lay at the heart of the various attacks on his publication—which routed pleasure and "jubilation" away from the legitimized productive ends of the heteronormative status quo.

The magazine frequently made clear that the constraints of its images—contorted poses to avoid full nudity and such tactics—were strictly a function of the prevailing obscenity regime and not the desire of the publisher or readership; inviting artists to submit in 1956, *Physique* clarified that they must "restrict themselves to the same pseudo-moral taboos required of photographers," including an avoidance of pubic hair and "sensual situations implying a primary carnal interpretation."[32] Again, it remained unspoken but evident that such material would be gladly included were it not for the restrictiveness of authorities.

If that stance followed a clear, pragmatic legal logic, it did not always satisfy *Physique*'s readers. In opening the magazine's pages to reader letters, Mizer further helped constitute a gay counterpublic with its own expression of interest and desire, not always in congruence with the positions of the homophile movement. From the start, *Physique* asked for reader input even on such matters as a 1955 inquiry on "the type of lighting you prefer," and over the years it printed dozens

---

[29] "Feisty Little Paper is Published in San Francisco," *Physique Pictorial* (May 1962), p. 7. See also: "Have You Submitted Your Application for Membership in the 'Anti-Fun' Club?" *Physique Pictorial* (May 1964), p. 23.

[30] "Big Brother is Still Eager to Control Your Life," *Physique Pictorial* (Summer 1957), p. 9.

[31] "Recruits Now Being Sought for the 'Anti-Pleasure League'!" *Physique Pictorial* (Fall 1955), p. 12.

[32] "New Artists are Invited to Market Their Work," *Physique Pictorial* (Summer 1956), p. 15.

of reader letters on various topics.[33] The strongest desire was for greater nudity. "RS" from Muskegon, Michigan canceled his subscription in 1955 because "I don't care for the amount of space taken up by 'editorials,'" and also because "the pictures have covering."[34] As "JL" from Athol, Washington put it in 1959, "You pious hypocrites at *Physique Pictorial* make me sick" and demanded that if the magazine refused to publish nudes, it at least supply addresses for companies that would. Mizer's remarkably even-keeled response acknowledged, "We cannot give logical answers to some of JL's questions" but only "feebly suggest" that society needed to be better educated before it would accept such representations.[35] Forced into the role of mediator, Mizer refused to dismiss or silence such critics, instead attempting to defuse their complaints by situating physique culture in the legal straits of inevitable prosecution were it to even publish the requested addresses, with the constant suggestion that political activity was necessary to change this.

Transmuting expressions of frustrated desire into concrete political avenues to demand change, Mizer supplied the unacknowledged erotic supplement to homophile respectability. Just as Daniel Hurewitz locates the interpellative "Althusserian moment" of gay identity formation through the state-sponsored police crackdowns of the 1930s in Los Angeles, Mizer harnessed the ubiquity of repressive censorship practices to solicit a politicized gay identity through the demand for the right to erotic self-fulfillment.[36] While homophile groups in many ways assumed pre-existing gay identities, Mizer deliberately coaxed them into being as intrinsically political entities, prodding readers to recognize (and resist) the criminality of their desires and consumer practices.

Police harassment extended beyond Mizer and the AMG studio, frequently targeting readers and subscribers. Again, Mizer consistently linked their plight to larger issues of civil liberties and encouraged their support for groups like the ACLU, which is what Mizer recommended when New Orleans reader "DS" asked for no further mailings to be sent his way after local post office officials threatened to "close down my box and literally destroy me and my business if I get any more of this kind of material whatsoever."[37] When readers complained of Mizer's incessant touting of the ACLU, he defended it (see Figure 9.4). To a Rochester, New York reader who accused the group of defending "known subversives who threaten the welfare of our country," Mizer replied that the United States was "strong enough ... to take any amount of criticism." When a priest from an undisclosed location found Mizer's political harangues tiresome and requested he "be more positive," Mizer offered a polite but uncompromising rejoinder that "we really believe that protest is essential." In the comment, Mizer added that he

---

[33] Untitled note, *Physique Pictorial* (Spring 1955), p. 6.

[34] RS, letter, *Physique Pictorial* (Winter 1955), p. 2.

[35] JL, letter, *Physique Pictorial* (Spring 1959), p. 13.

[36] Daniel Hurewitz, *Bohemian Los Angeles and the Making of Modern Politics* (Berkeley: University of California Press, 2007), pp. 115–50.

[37] Letter from DS, *Physique Pictorial* (May 1962), p. 16.

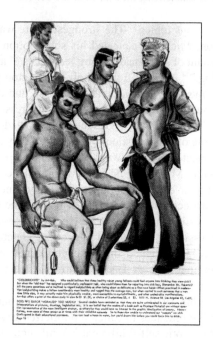

Fig. 9.4   *Physique Pictorial*, vol. 6, no. 1 (Spring 1956). Used with permission
of the Bob Mizer Foundation.

envisioned part of *Physique*'s role as "helping to wake our readers to the threat of
'the oppressors,'" in the hopes that they might "join effective groups which will
fight the wicked ones."[38]

If Mizer's editorial touch could at times verge on the heavy handed, *Physique
Pictorial* did nonetheless provide space—in fact, some of the *only* space in the
formal public sphere of Cold War America—for men to collectively negotiate a
print-culture eros. Expressing gratitude for a set of shower photos in 1960, a Duluth
reader praised the "pleasing, more natural type of posing" as superior to the usual
"stilted, phony muscle posing."[39] Not all readers approved: one 1961 published
letter began, "Oh, you think you're clever, but when I look at those pictures I
know exactly the filthy intention" and enlisted God in the quest to eliminate such
"filth peddlers."[40] Mostly, though, readers articulated specific desires, frequently
in the form of complaints. While a Delaware reader in 1955 supported "the current
de-emphasis on massive builds," a 1957 Cincinnati reader objected to the models'
posing straps, explaining, "it's just that trunks and levis seem more natural—like

---

[38]   Letter from LP, *Physique Pictorial* (July 1962), p. 31; letter from OR, *Physique
Pictorial*, p. 12.

[39]   Spring 1960 letter, quoted in Waugh, *Hard to Imagine*, p. 239.

[40]   Anonymous letter, January 1961, *Physique Pictorial*, p. 2.

the guy next door."[41] A Missouri reader lamented "the incongruity in physique magazines showing people eating their breakfast, vacuuming the floor, mowing the lawn, etc. all in jock straps." Articulating a specific calibration of the erotics of concealment and revealing, he reasoned that since "normal people don't do that sort of thing," clothes would "add a desirable, modest mystery." The very choice of terms in the suggestion belied any ostensible prudishness, instead framing modesty as itself erotic.[42]

In all of these letters, and even in such complaints as an alibi-laden inquiry, "Why don't you dig up some real men instead of a bunch of sallow faced babies. They all look like a bunch of fairies to me," a palpable sense of desire, collectively negotiated in the public sphere (albeit through initialized names, of necessity), permeated the pages of *Physique Pictorial*. While it certainly befitted Mizer's economic imperatives to generate that sense, the result was an admittedly editorially mediated, ongoing group dialogue that spanned the years, fostering precisely the sense of collectivity upon which community-building rests, with the feeling of belonging cultivated by the shared sense of pleasure and desire in looking at male bodies.[43]

The community had its limits. Exclusionary boundaries in physique culture paralleled those of homophile activism in many ways, privileging prevailing standards of "Americanness"—namely, a white leadership of activist groups and, in physique magazines, a racialized erotic imaginary of unmarked whiteness and exoticized bodies of color. Although David Johnson has recently tempered Tracy Morgan's powerful critique of physique culture's "abid[ing] by the rule of U.S. white supremacy," noting that when Latinos and mixed-race men are included, "the representations of minorities in physique magazines appears significantly better than most mainstream news of fitness magazines in 1950s and 1960s America," the glaring absence of bodies of color from *Physique*'s pages is undeniable.[44] The image of two loincloth-wearing "cowboys" surrounding a white "Indian" (in tribal headgear and loincloth, carrying a crossbow) in a 1958 photograph indicated the rather threadbare racial imagination of the magazine.[45]

The racial marking of men of color, when they appeared at all, did not go entirely unnoticed; one Ohio reader wrote to protest *Physique Pictorial*'s 1958 "all-negro" catalog as segregation. The magazine's editorial response reflected the facile liberal understanding of race sutured into both homophile and physique

---

[41] JB, letter, *Physique Pictorial* (Winter 1955), p. 2; CK, letter, *Physique Pictorial* (Spring 1957), p. 4.

[42] EC, letter, *Physique Pictorial* (Spring 1959), p. 4.

[43] DA, letter, *Physique Pictorial* (April 1961), p. 14.

[44] David Johnson, "Physique Pioneers," p. 887; Tracy Morgan, "The Pages of Whiteness: Race, Physique Magazines, and the Emergence of Public Gay Culture," in *Queer Studies: A Lesbian, Gay, Bisexual, and Transgender Anthology*, edited by Brett Beemyn and Mickey Eliason (New York: New York University Press, 1996), pp. 290–91.

[45] Untitled photograph, *Physique Pictorial* (Summer 1958), p. 9.

racialism: the catalog was "intended as a tribute, not a slight to that fine, healthy race ... we don't believe that all men are created equal—most of the colored boys we have met have definitely superior physiques to the average Caucasian."[46] Offensively awkward phrasing like "colored boys" did little to help the cause, but despite this, a glimpse of a more inclusive erotic imaginary was contained in D.E.H.'s letter, which Mizer dutifully entered into the public record.

Demands for gay visibility, coming from both homophile activists and physique readers and publishers, informed the cultural shifts of the 1960s sexual revolution, which in turn allowed for even greater visibility. A generation gap akin to that visible in civil rights, leftist, and feminist activism was pervasive in gay circles as well, and both homophile respectability and physique alibis appeared increasingly complacent to the new wave of proudly, openly gay activists. This shift would culminate in the claiming of the 1969 Stonewall rebellion for the cause of gay liberation, both openly sexual and radical in its agenda.[47]

Physique Pictorial navigated these developments somewhat uncomfortably; Mizer's arrests had left him frazzled, cautious about publishing nudes even as the dismantling of obscenity strictures allowed greater explicitness among his competitors.[48] When Philadelphia activist Clark Polak founded the openly gay *Drum* in 1964, he declared that "sexual stimulation is a valuable force," premising the magazine on an even bolder combination of eroticism and politics than Mizer had dared. When *Drum* published a critique of existing physique magazines, Mizer responded with a somewhat feeble rebuttal, explaining that "our portrayal of men in opposition to one another is done simply because it is one of the 'socially acceptable' ways for them to show off their muscles ... Photographing them in a display of affection would 'outrage' public decency."[49] Mizer was not entirely wrong—Polak's pioneering full-frontal nudes would prove lucrative but ultimately legally actionable—but he was, nonetheless, clearly on the defensive. By the time *Physique* finally announced it would feature nude photographs, in July 1968, it was far from a trailblazer, resting on the outcomes of legal battles fought by Polak and DSI, the Minneapolis firm of Lloyd Spinar and Conrad Germain.[50]

---

[46]   Letter from D.E.H. and response, *Physique Pictorial* (Spring 1958), p. 3.

[47]   Terence Kissack, "Freaking Fag Revolutionaries: New York's Gay Liberation Front, 1969–1971," *Radical History Review* 62 (1995), pp. 104–35.

[48]   Mizer discussed his self-described timidity regarding nudes in an oral history interview by Pat Allen and Valentine Hooven, 24 February 1992, audio cassette two of three, *ONE* National Gay and Lesbian Archives, Los Angeles, CA.

[49]   Clark Polak, "The Story Behind Physique Photography," *Drum*, October 1965; "Drum Tells What's Wrong with American Physique Magazines," *Physique Pictorial* (October 1965), p. 13.

[50]   Editor's note, *Physique Pictorial* (July 1968), p. 2. On Polak and *Drum*, see Marc Stein, *City of Sisterly and Brotherly Loves: Lesbian and gay Philadelphia, 1945–1972* (Philadelphia: Temple University Press, 2004), pp. 226–58. On the pivotal but mostly forgotten DSI, see Johnson, "Physique Pioneers," pp. 878–81.

Physique Pictorial's visual policy evolution followed its political self-positioning by several years. While remaining skittish about outright declarations of homosexual identity, Mizer grew less coy by the mid-1960s. In one typical Mattachine endorsement, he dismissed a Christian counselor's pamphlet on "How to Get Out of Gay Life" by recommending instead contacting the Mattachine to learn "How to Get the *Most* Out of Gay Life." A similar, even sharper tone was on display in a 1965 article cleverly declaring "Heterosexuality Can be Cured!" Presented as a future 2065 *Time* article, it began "Perhaps the most shocking thing about heterosexuality is its commonness," which included "at least one out of every six people." Looking back at an archaic twentieth-century institution, it tried to make sense of marriage: "this queer practice which is now recognized as being such a dangerous threat to our society that it could easily bring about our nation's downfall as it has that of so many former civilizations." Finally, leaving no antigay trope unturned on itself, the article concluded with a plea for tolerance, reminding readers that "it should be remembered that no one is born a hetero but rather picks up such bad habits because of unfortunate emotional experiences."[51]

Not only the sarcastic tone, but also the implicit notion of sexuality as a social construct, anticipated the radicalized gay liberation mindset of the late '60s/early '70s. Indeed, by the emergence of gay liberation, Mizer's vision of a desire-infused gay identity would resonate more with the youth generation than the perceived stodginess of the homophile movement. Certainly Mizer was no proto-liberationist, on many grounds; rarely did he challenge, or even acknowledge, the social constructions of race and gender that perpetuated various structures of hierarchy and privilege, and painfully tangible necessity contained his work within the antigay strictures of the Cold War era. Yet anticipatory glimpses of the "come out" mantras of gay liberation that linked the personal to the political were evident in Mizer's efforts to fuse desire and politics, using oppressive denials of consumer desire for nudity to encourage political consciousness and action, and in his insistence on gay erotics generally absent from the homophile movement—to which he nonetheless contributed, despite its intransigent refusal to acknowledge his efforts.

By the time of Stonewall, however, *Physique Pictorial* was something of a relic, a cultural position that helped relegate it to the margins of gay history by the generation of historians informed by the gay liberation activism of the 1970s. In the process, the ways in which *Physique* had helped cultivate the very development of a collective, public movement premised on both desire and resistance faded from view, as Mizer's efforts were superseded by more graphic, confrontational modes of textual pleasure and mobilization. By restoring *Physique* to its proper position alongside the homophile movement, we can better understand the conflicted genealogy of modern gay rights activism, rooted always in the interwoven political, commercial, and erotic spheres.

---

[51] Untitled editorial, *Physique Pictorial* (October 1964), p. 11; "Heterosexuality Can be Cured!" *Physique Pictorial* (June 1965), pp. 22–3.

Chapter 10
Calendar Art:
How the 1968 SNCC Wall Calendar
Brought Activism Indoors

Lián Amaris

In 1966 photographer, activist, and writer Julius Lester (*To Be A Slave*, 1969 Newbery Honor Book; *Day of Tears*, 2006 Coretta Scott King Award) joined the photography department of the Student Non-Violent Coordinating Committee (SNCC) and for documentation purposes spent several months traveling through Mississippi, Alabama, and Louisiana photographing black communities. During his time in those states, he saw many black families with walls postered in calendars, comic strips, and advertisements—but nowhere did he see images of black people represented. In a consciousness-raising effort to promote awareness and pride, Lester created a wall calendar using his own photographs and other photos from the SNCC files. The calendars included photographs of non-white people and important dates in black history and were distributed in 1967 to families in Mississippi. The statement on the last page of the calendar is as follows:

> The history of black people in the United States is the story of resistance, one of the longest stories of resistance in the history of man. Black people never accepted slavery or the involuntary servitude that followed slavery. From the rebellions on slave ships to the rebellions of today, our history is one of resistance. Nat Turner, Gabriel Prosser, Denmark Vessey, Frederick Douglass, W.E.B. DuBois [sic], Herbert Lee, Fannie Lou Hamer are just a few of the more well-known individuals who have fought in their own way.
>
> But our resistance struggle has taken many forms. During slavery it took the form of song and story and the ingratiating smile which disturbed the tranquility of many a white man. It also took the form of spiders in the soup, broken farm tools, accidental on purpose fires and murder.
>
> There were acts of resistance, as those above but blacks in America lived in such a way that their lives were an act of resistance. They used to say we were happy, because we sang, danced and made music with such zest, but they didn't understand our will to live, no matter how much they might consider us as property. They took away our drums; we just started clapping our hands. They took away our tribes and languages; we simply fashioned English to our own tongues and made our own new language, one that had the tonal variety of our mother tongues and one they could not understand. They tried to take from us

everything that told us who we were, but they couldn't. In our very souls we
resisted, biding our time, waiting for the day when we could strike the final blow
for our liberty.

This calendar marks the 349th year of our resistance struggle and is dedicated to
the solemn memory of those martyred in the rebellions of 1967 and to the lasting
glory of the heroes and heroines of those rebellions.

For the purposes of this essay, I analyze the SNCC calendar as a medium for
communication from a media ecology perspective, which as a discipline takes
as its main concern "how media of communication affect human perception,
understanding, feeling, and value; and how our interaction with media facilitates
or impedes our chances of survival."[1] My approach to the SNCC calendar is
consistent with the work of media ecologists such as Marshal McLuhan who, in his
most influential work, *Understanding Media: The Extensions of Man*, contributes
to a "broadening of the meaning of 'medium' ... [and] devotes chapters to media
such as the spoken word, roads, numbers, clothing, housing, money, clocks,
the automobile, games, and weapons, in addition to the major mass media and
communication technologies."[2] Through this lens, I will address how the SNCC's
utilization of calendars as "media of communication" functioned to create a
counter-archive of images of non-white people; to literally insert black identity into
the structural representation of time, thereby figuratively inserting black identity
into a daily experience; and to claim actual dates in a historical timeline in the
name of counter-hegemony, ostensibly rewriting history and actively combating
erasure. Also included in this essay are excerpts from an in-depth interview with
Julius Lester, the creator of the calendar, more than 40 years later, addressing his
experience as a black photographer during the Civil Rights Movement.

Lester spent the spring of 1966 under the auspices of the Newport Folk
Foundation traveling around the Mississippi delta, Alabama, and Louisiana
looking for people who "remembered the old music." He was trying to put together
festivals of indigenous music, and in the process of talking with people and doing
his research, Lester went into many homes on plantations. He recalled, "I noticed
that people had calendars on their walls, calendars that were often from previous
years. The walls of some of the homes were covered with the color comic strips
from Sunday papers. The calendars pictured white women, of course, but what
occurred to me was that the people wanted something 'beautiful' to look at, that
perhaps there is within all of us a need for, an instinct for, beauty."[3] A few months
later Lester went to work full time for the SNCC as a photographer. During his

---

[1]   Neil Postman, "The Reformed English Curriculum," in A.C. Eurich, ed., *High
school 1980: The shape of the future in American secondary education* (New York: Pitman,
1970), p. 161.

[2]   Lance Strate, "A Media Ecology Review," *Communication Research Trends* 23/2
(2004), p. 7.

[3]   Lester, Julius. Interview by author, November 2008.

Fig. 10.1   Julius Lester, "1968 Calendar: Student Nonviolent Coordinating Committee." © Julius Lester.

early time there, he went through the previous SNCC photo files and came across negatives and several prints made by SNCC photographers before him. It was then that Lester realized he wanted to "create a calendar that would have images of blacks and other non-whites and to give the calendars to poor blacks in Mississippi so they could look at people more like themselves."[4]

Janet Sternberg explains, "Media ecologists investigate how different media environments encourage and discourage, facilitate and impede, allow and deny, foster and prevent certain ways of perceiving, feeling, thinking, and evaluating ourselves and the world around us."[5] From this perspective we see that the print media environment of the Southern, rural, black family as Lester witnessed and described was limited at best and, at its worst, explicitly discouraged, impeded, denied, and prevented certain ways of addressing or seeing the world. As I will discuss, the calendar functioned on two levels, image and print, to act as a corrective to invisibility and socio-historical amnesia. Lester states,

---

[4]   Lester, Interview.

[5]   Janet Sternberg, *Misbehavior in cyber places: The regulation of online conduct in virtual communities on the Internet* (New York: New York University Press, 2001), p. 20.

... the images in the calendar are clearly documentary in nature. The concern of SNCC photography was to make a visual record of the lives of ordinary black people in the rural south, especially. These were the people who were the most invisible, so it was very important to create images that showed their resilience, their dignity, their strength, their joys. Art was used in the service of documenting these lives.[6]

It is within the print media environment that Lester and the SNCC clearly attempted to encourage, facilitate, allow, and foster a new way of "perceiving, feeling, thinking, and evaluating ourselves and the world around us," indeed, focusing attention on an inclusive "us" that meant to address those who were so limited in access both to and within print culture. Interestingly enough the "us" within the calendar extends beyond the Southern Black community: included in the calendar are two photographs of people in North Vietnam, which explicitly positions the calendar politically. Lester strategically included the photographs to "widen people's perceptions" on a global scale. He states, "The inclusion of the North Vietnam photos was an attempt to expand the consciousness of people about what they were a part of ... Blacks were a minority only in the US. In the world, blacks belonged to the majority because the majority of people in the world are not white."[7] Again, from a media ecological perspective, the SNCC calendar utilizes the print medium to foster a new way to see the world—the world that extends beyond the walls of a house and the streets of a neighborhood to even cross oceans consistent with media theorist Marshall McLuhan's concept of the "global village."[8] The calendar viewer is therefore entreated to engage on many levels as they see themselves in relation to the images the SNCC and Lester have provided, and it is within this context that "poor blacks in Mississippi" are identified by Lester as the intended audience.

In her comprehensive study of W.E.B. Du Bois, Shawn Michelle Smith "... models a critical methodology that sees race as fundamental to and defined by visual culture ... and that reads photographic archives as racialized sites invested in laying claim to contested cultural meanings."[9] It is within this methodology that I similarly situate the SNCC calendar as a photographic archive that attempts to re-imag(in)e representations of non-white people through the photographs taken by SNCC members. If visual culture has the ability to define race, as Smith suggests, then the SNCC took on a great responsibility certainly in their documentary photography, but even more so in the tangible object or artifact— a calendar—of this photography. That calendar-as-artifact enters into the schema of visual culture in direct opposition to other more mass-produced advertisements,

---

[6]   Lester, Interview.

[7]   Ibid.

[8]   Marshal McLuhan, *The Gutenberg Galaxy: The making of typographic man* (Toronto: University of Toronto Press, 1962), p. 43.

[9]   Shawn Michelle Smith, *Photography on the Color Line: W. E. B. Du Bois, race, and visual culture* (Durham, NC: Duke University Press, 2004), p. 3.

prints, clippings, and so on, that serve the dominant narrative as a kind of "beauty" that may also be pinned on a wall. Always strategic, Lester points out, "The beauty of the people I photographed in the south was not restricted to the young, was not restricted to the well-dressed. The beauty was one of character reflected in the faces of people who had been subjected to political and economic repression and they had not only endured but they had prevailed in a dignity I saw in their faces, in the joy they had wrested from a life that, seen from the outside, would define them only as being oppressed."[10] As Smith recommends, this engagement with visual culture, specifically through the documentary photographs, is indeed "laying a claim to contested cultural meanings" by challenging what images could be produced and reproduced in this archival form.

Similarly, Michael Harris proposes "… that images approximated texts in the sense that they were a means of writing the African [and African American] self into history and culture."[11] Indeed, Lester's observations of the walls of Southern rural homes reinforce the need for an inclusive visual history; therefore, the SNCC calendar specifically acts as a vehicle for insertion of the African American self not only into history but culture—insofar as culture can be disseminated through a visual print medium. Furthermore, because images of black people are sites of meaning-making in a white-dominated culture, influence over their production is imperative in order to challenge racism and redress image-based representation. Again, the strategic mission of the calendar itself was to produce and present content that clearly reflected the audience for which it was intended, with a kind of "by us, of us, for us" objective. Harris points out, "images are produced by the few to be consumed but seldom manipulated by the masses," but the SNCC calendar functioned as a corrective to that challenge.[12] Lester recalls, "One of the most interesting aspects of the experience for me was that people had never had their pictures taken. That's hard to believe now, but in 1966 images were not as ubiquitous as they are now, cameras were not common. So, the people were flattered that I would want to take their picture, and when I put the camera up to my eye, some of them would stand erect and look directly into the camera because this was an important occasion for them. This was especially true of the old people."[13] The subjects of Lester's photographs clearly understood the significance of this photographic event within their own lives; however, their images would also become part of an important new archive of black history. Smith warns, "if one cannot or does not produce an archive, others will dictate the terms by which one will be represented and remembered; one will exist, for the future, in someone else's archive."[14] Consistent with this anxiety over

---

[10]   Lester, Interview.

[11]   Michael Harris, *Colored Pictures: Race and visual representation* (Chapel Hill: University of North Carolina Press, 2006), pp. 252–3.

[12]   Harris, p. 15.

[13]   Lester, Interview.

[14]   Smith, p. 9.

representation and dissemination, Lester was critical of the Farm Security Administration's contribution to the photographic archive as they documented the black rural south:

> ... in the FSA photographs there are many images of black poverty, northern and southern, and those photographs were exposing conditions in the country that people didn't know about; it was protest photography. That's not what I was doing ... A photograph is always a picture of the relationship between the photographer and the person, object, landscape being photographed. So, a photograph tells you as much about the photographer as whatever is in the image. So, it is very easy to go to the black rural south and see the poverty if you have not been around poverty or black people ... I knew poverty because on rainy days the poor kids didn't come to school because their shoes had holes in them, or they didn't have the right clothes, or whatever. Because my grandmother lived in a house in Pine Bluff, Arkansas, much like the ones I saw in Mississippi, when I was photographing in the south I did not see the poverty. What I saw was the dignity and beauty of the people. A black or white photographer from the north would not have necessarily seen what I saw.[15]

Particularly resonant with Lester's critique is Du Bois's concept of "The Veil" that "shrouds African Americans in *in*visibility by making misrepresentations of blackness overwhelmingly *visible*."[16] This is not to suggest that the FSA photographs were inherently misrepresentational, but rather that, though they were widely available and provocative, they were limited in scope and agenda and specifically focused on poverty, rather than the breadth of experiences that Lester and the other SNCC photographers attempted to document. This apparent crisis over control of the image (both its production and its dissemination) implies that to produce images of oneself is an affirmation of selfhood that would otherwise be annihilated within white, hegemonic systems of representation. Therefore, the SNCC calendar, and the SNCC documentation efforts, recuperate selfhood and empower both the subject of the photograph and the viewer of the images.

John Berger, similarly to Harris, believes that if the "... language of images were used differently, it would through its use, confer a new kind of power ... Not only personal experience, but also the essential historical experience of our relation to the past: that is to say the experience of seeking to give meaning to our lives, of trying to understand the history of which we can become the active agents."[17] I wish to suggest that the alchemy of personal experience (the moment caught on camera) and the placement of those personal experiences within the SNCC calendar and within the larger context of the Civil Rights Movement, is precisely the kind of power that Berger suggests and that the SNCC manifested

---

[15]   Lester, Interview.

[16]   Smith, p. 40.

[17]   John Berger, *Ways of Seeing* (London: Penguin Group, 1972), p. 33.

Julius Lester
Atlanta, Georgia

Fig. 10.2   Julius Lester, "1968 Calendar: Student Nonviolent Coordinating Committee." © Julius Lester.

through the work. It is precisely at the juncture of personal and historical that I am able to locate the SNCC calendar as produced by politicized black activists who were able to "reconfigure the racialized structures of the gaze."[18] As I will discuss later in relation to the use of the calendar form, the images and historical dates used in the SNCC calendar informed new understandings of history with regard to personal experience and promoted an empowered agency of the viewer, performing the very things for which Harris, Smith, and Berger plead.

By placing the camera in the hands of politically and racially conscious photographers, the SNCC calendar functions as a corrective to "Du Bois' articulation of double consciousness as the 'sense of always looking at one's self through the eyes of others.'"[19] Lester addresses this directly as he acknowledges the advantages he had as a black photographer:

> ... because I was black, and there was an immediate comfort level between people and myself; I was connected to the civil rights movement, and this gave me immediate acceptance. In Mississippi, blacks called all of us "freedom riders." If you were a "freedom rider" you were "in." The other thing I had going for me was my youth. The older people especially related to me like I was a son

[18]   Smith, p. 3.
[19]   Ibid., p. 23.

or grandson, and the younger ones like I was a brother. So, all these elements gave me entree that might not have been extended to a white photographer. Also, my father was born in Mississippi, and my mother was from Arkansas and that was certainly something I would mention that helped create another level of comfort, so that people thought of me as being one of them rather than an outsider, a spectator.[20]

This idea that Lester was "one of [his photographic subjects] rather than an outsider" allowed him preliminary access but also offered an opportunity for a different kind documentation—one that could exist external to Du Bois's double consciousness. Outside of the "peremptory white glance of dismissal," the SNCC photographers were attempting to "recast a visual record" and thoughtfully reauthor images of non-whiteness through an empowering gaze that validated rather than vilified.[21]

Through this reauthoring, the SNCC calendar essentially functions as a counterarchive in Smith's definition. She states, "… visual archives reinforce the racialized cultural prerogatives of the gaze, which determine who is authorized to look, and what will be seen, such that looking itself is a racial act, and being looked at has racial effects … [the counterarchive] challeng[es] the continued authorization of a white gaze; indeed, such disruptions of a racialized normative gaze are central to the ways in which [Du Bois's] images function as a counterarchive."[22] In the spirit of Du Bois's work, Lester and the SNCC photographers recast the gaze, redetermining who was authorized to look (as they gave the calendars out to poor black families in rural Mississippi) and what would be seen (familiar images of their own communities). Therefore, the SNCC calendar prescribes the empowerment of the rural Southern black subject who is not captured by the white-supremacist photographer, but rather illuminated by the racially conscious photographer; both the photographers and the subjects of the photographs could "testify to and reinscribe their own embodied blackness, reclaiming an affirmative African American identity in the face of brutally dehumanizing forces."[23] In other words, the images move beyond a sensationalized poverty and into a testimonial of black experience promoting agency for both subjects and viewers alike.

Neil Postman describes media ecology as "the study of transactions among people, their messages, and their message systems"; analyzing the SNCC calendar within this mode offers an interesting perspective on the activist potential for the work itself.[24] In this case, the "message" consists of both photographic images and the dates, and the "message system" is the calendar itself. In strict literal terms, a transaction is an exchange of value, whether goods, services, information, or money; for the purposes of this essay, I would argue that the calendar functions

---

[20]   Lester, Interview.

[21]   Smith, p. 35, p. 98.

[22]   Ibid., p. 11.

[23]   Ibid., p. 117.

[24]   Neil Postman and Charles Weingartner, *The soft revolution: A student handbook for turning schools around* (New York: Delacorte, 1971), p. 139.

as a series of value exchanges between photographer and subject, subject and viewer, and producer and viewer. As I have suggested, the relationship between photographer and subject is one of a social value exchange: the subject is made to feel important as she is validated by the photographer's attention, while the photographer is able to contribute to a new kind of photographic archive. The relationship between subject and viewer is an exchange of a different kind of attention in relation to time: the subject gives their momentary image, which will live on in perpetuity, while the viewer gives their attention to the image in the time that they choose. This is a negotiation of trust, as we remember "that looking itself is a racial act, and being looked at has racial effects."[25] And finally, the exchange between producer and viewer is the first step in an ideological transaction wherein people exchange a place on their wall with a newly carved-out space in their mind. The calendar is the SNCC's investment in a stronger, more informed social group because accepting the calendar and placing it on one's wall means accepting a specific, newly articulated history that contributes to an ever-growing archive of knowledge and potential action. In this final transaction the SNCC offers 365 days of empowerment, agency, and information in exchange for a small amount of wall real estate.

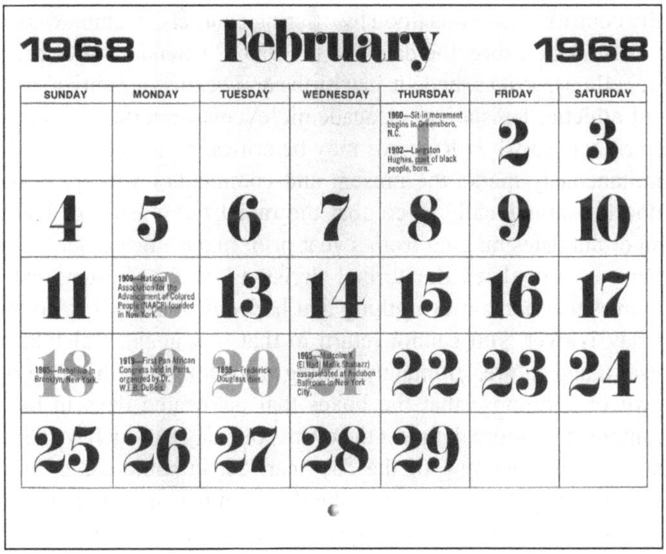

Fig. 10.3   Julius Lester, "1968 Calendar: Student Nonviolent Coordinating Committee." © Julius Lester.

---

[25]   Smith, p. 11.

As a medium for the communication of information, the calendar itself "… is a systematic way of naming the days by allocating each to a year and a month and maybe a week. It enables us to label the days in the past and in the future and to arrange them all in order."[26] But the SNCC's project took the mechanism of the calendar and renamed and reimag(in)ed it. Any physical calendar represents the struggle of humanity to concretize and delineate time, by arranging it into clearly designated sections. While the SNCC did not reorder time itself, they used time to reconstruct a missing history of resistance through events, birthdays, and holidays that addressed a black audience. Furthermore, aside from historical events, the calendar redressed a present that was blind to empowering images of non-whites. Together, these two elements of the calendar—the images and the historical dates—worked in tandem to describe "contested cultural space on the margins of official archives."[27] It is important to underscore the partnership of the word and image in this historical artifact because, though they are structurally different, they make stronger, and contribute equally to, the very counterarchive for which Smith calls.

Historian E.G. Richards argues that the contemporary proliferation of calendars is because, "as we approach the present, more and more original documents, reports, letters, and edicts survive. At the same time commentaries on texts ancient and modern appear. The supply of material on the calendar becomes a flood."[28] Strategically contributing to this flood by offering counter-hegemonic commentary to reverse historical erasure, the dates on the SNCC calendar were (re)named by historical rebellions, strikes, and sit-ins; births and deaths of political and cultural leaders; and athletic, legislative, or academic events important within the Civil Rights Movement. So while Richards may be critical of the flood of information which simultaneously marks the present and comments on the past, the SNCC calendar does so strategically to combat the racialized erasure of black history through important dates ranging from a year prior to a century prior.

D.E. Duncan articulates the formal divisions of the Western calendar as, "… small boxes that contain everything that happens in a day, but no more. And when that day is over, you cannot return to that box again. Calendar time has a past, present, and future, ultimately ending in death when the little boxes run out."[29] However, I propose that the boxes that delineated days in the SNCC's calendar contained far more than just the events of a day to which we never return; on the contrary, the renaming of the days carried, in some cases, hundreds of years of history. The actual marking of the day then becomes a record of history, and in the moment one looks at that day, history is reinvigorated in/as "today."

---

[26] E.G. Richards, *Mapping Time: The calendar and its history* (Oxford: Oxford University Press, 1998), p. 3.

[27] Smith, p. 158.

[28] Richards, p. 67.

[29] David Duncan, *Calendar: Humanity's epic struggle to determine a true and accurate year* (New York: Harper Perennial, 1998), p. xviii.

Moreover, "last month" is no longer just "June 1968" but is a month when 34 rebellions took place and are clearly marked on the calendar. Time in and of the calendar is no longer understood only in terms of a person's day-to-day experience, but rather situates her in a history that can make "today" more significant and perhaps prevent the viewer from "tak[ing] the mechanism of the calendar for granted, as we do the act of breathing and the force of gravity."[30] In that sense, the SNCC calendar redefines itself as a site for meaning-making, impossible to be taken for granted as "just a calendar" but rather as a tool for information dissemination, inspiration, and the possibility of action.

Insofar as a distinction is made between time represented on a calendar and time-as-lived, I propose that the SNCC calendar sutures "measured time" and "historical time" as articulated by Jacob Burckhardt in 1868. He claimed, "Historical time is not simply measured time. It is time that has been lived through, suffered, and experienced. It is determined not by the hand of the clock moving forwards minute by minute, but by the far more arhythmical clock of internal and external experiences."[31] Measured time is made up of the boxes on the calendar, the days and dates that segment the year; however, historical time, as Burckhardt describes it is evidently similar to the way Berger described the most powerful images as "not only personal experience, but also the essential historical experience of our relation to the past: that is to say the experience of seeking to give meaning to our lives, of trying to understand the history of which we can become the active agents."[32] Burkhardt's elucidation shows us that while the SNCC calendar presents important historical dates, they are more than just dates; they mark time that has been *experienced*. Similarly, the images are more than just documentary images of impoverished people; they are "images that showed their resilience, their dignity, their strength, their joys."[33] This layering of meaning and meaning-making is also perpetuated in each box that is marked by a significant date; as such, the SNCC calendar allows "today" to be rearticulated in terms of that historical date which connects history to lived experience. Burkhardt's use of the word "suffered" is particularly relevant here, as the SNCC calendar marks August 19th with the words "1619–20 Blacks exchanged for supplies by Dutch at Jamestown, Va., colony." Of course, an unsettling date on the calendar is April 4th, 1968, the day Martin Luther King, Jr. was assassinated, which has no event marked on it. On this day, the calendar functions as "both a miraculous tool and a cage of finite moments" that reports to us the past but cannot possibly foretell the suffering of the future.[34]

---

[30] Ibid.

[31] Arno Borst, *The Ordering of Time* (Chicago: University of Chicago Press, 1993), p. 119.

[32] Borst, p. 33.

[33] Lester, Interview.

[34] Duncan, p. 300.

Returning to the image and its unique relationship to time, Lester suggests, "Photography is the instrument that stops time. So a photograph becomes the ever-present and the ever-past at one and the same instant. It is ever-present for the fraction of a second the image is made, and it is ever-past for those who will look at that image years later." While this duality of the archive can provoke anxiety, especially within an archive that is defined by white history, the SNCC calendar meets that challenge directly by marrying the ever-present of the calendar box with the ever-past of that date in history. Similarly, Lester acknowledges his own relationship to time as a black man in the United States:

> As a black person (and as a Jew) I experience time as past and present, or to put it another way, I live not only in the present but I live in historical time, and I think that was true for any black person who grew up when I did. We lived with an awareness of being the victims of history—our skin color said we were the descendants of slaves, and at that time, this meant we were inferior. I also feel that growing up under racial segregation marked us/maimed us in such a way that what racial segregation did to those of my generation remains a part of us. One of the primary differences I feel between blacks and whites is that whites can live ahistorically, i.e. without any awareness of the history they move through. They can pretend to have an "innocence" which neither blacks nor Native Americans can have. In 1973 I was in Macon, Georgia and a pretty blue-eyed, blonde southern girl invited me to drive up to the northern part of Georgia. I knew that part of Georgia was Klan country, and I refused. She didn't understand why. I told her that if somebody saw me in a car with her in that part of Georgia, I could be killed or arrested. She looked at me with wide-eyed wonder and said, "That would never happen here." ... What amazed me was that 1973 was only nine years since the passage of the Civil Rights Act of 1964, but she had grown up in a world of integrated schools and buses and stores and that quickly, there was this white girl who had no knowledge of the segregation which had shaped my life in major ways. She and I lived in different time dimensions. One of my theories is that until white people make black history a part of themselves, there will always be a racial divide. Time for many whites is one-dimensional; for blacks and Native Americans time has many dimensions, and whites must learn to live in those other dimensions as well.[35]

At this point, I would like to return to Postman's early definition of media ecology as the study of "how media of communication affect human perception, understanding, feeling, and value; and how our interaction with media facilitates or impedes our chances of survival."[36] This word "survival" resonates deeply within the context of the SNCC calendar, within the story of Lester's refusal to go into Klan country with a white woman, within the poverty of the rural South. As the last page of the calendar states, "From the rebellions on slave ships to the rebellions of today, our history is one of resistance." That resistance, in its many

---

[35]   Lester, Interview.

[36]   Postman, *Reformed*, p. 161.

forms, has facilitated survival, and the documentation and dissemination of that history of resistance amplifies the possibilities for continued survival. The SNCC calendar itself is also an act of resistance wherein a counter-hegemonic history is authored through the use of photographic representations of non-white people and through the labeling of significant days that (re)present resistance to oppression. The calendar functions as both a historical document of a photographic archive and as a functional tool—because it will always mark the anniversaries of events prior to 1968, it still functions when "today" is matched against the anniversary marked in 1968. In this, it is a medium of communication that continues to speak to us today, as well as inform our "perception, understanding, feeling, and value." Through the complex spectra of black and white, poor and wealthy, image and text, personal experience and shared history, the calendar offers compelling representations of non-whites who now embody, mark, and represent 1968, the year that changed history.

Chapter 11
Amazon Quarterly:
Pre-Zine Print Culture and the
Politics of Separatism

Tirza True Latimer

Oakland, California, in the early 1970s looked a lot like what the radical feminist critic Jill Johnston famously described as a "Lesbian Nation."[1] In a collection of *Village Voice* essays published under this bold banner, Johnson outlined a lesbian separatist cultural agenda for lesbians building anti-patriarchal social, cultural, and economic networks. Her ideas were nourished by and resonated throughout lesbian popular culture. "They built their own houses and fixed their own bikes / Fulfilling our dream of a nation of dykes," the lyrics to "Sweet Betsy the Dyke," by the singer-songwriter Les B. Friends affirmed.[2] In the Bay Area, where gay men were restoring Victorians and reconfiguring San Francisco's Castro district, lesbians by the thousands settled in the East Bay. One entire row of 1920s stucco rental units on Sacramento Avenue was known as Amazon Acres for its dykey demographics. Berkeley and Oakland were honeycombed with such enclaves. Plaid-shirted dykes converged on the women's bookstores, women's centers, and lesbian restaurants and bars that cropped up to serve "the other side" of the Bay. Lesbian feminist publications both documented and contributed to the creation of alternative social structures and artistic economies. One of the first was the Oakland-based periodical *Amazon Quarterly: A lesbian feminist arts journal*, edited by Laurel Galana and Gina Covina.

The magazine's mission statement and table of contents reflected the preoccupations of the Lesbian Nation's constituents—women who converged on the Bay Area, Women's Lands to the north, and other promising territories to write poetry, to make art and music, to break into the trades and other traditionally male métiers, to escape their biological families or husbands, to achieve autonomy, to find soul mates, to make love with women, to build houses, to create intentional communities, to re-imagine the world. "Freed from male identification, lesbians are obviously in a very good position to be the ones to cross [freedom's] frontier," the first paragraph of *Amazon*'s inaugural issue declares.[3] The journal's utopian

---

[1]   Jill Johnston, *Lesbian Nation: The Feminist Solution* (New York: Simon and Schuster, 1973).

[2]   The lyrics are reproduced in full in *Amazon Quarterly: A lesbian feminist arts journal* 1:2 (February 1973), p. 25.

[3]   "Frontiers," *Amazon* 1:1 (Fall 1972), p. 5.

rhetoric should not be mistaken for naïveté. "Even after we are seemingly *free*, there remains only a patriarchal culture to be *free in*," *Amazon* cautioned. "We cannot just tackle the most visible institutions and 'equalize' them. We cannot stop short of a thorough knowledge of the extensions of the patriarchy, how and why it works, and ultimately a dismantling of the entire machine."[4] Every aspect of the journal—its facture, production values, literary and editorial contents, design, distribution, and economics—contributed to this project.

As a preliminary gesture, the magazine's co-editors, like many feminist contemporaries, dropped the patronymic from their signatures. Laurel's editorials, with titles such as "Toward a Woman Vision," emphasized that the deconstruction of the patriarchal apparatus, including its symbolic and psychic formations, was but a first phase of an exacting creative process. The lesbian feminist revolution called for the creation of new patterns of thought, relation, speech, action, and perception. Was it possible to make art, make love, make sense, make a living against the patriarchal grain? How would a future disentangled from masculinist schemas of power and the economic imperatives of capitalism look, sound, taste, smell, feel? Such questions interested the magazine's editors more than the coming out narratives and same-sex love stories that dominated lesbian feminist print culture throughout the 1970s. For *Amazon*, lesbianism was "a fait accompli, the background but not the message."[5]

> Though we define this as a lesbian-feminist magazine, we aren't interested solely in stories that tell of lesbian love, the problems of being a lesbian, or the joys. Most of us who read this magazine are quite familiar with all that on the personal front ... . [We imagine this magazine, instead, as a space for] launching out from all that we as women have been before into something new and uncharted ... . We are calling this an arts journal in the sense that art is communication ... . We simply want the best of communication from lesbians who are consciously exploring new patterns in their lives.[6]

Gina and Laurel aspired to create a context for the formation of revolutionary feminist networks to develop in dialogical exchange across disciplinary as well as social, sexual, and geographical boundaries. The magazine's title and the cover graphic for the first issue (a woman warrior astride her tightly reined and rearing steed) alerted readers to the militant character of the project. (See Figure 11.1)

The journal introduced work by contributors who deeply marked the history of feminism, lesbian feminism, publishing, literature, and the visual arts. An interview with Jan Oxenberg follows a review by the Women's Film Co-op of the filmmaker's early short *Home Movie*;[7] the lyrics to "A Woman's Love" by Michigan Womyn's

[4]   Laurel, "Toward a Woman Vision," *Amazon* 2:2 (December 1973), p. 18, p. 20.
[5]   Gina Covina and Laurel Galana, *The Lesbian Reader* (Berkeley: Amazon Press, 1975), inside front cover.
[6]   "Frontiers," *Amazon* 1:1 (Fall 1972), p. 5.
[7]   *Amazon* 2:2 (December 1973), pp. 53–5.

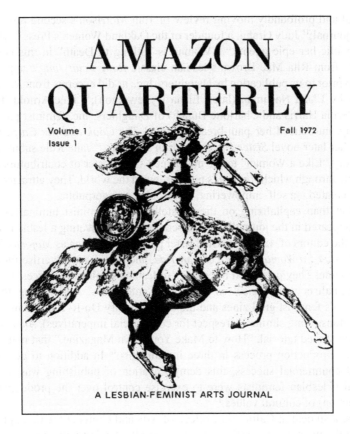

AMAZON QUARTERLY

Volume 1   Fall 1972
Issue 1

A LESBIAN-FEMINIST ARTS JOURNAL

Fig. 11.1   Unidentified artist, cover, *Amazon Quarterly: A Lesbian Feminist
Arts Journal*, Fall 1972.

Music Festival regular Alix Dobkin are preserved here as well;[8] Robin Morgan
(a generous financial backer of the magazine) published her keynote address to
the 1973 West Coast Lesbian-Feminist Conference, "Lesbianism and Feminism:
Synonyms or Contradictions?" in *Amazon*;[9] Adrienne Rich posted her statement to
the National Book Award assembly accepting a prize for *Diving into the Wreck* on
behalf of "all women whose voices have gone and still go unheard in a patriarchal
world";[10] Audre Lorde, who served for a time as *Amazon*'s poetry editor, composed

---

[8]   *Amazon* 2:3 (March 1973), p. 27.

[9]   *Amazon* 1:3 (May 1973), pp. 8–20.

[10]   The statement was prepared by three of the women nominated for the 1974
National Book Award for poetry (Audre Lorde, Adrienne Rich, and Alice Walker) "with
the agreement that it would be read by whichever of us, if any, was chosen … . We believe
that we can enrich ourselves more in supporting and giving to each other than by competing
against each other." *Amazon* 2:4 (July 1974), p. 71.

an artful and profoundly moving review of Toni Morrison's second novel, *Sula*, for the journal;[11] Judy Grahn, a founder of the Oakland Women's Press Collective, made public her epic poem, "A Woman is Talking to Death" in this context;[12] excerpts from Rita Mae Brown's lesbian classic *Ruby Fruit Jungle* appeared in *Amazon* prior to its publication by Daughters, Inc., as did excerpts from *Riverfinger Woman* by Elana Nachman (later, Elana Dykewomon);[13] June Arnold, founder (with Bertha Harris and Charlotte Bunch) of Daughters, Inc. feminist publishing company, introduced her path-breaking novel *The Cook and the Carpenter*, as well as her later novel *Sister Gin* to *Amazon*'s readers;[14] Jane Rule submitted her short story "Like a Woman" to the magazine.[15] This roster of contributors altered the frame through which *Amazon*'s public viewed the world. They attracted—and, indeed, created—a self-empowering, Amazonian counterpublic.

Rather than capitalizing on the constellation of feminist luminaries whose names appeared in the journal's table of contents by cultivating a lesbian "market niche," the editors of *Amazon* invited sister publications (such as *Majority Report*, *Herself*, *Ain't I a Woman?*, *The Lesbian Tide*, and *Sisters*) to advertise for free in the magazine. They published directories of lesbian feminist resources, including what capitalists would view as competing enterprises. Anticipating the next generation's feminist grrrl zines and the contemporary Do-It-Yourself movement (and demonstrating similar disrespect for commercial imperatives), *Amazon* even ran an illustrated tutorial, "How to Make Your Own Magazine," that mapped out *Amazon*'s production process in three installments.[16] In addition to defying the logic of commercial success, this demystification of publishing was tactically essential if lesbian feminists were to exercise control over the production (and reproduction) of cultural values.[17]

Gina, a student at California College of Arts and Crafts at the time, provided many of the illustrations for the journal, especially the first few issues. Seven out of the ten graphics in the inaugural number bear her signature. These include pen and ink vignettes capturing moments in the routines of couples whose reptilic hybridity completely queers the coziness of what otherwise appear to be quaint domestic scenes: lovers back-scrubbing in a claw-foot tub, curling up on the couch to watch TV, playing Scrabble in bed. (See Figure 11.2) These drawings, as well as others published in the journal, owe a visible debt to surrealism—one of the rare early twentieth-century movements to invite, albeit somewhat late in the day, the participation of women and to celebrate the strangeness/estrangement of their vision. Gina's flighty yet precise drafting, as well as her charismatically

---

[11] *Amazon* 2:3 (March 1974), pp. 28–30.

[12] *Amazon* 2:2 (December 1973), pp. 4–17.

[13] *Amazon* 1:2 (February 1973), pp. 6–18; *Amazon* 2:4 (July 1974), pp. 6–10.

[14] *Amazon* 2:2 (December 1973), pp. 44–5; *Amazon* 3:2 (March 1975), pp. 42–7.

[15] *Amazon* 1:2 (February 1973), pp. 18–23.

[16] See *Amazon*, vol. 2, issue 3; vol. 2, issue 4; vol. 3, issue 1.

[17] Gina Covina. Interview by author. December 26, 2007.

Fig. 11.2   Gina Covina, illustration, *Amazon Quarterly: A Lesbian Feminist Arts Journal*, February 1973.

monstrous iconography, call to mind Remedios Varo or even Frida Kahlo, two outsider artists loosely identified (for want of a more appropriate context) with the surrealist movement.

The ambition to subvert capitalism's cultural production apparatus aligns *Amazon* with vanguard art magazines of the surrealist era, such as *La Révolution surréaliste* and *Minotaure*. Like surrealist reviews, *Amazon* featured visual and literary material aligned with dissident political perspectives but bodied forth no unifying aesthetic. *Amazon* also shared certain objectives with contemporary artist-generated magazines—such as *Aspen, 0–9, Avalanche, FILE,* and *Art-Rite*—that arose during the same period to challenge "formalist models of medium specificity."[18] These magazines, as the historians of visual culture Gwen Allen and Cherise Smith have observed, set new standards "of self-reflexivity about institutions and audiences both inside and outside the so-called art world."[19] The phrase "alternative distribution,"

---

[18]   Gwen Allen and Cherise Smith, "Publishing Art Alternative Distribution in Print," *Art Journal* 66:1 (Spring 2007), p. 41.

[19]   Allen and Smith, p. 41.

which came into circulation at this time, connoted the creation of new patterns of cultural accessibility—a "desire to produce and exhibit art outside the mandates of profit and to reach a wider audience."[20] With hindsight, and against the backdrop of today's market-driven art scene, it is clear, Allen contends, that "to publish art, to literally 'make it public,' was a political act, one that challenged the art world and the world at large."[21] However, these rebellious pursuits contributed to forms of counter-publicity that often reinforced, via the dynamics of binary opposition, the very structures they contested. Moreover, they all but invited absorption, as the latest vanguard novelty, by the larger cultural economy.

Amazon strove to negotiate a way out of (or, more accurately, through) these binds by generating lesbian feminist counter-publicity and modeling forms of social and economic disentanglement from capitalism/patriarchy. What kind of a stance could a lesbian-feminist journal strike vis-à-vis the "man's world" from which it issued and in which it remained embedded, the editors wondered. Unlike artist magazines that bucked market forces to open alternative avenues of creativity and communication within mainstream culture, *Amazon* imagined social territories off the patriarchal grid as the proper domain of lesbian artists. Perhaps it then makes sense, in a perverse sort of way, that although *Amazon* operated on a strictly not-for-profit basis, it was denied official non-profit status because, according to the IRS, the lesbian readership it served could not be defined as "the public."[22]

Amazon, unlike most art magazines, however alternative, chose not to generate revenue through the publication of advertisements. Gina and Laurel produced the journal on a shoe-string with resources garnered from subscriptions, bookstore commissions, in-kind and cash donations. Low-quality paper stock, typewritten galleys, black and white illustrations, and low-cost photo offset printing technologies contributed to the viability of the enterprise. The resulting DIY aesthetic made a statement of non-complicity with a culture industry increasingly invested in packaging.

Less visibly, but perhaps even more significantly, the magazine relied heavily on an expansive volunteer labor pool for production and distribution. The editors offered thanks, for instance, to "a woman in Oklahoma who helped with typing ... and a woman in the East who is computerizing our subscription files"; they invited local readers to participate in an "all-you-can-drink mailing party" when it came time for distribution.[23] The editors themselves—subsisting on food stamps and occasional odd jobs—devoted all their free time ("free" in this case meaning both "available" and "gratis") to editorial and production tasks. They plowed any surplus funds they or the magazine earned into aligning the journal

---

[20]   Allen and Smith, p. 41.

[21]   Gwen Allen, *Artists' Magazines: An alternative space for art* (Cambridge, MA: MIT, 2011), p. 7.

[22]   Mentioned in "What You Can Do to Help Miss Q," *Amazon* 1:4/2:1 (October 1973), p. 13.

[23]   *Amazon* 2:2 (December 1973), p. 3; *Amazon* 3:1 (November 1974), p. 72.

ever more closely with their anti-market, anti-patriarchal, pro-social justice, and pro-environmentalist ideals. For instance, volume 2, issue 3 of *Amazon* was "dedicated to Trees" and printed on recycled paper, despite the additional expense.

In these ways, *Amazon* modeled editorial and production strategies redeployed by oppositional enterprises of the 1990s, when punk and grrrl zine makers turned to self-publishing. Print-culture activist Elke Zobl explains that this kind of self-publishing opened up "an outlet for creativity ... a network tool," and a forum for cultural resistance and political critique, while enabling social dissidents to narrate "an oppositional history and an alternative to the narrow and distorted mainstream representation of women [and] queer people ... an alternative that reflects and resists their cultural devaluation."[24] Zobl's remarks concern the grrrl zine movement, yet it is striking how accurately her observations about contemporary forms of counterpublicity describe *Amazon*'s ethos. Such resonances make *Amazon* accessible to a new generation of readers.

Reviewing *Amazon* through the lens of current events and preoccupations (such as climate change and the emergence of eco-feminism as a set of activist commitments and practices) reawakens latent content. For instance, reading the frontispiece of *Amazon*'s March 1975 issue in light of recent developments throws sustainability-related registers of meaning into heightened relief. (See Figure 11.3) The black-and-white photograph by Carol Newhouse pictures a wild-eyed woman—draped in a revealing shawl of macramé—emerging from a dense forest. Today's readers may laugh (or wince) at the picture's essentialist implications: Women (presumably because of their ability to generate life) have a privileged relationship with Mother Earth; women are, if you will, a force of nature. At the same time, this woman's don't-mess-with-me stance (she crouches as if to spring to action) and her expression (alert to potential danger) make it difficult to objectify her sleek, frontally exposed body. This 1970s Amazon looks like she can take care of herself. Her hand-crafted garment suggests autonomy from capitalist consumer economies. Indeed, the photograph's visual cues (the macramé, the massive tree trunk that serves as a backdrop) gesture toward a succession of eco-conscious historical trends—the back-to-the-land, DIY, and neo-craft movements among them.

Despite *Amazon*'s evident gynocentrism, the journal never fully subscribed to the essentialist programs of feminine representation advanced by many other lesbian and feminist publications of the 1970s. Indeed, the magazine's contributors regularly ratified the Beauvoirian notion that women, within patriarchy, were "man's first artificial product."[25] The editors of *Amazon* deliberately steered clear of images that appeared to reduce lesbianism (with its political potential) to sexuality, and sexuality to erotic zones of the body. Although Tee A. Corinne, known in both

---

[24] Elke Zobl, "Comparative Perspectives Symposium: Feminist Zines—Cultural Production, Transnational Networking, and Critical Reflection in Feminist Zines," *Signs: Journal of Women in Culture and Society* 35:1 (2009), p. 5.

[25] Jeanne Gallick, "Phallic Technology and the Construction of Women," *Amazon* 1:2 (February 1972), p. 62.

Fig. 11.3   Carol Newhouse, photograph, frontispiece for *Amazon Quarterly: A Lesbian Feminist Arts Journal*, March 1975.

the feminist art world and lesbian separatist communities for her photographs and texts celebrating lesbian eroticism, regularly submitted material to the magazine, she received nothing but polite rejection letters from the editors of *Amazon*.[26]

The artwork published in *Amazon* broadened the iconography of 1970s lesbian-feminism by pointing in less predictable directions. *Amazon*'s visual modes of address were as heterogeneous as the journal's imagined readership. The magazine, as the art historian Margo Hobbs Thompson has noted, offered "a visual lexicon of cultural forms."[27] It juxtaposed works as diverse as Gina's queer reptiles, Newhouse's Amazon, vintage photos donated by a subscriber, Kaymarion's stylized nudes, Judy Linhares's lesbianized day-of-the-dead vignettes, Diane Derrick's de-idealized Three Graces, and Louise Fishman's *Angry* paintings. The eclecticism of the visual program works against the kind of aesthetic of coherence to which magazine designers typically aspire. *Amazon*'s visual unevenness is productively unsettling, disrupting habits of seeing, and thus thinking. At the same time, this disturbing variety operates as a visual analogue for other forms of diversity.

---

[26]   Gina Covina. Interview by author. 26 December 2007.

[27]   Margo Hobbs Thompson, "'Dear Sisters': The Visible Lesbian in Community Arts Journals," *GLQ: Journal of Lesbian and Gay Studies* 12:3 (2006), p. 421.

Several of *Amazon*'s contributing artists went on to participate in other lesbian/ feminist art initiatives where representational diversity was a stated ambition. One was the "Great American Lesbian Art Show" of 1980. The show's organizers came up with a very concrete, non-elitist model for promoting the visibility of lesbian art and the celebration of lesbian culture in its multitude of forms. The show's curators conceived of a sort of DIY lesbian art exhibition kit and made it available to groups all over the country. The goal was to promote a nationwide art festival open to work by all lesbians. Fifty communities across the country participated; each local venue sent slides documenting their event to the GALAS collective, and the slides were shown at a gala invitational exhibition at the Women's Building in LA. This capstone exhibition honored artists whose careers had boosted lesbian visibility in the arts. Following in the footsteps of *Amazon*, lesbian feminist activists continued to use the arts to imagine and create non-competitive, non-commercial, lesbian-affirmative contexts within which to live and work.[28]

Harmony Hammond, organizer of "A Lesbian Art Show" at the 112 Greene St. Workshop in New York's Greenwich Village and member of the collective that produced the "Lesbian Art and Artists" issue of the feminist magazine *Heresies*, wondered if some sort of lesbian sensibility or aesthetic would become apparent in the course of these events.[29] It did not. Instead, GALAS, *Heresies*, and "A Lesbian Art Show," like *Amazon*, made visible a politicized lesbian presence within feminism. *Amazon*'s notes on contributors indicate that most did not draw sharp lines where their lesbian-feminist activism left off and their artistry began or prioritize one form of creative cultural engagement over the other. As one contributing artist explained,

> Art for us is a two-way communication in which both (all) participants are active. Instead of a given, objective, mechanical set of criteria, human, personal responses have become the means of our relationship to art. We do not, then, view, analyze or interpret art as a thing out there, separate from us. We engage it, in a process of communicative responses, and we use it … . We use art in our lives and our lives can become art. We participate in art.[30]

---

[28] GALAS arose in an environment enriched by earlier initiatives such as the Feminist Studio Workshop, of which the lesbian-feminist art critic and historian Arlene Raven was a founder. The Feminist Studio Workshop served as the educational center of the Los Angeles Women's Building, publishing *Chrysalis: A Magazine of Women's Culture* (1977–1980) and sponsoring the Natalie Barney Collective, a group committed to researching and documenting lesbian artists. Within the structure of the Feminist Art Workshop, Raven, in collaboration with the critic Terry Wolverton, also initiated the Lesbian Art Project (1977–1979), which hosted art discussion groups, writers' groups, and salons.

[29] Harmony Hammond. Interview by author. July 2007.

[30] Barbara Starrett, "I Dream in Female: The Metaphors of Evolution," *Amazon* 3:1 (November 1974), p. 21.

These are the tenets of what artists who produce social transactions rather than objects today describe as a "social practice." Distinctions of genre, medium, and even discipline fell away within *Amazon*'s conceptual framework, which emphasized art as a form of activism.

The journal's visual program offered points of access to the journal's underlying ideological positions and lesbian-feminist agenda. Gina's wrap-around cover graphic for the December 1973 issue is exemplary. (See Figure 11.4) The oblong line drawing traces the transition from the patriarchal present to a feminist future. The left half of the tableau (on the magazine's back cover) features a patriarchal deity who presides over a vertically organized social schema. Women, in the lower echelons, perform tasks of domestic labor—washing and hanging laundry at the river of life, children clinging to them. These working women bear working men upon their shoulders, and they, in turn, support male superiors. The bosses are held aloft in throne-like armchairs against a backdrop of skyscrapers and elevated roadways. In the distance, oil wells sprout up, mushroom clouds bloom. Downriver, the eye flows along the drawing's fluid lines to the right half of the drawing (on the magazine's front cover), where the freeway crumbles, broken up by roots and irrepressible shoots of vegetation. Women, washed downriver, naked now, free of gods and men, join hands and ride the current that buoys them up and carries them toward a post-apocalyptic, post-patriarchal future. Here, Nature—not some monotheistic deity or corporate boss—calls the shots. Since women, according to this scenario, have profited less from Nature's mastery (or destruction), they are transported and transformed, rather than stranded and crippled, by Nature's resurgence. This visual allegory again articulates lesbian-feminism within the more sweeping didactic program of sustainablity. The drawing also schematizes the kinetics of connection (among women) and disconnection (from the world of men) that generate *Amazon*'s intellectual dynamic.

The historian Martin Meeker, in his award-winning book *Contacts Desired*, stresses *Amazon*'s role in forging connections, knitting scattered outposts of lesbian feminists into a self-sufficient socio-economic complex. The lesbian feminist network, he writes,

> Could be built and could be robust without being tied to specific neighborhoods, cities, or regions; the lesbian-feminist network could be established through the interaction of close-knit and small-scale lesbian communities ... linked with others through newspapers, magazines, newsletters, collectives, distribution networks, telephone calls, live music festivals, conferences, and pen-pal clubs.[31]

Much evidence affirms the validity of Meeker's analysis, including *Amazon*'s spin-off publication *Connections* (a lesbian social networking directory) and the editors' 12,000-mile odyssey around North America to meet and converse with their subscribers.

---

[31]   Martin Meeker, *Contacts Desired: Gay and Lesbian Communications and Community, 1940s–1970s* (Chicago: University of Chicago Press, 2006), p. 232.

Fig. 11.4   Gina Covina, drawing, back and front cover of *Amazon Quarterly: A Lesbian Feminist Arts Journal*, December 1973.

Yet it is the disconnections that invest these connections with meaning. In the desire for disconnection from the patriarchy lies the specificity of lesbian-feminist "communications and community." That the connections proved fragile and the disconnections only partial, at best, does not detract from the force of *Amazon*'s moral impact. Indeed, *Amazon*'s very precariousness signals the force of its resistance to commercial expedients and compromise. The expectation of failure, as Gwen Allen convincingly argues, is narrowly associated with both alternative publication ventures and the concept of social revolution. Failures generate new ways of seeing, thinking, making, and thus living. "Such failure should be understood not as an indication of defeat, but as an expression of the vanguard nature of these publications and their refusal of commercial interests."[32] In other words, considering the prevailing standards of "success" (more money, more power, more possessions, more publicity), failure appears, not as a shameful outcome, but as a necessary condition of possibility for any truly anti-capitalist revolutionary process. Indifference to the terms of commercial success enabled *Amazon Quarterly* and other activist publications of the era to model anti-consumerist cultural practices and affirm alternative modes of circulation and reception. The fact that *Amazon*'s politics and production strategies resonate at key sites of cultural intervention today, despite the journal's limited circulation and relatively short publication history, suggests that the wheels of revolution may still be turning.

---

[32]   Allen, *Artists' Magazines*, p. 2.

Chapter 12
Crafting Public Cultures in Feminist Periodicals

Elizabeth Groeneveld

The early 1990s and 2000s saw the emergence of a cadre of independent periodicals, now associated with feminism's "third wave," a form of feminism viewed as distinct, but not completely divergent, from the "second wave" of feminism that developed during the 1960s and 1970s. The periodicals associated with third-wave feminism, such as *BUST* (1993–), *Bitch* (1996–), *HUES* (1992–1999), *ROCKRGRL* (1995–2006), *Venus Zine* (1994–), and *Shameless* (2004–), differed from earlier feminist periodicals like *off our backs* (1970–2008) or *Ms.* magazine (1970–) in a number of ways. Namely, this new cluster of feminist publications emerged out of 1990s zine[1] culture, and the content of these publications focuses primarily on cultural production by women.

While there are continuities between second-wave and third-wave feminism, the two categories are frequently set up in opposition to each other and figured as sites of inter-generational tension. Third-wave magazines are often used as evidence of the alleged turn away from the recognizably "political" feminist work of the second wave in ways that elide the points of alliance between these two sets of feminist waves and that place rigid boundaries on what can and should count as appropriately "political" work. Thus, in the mid-1990s and intensifying in the early 2000s, when many of these feminist periodicals began discussing and—in many cases—promoting the reclamation and repoliticization of crafting activities, this turn to craft has sometimes been read as a sign of this wave's difference from the second wave, positioned as a selling out of feminist principles or cited as further evidence of the political apathy of young women through its return to domesticity.[2] These periodicals, *BUST*, *Bitch*, *Venus Zine*, and *Shameless*, frequently cast

---

[1]   Zines are independently produced micro media in which the zine creator (or zinester) usually controls all aspects of the production process, which can include the writing, illustrations, layout, design, photocopying, and distribution of the zine. For further readings on zine culture, see Stephen Duncombe, *Notes From the Underground* (London: Verso, 1997) and Mark Todd and Esther Watson, *Whatcha Mean, What's a Zine? The art of making zines and mini-comics* (Boston: Graphia, 2006). For analyses of zines made by girls and women, see Mary Celeste Kearney, *Girls Make Media* (New York: Routledge, 2006) and Alison Piepmeier, *Girl Zines* (New York: New York University Press, 2009).

[2]   There are some ironies, here, in that within second-wave art history, crafting activities such as quilting were elevated to the status of high art.

knitting, sewing, and crocheting as new and fun ways of being hip and feminist. This paper thus considers the representation of crafting within feminist periodicals and, particularly, the ways that readers understand their relationships to both crafting and the magazines that promote craft. In what ways might crafting be feminist? How do these texts foster feminist craft cultures? Despite the frequent discursive appeals to the political potential of knitting, as evidenced by *BUST* editor Debbie Stoller's call to "join the knitting revolution,"[3] it is worth asking these questions about the reclamation of craft as political and as feminist, linking them to broader concerns regarding the productiveness of so-called third-wave feminism. Focusing primarily on reader response to feminist craft discourse helps to move beyond simplistic and binary modes of conceptualizing cultural production as either radical or complicit, or as either political or apolitical.

Despite the ways in which feminist crafting is often described as "new," however, the discourses on craft within these periodicals are frequently in dialogue with what is to some extent an imagined feminist past. Moreover, rather than serving as a radical break from their precursors, feminist periodicals that promote crafting carry on an engagement with do-it-yourself (DIY) principles that runs through the long history of feminist periodical publications. This chapter historicizes the promotion of craft in feminist periodicals by situating these publications within this long history, as well as within their more immediate contexts of contemporary women's culture and DIY punk and zine culture. Examining and drawing out these different lineages demonstrates the ways in which feminisms do not follow easy, linear progress narratives, but are rather shaped by, and feed back into, multiple contexts.

Late Twentieth-Century Feminist Periodicals

With the exception of *Shameless* (2004–), the feminist periodicals under consideration here—*BUST* (1993–), *Bitch* (1996–), and *Venus Zine* (1994–)— began as zine publications in the early to mid-1990s, and gradually grew into more widely circulating magazines.[4] The latter three are United States-based publications, while *Shameless* is published out of Toronto, Canada. *BUST*, *Shameless*, and *Venus Zine* are for-profit publications, while *Bitch* is a not-for-profit

---

3   Debbie Stoller, "The Shiz-Knit: Join the Knitting Revolution," *BUST* 19 (Spring 2002), p. 15.

4   These are not the only feminist periodicals that began publication at this time: the early and mid-1990s saw the rise of a vibrant feminist zine culture. Some of the most well-known feminist zines from this era include *Bamboo Girl*, *Bikini Kill*, *Doris*, and *Pagan's Head*. Other feminist periodicals that circulated more widely as magazines include *HUES* (1992–1999) and *Rockrgrl* (1995–2006); however, these publications did not include discussions of crafts. There is also a large number of small-scale zine publications devoted entirely to crafts: some are "one-offs" and others are serialized. Finally, there are also a handful of periodicals with higher circulation numbers (in the tens of thousands) devoted to crafting but without a feminist focus. These include *Make* (2005–) and *Craft* (2005–).

periodical; all four are published independently. Additionally, these periodicals share a focus on the activities of girls and young women (approximately ages 18–35), particularly in the realm of cultural production, including music, visual art, film, and, of course, craft.[5] All but *Venus Zine*, which confines its focus to women in the independent arts, examine contemporary women's culture from a feminist perspective. Frequently covered topics include motherhood, sex, style, and body politics.

BUST was created in New York City by Debbie Stoller and Marcelle Karp (playfully writing under the aliases Celina Hex and Betty Boob, respectively). The zine's initial editorial set out a manifesto-style statement asserting the need for a magazine that addresses the "groovy girl-women" of Generation X who couldn't quite get it together, a generation dubbed by Stoller and Karp "Generation XX."[6] The publication developed rapidly, from a black-and-white zine publication to a semi-glossy magazine with a circulation in the tens of thousands.[7] *BUST* introduced a "how-to" department related to crafting in 1997 and continues to offer instructions on how to make one handcrafted item in every issue. Overall coverage of crafting has intensified in *BUST* since the early 2000s: there was a significant rise in the advertising of hand-crafted items (or items that *appear* handcrafted) during this period, as well as more discussion of independent crafters and their handmade products in the pages of the publication. Stoller also launched her own line of knitting and crocheting books—the Stitch 'n Bitch series—which helped inspire a feminist knitting circle craze across the United States, Canada, Europe, and Australia.[8]

In contrast to *BUST*, *Bitch* is a journal-style publication devoted to feminist response to popular culture. Now published out of Portland, Oregon (and originally published in Oakland, California), each issue is organized around a central theme and includes feature-length articles, as well as short, pithy critical media commentary. One of *Bitch*'s long-time departments, Love It/Shove It, gives contributors the opportunity to either declare their love for, or disgust with, a recent pop culture text (such as a television commercial, music video, or

---

[5]   This focus is mirrored in the reading demographics for these periodicals. *Venus Zine*'s online press kit, for example, lists their readership as 92 percent female. *Venus Zine*'s readership has a median age of 26, and 76 percent are city dwellers (<http://venuszine.com/advertise>).

[6]   Debbie Stoller [Celina Hex] and Marcelle Karp [Betty Boob], Editorial, *BUST* 1 (1993); Stoller and Karp, eds., *The BUST Guide to the New Girl Order* (New York: Penguin Books [reprint], 1999), pp. x–xi.

[7]   The initial editorial mission, however, has stayed consistent: the publication serves as a feminist lifestyle publication for primarily urban, heterosexual, hipster women ranging in age from their early twenties to mid-thirties.

[8]   See Debbie Stoller, *Stitch 'n Bitch: The knitter's handbook* (New York: Workman Press, 2003); *Stitch 'n Bitch Nation* (New York: Workman Press, 2004); *Stitch 'n Bitch: The happy hooker* (New York: Workman Press, 2006); and *Stitch 'n Bitch: Advanced* (New York: Workman Press, 2009).

consumer product). In this sense, *Bitch*'s feminist stance is not entirely a negative one when it comes to the realm of the popular. *Bitch* acknowledges that pleasures can be derived from pop culture texts, even if they do not always (or rarely) live up to socially progressive principles. *Bitch*, unlike the other three periodicals, does not feature "how-to" articles. However, the periodical has featured coverage of, and discussion about, feminist crafting and its interface with other topics frequently discussed in the magazine, such as motherhood and domesticity.

Initially self-published once per year as a fanzine, *Venus Zine* was the creation of Amy Schroeder, who began circulating *Venus Zine* while majoring in Women's Studies at Michigan State University. Beginning in 2000 Schroeder began publishing *Venus Zine* quarterly, with an eye towards becoming a more widely circulating magazine devoted to covering women in music. Over time, the magazine expanded its mandate to include women in the independent arts, which allowed the magazine to devote space to handmade items. The first "how to" articles appeared in *Venus Zine* in the early 2000s.

Shameless is a magazine for teenage girls, which has included "how-to" crafting articles since its inception. Although the publication did not begin as a zine, it references many of the DIY principles that emerged out of feminist zine culture. For example, the cover of *Shameless*'s inaugural issue draws on the cut-and-paste aesthetics of zines, through its appearance of having been constructed out of cut up and reassembled strips of paper, as well as in the way that the font of the magazine title appears photocopied (see Figure 12.1). But *Shameless*'s commitment to DIY culture goes beyond its cover page: the publication is notable in its encouragement of readers to become producers of culture, an approach that is, according to Mary Celeste Kearney, often sadly lacking within media targeted towards girls and young women.[9] The magazine's original tagline, "for girls who get it,"[10] further constructs its readers as savvy, smart, and capable.[11]

BUST, *Bitch*, *Shameless*, and *Venus Zine* all currently remain in business; however, all have also struggled financially: *Bitch* launched a fundraising campaign in 2008 in order to help save it from going under and has massively restructured itself into more of a foundation model, of which the print magazine is simply one part. As co-founder and editor Andi Zeisler remarked in a 2007 interview,

---

[9]   See Kearney, *Girls Make Media*, pp. 1–16.

[10]   *Shameless* changed its tagline in the Spring of 2011 to "talking back since 2004" to reflect its mandate to be inclusive of transgender issues.

[11]   For additional critical work on late twentieth-century feminist periodicals, see Courtney Bailey, "*Bitch*ing and Talking/Gazing Back," *Women and Language* 26/2 (2003), pp. 1–8; Suzy D'Enbeau, "Feminine and Feminist Transformation in Popular Culture," *Feminist Media Studies* 9/1 (2009), pp. 17–36; Elizabeth Groeneveld, "Be a Feminist or Just Dress Like One," *Journal of Gender Studies* 18/2 (June 2009), pp. 177–90; Elizabeth Groeneveld, "Join the Knitting Revolution," *Canadian Review of American Studies* 40/2 (2010), 259–78; Rebecca Munford "Wake Up and Smell the Lipgloss," in *Third Wave Feminism: A Critical Exploration*, edited by Stacey Gillis, Gillian Howie, and Rebecca Munford (London: Palgrave Macmillan, 2004), pp. 142–54; and Piepmeier, *Girl Zines*.

Fig. 12.1   Norman Yeung, *Shameless* (cover), Summer 2004.

"it's just getting more and more difficult to publish a print magazine, financially. Everything gets more expensive every year—paper, postage, shipping, fuel … . Not to sound too pessimistic, but we always feel relieved when we look at our cash flow and see that we can make it to another issue."[12] *BUST* and *Venus Zine*, as for-profit periodicals that follow a commercial business model, have also had some difficulties. As of January 2011 *Venus Zine* has ceased publishing their print magazine.[13] Similarly, *BUST* now offers an online version of the magazine at a discounted subscription rate, and, in a 2009 editorial, Stoller appealed for subscriptions.[14] As the costs of producing a print magazine rise, these periodicals

---

12   Andi Zeisler. Interview by author. 20 November 2007.

13   Courtney Gillette. "R.I.P. Venus Zine," *AfterEllen*, <http://www.afterellen.com/people/2010/12/rip-venus-zine>. Published December 14, 2010. Accessed December 17, 2012.

14   See Debbie Stoller, "Future Shock," Editorial, *BUST* (January/February 2009), p. 6.

have adapted, and will continue to adapt, to the changing environment with new, hybrid forms of publication. Indeed, the promotion of crafting and the industry it has spawned have allowed feminist periodicals to adapt to and negotiate the changing demands of the capitalist marketplace, which is an increasingly difficult sphere for print periodicals and has always been a difficult sphere for feminist periodicals to operate within.

Feminist Crafting

The growth of interest in craft, which was fostered through the circulation of these print magazines, did not go unnoticed by the mainstream press. Beginning in the mid-2000s, for example, a spate of articles was published on the "new knitting," featuring titles such as: "Not Your Grandmother's Hobby"; "A Pastime of Grandma and the 'Golden Girls' Evolves Into a Hip New Hobby"; "Knitting: The New Yoga"; and "Rock-and-Roll Knitters: They May Have Blue Hair, But They're No Grannies."[15] As these titles demonstrate, the ways in which the resurgence of knitting was covered in the mainstream press emphasized the discourse of "newness" and trendiness, frequently at the expense of grannies (the "old knitters") who, as I have argued elsewhere, are "constructed as the antithesis of cool," a demographic figured here more in terms of hip replacements than as just plain "hip."[16] However, in examining the discursive construction of crafting in periodicals like *BUST*, *Bitch*, *Shameless*, and *Venus Zine*, what can be found in these feminist texts is a richer, more complex, and—at times—ambivalent relationship between crafters of different generations.

In comparison to more mainstream media publications, the relationship between younger and older generations is generally constructed more positively in *BUST*. For example, the author of one "how-to" article on rag rugs encourages readers to put "their own twists on old-school skills and crafts," with a pattern "inspired by one my grandmother made many years ago."[17] Within the letters to *BUST*, particularly, the potential for craft to link practitioners, particularly women, of different generations is emphasized. In letters to the editor about *BUST*'s craft content—and contrary to mainstream media accounts of "new" knitting—readers discuss the ways in which knitting has helped them connect

---

[15]   See Linda Greider, "Not Your Grandmother's Hobby," *Washingtonian* 36/5 (2001), pp. 136–40, <http://www.washingtonian.com/print/articles/20/99/6294.html> (accessed 29 January 2007); Carol E. Lee, "A Pastime of Grandma and the 'Golden Girls' Evolves Into a Hip New Hobby," *New York Times*, 30 March 2005, <http://www.nytimes.com/2005/03/30/opinion/30wed3.html?_r=1&sq=&st=nyt&oref=slogin> (accessed 2 August 2008); Eva Marer, "Knitting: The New Yoga," *Health* 16/2 (2002), pp. 76–80; and Julie Scelfo, "Rock-and-Roll Knitters: They May Have Blue Hair, But They're No Grannies," *Newsweek* (January 24, 2004), p. 54.

[16]   Groeneveld, "Join the Knitting Revolution," p. 272.

[17]   Jennifer Worick, "From Rags to Riches," *BUST* 47 (October/November 2007), p. 25.

to older family members. One letter writer claims to "love the warm, inclusive feminism of *BUST* and I think you have done brilliant work reclaiming knitting as a respected craft. My Grandma, who taught me to knit, is highly amused by the name Stitch 'n Bitch—her group is called Knit and Natter!"[18] These contributions to *BUST* emphasize the intergenerational aspects of craft and figure older women as sources of inspiration and knowledge, rather than as figures from whom distance needs to be kept.

The potential of craft to link different generations is also discussed in *Bitch*. An article on the reclamation of knitting, for example, takes to task those discursive constructions of craft that rely on "distance from the previous generations, and thus from knitters' own histories," citing, in addition to mainstream press coverage, indie website Craftster.org and craft bazaar Craftilicious, as evidence.[19] Indeed, *BUST*'s approach to knitting and generation can be less positive, at times, than the examples above indicate. For example, in one article on knitting, Stoller (writing as Celina Hex) and Amy Ray encourage readers to knit by stating that "knitting's not just for grannies anymore" and "don't let the old-lady aesthetic frighten you away," before adding parenthetically, "unless you find yourself drawn to things associated with old ladies."[20] This ambivalent statement about the association of craft with old ladies and grannies acknowledges the more mainstream construction of "new" knitting and upholds its ageist rhetoric, while simultaneously claiming to enjoy this same pastime *because* of its association with old ladies. The parentheses around this latter statement, however, minimize the value of this aspect of crafting, in this instance, likening the claim to more of a guilty admission than an embrace. In addition to showing up the more ambivalent relations between craft's association with older generations of women, both of these articles demonstrate not only that feminist periodicals are trend-setting, when it comes to the promotion of crafting, but that they also interact with and respond to the ways in which "new" craft practices are, in turn, discursively produced within mainstream, non-feminist publications. Rather than existing outside of mainstream culture, then, feminist periodicals overlap with this culture, shaping and responding to it.

According to Somerson, while many mainstream media accounts have framed knitting as a return to conservatism and the private sphere, "There's another way to look at the resurgence of knitting, one that focuses on its potential for building community, rejecting consumerist sweatshop culture, and encouraging creativity," an approach that Somerson finds preferable.[21] This emphasis is also found in the ways that periodical readers describe their own crafting practices. For example,

---

18　Anna Wise, Letter to the Editor, *BUST* 36 (December/January 2006), p. 8.

19　Wendy Somerson, "Knot In Our Name: Activism Beyond the Knitting Circle," *Bitch* 34 (Winter 2007), p. 39.

20　Debbie Stoller [Celina Hex] and Amy Ray, "She's Crafty: Knits are for Chicks," *BUST* 14 (Spring 2000), p. 17.

21　Somerson, "Knot In Our Name," p. 39.

one letter writer remarks that "Within the first week of being loaned a few of your back issues, I made no less than three snow globes, two rock T-shirt handbags, and two showy rings. I then proceeded to rave about you to all of my crafty homegirls who were not already informed."[22] Another letter writer, Sally Melville, herself the author of multiple knitting books, writes, "Congratulations on your discovery of knitting … . I find it fascinating that while many of us 'get it'—the intrinsic value of handmade things, the soothing nature of the activity, the community it engenders—there is still, so often, a note of apology surrounding the admission that one knits."[23] The apologetic tone cited by this letter writer, appearing, as it does, in a feminist magazine, references the broader discussions around the politics of crafting being debated within feminist print communities. There is a perception that a feminist has "sold out" if she has dropped her burning bra and is knitting one instead. Of course, the two positions encapsulated by these two caricatured figures (the bra burner and the knitter) are not incommensurable with each other.[24] One does not need to forsake volunteering at a women's shelter, marching in a protest, or advocating for equal pay for knitting. In fact, in some cases, the two may go together very well. In both of these letters, for example, the links between craft and community are emphasized; thus, although crafting is a pastime that can be practiced individually, within feminist periodicals it is the potential of crafting to foster friendships of many kinds that is valued.

The emphasis on creativity and productivity within feminist periodicals is also evidenced in the pages of *Shameless*. *Shameless*'s discursive framing of crafting frequently appeals to the creative and productive aspects of this pastime. The publication also constructs its readers as smart and thrifty for making handmade goods, a discourse that also circulates in *BUST* through, for instance, its repeated salutation of readers as "crafty." Indeed, the longtime title of *BUST*'s craft column, "She's Crafty," constructs readers as smart and subversive; further, as a reference to a Beastie Boys song with the same title,[25] the periodical figures female readers who craft as savvy about independent ("indie") culture and as attractive and sexually available to heterosexual men (perhaps particularly hipster "bad boys"). While much contemporary craft is explicitly queer in its focus and while much encourages the participation of all genders,[26] in *BUST*, the ways in which crafting

---

[22]   Christen McClellan Derr, Letter to the Editor, *BUST* 37 (December/January 2006), p. 8.

[23]   Sally Melville, Letter to the Editor, *BUST* 18 (Summer 2001), p. 6.

[24]   The stereotype of the feminist as bra burner stems from an inaccurate media report on a protest against the 1969 Miss America pageant: no bras were burned during this protest; yet, the figure endures within popular culture representations of feminists.

[25]   The chorus is as follows: "she's crafty / she gets around / she's crafty / she's always down / she's crafty / she's got a gripe / she's crafty / and she's just my type." Beastie Boys and Rick Rubin, "She's Crafty," *Licensed to Ill* (1986).

[26]   See, for example, the craftwork of Allyson Mitchell and Allison Smith, as well as craft groups such as the Washington, DC-based Queer Crafting Collective and the Calgary-based Revolutionary Knitting Circle.

is framed tends towards heteronormativity, which is in keeping with the overall flavor of the magazine—a tendency that has also been flagged by readers. In this sense, acts of reading should not be viewed as simply consuming information, but rather as processes yoked, as Pamela Butler and Jigna Desai put it, to subject formation and "(dis)identification."[27] Making the crafts described in feminist magazines, reading these magazines, discussing them, or even just having them lying around the house, therefore, become performances of feminism and of a particular kind of hipster feminist identity.

Like the DIY zine culture from which they emerged, crafting practices foster small-scale acts of friendship, care, and love not only among individuals, but—moreover—between individuals and feminist periodicals; these relationships between readers and texts can often be as intense, as caring, or as fraught as interpersonal ones. *Venus Zine*, for instance, regularly prints photographs of mail art and crafted items sent in by readers inspired by the magazine (see Figure 12.2), and *BUST* will publish photographs that readers have submitted of their completed craft projects. This practice of sharing cultivates a particular kind of relationship to texts, to crafts, and to community, creating a sense of discursive solidarity that has long been a hallmark of what Lauren Berlant calls "women's culture."[28] According to Berlant, "one of the main jobs of minoritized arts that circulate through mass culture is to tell identifying consumers that 'you are not alone (in your struggles, desires, pleasures)': this is something we know but never tire of hearing confirmed, because aloneness is one of the affective experiences of being collectively, structurally unprivileged."[29] Indeed, contemporary feminist periodicals often print letters that demonstrate the affective relationships between readers and texts that Berlant signals. Writes one reader, "You give me hope that the world isn't all right-wingers, and that there is a community for us 'indies.' I look to you for so many resources, and I can't thank you enough."[30] Moreover, this affection for texts is often figured through their personification, as readers frequently liken magazines to a friend or sister.[31]

As the above examples make clear, these periodicals help to produce particular kinds of affects through the act of reading, such as care, love, creativity, and thrift. These affects are tied to the production of crafts, but are, at the same time, thoroughly embedded in the realm of consumption. As Ann Cvetkovich argues, rather than providing "an alternative to market culture," crafting is more "an

---

[27] Pamela Butler and Jigna Desai, "Marriage, Manolos, and Mantras: Chick-Lit Criticism and Transnational Feminism," *Meridians: Feminism, race, transnationalism* 8/2 (2008), p. 27.

[28] Lauren Berlant, *The Female Complaint: The unfinished business of sentimentality in American culture* (Durham, NC: Duke University Press, 2008), p. 5.

[29] Ibid., p. ix.

[30] Jessica Clark, Letter to the Editor, *BUST* (Summer 2004), p. 7.

[31] See, for example, Stefanie Lenn, Letter to the Editor, *BUST* 42 (December/January 2007), p. 7.

Fig. 12.2   Page from *Venus*, issue 25 (Fall 2005), p. 6.

alternative market culture."[32] In *Venus Zine*, for example, it is this alternative economy that is primarily emphasized within the discursive construction of craft. Many of *Venus Zine*'s articles on crafting are written with an eye towards how handmade craft projects might be converted into small businesses. While certainly not radically challenging to capitalist consumer culture, this discourse represents an important intervention into the realm of commercial culture via the encouragement of women's entry into small businesses in a cultural context where corporate multinationals have the greatest stake in the marketplace; in which knowledge about how to start and maintain a business is less accessible to women; and in which women are frequently not actively encouraged to develop critical skills and knowledge around finance. While feminist crafting emerged out of the DIY ethos of punk music, particularly Riot Grrrl,[33] which has an implicit—and frequently explicit—anti-capitalist stance within feminist DIY periodical culture, the distinction between production and consumption becomes blurred, and the two practices come to exist in a reciprocal relationship. DIY, as Clive Edwards puts it, is "both a producing and a consuming culture," and this relationality is made more visible within, and capitalized upon, in feminist periodicals.[34] *BUST*'s introduction of a regular column, "Buy or DIY," through which readers can learn how to make a handcrafted item or where to purchase a similar one made by someone else, is emblematic in this regard.

Continuities

As the previous section demonstrates, there are differences between how crafting is presented in mainstream media texts and how it is depicted in feminist periodicals. Feminist periodicals typically present a broader discourse on craft that discusses it in terms of business, community, friendship, thrift, love, and care. But one of the most consistent aspects of craft discourse that appears across these media texts is the figuring of crafting hobbies as "new." Many of the letters cited above invoke this discourse through words such as "discovery" and "starting," and the articles in the periodicals reinforce this perspective. While there has been an intensification of crafting in recent years,[35] what is at stake in

---

[32] Ann Cvetkovich, "Depression: A public feelings project" (public lecture, Guelph, Ontario, University of Guelph, 20 March 2008).

[33] Riot Grrrl was (and continues to be) a feminist punk subculture that encouraged women and girls to pick up instruments and start bands, create zines, organize workshops, and make art.

[34] Clive Edwards, "'Home is Where the Art Is': Women, Handicrafts and Home Improvements 1750–1900," *Journal of Design History* 19/1 (2006), p. 11.

[35] According to the Craft Yarn Council of America, "the number of knitters and crocheters between the ages of 25 and 34 jumped 150 percent from 2002 to 2004, attracting 5.7 million people." See: Elizabeth Waickman, "Knitting Hobby Attracting More Men and Younger Devotees," *Point Park News Service* (24 September 2008), <http://pointparknewsservice.com/?p=247>.

continually figuring crafting practices as "new"? Certainly, such discourse allows media texts to self-construct as cutting edge and trendsetting, a journalistic craft tradition that Patricia Bradley dubs "the lure of the new."[36] But one effect of this persistent discourse of newness is that it also results in a distancing from the history of craft practices, eliding the important alliances—not just familial, but also political, aesthetic, and cultural—that might be forged in making these historical continuities more visible. This emphasis on newness is consistent with the ways in which "third-wave feminism" is often cast as a completely new form of feminism, rather than emerging out of and in response to other forms of feminist movements. Thus, within this context, the figuring of crafting as "new" distances contemporary feminist practices from the grassroots activities of previous feminist generations, activities that are not the same as current feminist practice associated with "third-wave feminism," but which share similarities and which might be put into dialogue with each other in fruitful ways. In this section, contemporary feminist crafting is situated within a set of contexts—the longer history of feminism, DIY and zine culture, and contemporary women's culture—that are germane to understanding the emergence of feminist craft cultures and their development.

The ways in which feminist crafting is promoted and discussed in feminist periodicals, particularly in the emphasis on the collective, community basis of craft, clearly resonate with the consciousness-raising (CR) groups established by radical feminists beginning in the 1960s and those which were established later within some Riot Grrrl chapters beginning in the 1990s. Stitch 'n Bitch groups, or other groups of crafters, offer sites for crafters to get together and discuss their lives, potentially linking their personal experiences with more structural and systemic problems. Indeed, the name "Stitch 'n Bitch" suggests that talking and griping (bitching) is as important as the stitching that takes place. While not all knitting circles are going to engage in radical politics, the simple act of making connections and creating community is, as Alison Piepmeier puts it, "meaningful for girls and women in a culture in which they are often figured as each others' competition rather than as allies."[37] In this sense, contemporary craft practices have the potential to unsettle conventionally held beliefs around what constitutes "the political" and how one engages in political practices.

There are also, of course, crafting groups that do engage in practices that are more recognizable as traditionally "political": these include "knit in" occupations and the use of collectively made knitted, sewed, or crocheted banners in protest marches. Beth Pentney's analysis of feminist crafting, for example, cites the Revolutionary Knitting Circle, the Cast Off Knitting Club, and Knit4Choice as groups that have engaged in political actions concerning the G8, militarism, and abortion

---

[36]   Patricia Bradley, *Mass Media and the Shaping of American Feminism, 1963–1975* (Jackson: University Press of Mississippi, 2003), p. 91.

[37]   Piepmeier, *Girl Zines*, p. 79.

rights, respectively.[38] Known as "craftivism," these political interventions are frequently feminist, genderqueer, anti-capitalist, and/or environmentalist in their orientations. In this sense, the political practices associated with traditional forms of feminist organizing find their way into, and are "recast" within, contemporary crafting. However, these kinds of actions also respond to the more immediate context of highly confrontational police violence that has come to mark mass protests in recent decades, with interventions that are marked by the softness of wool and the soothing clickety-clack sounds of knitting needles. The juxtaposition of craft and violence is also notable in the term "yarn bombing," a knitted version of graffiti.

The DIY spirit of contemporary crafting also shares continuities with grassroots feminist organizing that gained strength beginning in the 1960s. The emphasis on independently produced culture found within contemporary feminist craft has an ethos similar to the impetus that drove, for example, the establishment of feminist presses and a plethora of feminist periodicals in the 1960s, 1970s, and 1980s.[39] Another feminist continuity may be found in the links between crafting and Riot Grrrl and zine cultures. Being or becoming a professional musician, writer, or artist was not the point; rather, putting one's voice out into the world, whether through music, text, or art, in a culture that devalues or ignores such voices, was (and is) considered a profoundly political and radical act. The vibrant feminist zine culture spurred by Riot Grrrl continues to thrive and its energy has also inspired and found its way into feminist craft. Indeed, at zine fairs such as Toronto's Canzine, many of the zine makers are also crafters who sell both text and textile at their tables.

While feminist craft culture shares a lineage with feminist punk and zine subcultures, it can also not be divorced from the rise of "domestic goddess" figures like Martha Stewart and Nigella Lawson within popular culture, as well as an intensification of mainstream media coverage on women who "choose" to stay home.[40] Indeed, this continuity is observed by Justine Sharrock who writes in

---

[38]   See also the work of Cat Mazza: <http://post-craft.net/catmazza.htm> and <http://www.microrevolt.org>.

[39]   On feminist publishing, see Simone Murray, *Mixed Media: Feminist presses and publishing politics* (London: Pluto Press, 2004). On the growth of the feminist periodical press, see Kathleen Flannery, *Feminist Literacies, 1968–75* (Chicago: University of Illinois Press, 2005). Sourcebooks on feminist periodicals include Cynthia Ellen Harrison, *Women's Movement Media: A sourcebook* (New York: Bowker and Company, 1975) and Albert Krichmar, *The Woman's Rights Movement in the United States, 1848–1970: A bibliography and sourcebook* (Metuchen, NJ: Scarecrow Press, 1972). Also see Tirza Latimer's contribution to this volume for an example: "*Amazon Quarterly*: Pre-Zine Print Culture and the Politics of Separatism."

[40]   For analyses of the renewed interest in domesticity within the context of "postfeminism," see: Stéfanie Genz, "'I am Not a Housewife, but …' Postfeminism and the Revival of Domesticity," in *Feminism, Domesticity, and Popular Culture*, edited by Stacey Gillis and Joanne Hollows (New York: Routledge, 2009), pp. 49–62; Joanne Hollows, "Feeling Like a Domestic Goddess: Postfeminism and Cooking," *European Journal of Cultural Studies* 6/2 (2003), pp. 179–202.

Bitch that the advertising for household products appearing in *"Bust, Venus*, and, yes, *Bitch*, sometimes [makes] these magazines look more like *Martha Stewart Living* than *Ms.*"[41] Certainly, there is a link between the rise of crafting within feminist indie culture and the rise of neo-domestic celebrity figures. Arguably, however, in feminist periodicals the reclamation of domestic arts is frequently figured, at least aesthetically, as a more critical appropriation. For example, in the pages of *BUST* and *Venus Zine*, there is a reworking of images of women from the 1950s and 1960s, ironically recontextualized so that while the aesthetic elements of the 1950s housewife, for example, may be retained, her reframing within indie subculture creates an "as if-ness" to the image, as in, "as if it were ever really like this." The myth of the happy housewife is implicitly acknowledged as a myth, and yet, while the hard work and primarily invisible and always unpaid work performed by the housewife is not being reclaimed, the aesthetic stylings of this figure as retro kitsch are adopted.

Thus, in contrast to what the 1950s housewife represents—a selfless, tirelessly working figure dedicated to home, husband, and children—the ways in which crafts, linked as they are to the realm of domesticity, are being reclaimed pose key differences from this figure. First, broadly speaking, contemporary feminist crafting is much more closely tied to the public sphere, in terms of the kinds of political interventions performed by crafters, such as "yarn bombing" through which urban objects are "warmed" with handmade cozies. Second, in feminist periodicals, crafting is often figured as a leisure activity and as a way to unwind from the busy world of paid work. Crafting is thus a taste culture[42] coded in a way that has middle- or aspiring middle-class dynamics, given that crafting is usually a time-intensive activity, and resembles the more mainstream domestic goddess texts in this regard. What these continuities between feminist craft cultures and celebrity domestic goddess figures indicate is that—despite the ways in which feminism is often figured as at odds with, or outside of, mainstream culture— feminism and popular culture exist in a relationship of exchange and negotiation, albeit an unequal one.

This discussion also bears on the perceived tension between second- and third-wave feminisms. That is, while indeed many second-wave feminists were critical of domesticity, the kinds of domesticity being reclaimed are quite different from the domesticity critiqued by second-wave feminists, who were also not homogenous in their positions on this matter. In this sense, it is reductive and inaccurate to place these two waves in opposition to each other, when it comes to the matter of craft. One would be hard-pressed to find an article in a third-wave periodical advocating for the reclamation of toilet cleaning, vacuuming, window washing, dish drying, or floor mopping. Activities that are being promoted include knitting, sewing, and

---

41 Justine Sharrock, "The Revolution will not be Sanitized," *Bitch* 19 (Winter 2003), p. 60.

42 See Pierre Bourdieu, *Distinction: A Social Critique on the Judgment of Taste* (New York: Routledge and Keegan Paul, 1984), pp. 1–7.

soap, lamp, and jewelry making. Thus, it is domesticity as *leisure* and *pleasure* that is being advocated; the activities that allow most easily for creativity and the creation of a tangible product, rather than quotidian household tasks.

The multiple contexts out of which feminist craft cultures emerge challenge more straightforwardly linear histories of feminism, as well as the overdetermined wave categories. In principle, the watery-ness of the wave metaphor works well because it has the potential to invoke a language of feminist history that emphasizes fluidity, confluences, surges, tributaries, and slipperiness. Water is powerful: it can suddenly flood or it can gradually erode over time. And waves always have an undertow: water from previous waves running underneath the current ones, returning to a given body of water, a phenomenon that nicely emphasizes the ways in which waves connect with, and are supported by, each other. As Cecilia Chen, Janine MacLeod, and Astrida Neimanis argue, "water's importance to *language and metaphor* reveals how the continuity of watery materiality with meaning opens up thinking practices to great creative potential ... . [T]he movements and transformations of water emphasize shared cultures and unexpected communities."[43] In practice, however, the wave metaphor has become a highly problematic way of representing feminist histories: it tends to elide important "inter-wave" activities; it tends to overly emphasize the contributions of predominantly white middle-class US feminists as the catalyst events for each wave; and it often does not account for the important feminist work that is done in coalitional and in transnational contexts.[44]

Conclusion

Feminist periodicals and their readers offer complex and nuanced articulations of a particular set of activities that highlight the potential of craft to foster community. The development of feminist crafting emerges out of a nexus that includes DIY zine culture, popular women's culture, and feminism. These multiple contexts demonstrate the need for more complex ways of accounting for feminist histories, ones that acknowledge, for example, the ways in which feminism is not a pure space untouched by capital. These multiple contexts also highlight the ways

---

[43] Cecilia Chen, Janine MacLeod, and Astrida Neimanis, "Introduction: Towards a Hydrological Turn?" in *Thinking With Water* (Montreal: McGill University Press [forthcoming]).

[44] For critical writing on the limitations of the wave metaphor, particularly the ways in which it is generationally divisive, see Elizabeth Groeneveld, "Not a Postfeminism Feminist," in *Not Drowning But Waving: Women, Feminism, and the Liberal Arts*, edited by Susan Brown et al. (Edmonton: University of Alberta Press, 2011), pp. 271–84; Astrid Henry, *Not My Mother's Sister* (Bloomington: Indiana University Press, 2004); and Amber Kinser, "Negotiating Spaces For/Through Third-Wave Feminism," *NWSA Journal* 16/3 (Fall 2004), pp. 124–53.

in which the political efficacy of these print publications, in fostering feminist communities, relies on their circulation within a capitalist marketplace.

Third-wave feminist periodicals offer readers a space to enunciate and negotiate their relationships to crafting, in dialogue with each other, with older generations of crafters, with the periodical texts, and with their broader cultural milieu. In this sense, these periodicals serve as important media for the fostering of feminist craft communities and the many activisms generated within and through them. These magazines place more emphasis on the pleasurable, thrifty, creative, and do-it-yourself aspects of crafting, rather than the political activisms that might be fostered through craft. However, these discourses of pleasure, thrift, creativity, and DIY implicitly relate to and emerge out of anti-capitalist feminist politics, through their eschewing of products produced by multinational corporations and encouragement of readers to become producers rather than only consumers, even as these texts are thoroughly embedded within capitalism. In this way, the representation of feminist crafting in third-wave periodicals troubles easy binary distinctions between what is political and what is not, and between what is radical and what is complicit. Rather than taking an "either/or" position when it comes to these categories, third-wave periodicals demonstrate the inherently "both/and"-ness of political activism within the sphere of modern print culture.

Works Cited

Primary Sources

"$1000 Reward," *The Advocate and Family Guardian* (15 January 1849): 11.

Addams, Jane. *A New Conscience and an Ancient Evil* (New York: The Macmillan Company, 1912).

Aldington, Richard. "War Yawp," *Poetry* 5.2 (November 1914): 78–81.

Allen, James S. *The American Negro* (New York: International Publishers, 1932).

———. *Negro Liberation* (New York: International Publishers, 1938).

———. *Smash the Scottsboro Lynch Verdict* (New York: Workers' Library Publishers, 1933).

Anthony, Katharine. "The 'Sister Susie' Peril," *Four Lights: An Adventure in Internationalism* (July 14, 1917).

"As Seen in Court," *Milwaukee Sentinel* (6 December 1886).

"Asks Nation to Curb Maternity Deaths," *New York Times* (4 May 1931).

Bailey, Temple. "A Little Parable for Mothers," *Good Housekeeping* (May 1933).

Bair, Fred. *Does the USA need the KKK?* (Girard, Kansas: Haldeman-Julius, 1928).

Ball, Frank P. *Faults and Virtues of the Ku Klux Klan* (Brooklyn, New York: F.P. Ball, 1927).

"A Beautiful Example," *The Advocate and Family Guardian* (15 March 1884): 83–4.

Bell, Edward P. *Is the Ku Klux Klan Constructive or Destructive? A Debate between Imperial Wizard Evans, Israel Zangwill and Others* (Girard, Kansas: Haldeman-Julius, 1924).

Bentley, Max. "The Ku Klux Klan in Indiana," *McClure's Magazine* 57 (May 1924): 23–33.

———. "The Ku Klux Klan in Texas," *McClure's Magazine* 57 (May 1924): 11–21.

Bigelow, Frederick William. "A Day for Mothers," *Good Housekeeping* (May 1940).

———. "Fighting the Good Fight Again," *Good Housekeeping* (May 1930).

———. "Get Ready for Mother's Day," *Good Housekeeping* (April 1934).

———. "Mother's Day," *Good Housekeeping* (May 1931).

———. "Two Big Days," *Good Housekeeping* (May 1932).

———. "What the Editor has to Say," *Good Housekeeping* (March 1921).

Blake, Aldrich. *The Ku Klux Kraze* (Oklahoma City, Oklahoma: Blake, 1924).

Brooks, Christopher. "She Helped to Raise a Million Babies," *Good Housekeeping* (May 1940).

Browder, Earl. *The Communist Party and the Emancipation of the Negro People* (New York: Harlem Section of the Communist Party, 1934).

Brown, Egbert, *The Final Awakening: A story of the Ku Klux Klan* (Brunswick, Georgia: Overstreet & Co., 1923).

Brown, George Alfred. *Harold the Klansman* (Kansas City, MO: Western Baptist, 1923).

Campbell, Sam H. *The Jewish Problem in the United States* (Atlanta, GA: Knights of the Ku Klux Klan, 1923).

Canham, Erwin D. "It's Time Women Took Direct Action," *Ladies' Home Journal* (January 1952): 18, 108.

Catalogue of the Officers, Faculty, and Students of DeRuyter Institute, for the Year Ending November 29, 1848 (DeRuyter, NY: Cornelius B. Gould, 1848).

Ciolkowska, Muriel. "Fighting Paris," *The Egoist* 4:2.1 (April 1915): 62.

Clark, Jessica. "Letter to the Editor," *BUST* 28 (Summer 2004): 7.

Clark, William Lloyd. *The Devil's Prayer Book, or an Exposure of Auricular Confession as Practiced by the Roman Catholic Church: An Eye-Opener for Husbands, Fathers and Brothers* (Milan, IL: Rail Splitter Press, 1922).

Clason, George S., ed. *Catholic, Jew, Ku Klux Klan: What they Believe, Where they Conflict* (Chicago: Nutshell, 1924).

Cohen, Octavus Roy. "Mother's Day," *Good Housekeeping* (May 1926).

Communist International. "The Negro Question in the United States Resolution of the Communist International," *The Communist International Journal* 8 (1931): n.p.

Communist Party of the United States of America. *Race Hatred on Trial* (New York: Workers Library Publishers, 1931).

Covina, Gina, and Laurel Galana. *The Lesbian Reader* (Berkeley: Amazon Press, 1975).

C.P. "About Reading Story Books," *The Advocate and Family Guardian* (1 July 1885): 196–7.

Darrough, Rose. "To My Mother," *Good Housekeeping* (May 1935).

Derr, Christen McClellan. "Letter to the Editor," *BUST* 37 (December/January 2006): 8.

"DeRuyter Institute—Exhibition," *Sabbath Recorder* 8 (10 July 1851): 14.

Dever, Lem A. *Masks Off! Confessions of an Imperial Klansman* (Portland, OR: Dever, 1925).

Disney, Dorothy Cameron. "Escape to Freedom," *Ladies' Home Journal* (April 1952): 181–4, 192–5.

Dix, Dorothy. "Mirandy on Mothers," *Good Housekeeping* (May 1918).

———. "Mirandy on the Mother's Union," *Good Housekeeping* (May 1919).

Dodds, Harold W. "Women's Place in Politics," *Ladies' Home Journal* (August 1952): 47.

Doolittle, Hilda ("H.D."). Autograph letter signed to Marianne Moore, London, 21 August 1915. V:23:32. Marianne Moore Collection, Rosenbach Museum and Library, Philadelphia.

————. Autograph letter signed to Marianne Moore, London, 15 April 1916. V:23:32. Marianne Moore Collection, Rosenbach Museum and Library, Philadelphia.

————. "Marianne Moore," *The Egoist* 8.3 (August 1916): 118–19.

"Dr. Juliet H. Severance," *Facts* 1 (March and June 1882): 386.

Editors. "An Open Letter to Women in War Time," *The Woman Citizen* (13 April 1918).

Editors. "They Let Us Talk to the Russians," *Ladies' Home Journal* (June 1955): 50–51, 149–54.

Editors. "We Saw How Russians Live," *Ladies' Home Journal* (February 1955): 58–60, 170, 173–6, 179, 187.

Editors. "Who Cares?" *Ladies' Home Journal* (October 1951): 46–7.

Eliot, T.S. "The Love Song of J. Alfred Prufrock," *Poetry* 6.3 (June 1915): 130–35.

Estes, George. *The Roman Katholic Kingdom and the Ku Klux Klan* (Portland, OR: Empire, 1923).

Evans, Hiram Wesley. *The Attitude of the Ku Klux Klan toward the Roman Catholic Hierarchy* (Atlanta, GA: Knights of the Ku Klux Klan, 1927).

————. "The Ballots behind the Ku Klux Klan," *World's Work* 55 (1927): 243–52.

————. "The Catholic Question as viewed by the Ku Klux Klan," *Current History* (July 1927): 563–8.

————. "The Klan: Defender of Americanism," *Forum* 74 (December 1925): 801–14.

————. "The Klan's Fight for Americanism," *North American Review* 223 (Spring 1926): 33–63.

————. *The Menace of Modern Immigration* (Atlanta, Georgia: Knights of the Ku Klux Klan, 1924).

"The Eyes of the World are Upon Us," *Ladies' Home Journal* (September 1952): 50–51.

Florida Legislative Investigation Committee. *Homosexuality and Citizenship in Florida* (Tallahassee, 1964).

"For and Against the Ku Klux Klan," *Literary Digest* (24 September 1921): 34–40.

"Forbid Them Not," *The Advocate and Family Guardian* (15 August 1908): 253–4.

Ford, James, and James S. Allen. *The Negroes in a Soviet America* (New York: Workers' Library Publishers, 1935).

Foster, William Z. *Ford and Foster for Food and Freedom* (New York: Communist Party National Campaign, 1932).

Frost, Stanley. *The Challenge of the Klan* (Indianapolis: Bobbs-Merrill Company, 1924).

————. "When the Klan Rules: The Crusade of the Fiery Cross," *Outlook* 136 (January 1924): 20–24.

Fry, Henry Peck. *The Modern Ku Klux Klan* (Boston: Small, Maynard, 1922).

Fulbright, W.J. "How to Get Better Men Elected," *Ladies' Home Journal* (November 1951): 52, 218.

Glover, Katherine. "Making America Safe for Mothers," *Good Housekeeping* (May 1926).

Gordon, Eugene, and Cyril Briggs. *The Position of Negro Women* (New York: Workers' Library Publishers, 1935).

Grant, Madison. *The Passing of the Great Race; or the racial basis of European history* (New York: C. Scribner's Sons, 1921).

"Greenback Convention," *Milwaukee Sentinel* (25 May 1884).

"Guarding the Gates Against Undesirables," *Current Opinion* (April 1924): 400–401.

Guest, Edgar A. "The Girl He Left Behind," in *Over Here: War time rhymes* (Chicago: The Reilly & Britton Company, 1918).

Halle, Rita S. "Make Motherhood Safe; It Can Be Done!" *Good Housekeeping* (May 1934).

Hamilton, Gertrude Brooke, "Where is Your Mother?" *Good Housekeeping* (May 1920).

Hay, Austin. "Idealist of Imperial Germany," *The New York Times* (July 30, 1922).

Haywood, Harry. *Black Bolshevik* (Chicago: Liberator Press, 1978).

———. *The Road to Negro Liberation* (New York: Workers' Library Publishers, 1934).

———. *The South Comes North* (New York: National Office, League of Struggle for Negro Rights, 1934).

Haywood, Harry, and M. Howard. *Lynching* (New York: International Publishers, 1932).

Herndon, Angelo. *You Cannot Kill the Working Class* (New York: International Labor Defense and League of Struggle for Negro Rights, 1937).

Hickey, Margaret. "14 Points for Beginners in Politics," *Ladies' Home Journal* (February 1952): 49.

———. "Never Too Young," *Ladies' Home Journal* (November 1954): 37, 40.

———. "Teen-Age Citizens," *Ladies' Home Journal* (February 1956): 61.

———. "What's the U.S. to You?" *Ladies' Home Journal* (April 1950): 23.

Hillside, A. "The Unloved Wife," *Banner of Light* 2 (13 February 1858): 4.

"House Committee's Report," *The Advocate and Family Guardian* (16 January 1872): 24.

"Hygeio-Therapeutic College," *Water-Cure Journal* 26 (July 1858): 12.

International Labor Defense. *Death Penalty! The Case of Georgia against Negro and White Workers* (New York: International Labor Defense, 1930).

———. *The Story of Scottsboro* (New York: International Labor Defense, 1931).

Jackson, Helen. *Convent Cruelties or My Life in the Convent: Awful Revelations* (Toledo, OH: Helen Jackson, 1919).

Johnson, Guy B. "A Sociological Interpretation of the New Ku Klux Movement," *Journal of Social Forces* 1 (May 1923): 440–45.

Johnston, Jill. *Lesbian Nation: The Feminist Solution* (New York: Simon and Schuster, 1973).

Jones, Claudia. *An End to the Neglect of the Problems of Negro Women* (New York: National Women's Commission, C.P.U.S.A., 1949).

Jones, Rosemary. "Kefauver's Secret Weapon," *Ladies' Home Journal* (November 1954): 61, 208–11.

Jones, S.S. "Northern Illinois Association of Spiritualists," *Religio-Philosophical Journal* (25 October 1873): 4.

"Juliet H. Severance," *Medical Critic and Guide* 11 (1908): 276.

"Juliet H. Severance," *Slayton's Season Circular 1878–79* (Chicago: Slayton's, 1878): 36.

"Juliet H. Severance, M.D.," *The New York Times* (September 4, 1919): 13.

"Keep on Guarding the Gates," *Current Opinion* (June 1923): 652–4.

Kelly, June. "Mother Love," *Good Housekeeping* (May 1939).

Kenyon, Dr. Josephine H. "A Message to Prospective Mothers," *Good Housekeeping* (May 1938).

Keyes, Frances Parkinson. "Letters From a Senator's Wife," *Good Housekeeping* (March 1921).

King, L.J., ed. *The Converted Catholic and Protestant Missionary Annual* (Toledo, OH: L.J. King, 1924).

Kirk, Lydia. "Letters from Moscow," *Ladies' Home Journal* (April 1952): 62–3, 126–39.

———. "Letters from Moscow," *Ladies' Home Journal* (May 1952): 62–3, 211–20.

Kleeman, Rite Halle. "Seven Proud Women," *Good Housekeeping* (May 1937).

Knight, H.C. "Adeline, the Tailoress," *The Advocate and Family Guardian* (16 April 1849): 57–8.

Knights of the Ku Klux Klan, Inc. *Klan Building* (Atlanta, GA: Knights of the Ku Klux Klan, n.d.).

———. *Klansman's Manual* (Atlanta, GA: Buckhead, 1924).

———. *Kloran* (Atlanta, GA: Knights of the Ku Klux Klan, n.d.).

———. *Papers Read at the Meeting of Grand Dragons, Knights of the Ku Klux Klan at Their First Annual Meeting Held at Asheville, North Carolina, July 1923; Together with Other Articles of Interest to Klansmen* (Atlanta, GA: Knights of the Ku Klux Klan, 1923).

———. *The Practice of Klanishness* (Atlanta, GA: Knights of the Ku Klux Klan, 1924).

———. *Thirty-Three Questions Answered* (Atlanta, GA: Knights of the Ku Klux Klan, n.d.).

"Labor Men Meet," *Milwaukee Sentinel* (18 November 1887).

Lambert, William. Editorial, *ONE* (April 1958): 4–5.

Lawson, Elizabeth. *20 Years on the Chain Gang? Angelo Herndon Must Go Free!* (New York: International Labor Defense, 1935).

Lawson, Elizabeth, D.B. Amis, and League of Struggle for Negro Rights. *They Shall Not Die! The Story of Scottsboro in Pictures* (New York: League of Struggle for Negro Rights by Workers' Library Publishers, 1932).

League of Struggle for Negro Rights. *Equality, Land and Freedom: a Program for Negro Liberation* (New York: League of Struggle for Negro Rights, 1933).

Lenn, Stefanie. "Letter to the Editor," *BUST* 42 (December/January 2007): 7.

"Letter from Dr. A.B. Severance," *Religio-Philosophical Journal* (October 7, 1871): 2.

"Letter from Juliet H. Stillman, M.D.," *Religio-Philosophical Journal* (August 11, 1866): 3.

"Letter from Mrs. J.H. Stillman Severance," *Religio-Philosophical Journal* (August 20, 1870): 2.

Leventhal, Myrna. "Letter to the Editor," *Ladies' Home Journal* (February 1952): 5.

Levine, Nancy Jones. "Letter to the Editor," *Ladies' Home Journal* (February 1958): 4.

"The Liberal League," *Cincinnati Daily Gazette* (September 20, 1880): 2.

L.V.H. "A Plea for Some Girls," *The Advocate and Family Guardian* (16 July 1885): 212–13.

Mast, Blaine. *KKK Friend or Foe: Which?* (Kittanning, PA: Herbrick & Held, 1924).

"Maternal Instinct Run Riot," *Good Housekeeping* (March 1911).

Maternity Center Association. *Campaign Suggestions for Mother's Day, May 12, 1935* (1935).

———. *Maternity Center Association Log, 1915–1975* (1975).

———. *Maternity Center Association Log, 1918–1943* (1943).

———. *Publicity Kit for Mother's Day, May 10, 1931* (1931).

———. *Report of the Mother's Day Educational Activities, Maternity Center Association 1936* (1936).

———. *Six Years in Review 1930–1935* (1935).

———. *The Story of the New Mother's Day* (1935).

Mattachine Society of Washington. "Washington Section," *Eastern Mattachine Magazine* (November–December 1965).

McCracken, S.B. "Victoria C. Woodhull, Free Love, Spiritualism, and Several Other Things," *American Spiritualist* (April 13 1872): 4.

McDowall, John. "The Last Hope," *McDowall's Journal* (January 1833): 1.

———. *Magdalen Facts* (1832).

Mellor, William. *Direct Action* (London: Leonard Parsons, 1920).

Melville, Sally. "Letter to the Editor," *BUST* 18 (Summer 2001): 6.

Metropolitan Life Insurance Company Advertisement. *Good Housekeeping* (May 1931).

Millet, Millie. "Story Books Again," *The Advocate and Family Guardian* (15 August 1885): 246.

Modernist Journals Project (searchable database). Brown and Tulsa Universities, ongoing. <http://www.modjourn.org>.

Monroe, Anne Shannon. "Adventuring in Motherhood," *Good Housekeeping* (May 1920).

Monroe, Harriet. "The Audience—II," *Poetry* 5.1 (October 1914): 31–2.

———. "Editor's Note," *Poetry* 8.1 (October 1918): 55–8.

———. "Notes," *Poetry* 5.2 (November 1914): 96–7.

Monteval, Marion. *The Klan Inside Out* (Claremore, OK: Monarch, 1924).

Moore, Marianne. "Feed Me, Also, River God," *The Egoist* 8.3 (August 1916): 118.

———. "The Fish," *The Egoist* 7.5 (August 1918): 95.

———. "The Fish," Folder I:02:04, 1917. Marianne Moore Collection, Rosenbach Museum and Library, Philadelphia.

———. "He Made This Screen," *The Egoist* 8.3 (August 1916): 118.

———. "Jean De Bosschére's Poems," *Poetry* 12.1 (April 1918): 48–51.

———. "A Note on T.S. Eliot's Book," *Poetry* 12.1 (April 1918): 36–7.

———. *Observations* (New York: The Dial Press, 1924).

———. *Poems* (London: The Egoist Press, 1921).

———. "Pouters and Fantails: That harp you play so well, to an intra-mural rat, counseil to a bachelor, appelate jurisdiction, the wizard in words," *Poetry* 6.2 (May 1915): 70–72.

———. "Reinforcements," *The Egoist* 6.5 (June–July 1918): 21.

———. "Talisman," *The Egoist* 8.3 (August 1916): 118.

———. "To A Man Working His Way Through The Crowd," *The Egoist* 4:2 (April 1, 1915): 62.

———. "To A Screen-Maker," *Typn O'Bob* 6 (January 1909): 2–3.

———. "To A Screen-Maker," unpublished letter, Folder VI:15a:03 (4 February). Marianne Moore Collection, Rosenbach Museum and Library, Philadelphia.

———. "To a Steam Roller," *The Egoist* 10.2 (1 October): 158.

———. "To an Artificer" and "To A Screen-Maker" (in letter of December 12–13, 1908), reproduced in *The Selected Letters of Marianne Moore*, edited by Bonnie Costello, Celeste Goodridge, and Cristanne Miller (New York: Knopf, 1997), 52–3.

———. "To Art Wishing for a Fortress into Which / She may Flee from her Prosecutors, in- / stead of Looking for a Jail in Which to / Confine Them," n.d. Folder I:04:57. Marianne Moore Collection, Rosenbach Museum and Library, Philadelphia.

———. "To Be Liked By You Would Be A Calamity," *The Chimaera* 1.2 (July 1916): 56.

———. "To Military Progress," in *Observations* (New York: The Dial Press, 1924), 19.

———. "To Statecraft Embalmed," *Others* 1.6 (December 1915): 104.

———. "To the Soul of 'Progress,'" *The Egoist* 4.2 (1 April 1915): 62.

———. "To William Butler Yeats on Tagore," *The Egoist* 2.5 (1 May 1915).

———. "Wild Swans," *Poetry* 8.1 (October 1918): 42–4.

"Mother Love," *Good Housekeeping* (May 1910).

"Mother's Day," *American Journal of Nursing* 31.4 (April 1931): 449–50.

"Mother's Day," *Good Housekeeping* (May 1909).

"The Mother's Day Campaign," *American Journal of Nursing* 31.7 (July 1931): 839.

"Mother's Day, May 13," *American Journal of Nursing* 34.4 (April 1934): 342.

Mother's Day, SR. 16, 73rd Congress, 1st session, Congressional Record 77 (1 May 1933): 2615.

"Mrs. J.H. Stillman, M.D." [advertisement], *Dewitt (Iowa) Standard* (16 January 1861): 1.

"Mrs. J.H. Stillman, M.D." [advertisement], *Whitewater Register* (14 November 1862).

"Mrs. Juliet H. Severance, M.D., Milwaukee," *Facts* 1 (March and June 1882): 10–11.

"Mrs. Severance's Harangue," *Milwaukee Sentinel* (21 March 1888): 1–2.

New York World, *The Facts about the Ku Klux Klan* (New York: The World, 1921).

"Night-Sitting," *The Advocate and Family Guardian* (1 December 1844): 356.

Norris, Kathleen. "If You Are the Right Kind of Mothers, You Will Not Be Looking for Back Pay on Mother's Day," *Good Housekeeping* (May 1930).

North, Joseph. *Lynching Negro Children in Southern Courts* (New York: International Labor Defense, 1932).

Northrup, Elizabeth. "My Ideal Girl," *The Advocate and Family Guardian* (15 September 1908): 285–6.

"Nurses and Safe Maternity Care," *American Journal of Nursing* 37.4 (April 1937): 392–4.

"Our Fiction Magazines," *The Advocate and Family Guardian* (May 1925): 66.

"Our Own Four Walls: Where *Good Housekeeping* Readers, Writers and Editors Can Talk to One Another as Members of the Family," *Good Housekeeping* (April 1930).

Parlin, Charles C. "Women Versus the Kremlin," *Ladies' Home Journal* (October 1956): 46–50, 127.

Pattangall, William R. "Is the Ku Klux Klan Un-American?" *Forum* 74 (September 1925): 321–32.

"A Peculiar People," *St. Louis Globe-Democrat* (30 September 1882): 11.

"A Pink Carnation—or a Life on Mother's Day?" *New York Times* (12 May 1929).

Pound, Ezra. "The Audience—I," *Poetry* 5.1 (October 1914): 29–30.

———. "Dialogues of Fontanelle," *The Egoist* 8.3 (August 1916): 118–19.

———. *Pavannes and Divisions* (New York: Knopf, 1918).

"Prostitution in New-York," *New York Times* (10 November 1858).

Racism Research Project. *Critique of the Black Nation Thesis* (Berkeley: Racism Research Project, 1975).

Riley, Kay. "Mother's Day—of Reckoning," *Good Housekeeping* (May 1940).

Robinson, Eloise. "Fatherland," *Poetry* 8.1 (October 1918): 1–5.

"The Rockford Convention, Cont'd.," *Religio-Philosophical Journal* (12 July 1873): 8.

Roosevelt, Eleanor. "If You Ask Me," *Ladies' Home Journal* (April 1948): 77.

———. "My Day," *Good Housekeeping* (20 May 1936).

Rugel, Clara Hood. "Mothers are Funny: Maybe That's Why We Love Them So Much," *Good Housekeeping* (May 1936).

"Russell Trall," in *Appleton's Cyclopaedia of American Biography*, edited by Grant Wilson and John Fiske (D. Appleton, 1889), VI: 154.

Sangster, Margaret E. "Mother Memories: Is Today's Child Missing Something that Yesterday's Child Holds Dear?" *Good Housekeeping* (May 1936).

"Saving Mothers from Unnecessary Deaths," *American Journal of Nursing* 34.3 (March 1934): 272.

Saxon, A. *Knight Vale of the KKK: A Fiction Story of Love, Patriotism, Intrigue and Adventure* (Columbus, OH: Patriot, 1924).

Scottsboro Defense Committee. *Scottsboro: The Shame of America* (New York: Scottsboro Defense Committee, 1936).

Severance, J.H. "Farmers' Wives," *Transactions of the Wisconsin State Agricultural Society* 24 (1886): 274–5.

———. "An Important Question," *Truth Seeker* (11 October 1919): 655.

———. "Is the Present Marriage System a Failure," *Universe* (28 August 1869): 72.

———. "The 'Lucifer Match,'" *Truth Seeker* (20 January 1887): 71.

———. "Shall Such Things Continue," *Truth Seeker* (11 February 1893): 87–8.

———. "To my Fellow Workers," *Religio-Philosophical Journal* (19 November 1870): 2.

———. [Untitled letter], *American Journal of Eugenics* 1 (1907): 232.

———. "What Can Be Done," *Truth Seeker* (31 December 1887): 839.

Sharrock, Justine. "The Revolution will not be Sanitized," *Bitch* 19 (Winter 2003): 60–63, 93–4.

Shepard, William G. "The Fiery Double-Cross," *Collier's National Weekly* (28 July 1928): 8–9.

———. "How I Put Over the Klan," *Collier's National Weekly* (14 July 1928): 5–7.

———. "Ku Klux Koin," *Collier's National Weekly* (21 July 1928): 38–9.

Smith, Margaret Chase. "No Place for a Woman?" *Ladies' Home Journal* (February 1952): 50, 83.

"Some of the Consequences of Maternal Unfaithfulness," *The Friend of Virtue* (15 July 1847): 221.

Somerson, Wendy. "Knot In Our Name: Activism beyond the knitting circle," *Bitch* 34 (Winter 2007): 36–41.

Spivak, John Louis. *On the Chain Gang* (New York: International Publishers, 1932).

Stanton, E.F. *Christ and Other Klansmen, or Lives of Love: The cream of the Bible spread upon Klanism* (Kansas City, MO: Stanton & Harper, 1924).

Steinbeck, John. "Women and Children in the USSR," *Ladies' Home Journal* (August 1946): 44–59.

Stevens, Wallace. "Phases," *Poetry* 5.2 (November 1914): 70–71.

Stewart, Helen Campbell. "Big Flat," *The Advocate and Family Guardian* (16 April 1887): 125.

Stillman, J.H. "Experience in Hygeio-Therapeutics," *Water-Cure Journal* 29 (May 1860): 70.

———. "Hints to Reformers," *Water-Cure Journal* 26 (December 1858): 96.

———. "The Social Question," *Religio-Philosophical Journal* (7 July 1866): 3.

Stoller, Debbie. "Future Shock," *BUST* (January/February 2009): 6.

———. "The Shiz-Knit: Join the knitting revolution," *BUST* 19 (Spring 2002): 15–16.

———. *Stitch 'n Bitch: Advanced* (New York: Workman Press, 2009).

———. *Stitch 'n Bitch Nation* (New York: Workman Press, 2004).

———. *Stitch 'n Bitch: The happy hooker* (New York: Workman Press, 2006).

———. *Stitch 'n Bitch: The knitter's handbook* (New York: Workman Press, 2003).

Stoller, Debbie [Celina Hex], and Amy Ray. "She's Crafty: Knits are for chicks," *BUST* 14 (Spring 2000): 17.

Stoller, Debbie [Celina Hex], and Marcelle Karp [Betty Boob]. Editorial, *BUST* 1 (1993).

Stoller, Debbie, and Marcelle Karp, eds. *The BUST Guide to the New Girl Order* (New York: Penguin Books [reprint], 1999).

"Subscribe," *VenusZine.com*. <http://www.venuszine.com/subscribe> (accessed July 20, 2011).

"They Say it with Action," *Ladies' Home Journal* (February 1953): 62–3, 148–50.

Thompson, Dorothy. "America's Greatest Problem," *Ladies' Home Journal* (December 1946): 6, 228.

———. "The Challenge of a Soviet Education," *Ladies' Home Journal* (May 1956): 11–14, 225.

———. "Do American Educators Know What They Are Up To?" *Ladies' Home Journal* (February 1958): 11–14, 139.

———. "The Economical Man is the Patriot," *Ladies' Home Journal* (April 1948): 11–12.

———. "The Great Affirmative," *Ladies' Home Journal* (November 1953): 11, 14.

———. "I Write of Russian Women," *Ladies' Home Journal* (March 1952): 11–18.

———. "Liberty and Conformity in America," *Ladies' Home Journal* (October 1954): 18.

———. "On Loyalty," *Ladies' Home Journal* (June 1952): 11–12, 164.

———. "A Primer on the Cold War," *Ladies' Home Journal* (August 1950): 11–12, 134.

———. "Report on the American Communist," *Ladies' Home Journal* (January 1953): 12.

———. "The Soviet School Child," *Ladies' Home Journal* (February 1956): 25.

———. "To Protect Civil Liberties," *Ladies' Home Journal* (February 1952): 12.

———. "What Price Liberty?' *Ladies' Home Journal* (May 1958): 11, 14.

"To Help Mother," *Good Housekeeping* (May 1915).

Todd, Constance L. "Babies Without Pain," *Good Housekeeping* (November 1937).

Tomkins, Juliet Wilbur. "A Submerged Mother: A Tale for Mother's Day," *Good Housekeeping* (May 1911).

Trall, Russell T. *The Illustrated Hydropathic Review* (New York: Fowler and Wells, 1855).

"Truth," *The Advocate and Family Guardian* (December 1, 1885): 358.

VenusZine.com Press Kit. <http://venuszine.com/advertise> (accessed June 19, 2011).

"Visiting Committee's Report," *The Advocate and Family Guardian* (1 May 1849): 71.

Waickman, Elizabeth. "Knitting Hobby Attracting More Men and Younger Devotees," *Point Park News Service* (September 24, 2008). <http://point parknewsservice.com/?p=247> (accessed 19 June 2011).

Wells-Barnett, Ida. *Southern Horrors: Lynch Law in All Its Phases* (New York: The New York Age Print, 1892).

Welshimer, Helen, "16,000 New Mothers Will Die This Year, And—Two Out of Three Can Be Saved," *Good Housekeeping* (June 1936).

"What People Like to Read," *The Advocate and Family Guardian* (December 1925): 178.

White, Bishop Alma. *Heroes of the Fiery Cross* (Zarephath, NJ: The Good Citizen, 1928).

———. *Klansmen: Guardians of Liberty* (Zarephath, NJ: The Good Citizen, 1926).

———. *The Ku Klux Klan in Prophecy* (Zarephath, NJ: The Good Citizen, 1925).

Wing, Diana "Letter to the Editor," *BUST* 37 (February/March 2006): 8.

Wise, Anna. "Letter to the Editor," *BUST* 36 (December/January 2006): 8.

"A Woman Anarchist," *The [Oshkosh] Daily Northwestern* (2 December 1886): 1.

"Women Like You and Me in Politics," *Ladies' Home Journal* (February 1952): 48–9, 122–4.

Worick, Jennifer. "From Rags to Riches," *BUST* 47 (October/November 2007): 25–6.

"You Can Ask Questions," *Ladies' Home Journal* (March 1952): 62, 164.

Zeisler, Andi. Email Interview with Elizabeth Groeneveld. 20 November 2007.

Secondary Sources

Aboulafia, M., M. Bookman, and C. Kemp. *Habermas and Pragmatism* (New York: Routledge, 2002).

Allen, Gwen. *Artists' Magazines: An Alternative Space for Art* (Cambridge, MA: MIT Press, 2011).

Allen, Gwen, and Cherise Smith. "Publishing Art Alternative Distribution in Print," *Art Journal* 66.1 (Spring 2007): 41–5.

Allen, James S. *Organizing in the Depression South: A Communist's memoir* (Minneapolis, MN: MEP Publications, 2001).

Alonson, Harriet Hyman. *Peace as a Women's Issue* (Syracuse, NY: Syracuse University Press, 1993).

Altieri, Charles. *The Art of Twentieth-Century American Poetry: Modernism and after* (Oxford: Blackwell, 2006).

Anderson, Benedict R. *Imagined Communities: reflections on the origin and spread of nationalism* (London: Verso, 1991).

Antolini, Katharine. "Memorializing Motherhood: Anna Jarvis and the Struggle for Control of Mother's Day" (dissertation, West Virginia University, 2009).

Apple, Rima D. "Constructing Mothers: Scientific Motherhood in the Nineteenth and Twentieth Centuries," in *Mothers and Motherhood: Readings in American History*, edited by Rima Apple and Janet Golden (Columbus: Ohio State University Press, 1997): 90–110.

Aptheker, Bettina, ed. *Lynching and Rape: an exchange of views by Jane Addams and Ida B. Wells* (New York: American Institute for Marxist Studies, 1982).

Bailey, Courtney. "Bitching and Talking/Gazing Back: Feminism as Critical Reading," *Women and Language* 26.2 (2003): 1–8.

Barker, Kristen. "Birthing and Bureaucratic Women: Needs Talk and the Definitional Legacy of the Sheppard-Towner Act," *Feminist Studies* 29.2 (Summer 2003): 333–55.

Barnes, Elizabeth. *States of Sympathy: Seduction and democracy in the American novel* (New York: Columbia University Press, 1997).

Bazin, Victoria. *Marianne Moore and the Cultures of Modernity* (Aldershot, UK and Burlington, VT: Ashgate Publishing, 2010).

Beastie Boys and Rick Rubin. "She's Crafty," in *Licensed to Ill* (Columbia Records, 1986) [audio recording].

Beatty, Barbara, Emily D. Cahan, and Julia Grant, eds. *When Science Encounters the Child: Education, Parenting, and Child Welfare in 20th-Century America* (New York: Teachers College Press, 2006).

Berger, John. *Ways of Seeing* (London: Penguin Group, 1972).

Berlant, Lauren. *The Female Complaint: The unfinished business of sentimentality in American culture* (Durham, NC: Duke University Press, 2008).

Blee, Kathleen M. *Women of the Klan: Racism and Gender in the 1920s* (Berkeley: University of California Press, 1991).

Bollman, Don. *Run for the Roses: A 50 Year memoir* (Mecosta, MI: Canadian Lakes, 1975).

Bornstein, George. *Material Modernism: The politics of the page* (Cambridge: Cambridge University Press, 2001).

Borst, Arno. *The Ordering of Time From the Ancient Computus to the Modern Computer* (Chicago: University of Chicago Press, 1993).

Bourdieu, Pierre. *Distinction: A social critique on the judgment of taste*. Trans. Richard Nice (New York: Routledge and Keegan Paul, 1984).

Boyer, Paul. "Gilded-Age Consensus, Repressive Campaigns, and Gradual Liberalization: The shifting rhythms of book censorship," in *Print in Motion: The expansion of publishing and reading in the United States, 1880–1940, A history of the book in America, Volume IV*, edited by Carl F. Kaestle and Janice A. Radway (Chapel Hill: University of North Carolina Press, 2005), 276–98.

Bradley, Patricia. *Mass Media and the Shaping of American Feminism, 1963–1975* (Jackson: University Press of Mississippi, 2003).

Braude, Ann. *Radical Spirits: Spiritualism and Women's Rights in Nineteenth-Century America* (Bloomington: Indiana University Press [second edition], 2001).

Butler, Pamela, and Jigna Desai. "Marriage, Manolos, and Mantras: Chick-lit criticism and transnational feminism," *Meridians: Feminism, Race, Transnationalism* 8.2 (2008): 1–31.

Cahill, Daniel. *Harriet Monroe* (New York: Twayne, 1973).

Calomiris, Charles W., and Larry Schweikart. "The Panic of 1857: Origins, Transmission, and Containment," *Journal of Economic History* 51.4 (December 1991): 807–34.

Capozzola, Christopher. *Uncle Sam Wants You: WWI and the making of the modern American citizen* (Oxford: Oxford University Press, 2008).

Carter, Dan T. *Scottsboro: A tragedy of the American South* (Baton Rouge: Louisiana State University Press, 1979).

Cayleff, Susan. *Wash and Be Healed: The water-cure movement and women's health* (Philadelphia: Temple University Press, 1987).

Chalmers, David M. *Hooded Americanism: The history of the Ku Klux Klan* (New York: Franklin Watts [second edition], 1976).

Chen, Cecilia, Janine MacLeod, and Astrida Neimanis. "Introduction: towards a hydrological turn?" in *Thinking With Water* (Montreal: McGill University Press [forthcoming]).

Chomsky, Noam. *Media Control: Spectacular achievements of propaganda* (New York: Seven Stories, 1991 [2002]).

Chuppa-Cornell, Kim. "Filling a Vacuum: Women's Health Information in *Good Housekeeping*'s Articles and Advertisements, 1920–1965," *Historian* 3 (2005): 454–73.

Churchill, Suzanne W. *The Little Magazine "Others" and the Renovation of Modern American Poetry* (Aldershot, UK and Burlington, VT: Ashgate Publishing, 2006).

Churchill, Suzanne W., and Adam McKible, eds. *Little Magazines and Modernism: New Approaches* (Aldershot, UK and Burlington, VT: Ashgate Publishing, 2007).

Clark, Lynn Schofield. *From Angels to Aliens: Teenagers, the media, and the supernatural* (New York: Oxford University Press, 2005).

Clement, Elizabeth Alice. *Love for Sale: Courting, treating, and prostitution in New York City, 1900–1945* (Chapel Hill: University of North Carolina Press, 2006).

Clews, John C. *Communist Propaganda Techniques* (New York: Frederick A. Praeger, 1964).

Conlin, Joseph R. *American Anti-War Movements* (Beverly Hills: The Glencoe Press, 1968).

Connelly, Mark Thomas. *The Response to Prostitution in the Progressive Era* (Chapel Hill: University of North Carolina Press, 1980).

Cott, Nancy. *The Bonds of Womanhood: "Women's Sphere" in New England, 1780–1835* (New Haven, CT: Yale University Press, 1977).

———. *The Grounding of Modern Feminism* (New Haven, CT: Yale University Press, 1987).

Coughlan, Robert. "Konklave in Kokomo," in *The Aspirin Age: 1919–1941*, edited by Isabel Leighton (New York: Simon and Schuster, 1949), 105–29.

Cruse, Harold. *Crisis of the Negro Intellectual* (New York: William Morrow & Company, 1967).

Cvetkovich, Ann. "Depression: A public feelings project" (public lecture, Guelph, Ontario, University of Guelph, March 20, 2008).

Davies, Carole Boyce. *Left of Karl Marx: The political life of Black Communist Claudia Jones* (Durham, NC: Duke University Press, 2007).

Davis, Angela. *Women, Race, and Class* (New York: Vintage Books, 1983).

Davis, David Brion. "Some Themes of Counter-subversion: An analysis of Anti-Masonic, Anti-Catholic and Anti-Mormon literature," *Mississippi Valley Historical Review* 47 (1960): 205–24.

D'Emilio, John. *Sexual Politics, Sexual Communities: The making of a homosexual minority in the United States, 1940–1970* (Chicago: University of Chicago Press, 1983).

D'Enbeau, Suzy. "Feminine and Feminist Transformation in Popular Culture: An application of Mary Daly's Radical Philosophies to Bust Magazine," *Feminist Media Studies* 9.1 (2009): 17–36.

Desmond, Humphrey J. *The Know-Nothing Party* (New York: Arno Press [reprint], 1969).

Dobson, Joanne. "Reclaiming Sentimental Literature," *American Literature* 69 (1997): 263–88.

Dodge, Mara L. *"Whores and Thieves of the Worst Kind": A study of women, crime, and prisons, 1835–2000* (DeKalb: Northern Illinois University Press, 2002).

Donegan, Jane. *Hydropathic Highway to Health: Women and water-cure in antebellum America* (New York: Greenwood Press, 1986).

Donovan, Brian. *White Slave Crusades: Race, gender, and anti-vice activism, 1887–1917* (Urbana: University of Illinois Press, 2006).

Doob, Leonard W. *Propaganda: Its psychology and technique* (New York: Henry Holt and Company, 1935).

Dray, Philip. *At the Hands of Persons Unknown: The lynching of Black America* (New York: Random House, 2002).

Du Bois, W.E.B. *Black Reconstruction in America* (New York: The Free Press, 1935 [1998]).

Duncan, David Ewing. *Calendar: Humanity's epic struggle to determine a true and accurate year* (New York: Harper Perennial, 1998).

Duncombe, Stephen. *Notes from the Underground: Zines and the politics of alternative culture* (London: Verso, 1997).

Early, Frances H. *A World without War: How U.S. feminists and pacifists resisted World War I.* (Syracuse, NY: Syracuse University Press, 1997).

Edwards, Clive. "'Home is Where the Art Is': Women, Handicrafts and Home Improvements 1750–1900," *Journal of Design History* 19.1 (2006): 11–21.

Endres, Kathleen L., and Therese L. Lueck. *Women's Periodicals in the United States: Social and political issues* (Westport, CT: Greenwood Press, 1996).

Enke, Anne. *Finding the Movement: Sexuality, contested space, and feminist activism* (Durham, NC: Duke University Press, 2007).

Escoffier, Jeffrey. *Bigger Than Life: The history of gay porn cinema from beefcake to hardcore* (Philadelphia: Running Dog Press, 2009).

Ettinger, Laura E. *Nurse-Midwifery: The birth of a new American profession* (Columbus: Ohio State University Press, 2006).

Faderman, Lillian, and Stuart Timmons. *Gay L.A.: A history of sexual outlaws, power politics and lipstick lesbians* (New York: Basic Books, 2006).

Fink, Leon. *Workingmen's Democracy: The Knights of Labor and American politics* (Urbana: University of Illinois Press, 1983).

Finnegan, Margaret. *Selling Suffrage: Consumer culture and votes for women* (New York: Columbia University Press, 1999).

Fisher, Philip. *Hard Facts: Setting and form in the American novel* (New York: Oxford University Press, 1985).

Flannery, Kathryn. *Feminist Literacies, 1968–75* (Chicago: University of Illinois Press, 2005).

Foner, Philip S. *American Socialism and Black Americans: From the age of Jackson to World War II* (Westport, CT: Greenwood Press, 1977).

Forman, James. *Self-determination and the African-American people* (Seattle: Open Hand Publications, 1981).

Foster, Carrie A. *The Women and the Warriors: The U.S. section of the Women's International League for Peace and Freedom, 1915–1946* (Syracuse, New York: Syracuse University Press, 1995).

Foster, William Z. *History of the Communist Party in the United States* (New York: Greenwood Press, 1968).

———. *The Negro People in American History* (New York: International Publishers, 1954).

Fox, Craig. *Everyday Klansfolk: White Protestant life and the KKK in 1920s Michigan* (East Lansing: Michigan State University Press, 2011).

Fraser, H. *Gender and the Victorian Periodical* (Cambridge: Cambridge University Press, 2003).

Friedan, Betty. *The Feminine Mystique* (New York: W.W. Norton and Company, 1997).

Genz, Stéfanie. "'I am Not a Housewife, but …': Postfeminism and the revival of domesticity," in *Feminism, Domesticity, and Popular Culture*, edited by Stacey Gillis and Joanne Hollows (New York: Routledge, 2009), 49–62.

Giddings, Paula J. *Ida: A sword among lions: Ida B. Wells and the campaign against lynching* (New York: Amistad, 2008).

Gilfoyle, Timothy J. *City of Eros: New York City, prostitution, and the commercialization of sex, 1790–1920* (New York: W.W. Norton and Company, 1992).

Gilmore, Glenda Elizabeth. *Defying Dixie: The radical roots of Civil Rights, 1910–1950* (New York: W.W. Norton & Co., 2008).

Goodman, James E. *Stories of Scottsboro* (New York: Pantheon Books, 1994).

Gould, Bruce, and Beatrice Blackman Gould. *American Story: Memories and reflections of Bruce Gould and Beatrice Blackman Gould* (New York: Harper and Row Publishers, 1968).

Grant, Julia. *Raising Baby by the Book: Education of American Mothers* (New Haven, CT: Yale University Press, 1998).

Grayzel, Susan R. *Women's Identities at War: Gender, motherhood, and politics in Britain and France during the First World War* (Chapel Hill: University of North Carolina Press, 1999).

Greider, Linda. "Not Your Grandmother's Hobby," *Washingtonian* 36.5 (2001): 136–40. <http://www.washingtonian.com/print/articles/20/99/6294.html> (accessed 29 January 2007).

Groeneveld, Elizabeth. "Be a Feminist Or Just Dress Like One," *Journal of Gender Studies* 18.2 (June 2009): 177–90.

———. "'Join the Knitting Revolution': Third-wave feminist magazines and the politics of domesticity," *Canadian Review of American Studies* 40.2 (2010): 259–78.

———. "'Not a Postfeminism Feminist': Feminism's third wave," in *Not Drowning But Waving: Women, Feminism, and the Liberal Arts*, edited by Susan Brown et al. (Edmonton, Alberta: University of Alberta Press, 2011).

Gruber Garvey, Ellen. *The Adman in the Parlor: Magazines and the gendering of consumer culture, 1880s to 1910s* (Oxford: Oxford University Press, 1996).

Habermas, Jürgen. "The Public Sphere: An Encyclopedia Article," *New German Critique* 3 (Autumn 1974): 49–55.

———. *The Theory of Communicative Action Volume 1: Reason and the Rationalization of Society*. Trans. Thomas McCarthy (Boston: Beacon Press, 1984).

Hall, Jacquelyn Dowd. *Revolt Against Chivalry: Jessie Daniel Ames and the women's campaign against lynching* (New York: Columbia University Press, 1993).

Haltunnen, Karen. *Confidence Men and Painted Women: a study of middle-class culture in America, 1830–1870* (New Haven, CT: Yale University Press, 1982).

Hamm, Thomas D. *The Quakers in America* (New York: Columbia University Press, 2003).

Hanson, Dian. *Bob's World: The life and boys of AMG's Bob Mizer* (Koln, Germany: Taschen, 2009).

Harris, Michael. *Colored Pictures: Race and visual representation* (Chapel Hill: University of North Carolina Press, 2006).

Harrison, Cynthia Ellen. *Women's Movement Media: A sourcebook* (New York: Bowker Company, 1975).

Hayden, Michael J. "The Uses of Political Pamphlets: The Example of 1614–1615 in France," *Canadian Journal of History/Annales Canadiennes d'Histoire* 21 (August 1986): 143–65.

Hays, Sharon. *The Cultural Contradictions of Motherhood* (New Haven, CT: Yale University Press, 1996).

Haywood, Harry. *Black Bolshevik* (Chicago: Liberator Press, 1978).

Hendler, Glenn. *Public Sentiments: Structures of feeling in nineteenth-century American literature* (Chapel Hill: University of North Carolina Press, 2001).

Henry, Alice. *The Trade Union Woman* (New York: D. Appleton and Co., 1915).

Henry, Astrid. *Not My Mother's Sister* (Bloomington: Indiana University Press, 2004).

Heuving, Jeanne. *Omissions are not Accidents: Gender in the art of Marianne Moore* (Detroit, MI: Wayne State University Press, 1992).

Hobson, Barbara Meil. *Uneasy Virtue: The politics of prostitution and the American reform tradition* (New York: Basic Books, 1987).

Hollows, Joanne. "Feeling Like a Domestic Goddess: Postfeminism and Cooking," *European Journal of Cultural Studies* 6.2 (2003): 179–202.

Hooven, F. Valentine. *Beefcake: The muscle magazines of America: 1950–1970* (Koln, Germany: Taschen, 1995).

Horne, Gerald. *Black Liberation/Red Scare: Ben Davis and the Communist Party* (London: Associated University Presses, 1994).

Hotelling Zona, Kirstin. *Marianne Moore, Elizabeth Bishop, and May Swenson: The feminist poetics of self-restraint* (Ann Arbor: University of Michigan Press, 2002).

Howard, Esme J. "Navigating the Stormy Sea: The Maternity Center Association and the Development of Prenatal Care 1900–1930" (master's thesis, Yale University School of Nursing, 1994).

Howard, Walter. *Black Communists Speak on Scottsboro: A documentary history* (Philadelphia: Temple University Press, 2008).

Hurewitz, Daniel. *Bohemian Los Angeles and the Making of Modern Politics* (Berkeley: University of California Press, 2007).

Hutchinson, Earl Ofari. *Blacks and Reds: Race and class in conflict 1919–1990* (East Lansing: Michigan State University Press, 1995).

Ingle, H. Larry. *Quakers in Conflict: The Hicksite Reformation* (Philadelphia: Pendle Hill, 1998).

Jackson, Kenneth T. *The Ku Klux Klan in the City, 1915–1930* (Chicago: Ivan R. Dee [second edition], 1992).

Johnson, David. *The Lavender Scare: The Cold War persecution of gays and lesbians in the Federal Government* (Chicago: University of Chicago Press, 2004).

———. "Physique Pioneers: The politics of 1960s gay consumer culture," *Journal of Social History* 43.4 (2010): 867–92.

Johnson, Manning. *Color, Communism, and Common Sense* (Belmont, MA: American Opinion, 1963).

Joost, Nicholas. *Scofield Thayer and The Dial: An illustrated history* (Carbondale, IL: Southern Illinois University Press, 1964).

Jowett, Gareth S., and Victoria O'Donnell. *Propaganda and Persuasion* (London: Sage Publications [third edition], 1999).

Kearney, Mary Celeste. *Girls Make Media* (New York: Routledge, 2006).

Kelley, Robin D.G. *Hammer and Hoe: Alabama Communists during the Great Depression* (Chapel Hill: University of North Carolina Press, 1990).

Kennedy, Elizabeth Lapovsky, and Madeline Davis. *Boots of Leather, Slippers of Gold: The history of a lesbian community* (New York: Routledge, 1993).

Kinser, Amber E. "Negotiating Spaces For/Through Third-Wave Feminism," *NWSA Journal* 16.3 (Fall 2004): 124–53.

Kissack, Terence, "Freaking Fag Revolutionaries: New York's Gay Liberation Front, 1969–1971," *Radical History Review* 62 (1995): 104–35.

Kitch, Carolyn. *The Girl on the Magazine Cover* (Chapel Hill: University of North Carolina Press, 2001).

Klaus, Alisa. *Every Child a Lion: The origins of maternal and infant health in the United States and France 1890–1920* (Ithaca, NY: Cornell University Press, 1993).

Kreymborg, Alfred. *Troubadour: An American autobiography by Alfred Kreymborg* (New York: Sagamore Press, 1925).

Krichmar, Albert. *The Woman's Rights Movement in the United States, 1848–1970: A bibliography and sourcebook* (Metuchen, NJ: Scarecrow Press, 1972).

LaRossa, Ralph, and Jaimie Ann Carboy. "A Kiss for Mother, a Hug for Dad," *Fathering* 6.3 (Fall 2008): 249–65.

Lasswell, Harold D., and Dorothy Blumenstock. *World Revolutionary Propaganda: A Chicago study* (New York: Alfred A. Knopf, 1939).

Latham, Sean, and Robert Scholes. "The Changing Profession: The Rise Of Periodical Studies," *PMLA* 121 (March 2006): 517–31.

Lay, Shawn, ed. *The Invisible Empire in the West: Toward a new historical appraisal of the Ku Klux Klan of the 1920s* (Urbana: University of Illinois Press, 1992).

Leavell, Linda. "Marianne Moore and Georgia O'Keeffe: The Feelings of a Mother—A Woman Or A Cat," in *Marianne Moore: Woman and Poet*, edited by Patricia C. Willis (Orono, ME: National Poetry Foundation, 1990).

Leavell, Linda, Cristanne Miller, and Robin G. Schulze, eds. *Critics and Poets on Marianne Moore: "A Right Good Salvo of Barks"* (Lewisburg, PA: Bucknell University Press, 2005).

Lee, Andrew, ed. *Scottsboro Alabama: A story in linoleum cuts*, foreword by Robin D.G. Kelley (New York: New York University Press, 2008).

Lee, Carol E. "A Pastime of Grandma and the 'Golden Girls' Evolves Into a Hip New Hobby," *New York Times* (March 30, 2005), <http://www.nytimes.com/2005/03/30/opinion/30wed3.html?_r=1&sq=&st=nyt&oref=slogin> (accessed 2 August 2008).

Leyland, Winston, ed. *Physique: A pictorial history of the Athletic Model Guild* (San Francisco: Gay Sunshine Press, 1982).

Lindenmeyer, Kriste. *"A Right to Childhood": The U.S. Children's Bureau and Child Welfare 1912–1946* (Urbana: University of Illinois Press, 1997).

Lynd, Robert S., and Helen M. Lynd. *Middletown: A study in contemporary American culture* (London: Constable, 1929).

MacBride, Genevieve G. *On Wisconsin Women: Working for their rights from settlement to suffrage* (Madison: University of Wisconsin Press, 1993).

Marchand, C. Roland. *The American Peace Movement and Social Reform, 1898–1918* (Princeton, NJ: Princeton University Press, 1972).

Marek, Jayne. *Women Editing Modernism* (Lexington: University of Kentucky Press, 1995).

Marer, Eva. "Knitting: The New Yoga," *Health* 16.2 (2002): 76–80.

Margolis, Maxine. *Mothers and Such: Views of American women and why they changed* (Berkeley: University of California Press, 1985).

Marshall, Nicholas. "The Rural Newspaper and the Circulation of Information and Culture in New York and the Antebellum North," *New York History* 88 (Spring 2007): 133–51.

May, Elaine Tyler. *Homeward Bound: American families in the Cold War era* (New York: Basic Books, 1988).

Mayes, Herbert R. *The Magazine Maze: A Prejudiced Perspective* (Garden City, NY: Doubleday and Company, Inc., 1980).

Mazza, Cat. "Cat Mazza," <http://post-craft.net/catmazza.htm> (accessed 18 August 2011).

———. "Microrevolt," <http://www.microrevolt.org/> (accessed 18 August 2011.

McClintock, Anne, Aamir Mufti, and Ella Shohat, eds. *Dangerous Liaisons* (Minneapolis: University of Minnesota Press, 1997).

McDonald, P.D. "Modernist Publishing: 'Nomads and Mapmakers,'" in *A Concise Companion to Modernism*, edited by D. Bradshaw (Malden, MA: Blackwell Publishing, n.d.)

McDuffie, Erik S. *Sojourning for Freedom: Black Women, American Communism, and the making of Black left feminism* (Chapel Hill, NC: Duke University Press, 2011).

McLuhan, Marshall. *The Gutenberg galaxy: The making of typographic man* (Toronto, Ontario: University of Toronto Press, 1962).

Meckel, Richard A. *Save the Babies: American public health reform and the prevention of infant mortality, 1850–1929* (Ann Arbor: University of Michigan Press, 1990).

Meeker, Martin. "Behind the Mask of Respectability: Reconsidering the Mattachine Society and Male Homophile Practice, 1950s and 1960s," *Journal of the History of Sexuality* 10.1 (2001): 78–116.

———. *Contacts Desired: Gay and Lesbian Communications and Community, 1940s–1970s* (Chicago: University of Chicago Press, 2006).

Meer, Sarah. *Uncle Tom Mania: Slavery, minstrelsy, and transatlantic culture in the 1850s* (Athens: University of Georgia Press, 2005).

Meggs, Philip B. *A History of Graphic Design* (New York: Van Nostrand Reinhold Press, 1983).

Messer-Kruse, Timothy. "Memories of the Ku Klux Klan Honorary Society at the University of Wisconsin," *The Journal of Blacks in Higher Education* 23 (Spring 1999): 83–93.

Meyer, Richard. "Gay Power Circa 1970: Visual strategies for sexual revolution," *GLQ: A Journal of Lesbian and Gay Studies* 12.3 (2006): 441–64.

Meyer, Susan. *James Montgomery Flagg* (New York: Guptill Publications, 1974).

Meyerowitz, Joanne. "Beyond the Feminine Mystique: A reassessment of postwar mass culture, 1946–1958," *Journal of American History* 79 (March 1993): 1455–82.

Miller, Cristanne. *Marianne Moore: Questions of authority* (Cambridge, MA: Harvard University Press, 1995).

Miller, James. *Remembering Scottsboro: The legacy of an infamous trial* (Princeton, NJ: Princeton University Press, 2009).

Mizruchi, Susan L. *The Rise of Multicultural America: Economy and Print Culture, 1865–1915* (Chapel Hill: University of North Carolina Press, 2008).

Molesworth, Charles. *Marianne Moore: A literary life* (New York: Atheneum, 1990).

Monroe, Harriet. *A Poet's Life: Seventy years in a changing world* (New York: Macmillan, 1938).

Moore, Leonard J. *Citizen Klansmen: The Ku Klux Klan in Indiana, 1921–1928* (Chapel Hill: University of North Carolina Press, 1991).

Moore, Marianne. *Becoming Marianne Moore*, edited by Robin Schulze (Berkeley: University of California Press, 2002).

——. *Selected Letters of Marianne Moore*, edited by Bonnie Costello, Celeste Goodridge, and Cristanne Miller (New York: Knopf, 1997).

Morgan, Tracy. "The Pages of Whiteness: Race, Physique Magazines, and the Emergence of Public Gay Culture," in *Queer Studies: A Lesbian, Gay, Bisexual, and Transgender anthology*, edited by Brett Beemyn and Mickey Eliason (New York: New York University Press, 1996), 280–97.

Morrisson, Mark S. *Pluralism and Counterpublic Spheres: Race, radicalism, and the "Masses"* (Madison: University of Wisconsin Press, 2001).

Mott, Frank Luther. *A History of American Magazines*, vol. 5 (Cambridge, MA: Harvard University Press, 1968).

Munford, Rebecca. "'Wake Up and Smell the Lipgloss': Gender, generation and the (a)politics of girl power," in *Third Wave Feminism: A Critical Exploration*, edited by Stacey Gillis, Gillian Howie, and Rebecca Munford (London: Palgrave Macmillan, 2004), 142–54.

Murray, Simone. *Mixed Media: Feminist presses and publishing politics* (London: Pluto Press, 2004).

Nadel, Alan. *Containment Culture: American narratives, postmodernism and the atomic age* (Durham, NC: Duke University Press, 1995).

Naison, Mark. *Communists in Harlem during the Depression* (Chicago: University of Illinois Press, 1983).

Newman, Richard, Patrick Rael, and Philip Lapsansky, eds. *Pamphlets of Protest* (London: Routledge, 2001).

Nord, David. *Faith in Reading: Religious Publishing and the Birth of Mass Media in America* (New York: Oxford University Press, 2007).

North, Michael. *The Political Aesthetic of Yeats, Eliot, and Pound* (Cambridge: Cambridge University Press, 1991).

Northrup, Flora L. *The Record of a Century, 1834–1934* (New York: American Female Guardian Society, 1934).

Odem, Mary E. *Delinquent Daughters: Protecting and policing adolescent female sexuality in the United States, 1885–1920* (Chapel Hill: University of North Carolina Press, 1995).

Ohmann, Richard. *Selling Culture: Magazines, markets and class at the turn of the century* (London: Verso, 1996).

Orwell, George. *All Art is Propaganda: Critical essays* (Boston: Mariner Books, 2009).

Passet, Joanne E. *Sex Radicals and the Quest for Women's Equality* (Urbana and Chicago: University of Illinois Press, 2003).

Pentney, Beth Ann. "Feminism, Activism, and Knitting: Are the fibre arts a viable mode for feminist political action?" *thirdspace* 8.1 (Summer 2008). <http://www.thirdspace.ca/journal/article/viewArticle/pentney/210> (accessed 1 July 2011).

Pfannestiel, T.J. *Rethinking the Red Scare: The Lusk Committee and New York's crusade against radicalism, 1919–1923* (New York: Routledge, 2003).

Phillips, J.B. "Typical Woman of Postwar Moscow," *Newsweek* 28 (4 November 1946): 52.

Piepmeier, Alison. *Girl Zines: Making media, doing feminism* (New York: New York University Press, 2009).

Pierson, Ruth Roach, ed. *Women and Peace: Theoretical, historical, and practical perspectives* (London: Croom Helm, 1987).

Plant, Rebecca Jo. *MOM: The Transformation of Motherhood in Modern America* (Chicago: University of Chicago Press, 2010).

Porter, Dorothy. *Negro Protest Pamphlets* (New York: Arno Press, 1969).

Postman, Neil. "The reformed English curriculum," in *High school 1980: The shape of the future in American secondary education*, edited by A.C. Eurich (New York: Pitman, 1970), 160–68.

Postman, Neil, and Charles Weingartner. *The Soft Revolution: A student handbook for turning schools around* (New York: Delacorte, 1971).

Radway, Janice. *Reading the Romance: Women, patriarchy, and popular literature* (Chapel Hill: University of North Carolina Press, 1984).

Rainey, Lawrence. "The Cultural Economy of Modernism," in *Cambridge Companion to Modernism*, edited by Michael Harry Levenson (Cambridge: Cambridge University Press, 1999).

———. *Institutions of Modernism: Literary elites and public culture* (New Haven, CT: Yale University Press, 2005).

Reumann, Miriam. *American Sexual Character: Sex, gender, and national identity in the Kinsey Reports* (Berkeley: University of California Press, 2005).

Richards, E.G. *Mapping Time: The calendar and its history* (New York: Oxford University Press, 1998).

Ritter, Gretchen. "Gender and Citizenship after the Nineteenth Amendment," *Polity* 32.3 (2000): 345–75.

Rivera, David Allen. *Final Warning: A history of the new world order* (Oakland, CA: Conspiracy Books, 1984 [2004]).

Robinson, Cedric J. *Black Marxism: The making of the Black radical tradition* (Chapel Hill: University of North Carolina Press, 1983 [2000]).

Rogin, Michael. *Ronald Reagan, the Movie and Other Episodes in Political Demonology* (Berkeley: University of California Press, 1987).

Rosenberg, Emily S. "Foreign Affairs After World War II: connecting sexual and international politics," *Diplomatic History* 18.1 (January 1994): 59–70.

Ryan, Mary P. *Women in Public: Between Banners and Ballots, 1825–1880* (Baltimore: Johns Hopkins University Press, 1992).

Sánchez, María Carla. *Reforming the World: Social activism and the problem of fiction in nineteenth-century America* (Iowa City: University of Iowa Press, 2008).

Sanford, Don A. *A Choosing People: The history of Seventh Day Baptists* (Nashville, TN: Broadman Press, 1992).

Sangrey, Trevor Joy. "'Put One More "S" in the USA': Pamphlet Literature and the Productive Fiction of the Black Nation Thesis" (dissertation, University of California, Santa Cruz, June 2012).

Scelfo, Julie. "Rock-and-Roll Knitters: They may have blue hair, but they're no grannies," *Newsweek* (January 24, 2004): 54.

Scholes, Robert, and Clifford Wulfman. *Modernism in the Magazines: An introduction* (New Haven, CT: Yale University Press, 2010).

Schreiber, Rachel. "Before their Makers and their Judges: Prostitutes and White Slaves in the Political Cartoons of the *Masses*," *Feminist Studies* 35.1 (Spring 2009): 161–93.

———. *Gender, Activism, and a Little Magazine: the modern figures of the "Masses"* (Aldershot, UK and Burlington, VT: Ashgate Publishing, 2011).

———. "George Bellows's Boxers in Print," *Journal of Modern Periodical Studies* 1.2 (2010): 159–81.

Schudson, M. *Discovering the News: A Social History of American Newspapers* (New York: Basic Books, 1978).

Schweik, Susan. "Writing War Poetry Like a Woman," *Critical Inquiry* 13.3 (1987): 532–56.

Seidman, Steven A. *Posters, Propaganda, and Persuasion in Election Campaigns Around the World and Through History* (New York: Peter Lang, 2008).

Shakespeare, William. *The Tempest*, edited by Virginia Mason Vaughan and Alden T. Vaughan (London: Arden Shakespeare, 1999).

Shalin, D.N. "Critical Theory and the Pragmatist Challenge," *American Journal of Sociology* 98.2 (1992): 237–79.

Sherry, Michael. *Gay Artists in Modern American Culture: An imagined conspiracy* (Durham, NC: Duke University Press, 2007).

Sherry, Vincent. *The Great War and the Language of Modernism* (New York: Oxford University Press, 2003).

Slatin, John M. *The Savage's Romance: The poetry of Marianne Moore* (University Park, PA: Pennsylvania State University Press, 1986).

Smith, Shawn Michelle. *Photography on the Color Line: W.E.B. Du Bois, race, and visual culture* (Durham, NC: Duke University Press, 2004).

Smith-Rosenberg, Carroll. "Misprisioning *Pamela*: Representations of Gender and Class in Nineteenth-Century America," *Michigan Quarterly Review* 26 (Winter 1987): 9–28.

Snyder, Timothy. *Bloodlands: Europe between Hitler and Stalin* (New York: Basic Books, 2010).

Solomon, Mark. *The Cry was Unity: Communists and African Americans 1917–1936* (Jackson: University Press of Mississippi, 1998).

Stansell, Christine. *American Moderns: Bohemian New York and the Creation of a New Century* (New York: Henry Holt and Company, 2000).

Stein, Marc. *City of Sisterly and Brotherly Loves: Lesbian and Gay Philadelphia, 1945–1972* (Philadelphia: Temple University Press, 2004).

Sternberg, Janet. *Misbehavior in cyber places: The regulation of online conduct in virtual communities on the Internet* (New York: New York University, 2001).

Still, Bayrd. *Milwaukee: The history of a city* (Madison: The State Historical Society of Wisconsin, 1948).

Strate, Lance. "A Media Ecology Review," *Communication Research Trends* 23.2 (2004): 1–48.

Strub, Whitney. "The Clearly Obscene and the Queerly Obscene: Heteronormativity and Obscenity in Cold War Los Angeles," *American Quarterly* 60.2 (2008): 373–98.

Taylor, Georgina. *H.D. and the Public Sphere of Modernist Women Writers, 1913–1946* (New York: Oxford University Press, 2001).

Tebbel, John, and Mary Ellen Zuckerman. *The Magazine in America, 1740–1990* (New York: Oxford University Press, 1991).

Thompson, Margo Hobbs. "'Dear Sisters': The visible lesbian in community arts journals," *GLQ: Journal of Lesbian and Gay Studies* 12.3 (2006): 405–23.

Todd, Mark, and Esther Pearl Watson. *Watcha Mean, What's a Zine? The art of making zines and mini-comics* (Boston: Graphia, 2006).

Trachtenberg, Alan. *Reading American Photographs: Images as history* (New York: Hill and Wang, 1989).

244 Modern Print Activism in the United States

10

Twerdon, Sarah, "The Maternity Center Association as a Vehicle for the Education of Motherhood" (master's thesis, Columbia University, 1947).

Van Wienen, Mark. "Poetics of the Frugal Housewife: A modernist narrative of the Great War in America," *American Literary History* 7.1 (1995): 55–91.

Warner, Michael. *Publics and Counterpublics* (New York: Zone Books, 2005).

Warren, Sidney. *American Freethought, 1860–1914* (New York: Columbia University Press, 1943).

Wasserstrom, William. *The Time of The Dial* (Syracuse, NY: Syracuse University Press, 1963).

Waugh, Thomas. *Hard to Imagine: Gay male eroticism in photography and film from their beginnings to Stonewall* (New York: Columbia University Press, 1996).

West, William Lemore. "The Moses Harman Story," *Kansas Historical Quarterly* 37.1 (Spring 1971): 41–63.

White, C. Todd. *Pre-Gay L.A.: A social history of the movement for homosexual rights* (Urbana: University of Illinois Press, 2009).

Whitfield, Stephen J. *The Culture of the Cold War* (Baltimore: Johns Hopkins University Press, 1991).

Wiegand, W.A. "Introduction: Theoretical Foundations for Analyzing Print Culture as Agency and Practice in a Diverse Modern America," in *Print Culture in a Diverse America*, edited by J.P. Danky and W.A. Wiegand (Urbana and Chicago: University of Illinois Press, 1998).

Wiegman, Robyn. "The Anatomy of Lynching," *Journal of the History of Sexuality* 3.3 (January 1993): 445–67.

Williams, Michael. *The Shadow of the Pope: The story of the anti-Catholic movement in America* (New York: Whittlesey House, McGraw-Hill, 1932).

Williams, Raymond. *The Long Revolution* (London: Chatto & Windus, 1961).

Willis, Deborah. *Reflections in Black: A history of Black photographers 1840 to the present* (New York: W.W. Norton & Company, 2000).

Wolfe, Howard. *Behold Thy Mother: Mother's Day and the Mother's Day Church* (Kingsport, TN: Kingsport Press, 1962).

Zobl, Elke. "Comparative Perspectives Symposium: Feminist Zines—Cultural Production, Transnational Networking, and Critical Reflection in Feminist Zines," *Signs: Journal of Women in Culture and Society* 35.1 (2009): 1–12.

Zuckerman, Mary Ellen. *A History of Popular Women's Magazines in the U.S., 1792–1995* (Westport, CT: Greenwood Press, 1998).

Index

Page numbers in italics refer to figures.

abolitionism 17, 32, 55n9
ACLU, 173
activism; *see also* print activism
    abolitionist 17, 32, 55n9
    art as 202
    consumerism contrasted with 163
    craftivism 217
    cultural 163
    direct action 6, 122, 151
    origins of term 5–7, 67
    pragmatism and Eucken on 5
    radicalism associated with 6–7
    as response to modern life 7
Addams, Jane 42, 47
Adonis (magazine) 170
advertising 2–3, 28, 118
Advocate and Family Guardian, The
    (newspaper) 29–42
    as all-female enterprise 33
    on bad literature's effects 39–41
    circulation 32
    fallen women as depicted in 33–8
    and Modernism 30, 31, 39, 42
    sentimental narratives in 37–9
    span of 31
    as in tune with its times 41–2
African Americans
    Communist Party's Black Nation
        Thesis 125, 127–8, 133, 136–43
    double consciousness 185, 186
    Physique Pictorial's "all-negro"
        catalog 175–6
    Scottsboro Boys 123–7, 130–35, 142
    SNCC 1968 wall calendar 179–91
African Blood Brotherhood 127
Aldington, Richard 68, 70, 71, 78, 81
Allen, James S. 128, 137–42
*Amazon Quarterly: A lesbian feminist arts
    journal* 191–203

artwork 196–7, 200–202
    economic disentanglement from
        capitalism/patriarchy 198, 203
    editorials 194
    gynocentrism 199–200
    mission statement 193–4
    vanguard art magazines
        compared 197–8
    volunteer labor 198–9
American Female Guardian Society 30n3,
    32–3, 35, 36, 37, 41
American Journal of Eugenics 20n18, 26
*American Negro, The (Negro
    Liberation)* (pamphlet, Allen) 128,
    137–9, 143
American Secular Union 26
American Spiritualist (journal), 22n25
Anderson, Benedict 4, 19
Anthony, Katharine 62
anti-vice movements 41
"Appellate Jurisdiction" (Moore) 78
"Arms vs. Army" (Rogers) 43, *44*, 45
Arnold, June 196
Athletic Model Guild (AMG) 166, 168

Banner of Light, The (periodical) 16, 19
Barnett, Ida B. Wells 125
Batchelor, Clarence Daniel 52–3, *54*,
    57–62
Bigelow, William Frederick 95–6, 97–8,
    99, 100, 101–2
*Bitch: Feminist Response to popular
    culture* (periodical) 205–11, 218
Black Nation Thesis 125, 127–8, 133,
    136–43
Blake, Aldrich 116
Boston Investigator (newspaper) 16,
    23, 26
Briggs, Cyril 127, 135, 137, 138
Brown, Rita Mae 196
BUST (periodical) 205–13, 215, 217–18

calendars
    as hybrids 11
    proliferation 188
    SNCC 1968 wall calendar 179–91
Canzine (Toronto) 217
capitalism
    Amazon Quarterly seeks
        disentanglement 198, 203
    coming together of print and 4
    feminist crafting and 215, 217
    periodicals become expressions of
        capitalist culture 3
Carr, Joe 132–3
Cast Off Knitting Club 216
Catt, Carrie Chapman 56
childbirth, women's deaths in 87–90, 98
Christy, Howard Chandler 47
Churchill, Suzanne W. 67n8, 83n54, 84
citizenship, gendered notions of 43,
    44–5, 63
Coates, Paul 167
Cold War
    containment culture 145–59
    gay life during 161, 166, 168, 177
    "happy housewife heroine" image
        permeates 145–6
    religion in 158
communism; *see also* Communist Party
    (CPUSA)
    homosexuality conflated with 168
    Ladies' Home Journal in Cold War
        145–59
    Red Scare of 1919–1920 5–6
Communist Party (CPUSA) 123–43
    black membership 127
    Black Nation Thesis 125, 127–8, 133,
        136–43
    functions of pamphlets 125
    origins 127
    Scottsboro Boys case 123–7,
        130–35, 142
    varieties of pamphlets 129–30
Comstock Act of 1873 15, 16, 21, 23, 26
Connections (directory) 202
Corinne, Tee A. 199–200
"Counseil To A Bachelor" (Moore) 78,
    80–81
counter-public spheres
    The Egoist facilitates 66–7, 70, 77

gay 161, 168, 172
Ku Klux Klan as 116
radical publications form 3
Covina, Gina 193, 194, 196–7, 198,
    200, 202
Craddock, Ira 15, 26
crafting, feminist 205–20
craftivism 217
"cult of true womanhood" 35

Dawn (periodical) 109, 114, 120
De Cleyre, Voltairine 6, 26
Dearborn Independent (newspaper) 110,
    110n12
*Death Penalty! The Case of Georgia
    Against Negro and White Workers*
    (pamphlet) 132–4
Derrick, Diane 200
Dial, The (periodical) 67, 78n38
direct action 6, 122, 151
Do-It-Yourself (DIY) movement
    Amazon Quarterly and 196, 198,
        199, 201
    feminist crafting 206, 208, 213, 215,
        216, 217, 219, 220
Dobkin, Alix 195
domesticity 10, 145–6, 148–9, 217–19
Drum (magazine) 176
Du Bois, W.E.B. 179, 184, 185, 186

Eastman, Crystal 56
Egoist, The (periodical)
    as counter-public sphere 66–7, 70
    folds 78n38
    format 69n20, 79
    H.D. reviews Moore's poems 70–74
    Moore's final poems 74–7
    Moore's first published poems
        68–70, 82
    Others magazine compared 83
Eliot, T.S. 71, 74, 78
Espionage Act of 1917 56, 63
Eucken, Rudolf 5
eugenics 22, 107, 112
Evans, Hiram 106, 107, 108n6, 110,
    113, 115

"fallen" women, reform press on 29–42
Farm Security Administration 184

"Feed Me, Also, River God" (Moore) 70
Fellowship Forum (periodical) 114
Feminine Mystique, The (Friedan) 145, 159
feminist periodicals
  Amazon Quarterly's lesbian separatism
    193–203
  crafting in 205–20
"Fish, The" (Moore) 75–7
Fishman, Louise 200
Flagg, James Montgomery 47, *48*, 56
Fletcher, Lucy Walton 36–7, 41
Florida Legislative Investigation
  Committee 165
Ford, Henry 110, 110n12
Ford, James 128, 137–8, 139–42
Foringer, Alonzo Earl 49, *50*
Fort-Whiteman, Lovett 127n12, 137
Forum (periodical) 115
Foster, Laura 45, *46*, 47, 63n18
Foster, William 128
*Four Lights: An Adventure in
    Internationalism* (periodical) 56,
    62, 63
free love 21, 22, 23, 25
freethought 15, 16, 17, 22, 23, 26
Freewoman, The (periodical) 66, 69n20
Friedan, Betty 145, 159
Friend of Virtue, The (periodical) 35n21

Galana, Laurel 193, 194, 198
gay politics; *see also* homophile movement
  Amazon Quarterly's lesbian separatism
    193–203
  consumerism and activism in 163
  generation gap 176, 177
  male physique magazines and 161–77
  Physique Pictorial routes readers
    toward activism 166, 171–2
Gibson, Charles Dana 47, *48*, 60
"Gibson Girl" 47, *48*, 49, 60, 62
"girl he left behind" theme 50–53
Glintenkamp, H.J. 52, *53*, 54
Good Housekeeping (magazine) 87–104
  on good mothers 96–7
  joins Mother's Day campaign 91,
    98–9, 101–2
  May Mother's Day articles 95–6,
    99–100, 103
  resident medical experts 102

sets boundaries on Mother's Day
    campaign 95, 98
  Sheppard-Towner Act supported 97–8
  twilight sleep endorsed 104
Gordon, Eugene 135
Gould, Bruce and Beatrice 155, 158
Grahn, Judy 196
Great American Lesbian Art Show
    (1980) 201
Greenback party 24
grrrl zines 196, 199
Guenther (artist) 51, *51*, 54
Guest, Edgar A. 50–51

Habermas, Jürgen 3–5, 7, 28, 65n3
Haggard, Howard W. 87–8
Hall, Otto 137
Hammond, Harmony 201
"Hand in Hand" (Foster) 45, *46*, 47
Harman, Moses 15, 26, 27
Harold the Klansman (Brown) 109
Hay, Harry 171
Haywood, Harry 128, 136n36, 137
H.D. (poet) 65, 66, 70–74, 77, 78, 78n38
"He Made This Screen" (Moore) 72–4
Hecht, George 92
Heresies (magazine) 201
heteronormativity 47, 163, 166, 169, 213
Heywood, Ezra 15, 27
homophile movement
  generation gap in gay politics 176, 177
  male physique magazines excluded
    161–2, 163–4, 166
  Mattachine Society 164–5, 166, 167,
    171, 177
  obscenity charges against physique
    distributors ignored 169
  obscenity charges against publications
    165–6
  open but desexualized homosexuality
    of 169
  Physique Pictorial routes readers
    toward 166, 171–2
  respectability sought 164–6, 176
homosexuality; *see also* gay politics
  in Cold War context 161, 166, 168, 177
  lavender scare 164
  Los Angeles police crackdowns of
    1930s 173

male physique magazines associated
with 161, 165
Physique Pictorial goes beyond peer
publications in acknowledging
170–71
Homosexuality and Citizenship in Florida
(report) 165
Howard, M. 128
HUES (periodical) 205, 206n4
Huiswoud, Otto 137
hydropathy (water cure) 18–19, 27

"If the Public Only Knew! Editors Can
Help Mothers on Mother's Day"
(pamphlet, MCA) 92, *93*
Illustrated Hydropathic Review, The 19n14
Imperial Night-Hawk (periodical)
113–14, 117
International Labor Defense (ILD) 124,
126, 130–35
Iron Man (magazine) 171

Jackson, Helen 109–10
Jarvis, Anna 95, 96, 98–9, 100
Jones, Claudia 135, 138, 142n57
Judge (periodical) 45, *46*, 47
Junior Klansman (periodical) 120

Karp, Marcelle 207
Kenyon, Josephine H. 102
King, L.J. 109–10
Kinsey reports 170
Kirk, Lydia 154
Knight Vale of the KKK (Saxon) 108–9
Knights of Labor 24–5
"knit in" occupations 216
Knit4Choice 216
knitting 206, 210–12, 216, 217, 219
Kourier (magazine) 114, 117, 121
Kreymborg, Alfred 82
Ku Klux Klan (KKK) 105–22
anti-Catholic conspiracy theories
110–11
Catholic immigrant opposition to
106–8, 109, 122
as commercially minded 112–13
community-building activities
117–21, 122
laudatory literature 108–9

mainstream press attention 115–16
membership 116
official press 113–14, 117–18
pageants 120–21, 122
popularity in 1920s 105, 112, 113,
114, 121
Protestant ministers in recruitment
118–19
ritual 118, 119
youth movement 120

labor unions
Bolshevism associated with 6
Knights of Labor 24–5
Ku Klux Klan on immigrants and 106
publications 3
Severance supports 23
Ladies' Home Journal 145–59
circulation 146
on circumstances of Cold War
period 146–8
discourse of domesticity promoted 10,
145, 146, 148–9
on emigrants from Soviet Union 156–7
"If You Ask Me" column 148
"Letters from Russia" series, 154
life in Soviet Union described 153–6
"Political Pilgrim's Progress"
column 151–2
on religion in Soviet Union 157–8
on Soviet women 155–9
women's political participation
encouraged 148–52, 154
youth political participation
encouraged 152–3
Lawson, Elizabeth 130
League for Civil Education 171–2
League of Struggle for Negro Rights 137
Lesbian Art Show (1978) 201
lesbian separatism 193–203
Lester, Julius 179, 180–81, 182, 183–4,
185–6, 190
Linhares, Judy 200
Literary Digest 115
little magazines
as distinct from commodity culture 8
Moore publishes in 65–85
as site for discursive interaction
between poetics and politics, 66

Lorde, Audre 195–6
Lucifer, the Light-Bearer (periodical) 16, 26
lynching 125–6, 130, 135
Lynching (pamphlet, Haywood and
 Howard) 128

Macauley, Charles R. 93–4
McClure's (magazine) 115–16
McDowall, John 37, 39
McDowall's Journal 37
McKible, Adam, 84
magazines; *see also* little magazines; male
 physique magazines; women's
 magazines
 Advocate and Family Guardian
  newspaper on fiction in 40
 golden age 17
male physique magazines; *see also*
 Physique Pictorial (magazine)
 homophile movement excludes 161–2,
  163–4, 166
 Mizer on critics of 168
 popularity 161
 racial aspect 175–6
 seen as evidence of perversity 165
Masses, The (periodical) 52, *53*, 59, 68
Maternity Center Association (MCA)
 87–96, 98, 100–104
Mattachine Society 164–5, 166, 167,
 171, 177
Maugham, W. Somerset 168
media; *see also* periodicals
 corporatization 4
 media ecology 180, 181, 186, 190
Mellor, William 6
Mizer, Bob
 Athletic Model Guild 166, 168
 avoids direct acknowledgment of
  homosexuality 169
 on *Drum* critique 176
 on *Iron Man* article 171
 as no proto-liberationist 177
 obscenity charges 166, 167, 176
 Physique Pictorial magazine
  founded 161
 pleasure endorsed 172
 politicized editorial voice 161–2, 164,
  166, 167–8
 reader questions answered 173, 176

Modernism
 Advocate and Family Guardian
  newspaper and 30, 31, 39, 42
 conversational model 84–5
 Moore 67, 84
 print activism as phenomenon of 7–9
Monroe, Harriet 66, 78, 79, 81, 82
Moore, Marianne 65–85
 attention given to her publications 67–8
 in Bryn Mawr publications 68, 72
 as *Dial* editor 67, 78n38
 distinct oeuvres 65
 as "fighting spirit" 65, 78, 85
 final poems in *The Egoist* 74–7
 H.D. as sponsor 77
 H.D. reviews poems 70–74
 as Modernist 67, 84
 Others magazine publishes 82–5
 Poetry magazine publishes 78–82
Morgan, Robin 195
Morrisson, Mark 8, 66, 70, 116
motherhood
 call for new meaning for Mother's Day
  87–104
 patriotism associated with 47, 49
 scientific view 90, 94, 102–4, 103n49
 as unifying identity of all women
  56, 64
 Victorian image 96–7, 102
Mother's Day
 campaign for new meaning for 87–104
 congressional resolution on 91
 sentimental traditional celebrations 90,
  91, 95, 99, 101, 104
Ms. (magazine) 12n24, 205, 218

Nachman, Elana (Elana Dykewomon) 196
National American Woman Suffrage
 Association (NAWSA) 55–6
National Liberal League 23–4
Negroes in a Soviet America, The
 (pamphlet, Allen and Ford) 137–8,
  139–42
New England Female Moral Reform
 Society 35
New Freewoman, The (periodical) 66,
 69n20
new woman 45, 49, 54, 60
Newhouse, Carol 199, 200

newspapers
    evolution 2–3
    moral reform movement 32
    radical 16
Nineteenth Amendment 63
Norris, Kathleen 99–100, 100n38

Observations (Moore) 78n38
off our backs (periodical) 205
On the Chain Gang (pamphlet, Spivak)
    128, 130
ONE (magazine) 165–6, 167
Others (periodical) *83*
    austere ideal 82–3
    Moore published 82–5
    as socially hospitable 66
Oxenberg, Jan 194

pamphlets 124
    African American 129
    Communist Party 123–43
    emergence 2, 129
    functions 125
    industrialized printing 3
    Ku Klux Klan 115
    as non-periodical forms 11
peace movement 43–4, 54–5, 63
penny press, 2
periodicals; *see also* magazines;
        newspapers
    become expressions of capitalist
        culture 3
    emergence of 3
    freethought 16, 23
    Ku Klux Klan propaganda 105–22
    as sites of print activism 1
    suffragist 44–5
Philadelphia Magdalen Society 34–5
Phillips, Joseph 154
photography
    Farm Security Administration's 184
    SNCC 1968 wall calendar's use of
        179–91
    stops time 190
Physique Pictorial (magazine) 161–77
    "all-negro" catalog of 1958 175–6
    counterpublic created 168
    as cultural activism 163

goes beyond peer publications in
        acknowledging homosexuality
        170–71
    nudes published 176–7
    obscenity charges 167
    pleasure endorsed 172
    politicized editorial voice 161–2, 164,
        166, 167–8
    reader input 172–6
    reports obscenity charges against
        physique distributors 168–9
    routes readers toward gay rights
        activism 166, 171–2
    spartan aesthetic 166–7
    visual policy evolution 177
Physique World (magazine) 170–71
Playboy (magazine) 167
Poems (Moore) 78n38
Poetry (magazine)
    aesthetic glosses to materials published
        66, 81
    establishment 78–9
    format 79
    Moore's poems published 78–82
    Others magazine compared 83
    war poetry *80*, 81–2
Polak, Clark 176
Position of Negro Women, The (pamphlet,
        Gordon and Briggs) 135
Pound, Ezra 39, 73–4, 79n44, 82
"Pouters and Faintails" (Moore) 78, 79–80
Powers, M.H. 132–3
pragmatism 5
print activism
    on all points of political spectrum 7
    assessing efficacy 12
    in commodified medium 8, 12
    declines due to monopolization of
        public media 4
    as Modernist phenomenon 7–9
    periodicals as sites 1
    strategies 12
    as twentieth-century phenomenon 1
print culture
    coming together of capitalism and
        print 4
    as commodity 8, 12
    democratization of the press 28

as means of coping with modernity 7–8
as political force 9
print as form of activity 4–5
as site of record for social and political
    movements 7
technological developments in
    production and distribution 1–3
productive fiction (in pamphlets of the
    Communist Party) 125, 135,
    136, 143
Progressives
    Advocate and Family Guardian
      newspaper and 30, 31, 32, 42
    Good Housekeeping magazine on 97
    influences that shaped worldview of 16
    as middle class 1
propaganda 134
    Communist Party pamphlets 123–43
    Ku Klux Klan 105–22
prostitution
    Advocate and Family Guardian
      newspaper on 30–34
    increasing presence in mainstream
      media 41
public spheres 3–4, 7, 66, 70, 116–17, 146

Race Hatred on Trial (pamphlet,
    Yokinen) 128
radical press 3; *see also* socialist press
    Communist Party pamphlets 123–43
    newspapers 16
    Severance in 15–28
Ray, Amy 211
Raymond, Kaymarion 200
Red Scare of 1919–1920 5–6
reform press
    anti-war graphic satire of American
      suffrage press 43–64
    on "fallen" women 29–42
    Severance in 15–28
Refregier, A. (Anton) 130, *131, 132, 133*
"Reinforcements" (Moore) 74–5, 74n34,
    75n35
Religio-Philosophical Journal 16, 22
"Resolution on the Negro Question"
    (Comintern) 127–8, 137
Revolutionary Knitting Circle 216
Rich, Adrienne 195
Riot Grrrl 215, 216, 217

ROCKRGRL (periodical) 205, 206n4
Rogers, (Annie) Lou 43, *44*, 45, 53–4, *55*,
    56, 62, 63
Roosevelt, Eleanor 95, 148
Rule, Jane 196

Sangster, Margaret E. 103
Schroeder, Amy 208
Scottsboro Boys 123–7, 130–35, 142
Searchlight, The (periodical), 113n25
"second wave" feminism 205, 218–19
Severance, Juliet H. 15–28
    in American Secular Union 26
    background 17–18
    Comstock Act opposed 15, 21, 23, 26
    death 27
    free love supported 21, 22, 23
    in Greenback party 24
    hydropathy studied 18–19, 27
    influences on 27
    Knights of Labor supported 24–5
    leaves Severance 26
    as lecturer 20–21, 23
    on marriage 20, 21–2
    marriage to Anson B. Severance 21
    marriage to John D. Stillman 18–19
    on monopolistic power 20, 23
    in National Liberal League 23–4
    oratory 18, 28
    as outsider 16, 27
    as physician 20, 27
    on separation of church and state 25–6
    in Spiritualism 19, 21, 22, 27
    in Union Labor Party 25
    Woodhull supported 22
Shameless: For girls who get it (periodical)
    205–7, 208, *209*, 210, 212
"She Will Spike War's Gun" (Rogers)
    45, *46*
Sheppard-Towner (Maternity and Infancy)
    Act 92, 97–8
SNCC (Student Non-Violent Coordinating
    Committee) 1968 wall calendar
    179–91
    as act of resistance 191
    as counterarchive 186, 188
    juncture of personal and historical 184–5
    measured and historical time
      sutured 189

media ecology approach to 180, 181, 186, 190
partnership of word and image 188–9
as photographic archive 182
as series of value exchanges 186–7
as site for meaning-making 189
statement on last page 179–80, 190–91
strategic mission 183
socialist press
   Masses 52, *53*, 59, 68
   on women's wartime roles 49
Southern Worker, The (periodical) 137
Spiritualism 16, 19, 21, 22, 27
Spivak, John 128, 130
Steinbeck, John 153, 154, 155
Stitch 'n Bitch groups 216
Stoller, Debbie 206, 207, 209, 211
Stonewall rebellion 176, 177
Stowe, Harriet Beecher 18, 19, 37–8
suffrage movement *see* women's suffrage movement
suffrage press, 43–64
Suffragist, The (periodical) 55, 56

"Talisman" (Moore) 70
temperance movement 17, 18, 21, 22, 32
"That Harp You Play So Well" (Moore) 78
They Shall Not Die! The Story of Scottsboro in Pictures (pamphlet, Lawon and Refregier) 130–31, *131, 132, 133*
"third wave" feminism 205, 216, 218–19, 220
Thompson, Dorothy 147, 153, 155–6
"To A Man Working His Way Through The Crowd" (Moore) 68–9
"To A Screen-Maker" (Moore) 70, 72
"To An Intra-Mural Rat" (Moore) 78
"To Statecraft Embalmed" (Moore) 69, 84, *85*
"To the Soul of 'Progress'" (Moore) 68, 69–70, 72
Tomorrow's Man (magazine) 170
Truth Seeker (newspaper) 15, 16, 23, 26

Uncle Tom's Cabin (Stowe) 37–8
Union Labor Party 25
unions *see* labor unions
Universe (periodical) 20
Urban, Al 169

Venus Zine (periodical) 205–10, 213, *214,* 215, 217–18

Waisbrooker, Lois 15, 21, 27
"War Yawp" (Aldington) 81
Water-Cure Journal 16, 18, 20
"win the war women" theme 59–62
"Wizard in Words, The" (Moore) 78
Woman Citizen, The (periodical) 47, *48,* 49, 52–4, *55,* 56–64
Woman's Journal, The 43, *44*
women's suffrage movement
   anti-war graphic satire of American suffrage press 43–64
   emerges from nineteenth-century reform culture 32
   splinters over World War I 44
women's magazines; *see also Good Housekeeping* (magazine); *Ladies' Home Journal*; suffrage press
   in acceptance of prenatal and postnatal care 104
   balance between following and leading public opinion 90–91
   domestic ideal promoted 145–6, 159
   as site of commodification 8
Woodhull, Victoria 15, 21, 22
Woodhull & Claflin's Weekly 16, 22
World War I
   anti-war graphic satire of American suffrage press 43–64
   Moore's poetry during 65–85
   Poetry magazine war poems *80,* 81–2
   propaganda 134

yarn bombing 217
Yokinen, August 128

Zeisler, Andi 208–9
zine culture 205, 206, 213, 216, 217, 219

For Product Safety Concerns and Information please contact our
EU representative GPSR@taylorandfrancis.com Taylor & Francis
Verlag GmbH, Kaufingerstraße 24, 80331 München, Germany